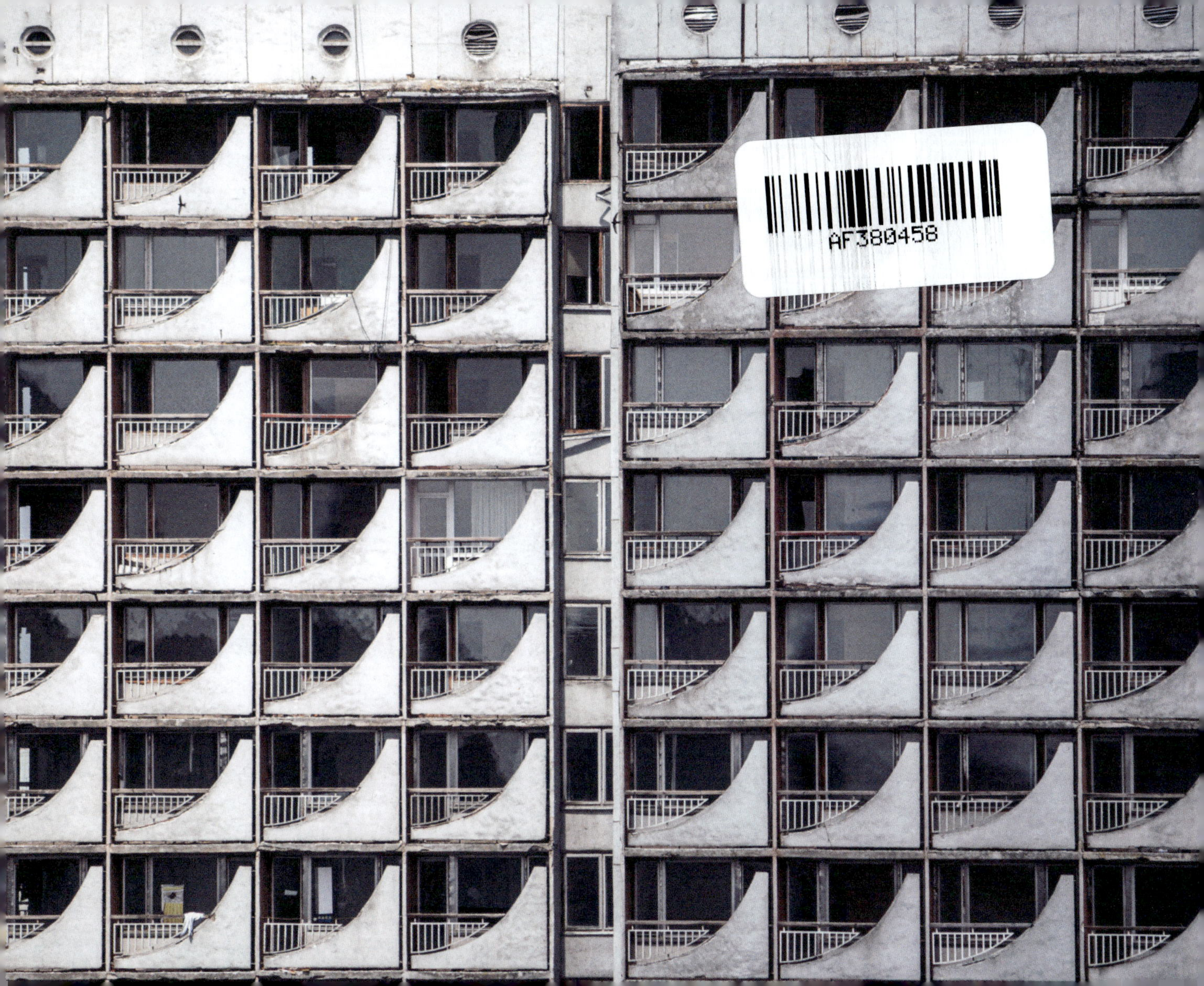
AF380458

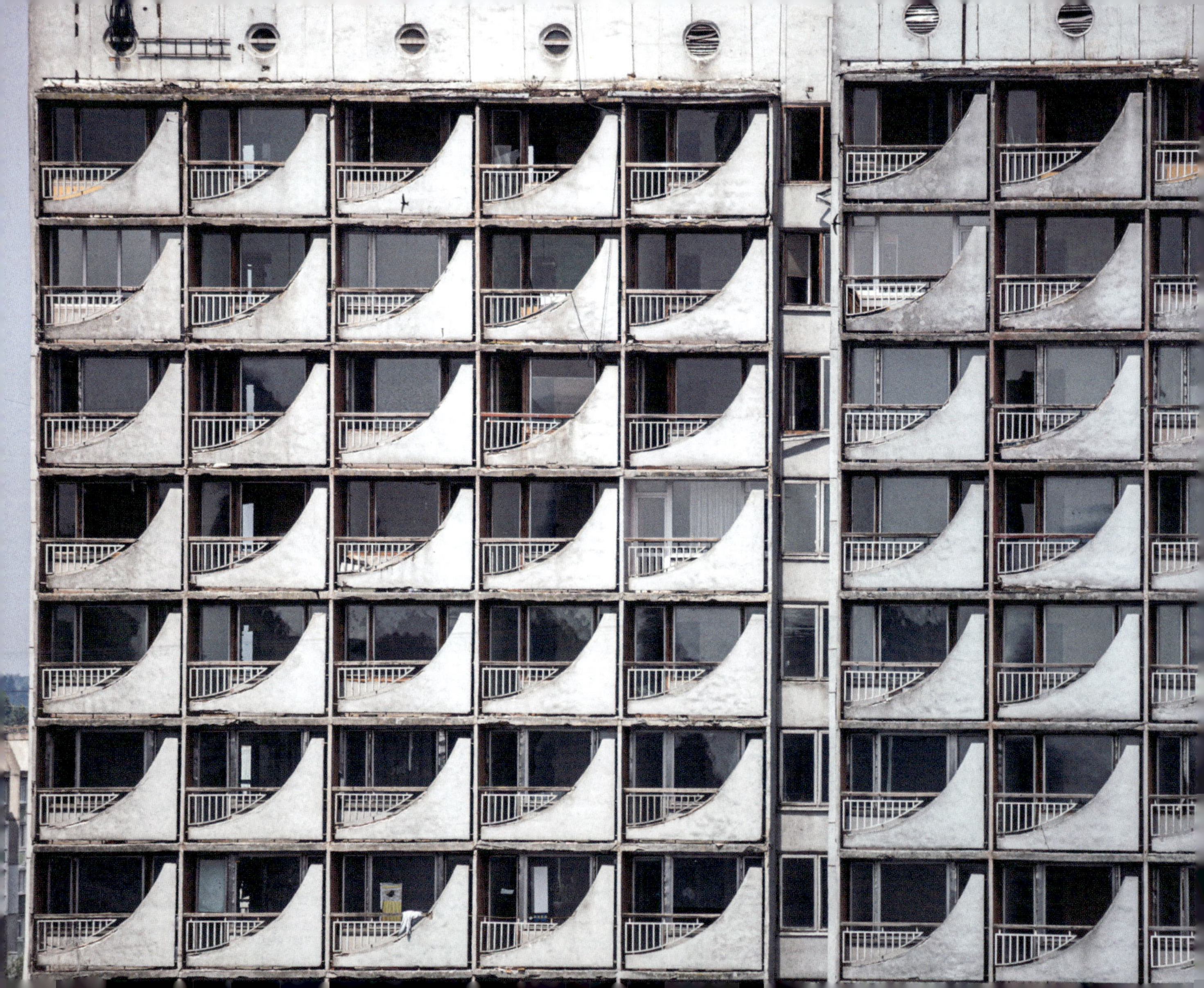

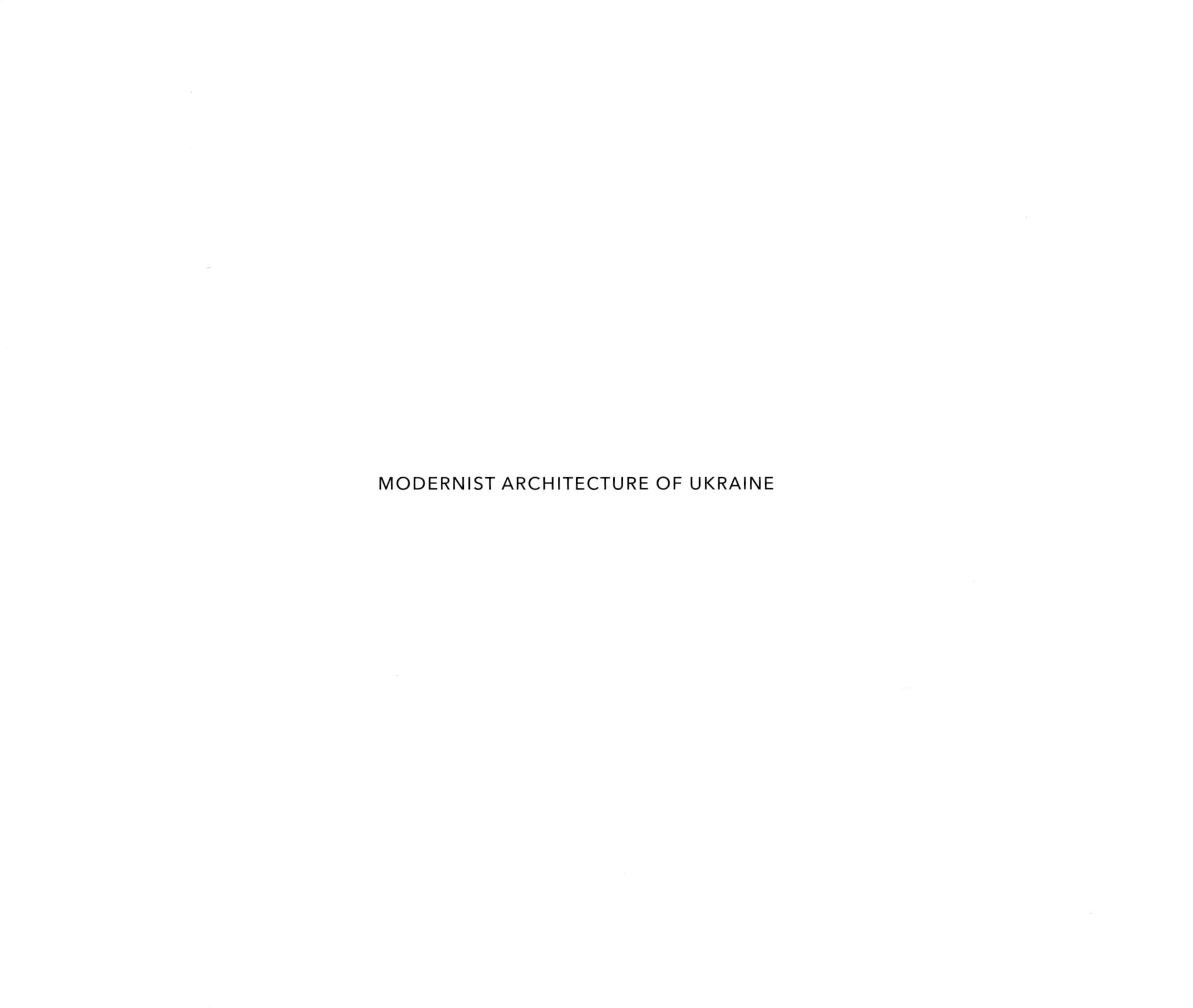

MODERNIST ARCHITECTURE OF UKRAINE

UKRAIN IAN MODERN ISM

DMYTRO SOLOVIOV

INTRODUCTION BY
OWEN HATHERLEY

FUEL

OWEN HATHERLEY

PALACES OF CULTURE IN A TIME OF BARBARISM
Ukrainian modernist architecture, after, before, and during war

When the Russian Federation launched its full-scale invasion of Ukraine in early 2022, there was soon an awareness in the west of the architectural treasures it put under threat. Scholars, art historians and activists shared images of gold-encrusted Orthodox cathedrals, brightly painted baroque streets, wooden houses and churches, at least some of which had been damaged or destroyed by Russian rockets. To anyone that knows the country, this presented a seductive but rather partial picture, a kitsch land of gold and domes and the Virgin Mary that had fairly little correspondence with anywhere most Ukrainians actually lived. In this book you'll find something else – a built landscape that is much more poorly understood, both outside Ukraine and, to a degree, even in Ukraine itself. Here, the Ukraine under threat is one of the most modernist of European countries, a place full of vast, ambitious, futuristic public buildings, mass produced public housing, cosmic public art and neglected public spaces where plants break through granite and concrete. Put together by the photographer, tour guide and activist Dmytro Soloviov, these images complicate many assumptions surrounding the country and its fight for survival. Rather than an intrinsically anti-communist, anti-Soviet history, they reveal the achievements of Ukrainians in the Soviet period. And given that this architecture, much more than the country's official historic heritage, comprises the country most people live in, it is ultimately these places that the missiles and mortars of Russia's 'anti-fascist' war, its 'special operation', are aimed at.

Ukrainian Modernism, the title of this book (and of Soloviov's Instagram account, from which he organises popular 'Excursions' to many of these buildings and places) is not a historical term – at the time the buildings in this book were constructed, nobody would have used it – 'it's modern architecture, and it's in Ukraine, that's basically it', as Soloviov tells me. In Ukrainian, as in Spanish or Russian, 'Modernism' usually means Style Moderne, what in other languages is called Art Nouveau, Jugendstil or Secession, the decadent, experimental, decorative architecture of the end of the 19th century and the very start of the 20th. So the term is rooted in another altogether, which was popular in the 1930s and beyond – 'The Modern Movement'. This 'movement' began in continental Europe in the aftermath of World War I – De Stijl in the Netherlands, the Neue Sachlichkeit and the Bauhaus in the Weimar Republic, Poetism in Czechoslovakia, and of course Constructivism in the new Soviet Union. Although it has extremely deep roots in Ukrainian cities like Kharkiv, Kyiv, Dnipro and Odesa, the Modern Movement's story as told by historians like Nikolaus Pevsner, Siegfried Giedion or Reyner Banham, has tended to misunderstand or overlook what happened here. The reason for this is that the Modern Movement's 'first wave' was violently interrupted in Ukraine, and not resumed until a 'second wave' decades later, a process of building, rejection and destruction that seems to recur and recur.

'The first wave of modernism in Ukraine, Constructivism, and the second wave after the 1950s, can both be attributed to a global modernist movement', says Soloviov, a movement which he finds in Ukrainian buildings as far back as the Philharmonic in Dnipro, dating from 1913. After 1917, a multi-front war that lasted four years pitted against each other Ukrainian nationalists of the left and right, Anarchists and Marxists, Russian Tsarists and Bolsheviks, Poles and Czechs and a French army of intervention, in competing alliances until an eventual Bolshevik victory at the start of the 1920s.

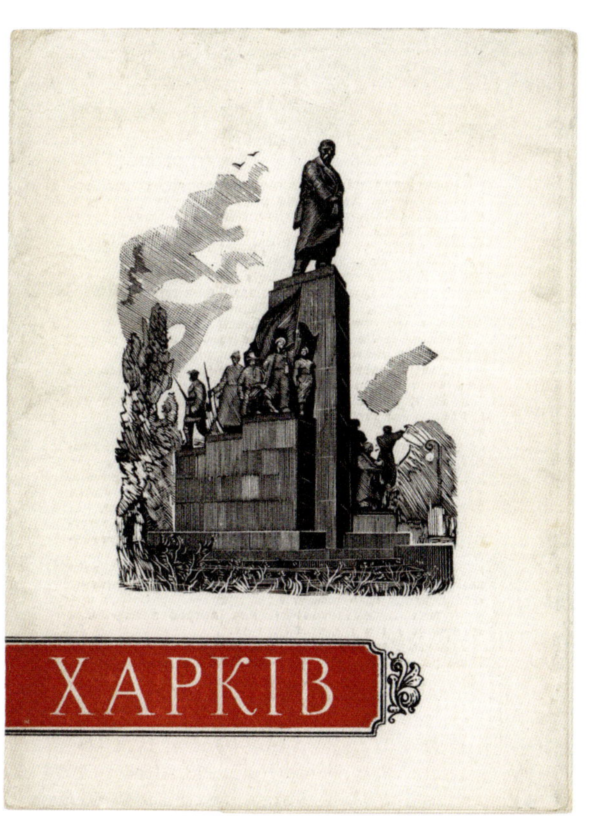

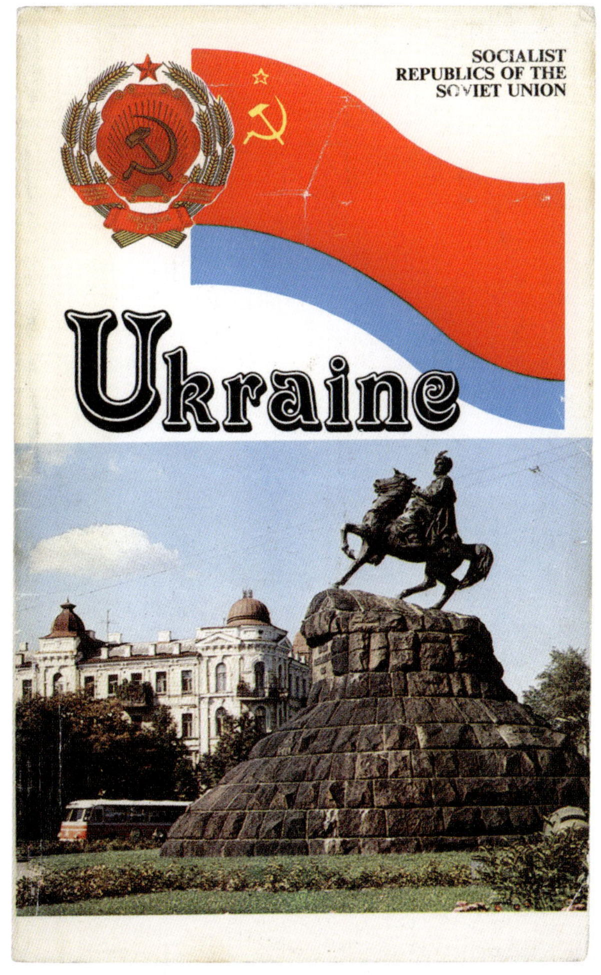

above: Kharkiv booklet, 1957
right: Ukraine guide book, 1987

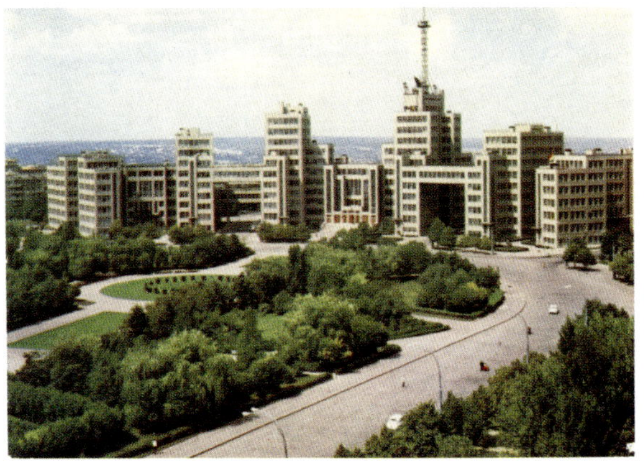

For the first decade of Soviet power, Ukraine had significant political and cultural autonomy: Kyiv and especially the capital at the time, Kharkiv, developed into centres of the European avant-garde, with filmmakers, painters, designers and architects achieving extraordinary work – some of which, like the multi-level mini-skyscraper complex of the Derzhprom Building in Kharkiv, attained international fame. Central, eastern and southern Ukraine have scores of Constructivist buildings, and you can see one of the most dramatic in this book, the Ilyich Palace of Culture in Dnipro, a building of sweeping curves and expressive angles, with all the abstraction and activity of the avant-garde abstract paintings of a Kasimir Malevich or an El Lissitzky, something only partly hidden by the pervasive neglect the building has suffered.

Soloviov grew up in Zaporizhzhia – a south-eastern industrial city located in what was a centre for Ukraine's once-autonomous Cossacks, which became the town of Oleksandrivsk in the Tsarist Empire before being built up into a major industrial metropolis during the first Five-Year Plan of 1928–32. During that period, Zaporizhzhia was filled with Constructivist buildings, including the 'Sotsmisto', the Socialist City, a series of Bauhaus-style blocks in open space, and the DniproHES dam, designed by the Constructivist team of the Vesnin Brothers. In the original drawings, these buildings glitter with glass and smooth concrete, but by the time they were completed in the mid-1930s they were clad in heavy purple and brown stone, sometimes acquiring neoclassical details, so their original modernism was obscured. During the Five-Year Plan, Ukrainian autonomy was suddenly and brutally curtailed, and a famine inflicted on the peasantry which killed millions. The Ukrainian artists who had made the country such a centre for the avant-garde were, for the most part, murdered under Stalin, then gradually forgotten, as Russification increased and a neo-Tsarist neoclassicism came to constitute 'socialist' architecture.

There have been efforts to explain this complicated modernist history in recent years, including the research project *Bauhaus Zaporizhzhia*, and another colloquium in the same city *on Atomic Cities*, which Soloviov attended, encountering the work of Ukrainian and Soviet modern architecture historians, such as the Kharkiv-based Ievgeniia Gubkina and the Belarusian Dmitri Zadorin. 'I never thought of these buildings as modernism', he recalls, so hidden were they by neglect and classicising cladding; 'I hadn't heard the word Bauhaus in the 25 years I lived in Zaporizhzhia, from my birth in 1990 to leaving in 2015'. It was visiting Warsaw and later, living in Kyiv, both cities with major architectural activist movements, that brought him to an enthusiasm for modern architecture.

For the most part, the Ukrainian modernism you can find here is from what Soloviov calls 'the second wave'. Gradually, after the death of Stalin in 1953, the Soviet Union's architects, artists and planners were able to re-connect themselves with the Modern Movement that their forebears in the 1920s had helped inspire in the first place. Trends which owed more than a little to the likes of the Derzhprom Building, like the International Style and the New Brutalism, were imported back into the USSR and re-interpreted. Given that Ukraine, especially Kyiv and the southern and eastern urban centres, were among the most populous and modern parts of the Soviet Union, there's a particularly large amount of it to be found, though it often existed in a complicated game of the permitted and the not-permitted, given that during the 1956–91 period de-Stalinisation and de-Russification were frequently interrupted by waves of Russification and re-centralisation. In general, Ukraine was one of the more repressive parts of the USSR during this era, contrasting with places like Estonia or Georgia, where it was easier to escape the supervision of Moscow. This is due in part to Ukraine's expansion at the end of World War II, with Western Ukraine – previously part of Romania, Czechoslovakia, and mainly, Poland – annexed to the Soviet republic. The Western regions bitterly resisted incorporation into the USSR, with a guerrilla war continuing right until the middle of the 1950s in and around Galicia and Volhynia (today, the Lviv, Volyn, Rivne, Ivano-Frankivsk and Ternopil Oblasts), leading to a lasting distrust of Ukrainians on the part of Moscow. Accordingly,

left: Derzhprom postcard, 1970
below: Zaporizhzhia postcard book, 1981

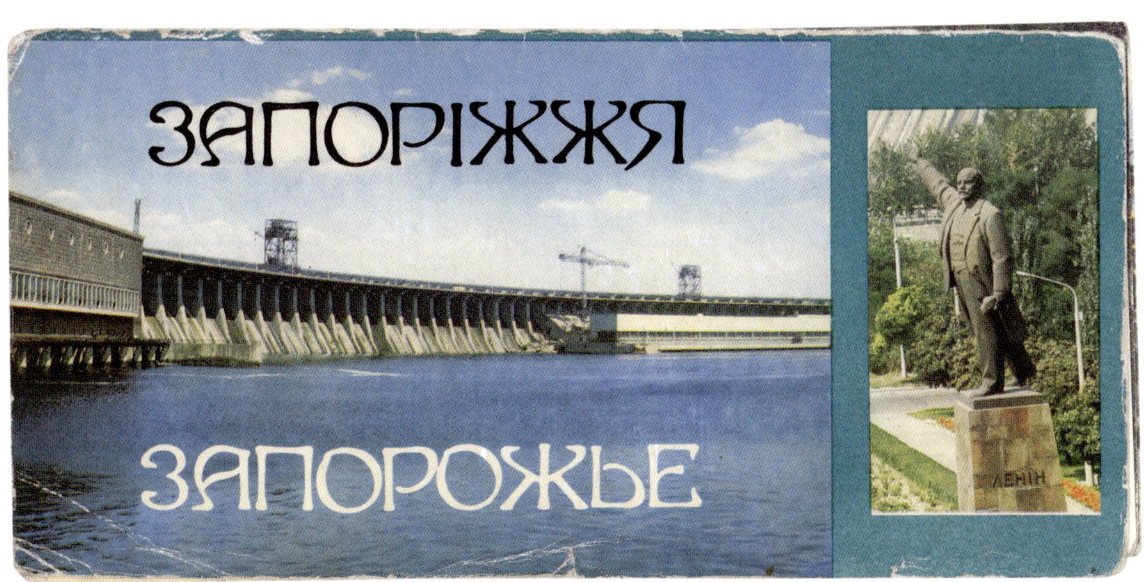

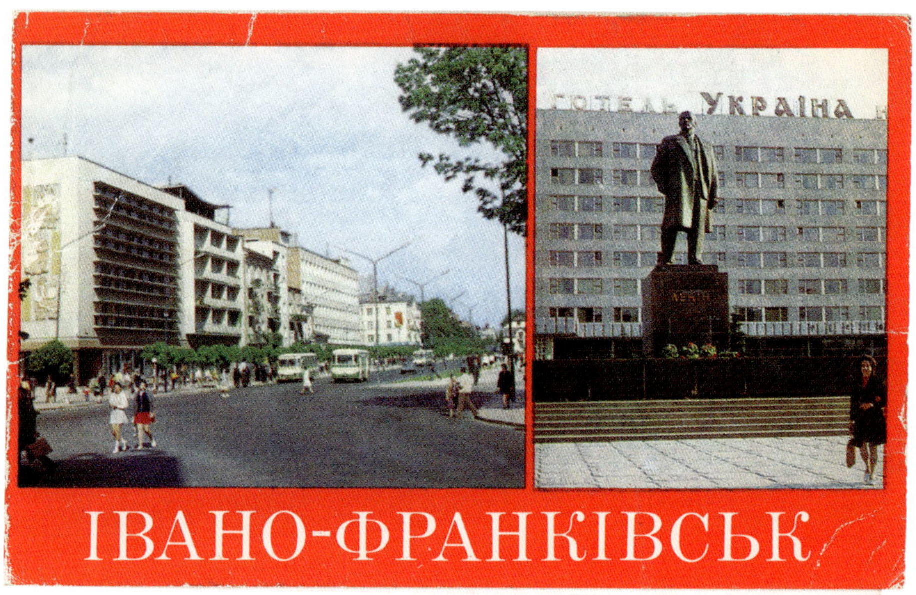

Ukrainian cultural expression was acceptable as folk art and kitsch, but much more suspicious was anything resembling the autonomous modernist culture of the 1920s. Some of the buildings in this book had artworks which were covered or altered while under construction; some took decades to build, as Soviet bureaucracy blocked or slowed the more complicated and ambitious projects.

The buildings of the sixties will, however, have seemed incredibly lightweight and optimistic after two ponderous, pompous decades of Stalinist neoclassicism, with its sense of immense, stone-clad heaviness and ornamental weight, all pinnacles, colonnades and pediments. Soloviov points out that 'the light, airy functionalism' of the 1960s and early 1970s is difficult to 'experience as it was intended' because of it being 'especially susceptible' to poor quality renovations, but you can see some of its qualities in the buildings in this book, such as the delicately constructed hyperbolic paraboloid of the Yuvileinyi Cinema and Concert Hall in the Black Sea port city of Kherson, one of several Ukrainian buildings influenced by the oyster-like concrete construction of the Polish-American architect Maciej Nowicki's Dorton Arena in Raleigh, North Carolina.

But it is the 'more imaginative', more monumental modern architecture of the 1970s and 1980s which has in recent years become famous in and outside of Ukraine. There was a lot of it – Dnipro, in particular, as the hometown of Leonid

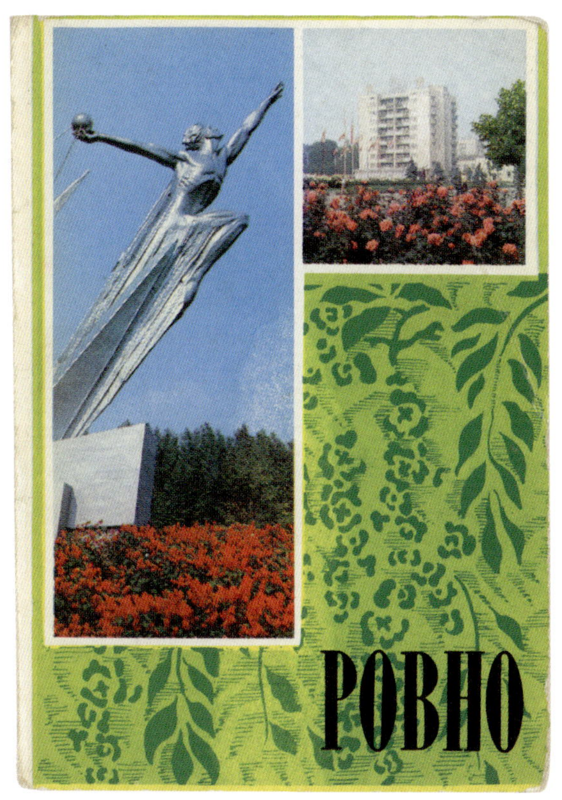

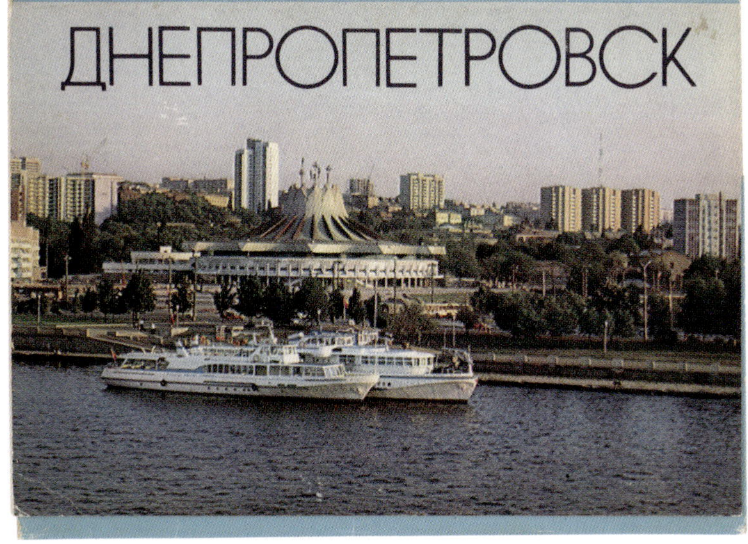

left: Ivano-Frankivsk postcard book, 1977
above: Rivne postcard book, 1989
right: Dnipropetrovsk postcard book, 1982

Brezhnev and a centre for rocket production, became a showcase for vast, experimental modern structures. This work is remarkable both for the fearless, cosmic scale of its architecture and for its incorporation, unusual in Western Europe or North America at the time, of monumental propaganda art – mosaics, sculptural reliefs – which show a sometimes-breathtaking fusion of Mexican muralism, Constructivist and Suprematist abstraction, children's book illustration, Orthodox mosaic traditions and the 'severe' style of post-Stalin realist painting. Sculptural, Brutalist-inspired structures such as the Dnipro Circus and Accommodation Building or the jagged, vertiginous buildings of the Taras Shevchenko National University of Kyiv draw, much more than architecture of the Stalin years, on international sources. The Brazilian modernism of Oscar Niemeyer, the Japanese Metabolism of Kenzo Tange or the British New Brutalism of James Stirling, were all published in Soviet magazines and books, and all had obvious effects on Soviet architecture of the Brezhnev years – but the end result is oddly specifically Soviet, with references to space exploration and communist millenarianism, with utopia always just around the corner. Also Soviet perhaps is the avoidance of 'truth to materials', the unclad concrete surfaces of European or Japanese Brutalist buildings. Soviet architects and engineers were not so confident of the quality of their concrete work, so tended to clad concrete-framed or precast concrete panel buildings in tile or mosaic – which in turn, provided possible surfaces for monumental art.

You can see traces too, in the unexpectedly heroic architecture of the Brezhnev years in Ukraine, of what was happening in the 1920s, as with the glass cylinder towers of the canteen at the Kyiv Polytechnical Institute or the Control Tower of the Hydroelectric Power Plant in Kaniv, and a gradual appreciation started to form about what had happened in Ukraine in the avant-garde years. Interest in the past also thrived in the last Soviet buildings, which delved into local

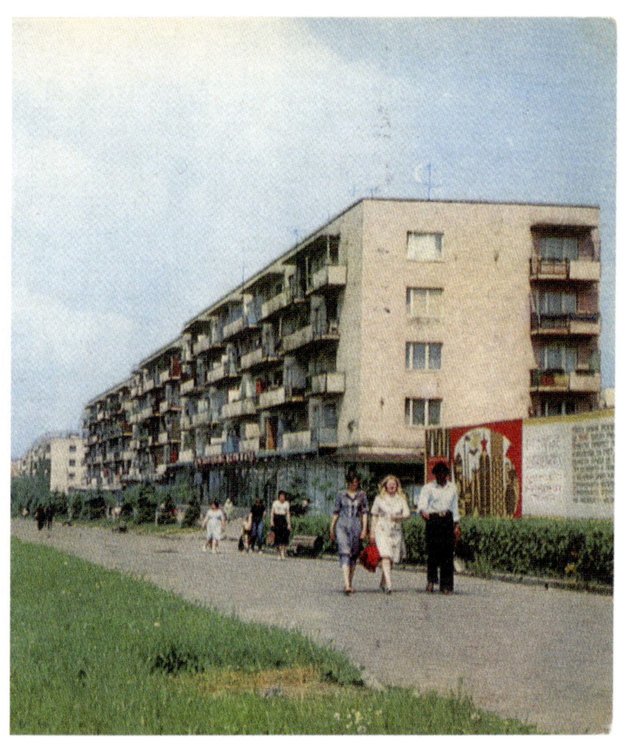

above: Chernivtsi postcard, 1982
right: Lviv bus station postcard, 1980s

and international forms of Postmodernism. Some of these still look futuristic, like the Palace of Pioneers in Dnipro, completed in 1991, which shows some awareness of the High-Tech of Richard Rogers and Norman Foster, but others are specifically regional. Among these are the international collaboration of Slavutych, the town built for Chernobyl employees who had to be moved out of the contaminated new town of Pripyat, with its specially designed Baltic and Caucasian 'quarters', their Hanseatic or Persian details executed in concrete panels. Similarly, a trend began towards regional modernism in particularly rural Western Ukraine, when architects carried on a dialogue with Hutsul folk traditions. This, for Soloviov, is probably the 'most distinct and original' modern design trend of Soviet Ukraine, and you can see a little of it here, in the steep roofs and peculiar angles of the 'Romantyk' Palace of Youth in Lviv or the Verkhovyna Sanatorium and Administrative Building in Mizhhiria, Zakarpattia.

Soloviov developed his enthusiasm for this architecture into work as a tour guide, beginning with a tour of 'Late Soviet Podil', the lower town area of Kyiv, a place of great architectural variety, ranging from Ukrainian baroque to neoclassicism to Constructivism, lined by tall 19th-century tenements. In the 1980s, these were supplemented with brick flats and offices that had a fragmentary but complementary relationship to the historic buildings, rather than simply shunning them in the modernist style. This, for Soloviov, was an interesting moment because the architecture isn't banal Postmodernism, not just 'towers of glass' or neoclassical kitsch, but 'good Postmodernism', where modernism was 'still playing the main part'. The tour was a success, and it as a tour guide that Soloviov has become well-known in Kyiv and in Ukraine more generally.

For a campaigner for modern architecture in Ukraine, things were difficult already before the full-scale Russian invasion of 2022. Ukrainian capitalism since 1991 has been dominated by oligarchs, equally brutal and rapacious with or

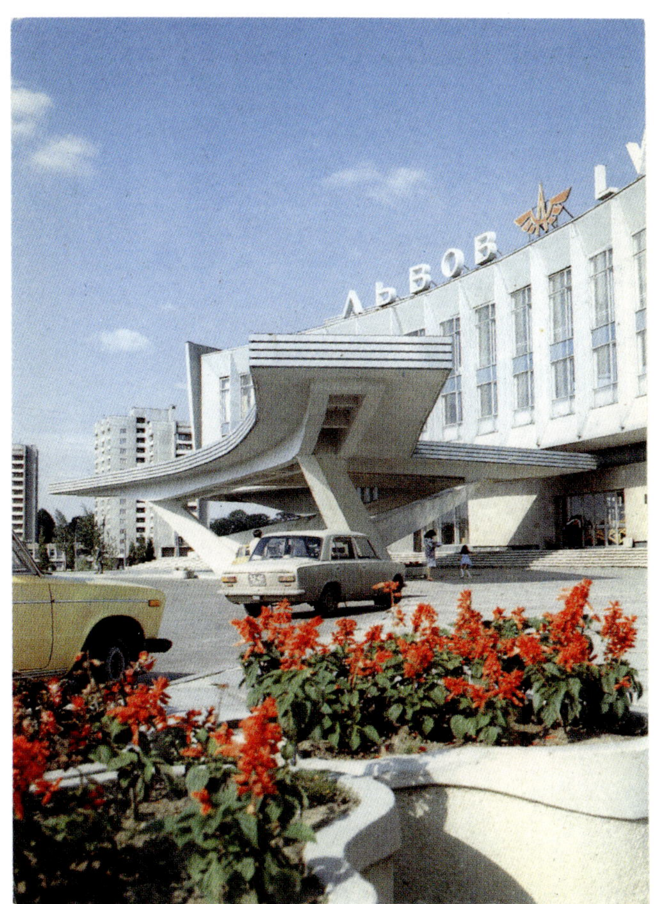

without ties to Moscow, and these huge, mainly public buildings, mainly serving the Brezhnev-era welfare state, have been an encumbrance to property development; their materials and artworks can be expensive to conserve, or require expertise to do so. Much as it's hard to find many Ukrainian buildings of note from the 1990s and 2000s, Soloviov is hard-pressed to come up with a positive example of renovation; he names the Kyiv Tramway Dispatch building, a punchy little structure of brick with porthole windows: 'they just washed it and removed the plastic siding, which is the best renovation you can do with a building that is structurally OK.' Elsewhere, neglect, demolition or hugely insensitive renovations have been a common fate, including, imminently, one of the finest of Kyiv's modernist buildings, the Koroliov Palace of Culture.

But this process has been made immeasurably worse by the Russian invasion. In 2022, when I interviewed him for an article about the effects of the war on the architectural activist community in Ukraine, Soloviov told me that 'since the war started, I've been posting only buildings and monuments that suffered during the Russian invasion.' Rather than seeing these as monuments to Soviet oppression, 'responses for the buildings were exclusively sympathetic', though he counted out 'some omnipresent Russians who are ready to justify any war crime'. However, this 'got trickier when Ukrainian officials started demolishing Soviet monuments, including World War II memorials.' Then, most of his Instagram followers 'opposed destruction and called for preservation or at least civilised removal', he said, 'but there has been a vocal minority who saw this destruction as a vital part of the war effort, and branded preservationists as "pro-Russian".' As awareness of the magnitude of what was happening became clearer to outside observers, Soloviov moved back to documenting modern buildings and advocating for their preservation, but even then, during the war it has been difficult to actually photograph many buildings, ruined or

otherwise, given the roadblocks and checkpoints between Ukrainian towns and cities. Even with press accreditation, there is an understandable suspicion of anyone roaming around with a camera. So there is no ruin porn in this book, no images that rub your face in the misery and horror of Russia's invasion; there are traces of the war and of wartime destruction to be found here, but only if you look very closely.

There is a link between the war and Soloviov's tours, which have become a much bigger part of his life since the invasion. Talking to me in summer 2024, he says, 'at the start of the war I thought "what can I do here, how can I help?", so I focused on bringing international attention to what is happening, doing posts about the destruction'; but he then thought 'why should I halt my tours because of the war? – matters of culture and heritage are most relevant now. And people might need moments of normality, too'. In April 2022 he led tours of the western city of Ivano-Frankivsk, where he was based at the time with his girlfriend, whose family had fled to the city to shelter from the bombardment of Kyiv. That year, Soloviov described the reception of the tours to me as: 'Very warm. People seemed gleeful and were laughing happily at my jokes. The feedback I received afterwards was nothing short of inspiring. To quote a few people's Instagram stories, my tours were "the happiest moment since the war started", and "a great way to reduce anxiety and distract from 24/7 news consumption".'

Today, he says that he was motivated to start the tours because 'I wanted to find like-minded people, and just find friends. I can hang out with these bright people, and I can make money, which is important if I want to dedicate my life to this stuff' – particularly as he lost his job in 2022, which meant that 'tours have become my main source of income, and my main source of socialisation in Kyiv'. Recently, he was even able to take a now-rare western visitor on a commissioned tour of Kyiv, and then to the extraordinary nuclear new town of Slavutych.

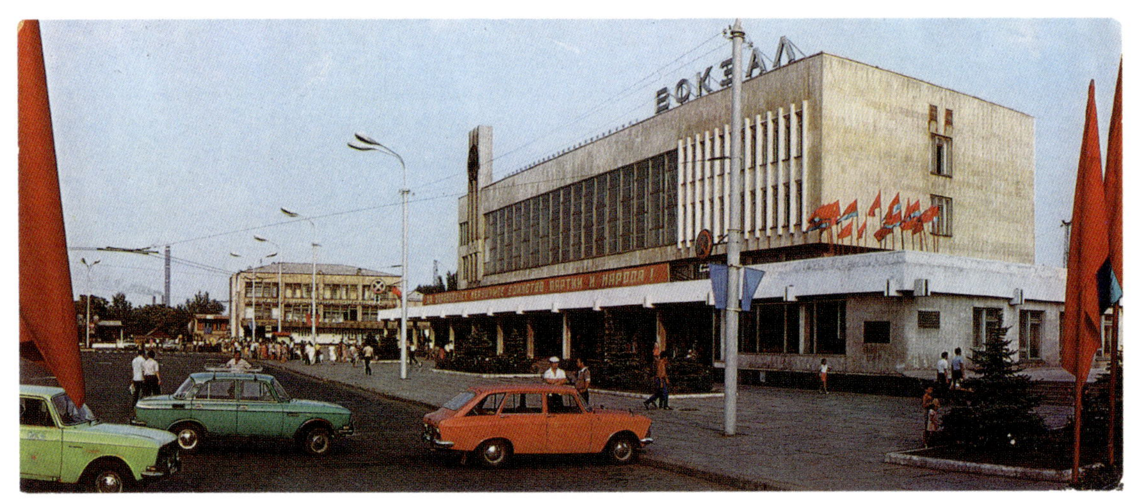

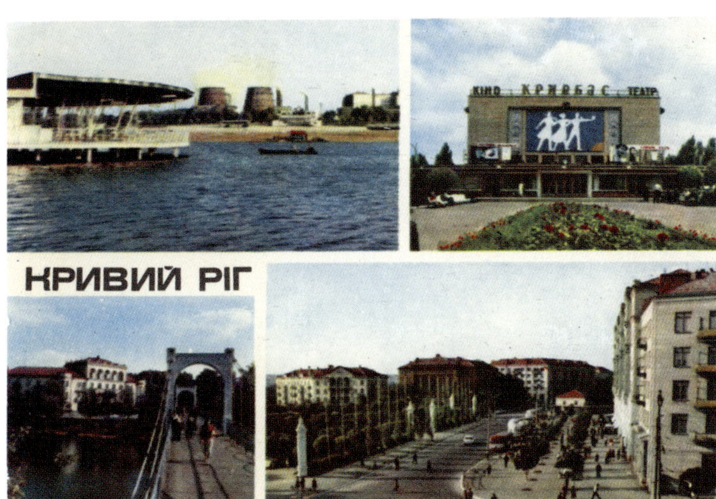

top: Mariupol train station postcard, 1970s
bottom: Kryvyi Rih postcard, 1969

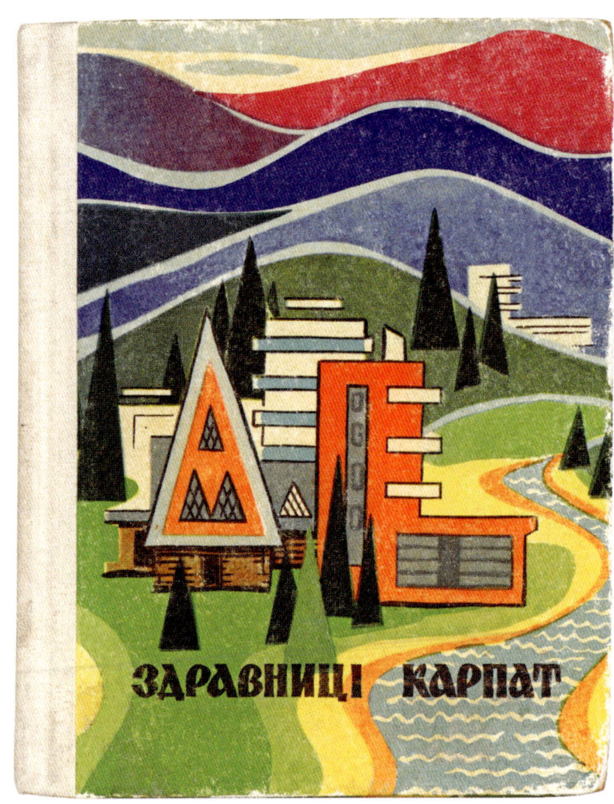

above: *Health Resorts of the Carpathians*, 1975
right: *Ukrainian Language*, school book, 1987

The tours attract 'a diverse group, but mainly young adults, and they're very inspiring for me'; at the end of each one there are 'after-parties', where participants have tea and dinner, and there's a Telegram group for tour regulars to chat to each other. There's also a politics to this, in exploring these public spaces in the context both of the war and of a renewed and understandable disgust at a period in which Ukrainians and Russians were, according to official propaganda, 'brotherly nations' (with Russia of course the overbearing elder brother). 'It was important', Soloviov says, 'to be able to express my views' on the tours, 'and to help people appreciate this often-despised architecture'. 'I talk a lot about politics, since it is inseparable from the built environment. I often point out the benefits of socially oriented, progressive policies as opposed to neoliberal capitalist ones, which enrich the rich and subdue everyone and everything else.' In this context, the architecture is a way into talking about political change: 'in Ukraine, it's not only socialist architecture that is stigmatised, but the whole leftist ideology is frowned upon', given that 'people here often have trouble distinguishing between the retrograde dreams of bringing back the Soviet Union and the desire to evolve our independent, peaceful, democratic Ukraine into a welfare state. They might often agree with the latter, but the ingrained aversion to the word "socialism" is just too strong. I try to work with that.'

For Soloviov, this project means taking a nuanced, but not uncritical, look at the structures and functions thrown up by late Soviet modernism in Ukraine, which have been very hard to find in post-Soviet Ukraine. That is, all that affordable mass housing, all those 'Palaces of Culture', all that public transport infrastructure, the functions of which were hardly the focus of oligarchic capitalism of the 1990s and since, as inequalities have skyrocketed and construction has pursued the path of luxury housing for the minority, and notorious boondoggles such as the grotesque 'palace' of president Viktor Yanukovych, overthrown by the protests on Kyiv's Maidan in 2014.

I wondered whether the tours were more or less difficult in different parts of the country. Soloviov replied that 'in the Western regions there is slightly more spite towards that period, while in Kyiv slightly less spite, but nonetheless, since 2022 the amount of hate and hostility towards that period increased a hundredfold'. This hostility has been rife on the internet, but has only come up once on the tours – 'it's mostly enthusiasts, and there's only been one or two negative comments on a tour'. This was in the Kyiv canalside suburb of Rusanivka, where one of the group took offence at his drawing attention to a mosaic of Young Pioneers in a school, which was scheduled to be covered by insulation. 'One lady said, "They're right to destroy it," but back in the day, almost everyone was a Pioneer', he recalls. 'Even my mother was a Pioneer – do I need to burn pictures of her in a red scarf, too? Those mosaics are part of our material history – the only truthful one. Apart from their artistic merit and cultural value, and – with the rate we destroy them – almost archaeological significance, at the very least we should keep them for posterity, for future generations to learn about the past and to be able to make their own judgments about it, providing an opportunity for critical reflection.'

A popular post on Soloviov's Instagram account catalogued images of Soviet mosaics in Mariupol, many of which will have been destroyed during the apocalyptic assault on the city by the Russian army in 2022. For Soloviov, rather than seeing Putin's Russia as an upholder of the Soviet legacy, his rule is actually the negation of anything that was progressive or valuable in it. In 2022, he told me, 'It's easy to think of contemporary Russia as a direct descendant of the Soviet Union, the same country under a different flag. Nothing can be further from the truth. Putin's Russia is a kleptocratic empire, driven solely by his expansionism and hunger for power, while the Soviet Union had a different agenda, driven by communist ideology. It's obvious Putin doesn't follow any ideology, nor does he care about Soviet

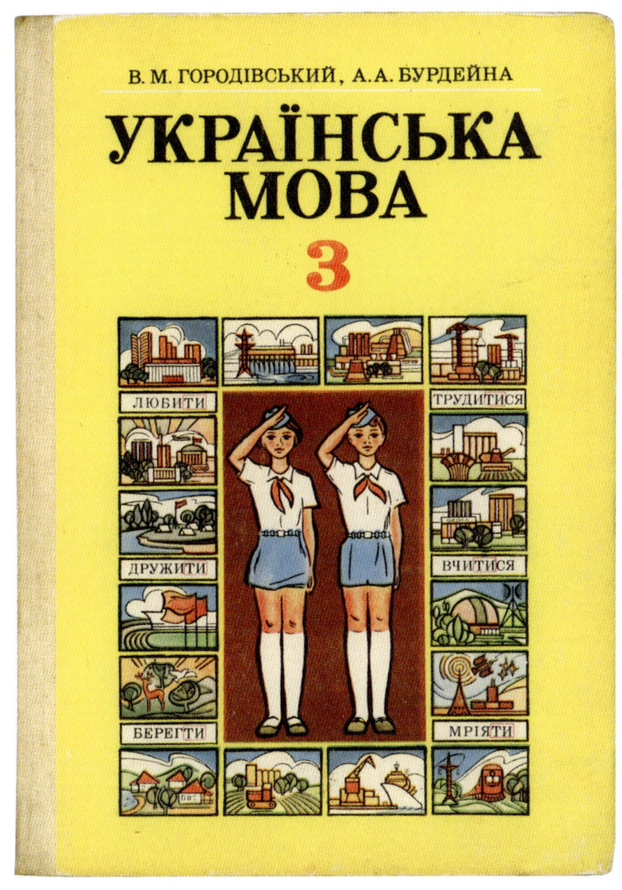

heritage. Take Soviet architecture, which was demolished en masse in Moscow, or destroyed by Russian rockets in Ukraine.' He does note that Putin's statements make this matter 'pretty confusing for an outside observer, with all his shenanigans, like his constant whining about the dissolution of the Soviet Union [and] occasional brandishing of Soviet flags on the battlefield' – though he points out that at the start of the war, Putin blamed Lenin for the 'crime' of the creation of a large, autonomous Ukrainian state within the Soviet Union a century ago.

Instead of seeing Putin as 'Soviet', Soloviov says, 'if one feels the urge to connect contemporary Russia to something, the Tsarist Russian Empire seems less far-fetched to me'. He connects this to some of the far-right cultists that have been deeply involved in the invasion of Ukraine – from Russian Minister of Defence Sergei Shoigu, a 'huge fan of Roman von Ungern-Sternberg', a proto-fascist general and monarchist, who fought to restore the Tsarist Empire in the Civil War of 1917–21; to the fascist LARPer Igor 'Strelkov' Girkin, who spearheaded the 2014 invasion of eastern Ukraine. He quotes the Ukrainian leftist Taras Kuzio's pinpointing of the Russian government's actual politics: 'most definitions of fascism would indicate a dictatorial system of government marked by nationalism, militarism, xenophobia, revisionism and expansionism. Putin's Russia unquestionably ticks all of these boxes.' Soloviov 'would only add one more important trait of fascist ideology – anti-communism.'

In those first months of the war, Soloviov told me he was 'confident it is vital to separate the Soviet Union from Russian imperialism. In the very least to ensure the survival of Soviet Ukrainian heritage – the result of 70 years of labour by Ukrainian artists and architects.' This has become increasingly difficult, both due to the pace of destruction and the desire of Ukrainians to decouple themselves from any relationship to a historical state with its capital in Moscow. While taking his images of the Uzhhorod Palace of Children and Youth in Western Ukraine, near the EU border, Soloviov could see women sewing nets for the military, a small reminder of the mass participation of civil society in the war effort that helped Ukrainians, to the surprise of everyone else, to push back what Putin expected to be an easy victory in 2022. But the image in this book that perhaps most sums up the efforts to retain the memory of a Ukrainian modernism is of the Kyiv Crematorium, an extraordinary piece of organic architecture in concrete, designed at the end of the sixties by Avraam Miletskyi and completed over a decade later. It is now a fairly well-known building, shared all over Instagram and featuring on the covers of photobooks, but there are elements to it that bear very close examination.

Surrounding the hauntingly abstract domes of the Crematorium is a sculptural wall, both figurative and abstract, cathartic and expressionistic, which was intended to represent the horrors which Kyiv had been subjected to in the 20th century, through war, fascism, and Stalinism. The form and the content of the sculpture was more than a little too close to the bone for the bureaucrats of Brezhnev-era Soviet Ukraine, and they ordered it to be covered with concrete. In the last few years, activists have been gradually chipping away at this surface to expose the sculpture, and it can be seen in the foreground of Soloviov's photograph. At the Kyiv Crematorium, activists were able not merely to celebrate Ukrainian Soviet architects' – here, very real – achievements, but also to emphasise what had to be concealed and obscured in the Soviet era. It is not just conservation, but a widening out from there to do what the Soviets couldn't: start an honest conversation about the forces that have time and again subjected this country to needless suffering – dictatorship, militarism, nationalism, the bullying chauvinism of the world's 'great powers'. That should not be covered over again.

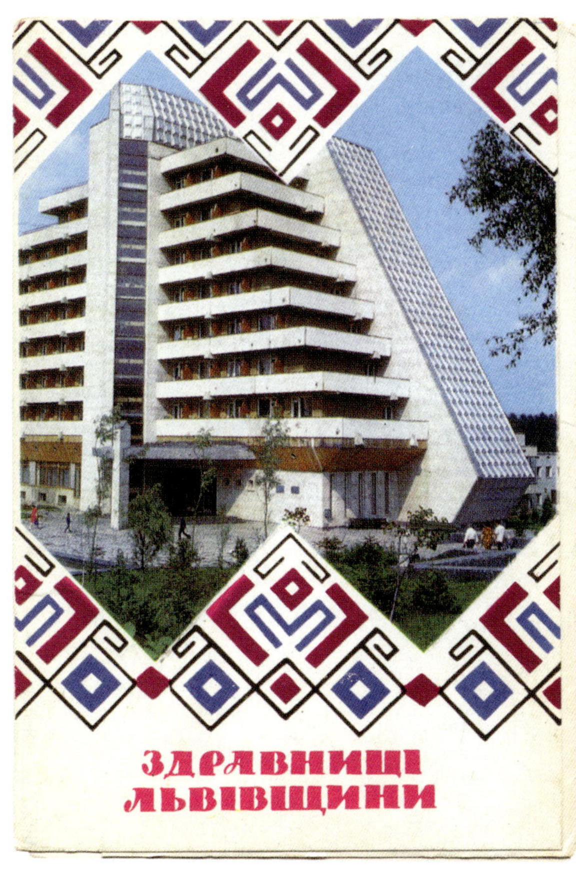

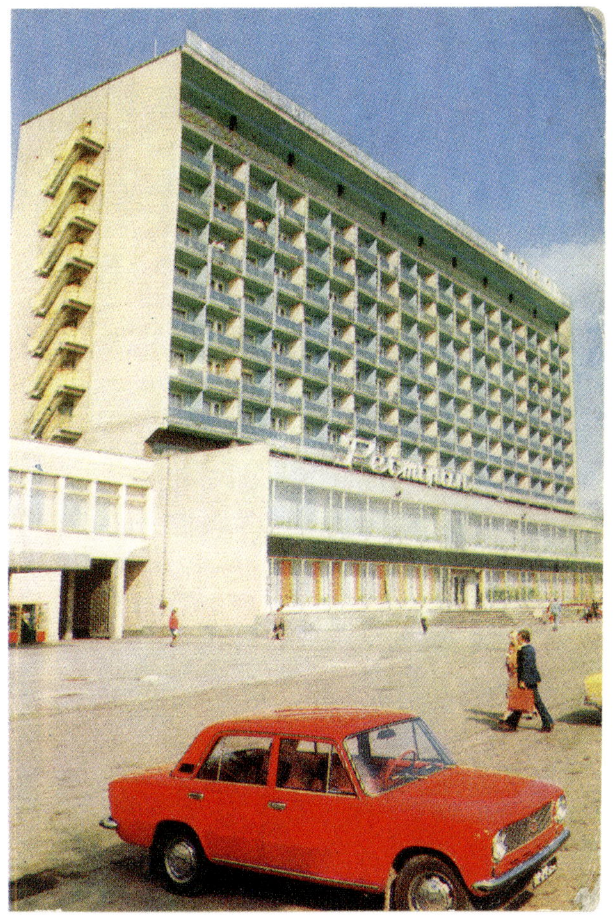

above: *Health Resorts of the Lviv Region*, 1980s
right: Zaporizhzhia postcard, 1980

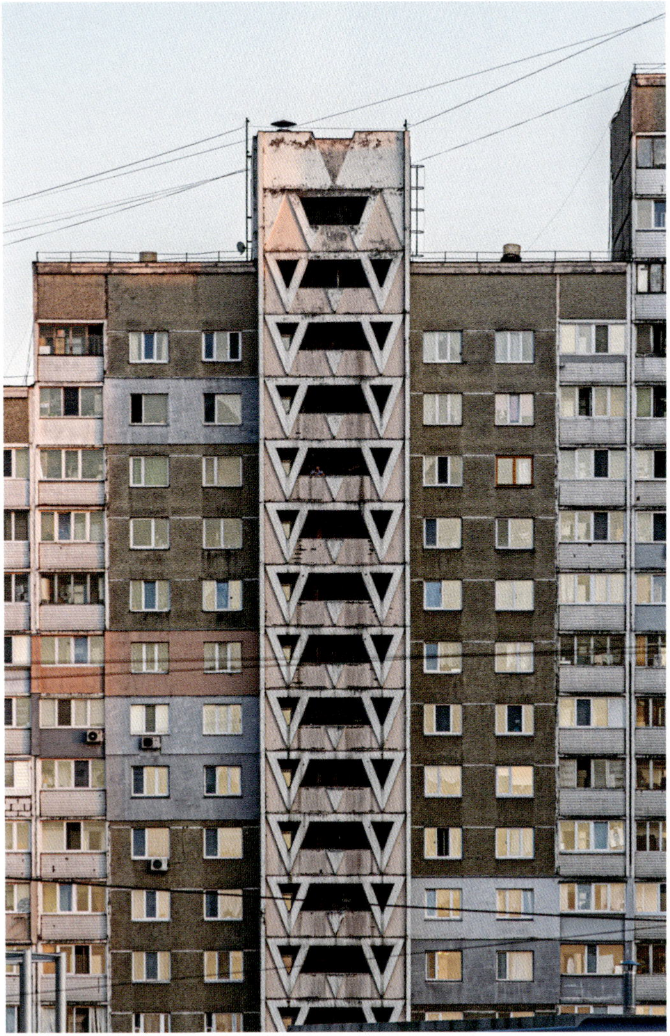

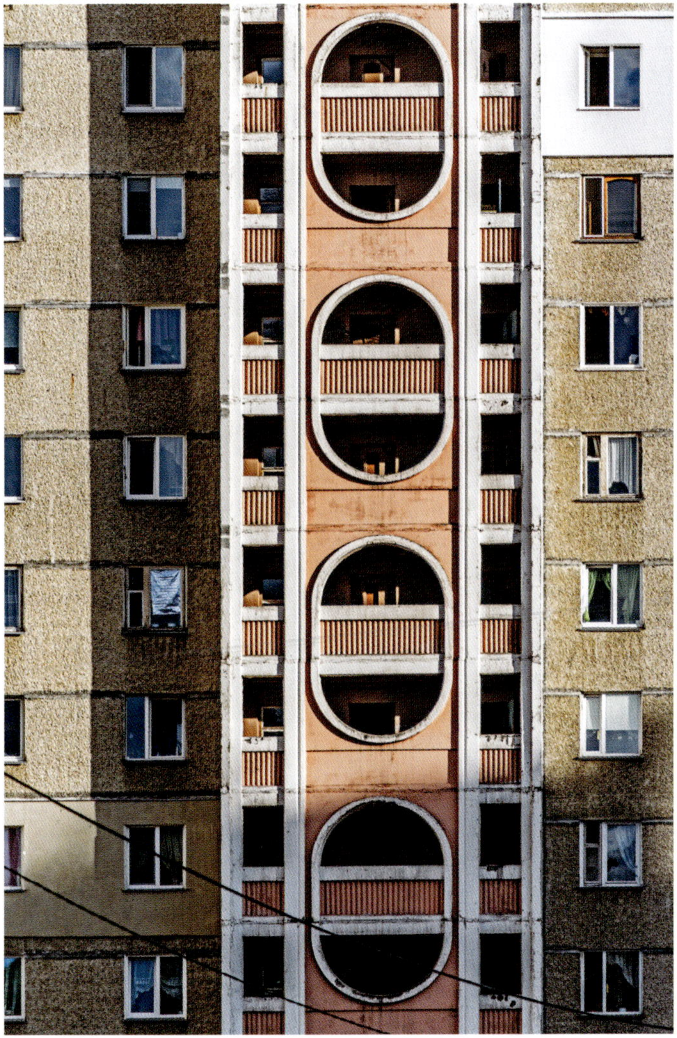

    Residential buildings, Kyiv

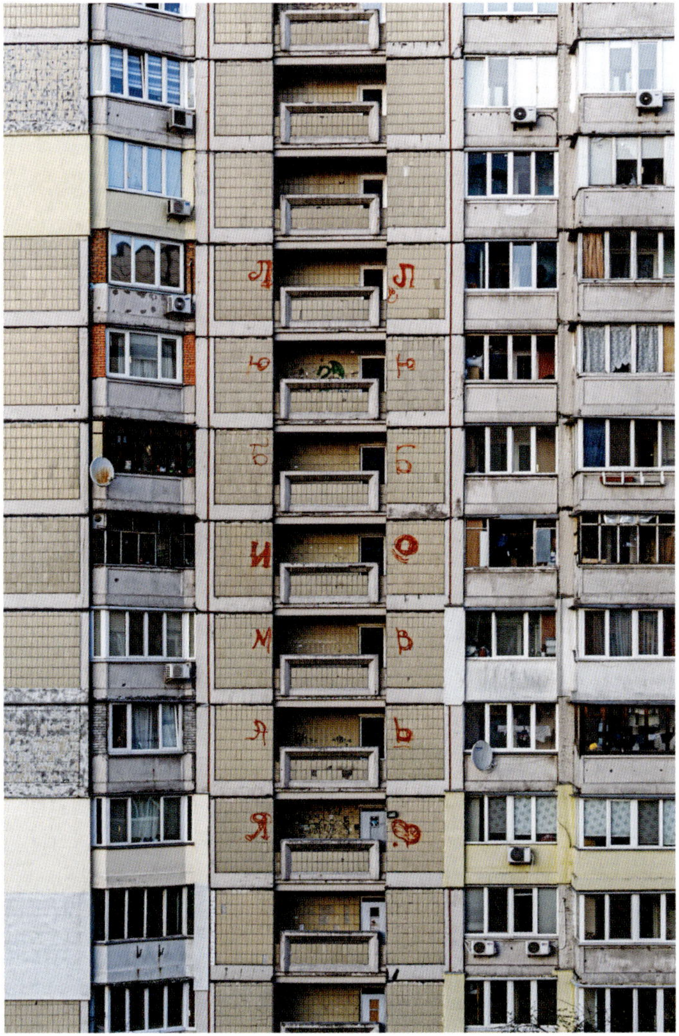

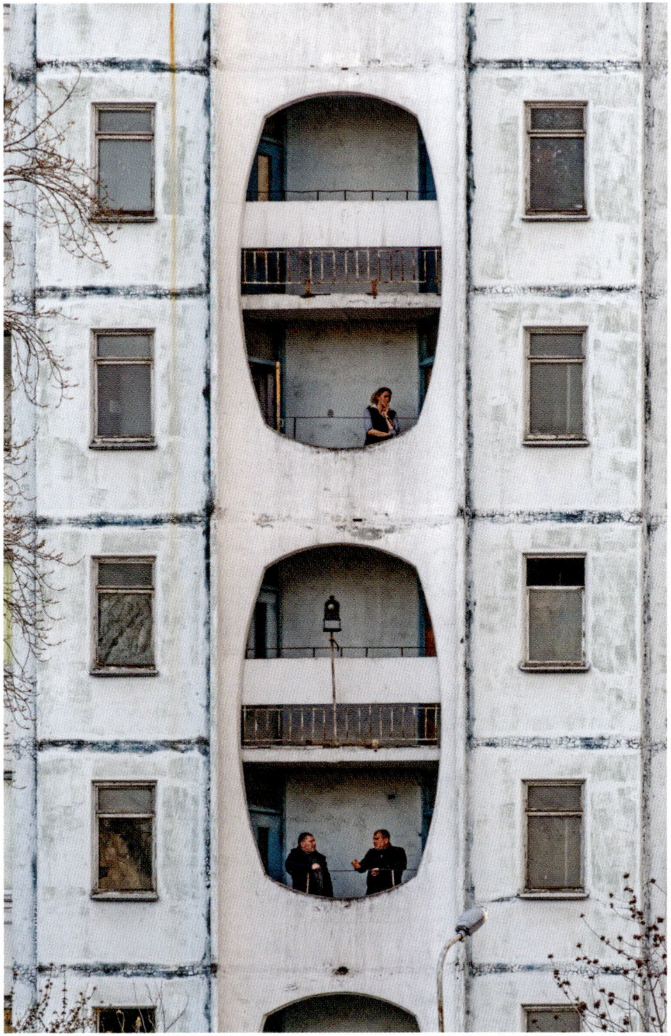

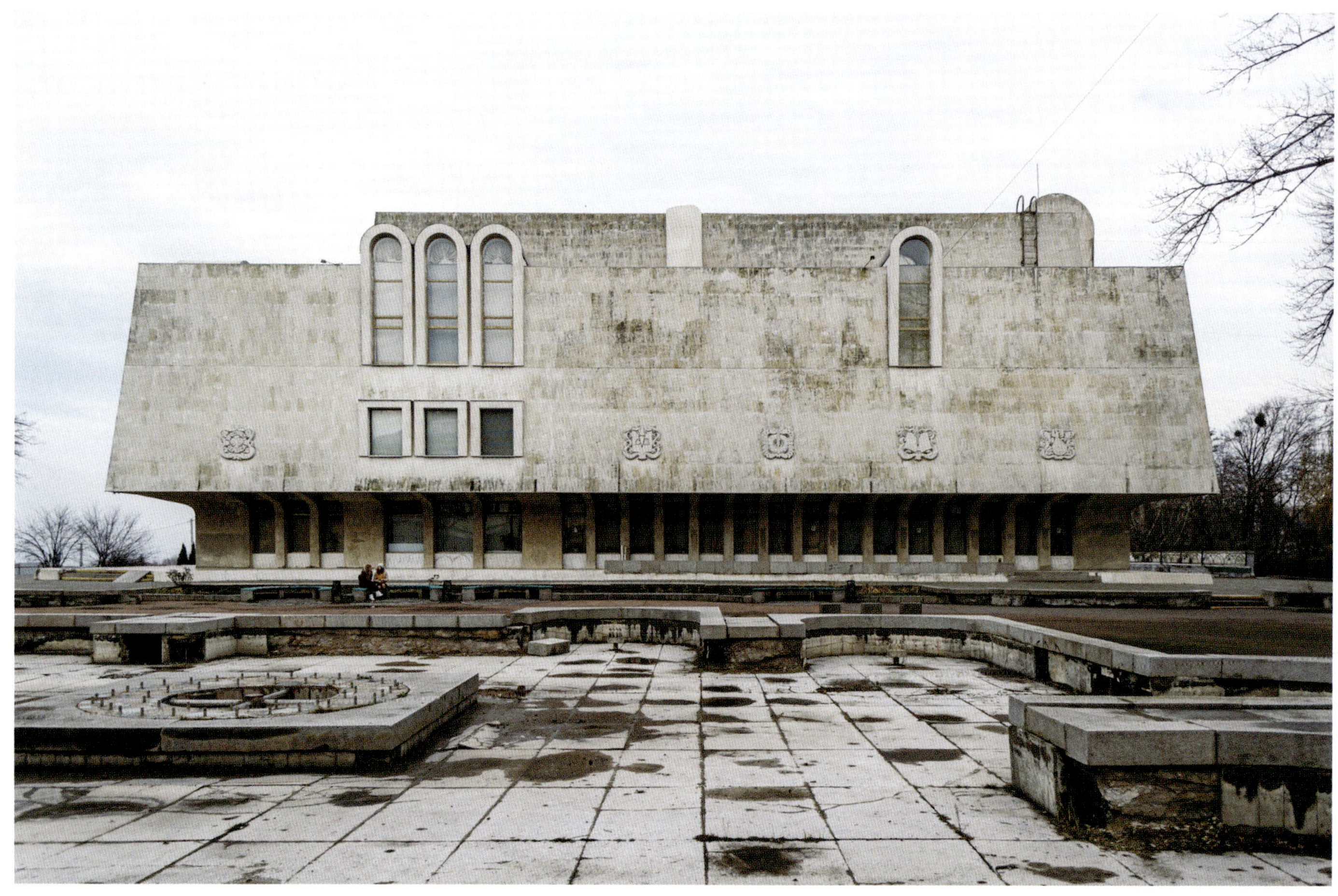

Cherkasy Local History Museum
Cherkasy
1978–83
Architects: Leonid Konatskyi, Mykola Sobchuk, Serhii Fursenko

Engineer: Oleksandra Stetsenko
Artists: Nataliia Borysenko, Anatolii Kushch, Volodymyr Priadka, Ivan Lytovchenko, Nataliia Lytovchenko, Liudmyla Zhohol

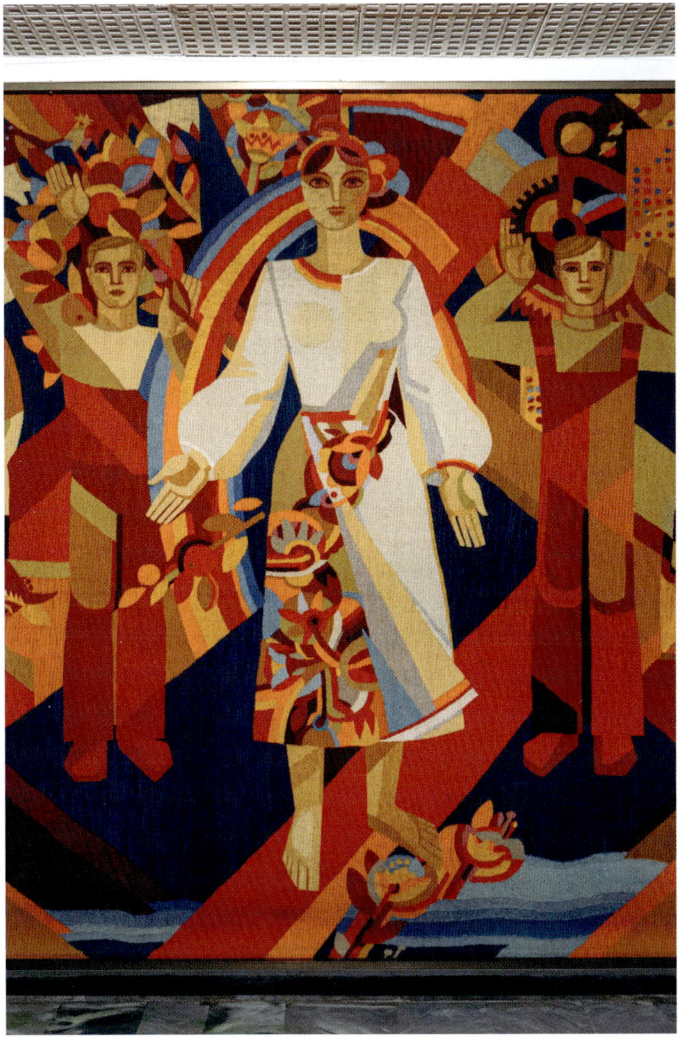

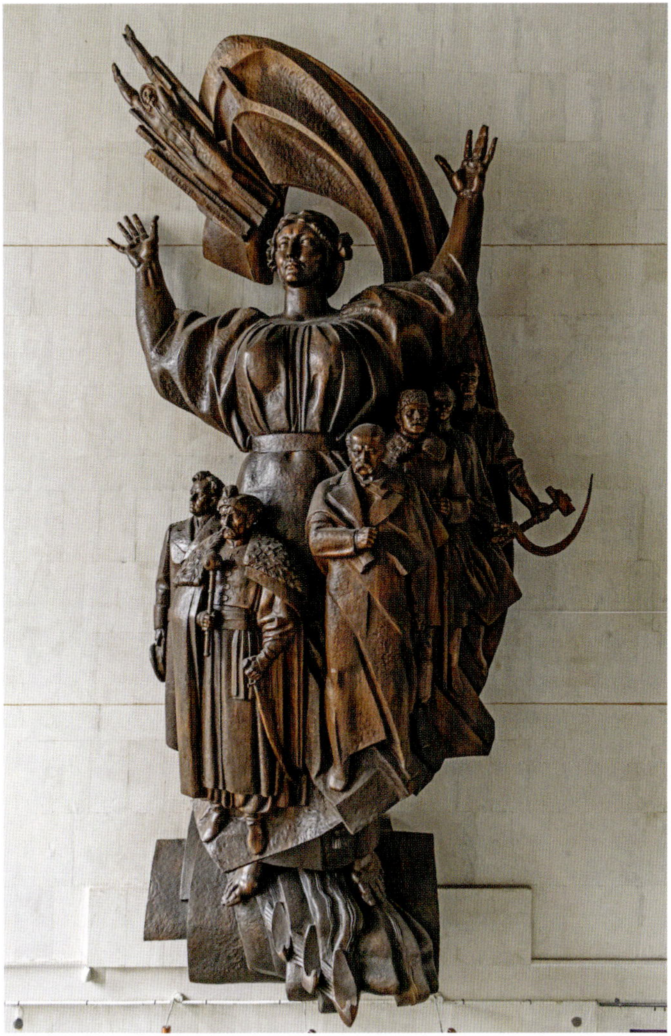

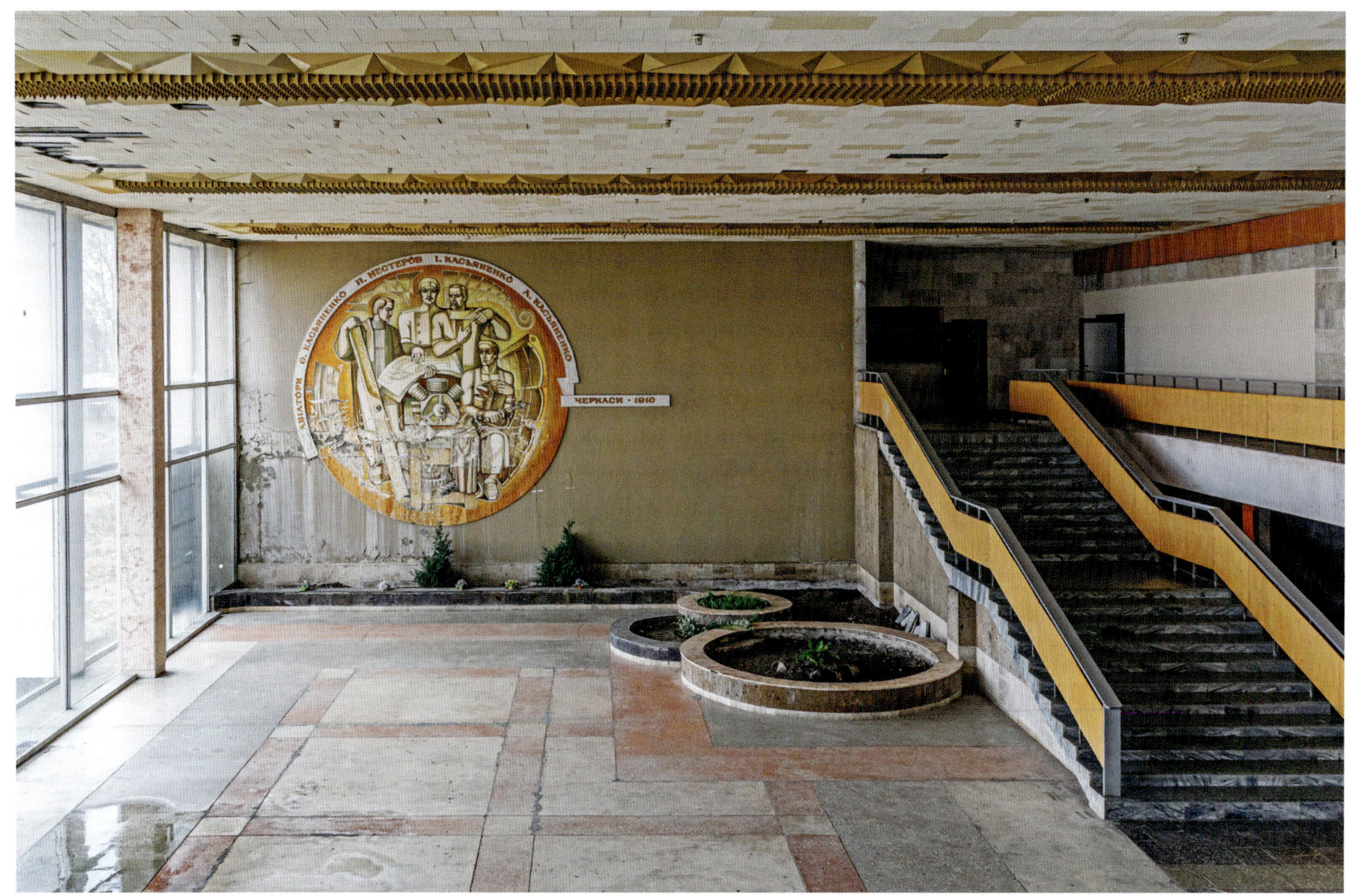

Cherkasy Airport Terminal
Cherkasy
1985
Architect: Ivan Pomazan

At the time of its completion Cherkasy Airport was one of the largest in the USSR with around 80 flights a day, including to international destinations. In 1992, after struggling to maintain services following the fall of the USSR, operations were reduced to domestic flights only.

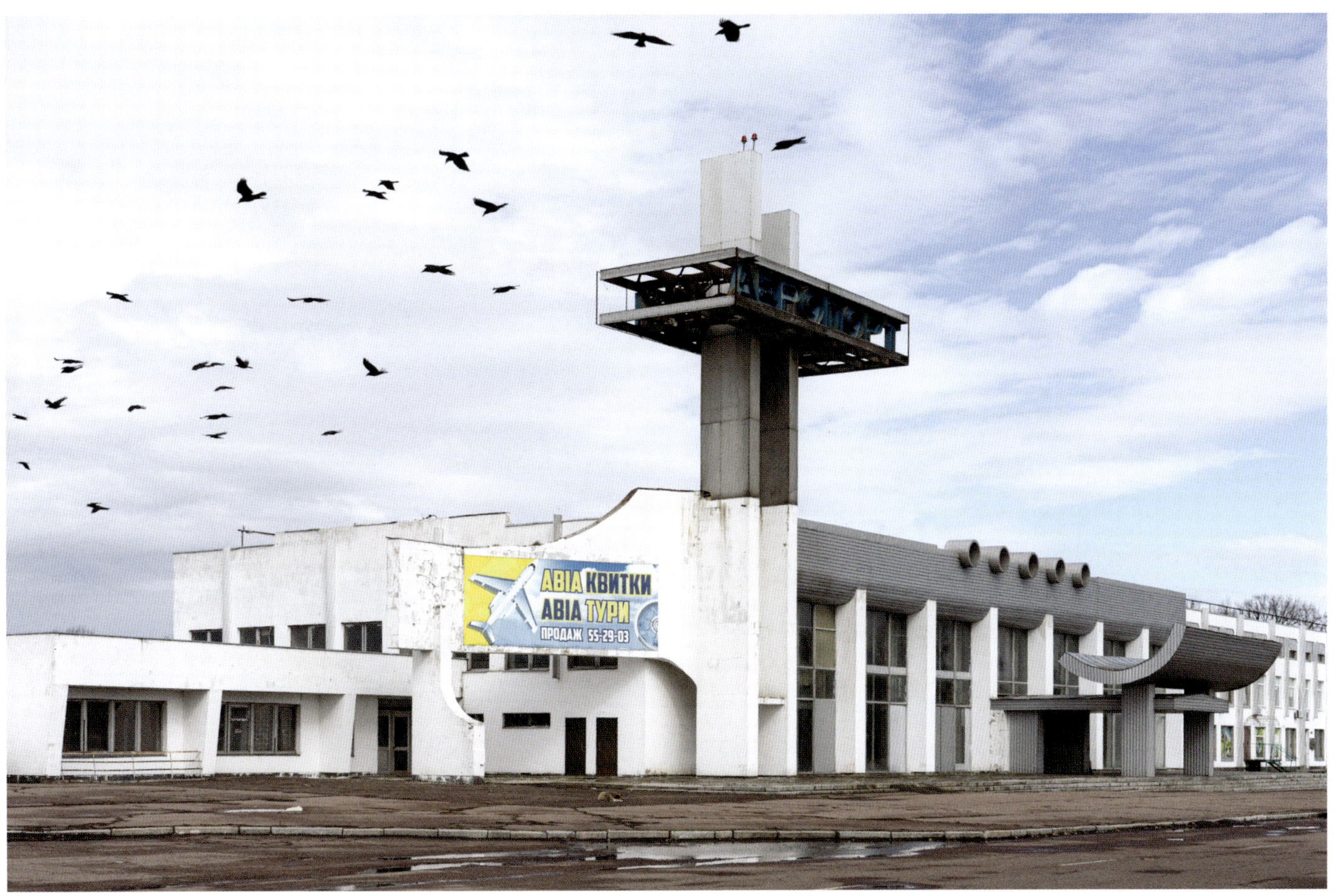

АВІА КВИТКИ
АВІА ТУРИ
ПРОДАЖ 55-29-03

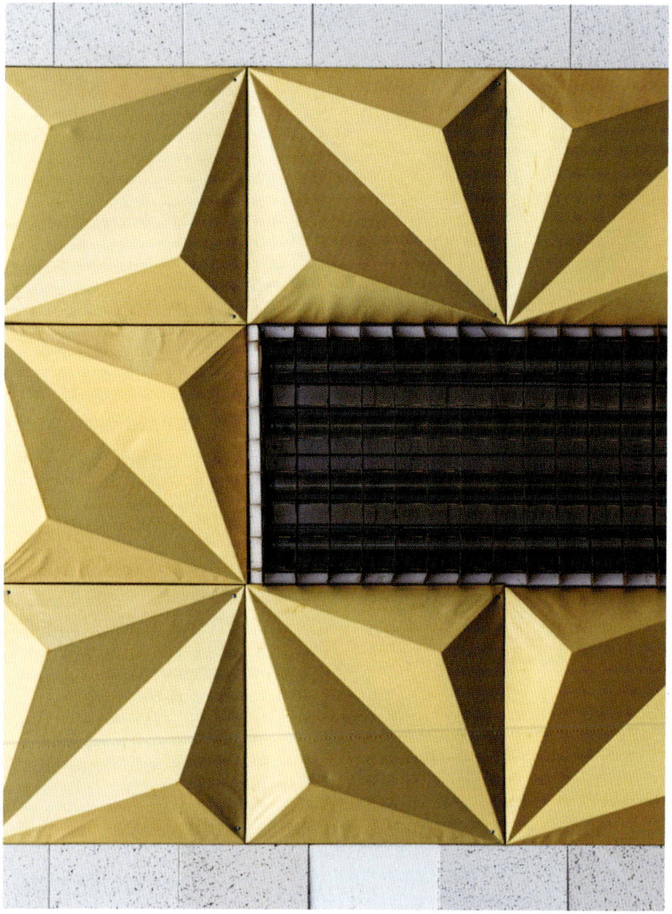

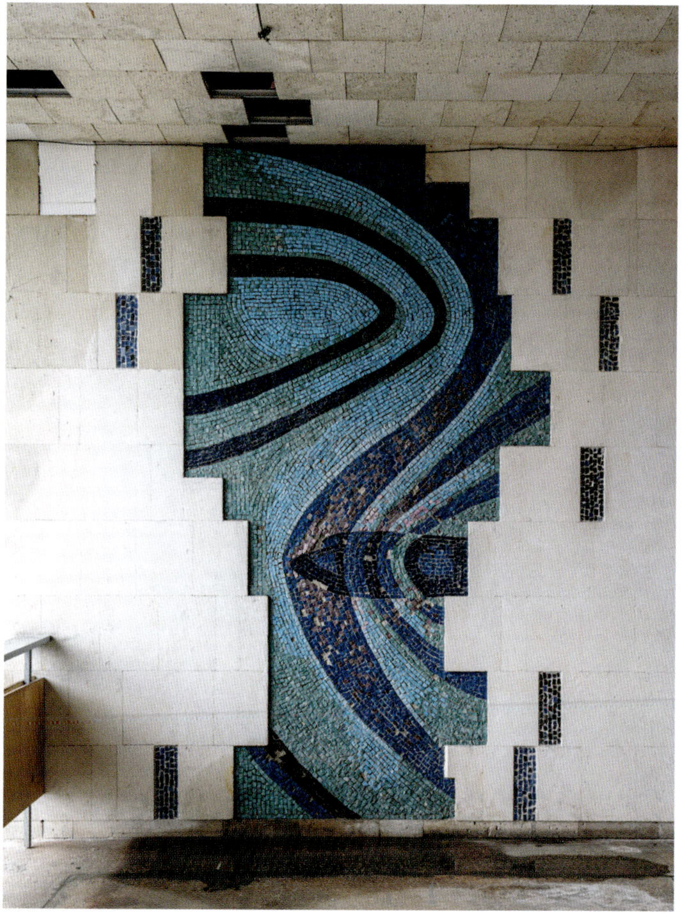

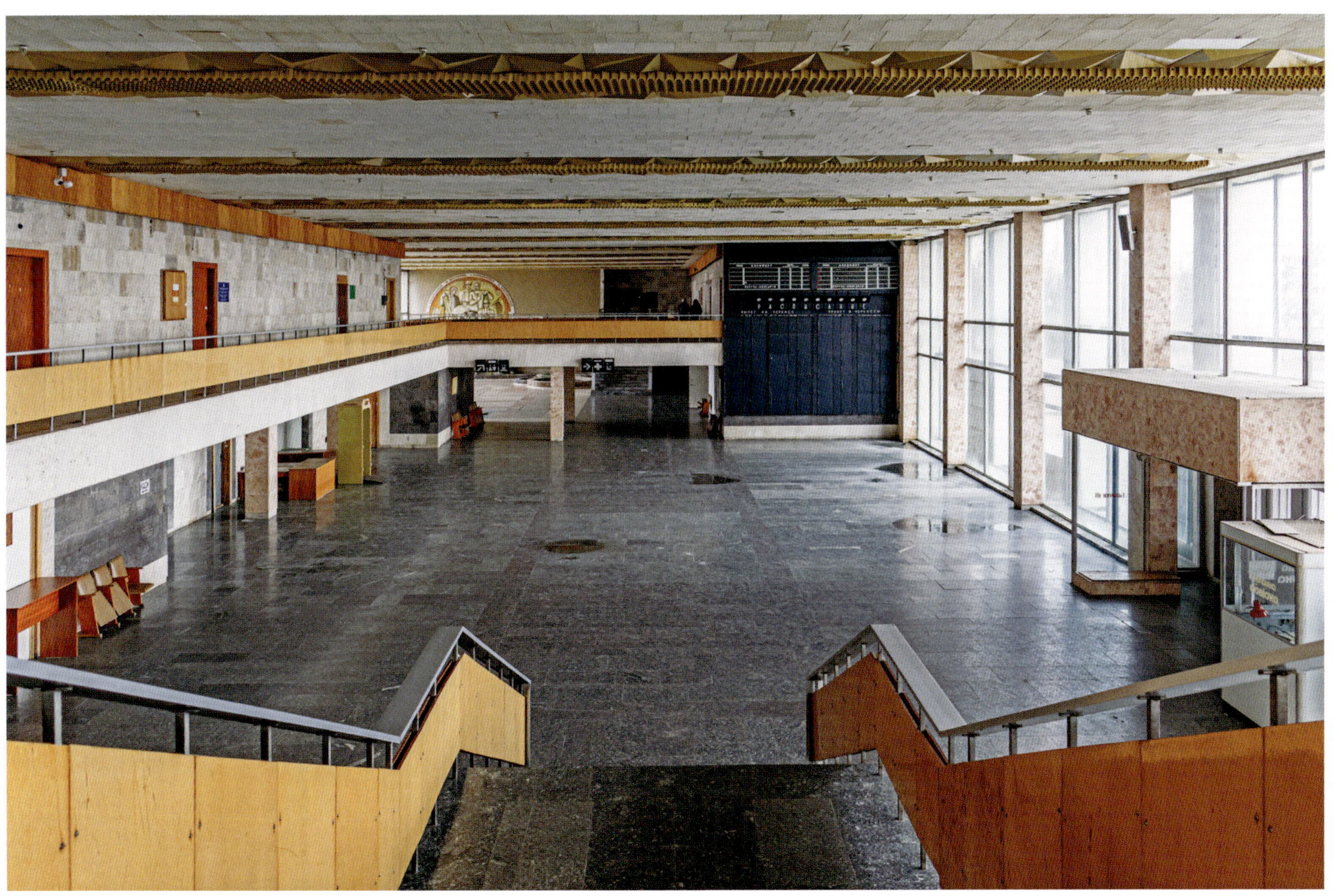

The airport ceased operations between 1997 and 2007, closing again in 2011, and has not operated as an airport since. For this reason, the building has been preserved almost entirely in its original form, including its wayfinding pictogram signage.

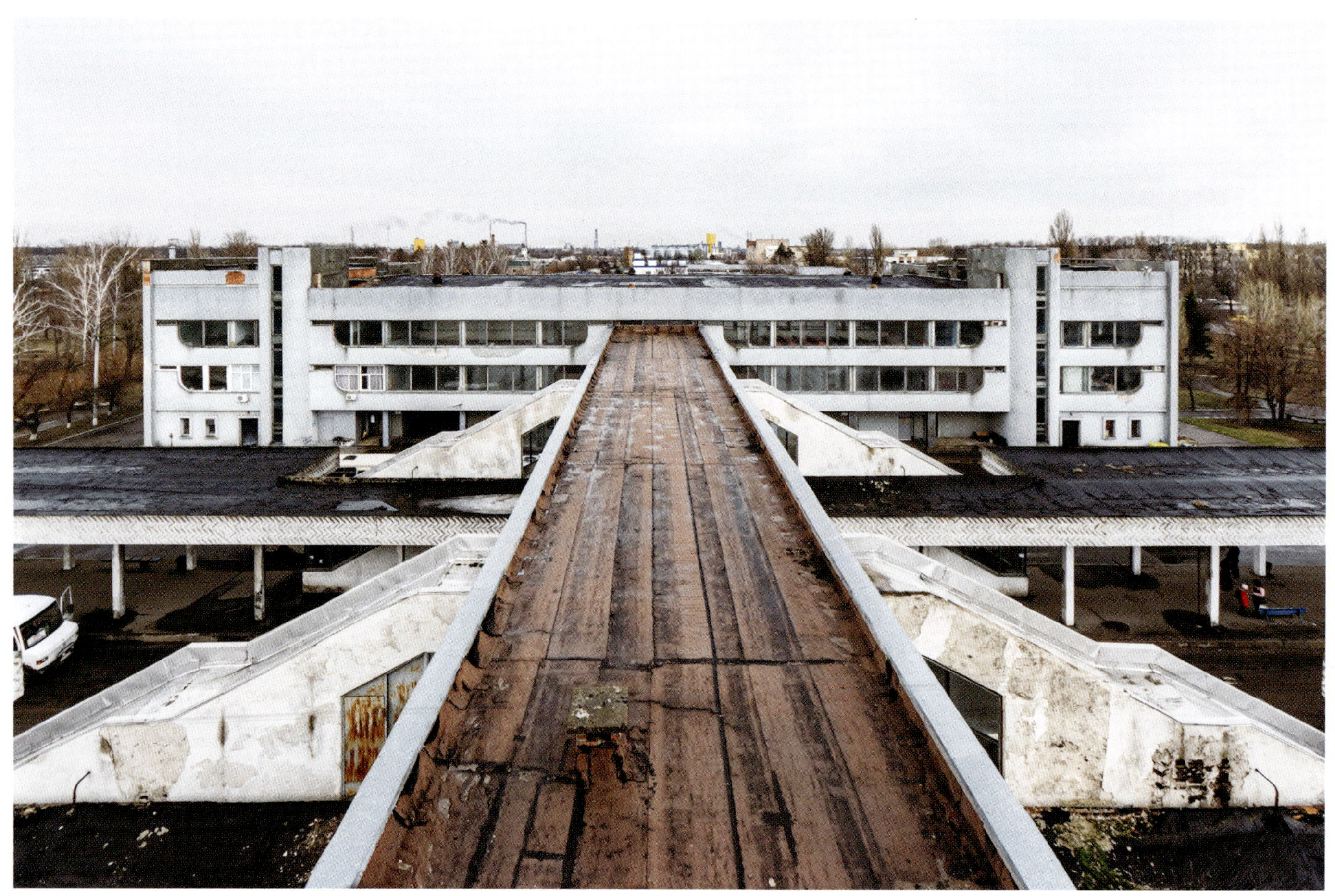

Cherkasy Bus Station
Cherkasy
1985
Architects: L. Kachurynets, A. Kolosov

Engineers: Oleksandra Stetsenko, I. Tiutiunnyk
Artists: Neonila Nedoseko, Albert Nedoseko
Damaged on 23 October 2024 by a Russian explosive drone.

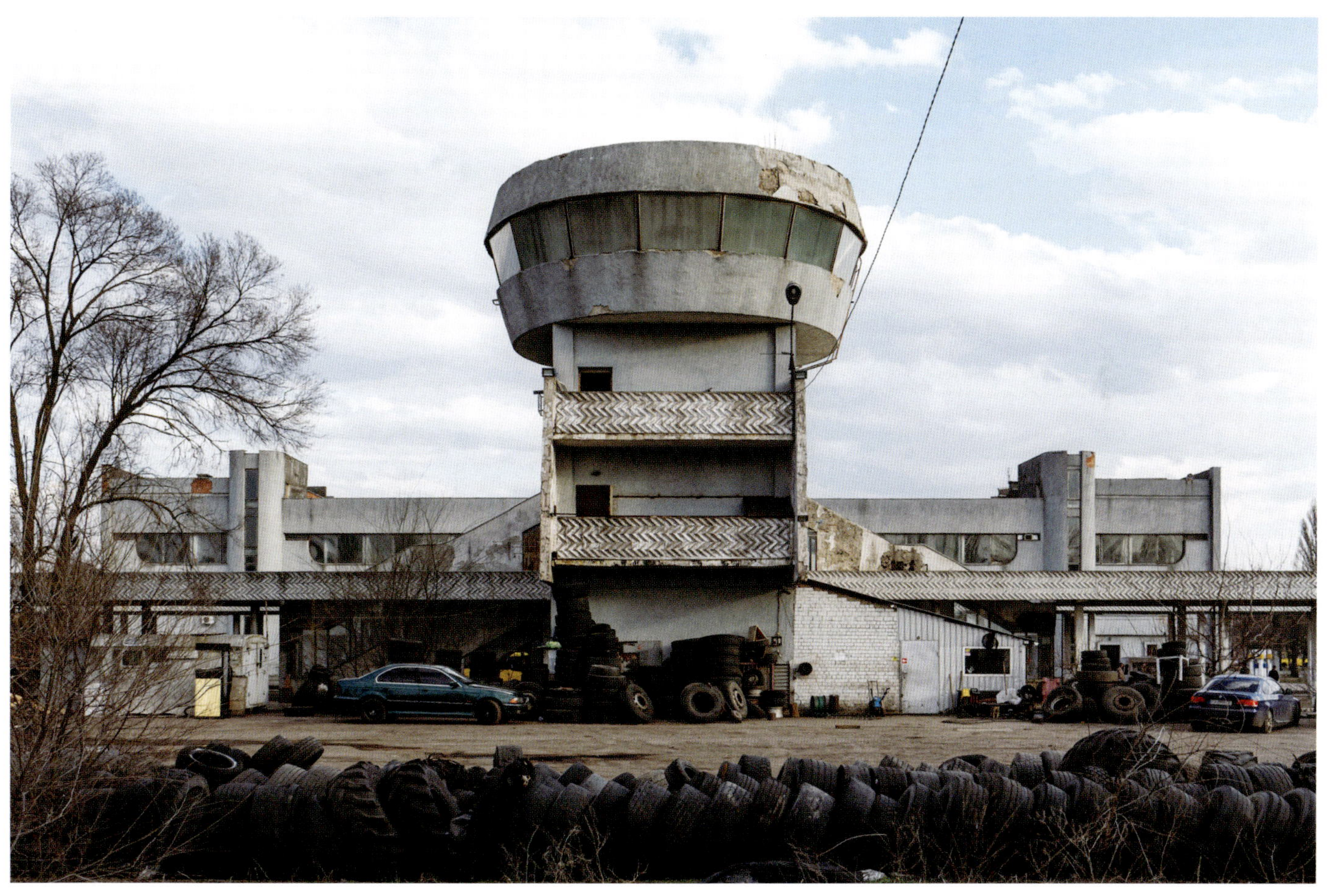

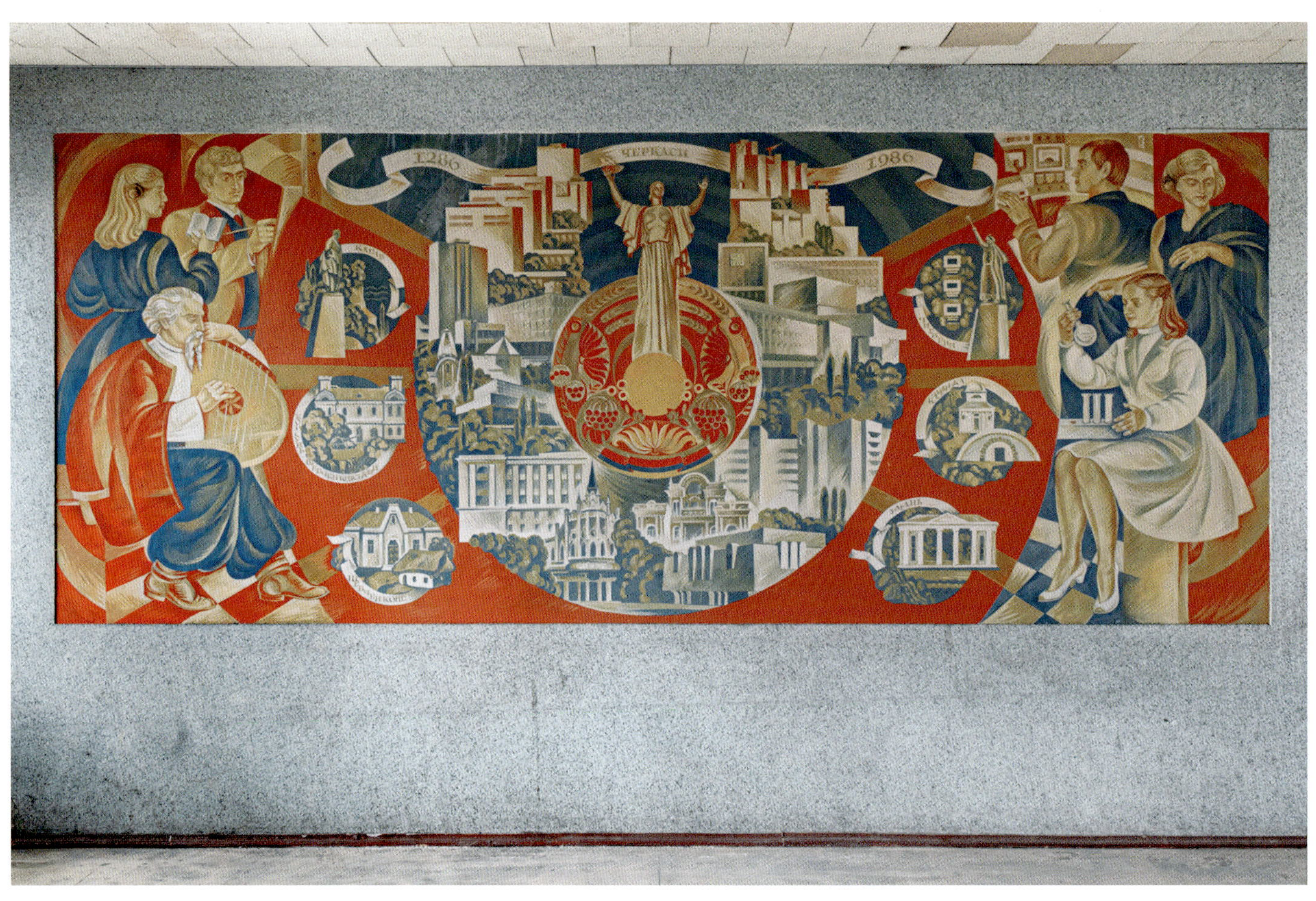

1286
ЧЕРКАСИ
1986

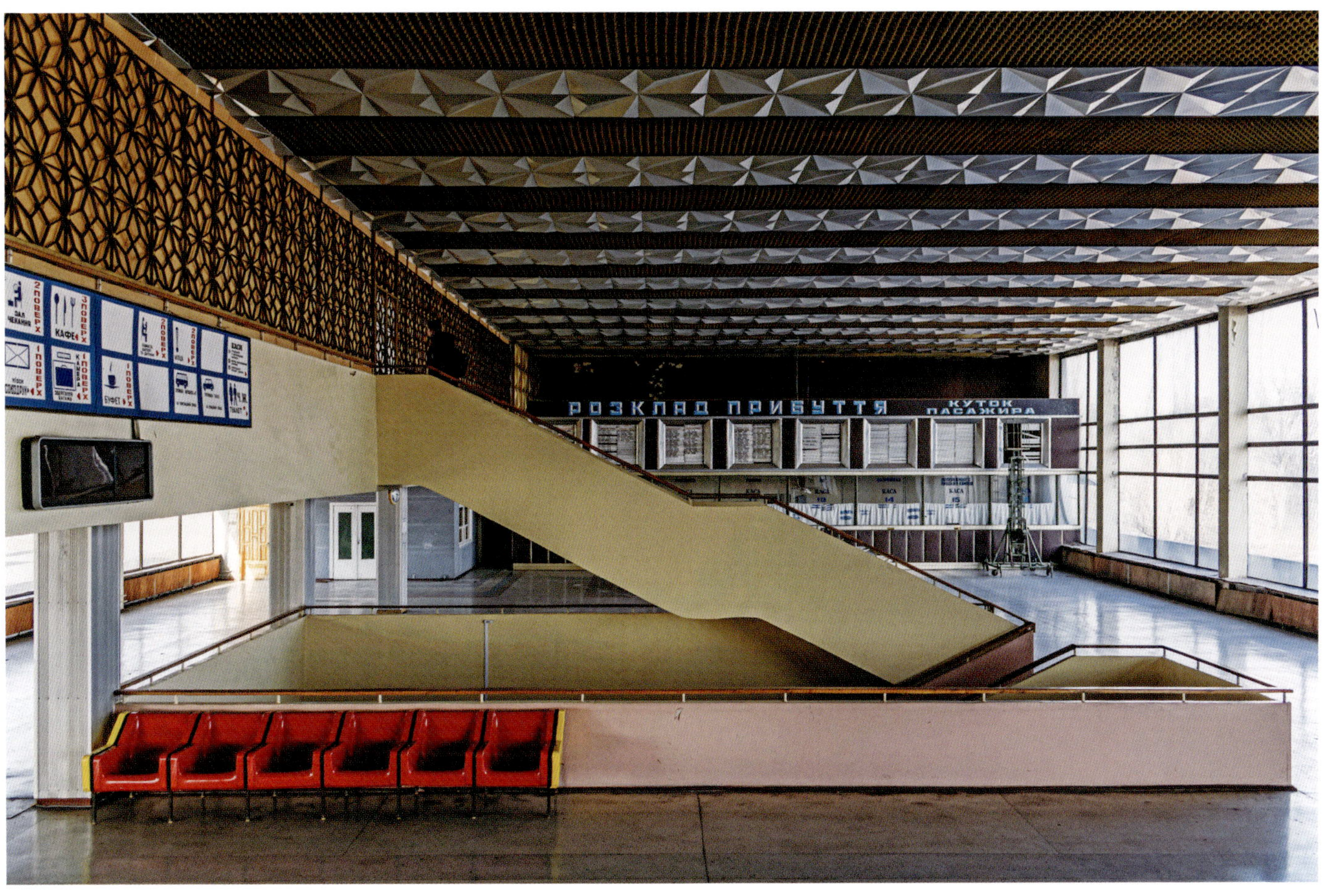
РОЗКЛАД ПРИБУТТЯ
КУТОК ПАСАЖИРА
КАФЕ
БУФЕТ
КАСА

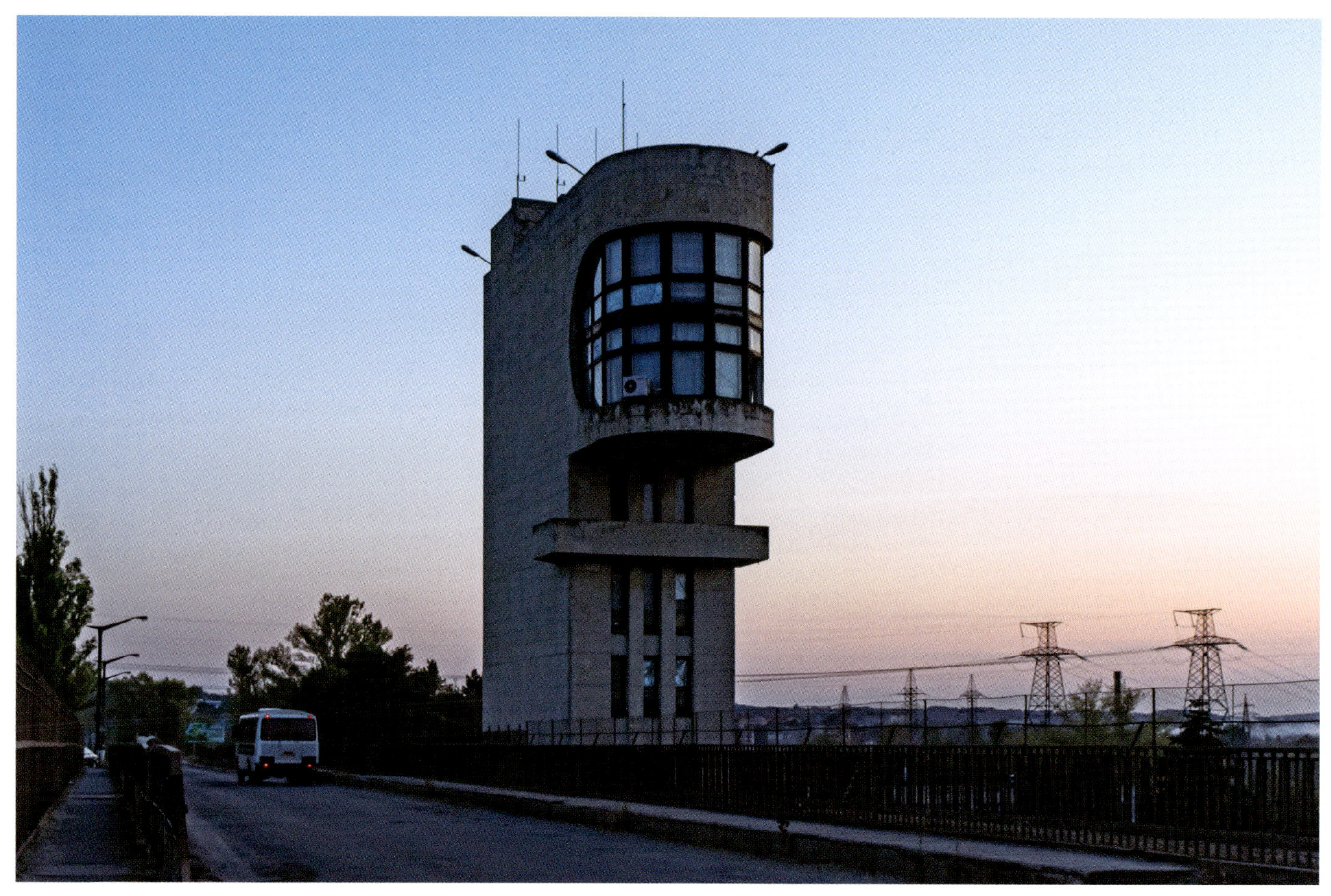

Lock Control Building, Kaniv Hydroelectric Power Plant
Kaniv, Cherkasy Oblast
1964–72
Designed by UkrHydroProject (hydropower facilities design institute)

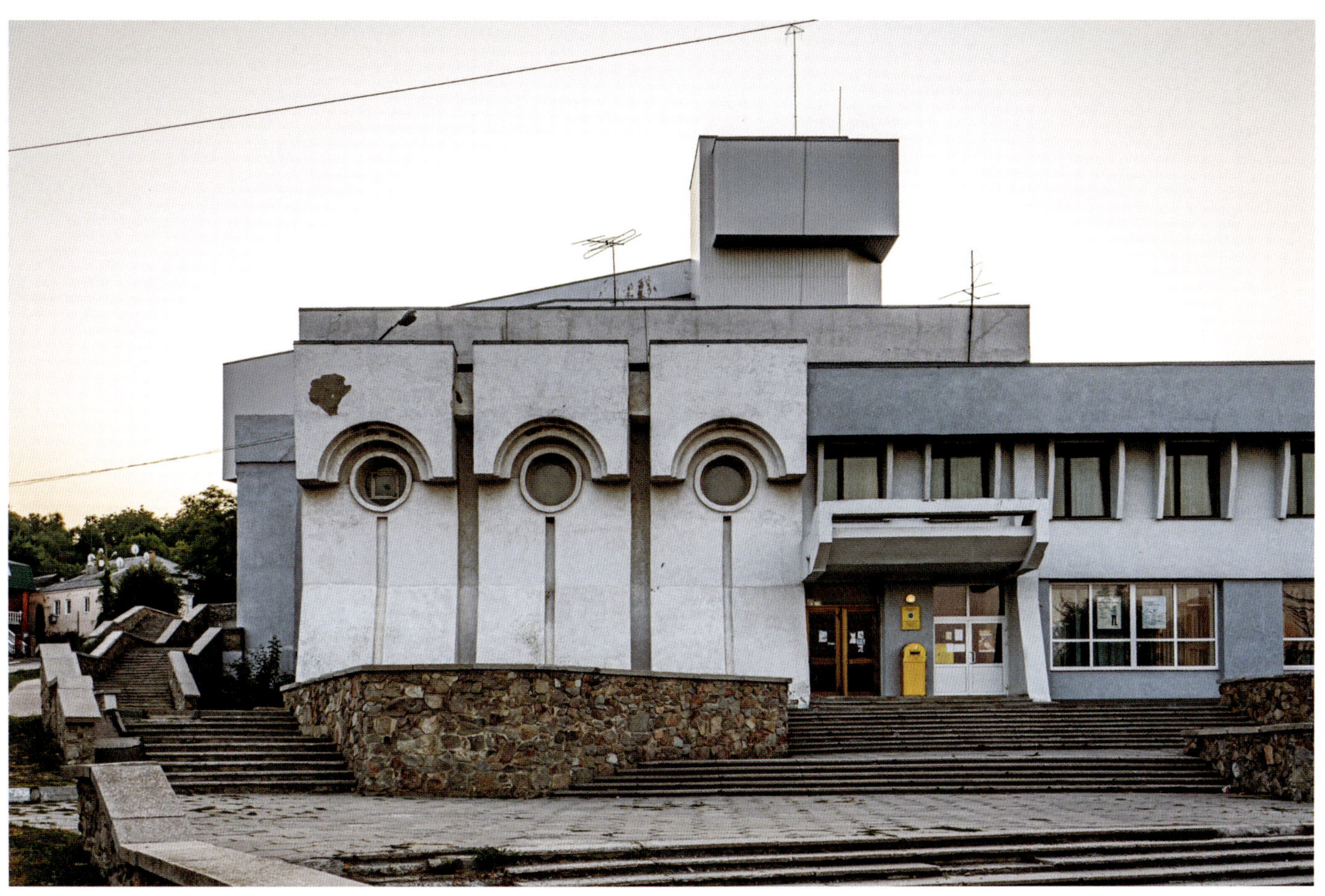

Kaniv Post Office
Kaniv, Cherkasy Oblast
1980s

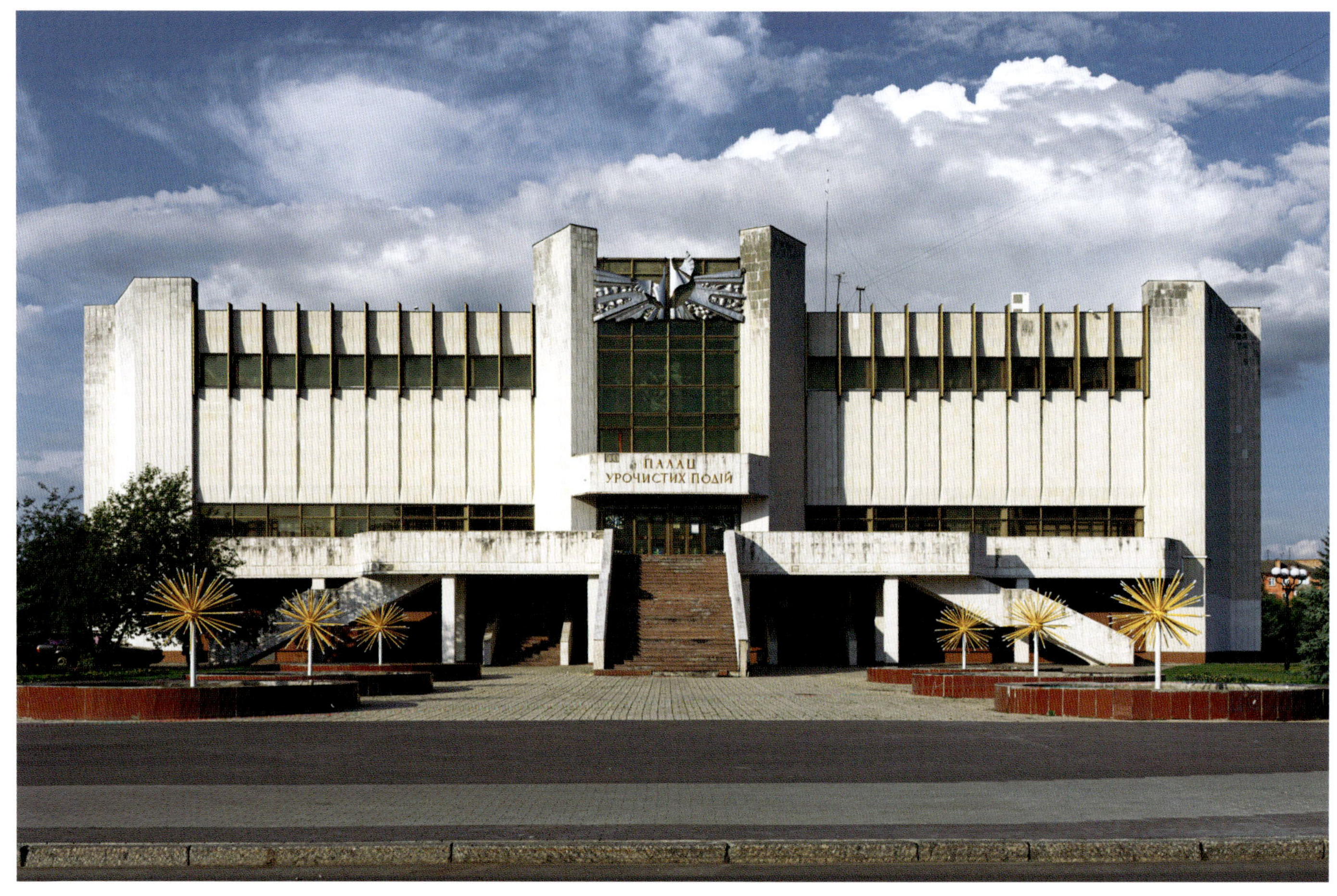

Chernihiv Palace of Weddings
Chernihiv
1985–88
Architect: Viacheslav Pavliukov

Artists: Tetiana Fedorytenko, Tetiana Diedova, Vitalii Vasylevskyi, Vitalii Omelianenko, Ivan Stetsenko

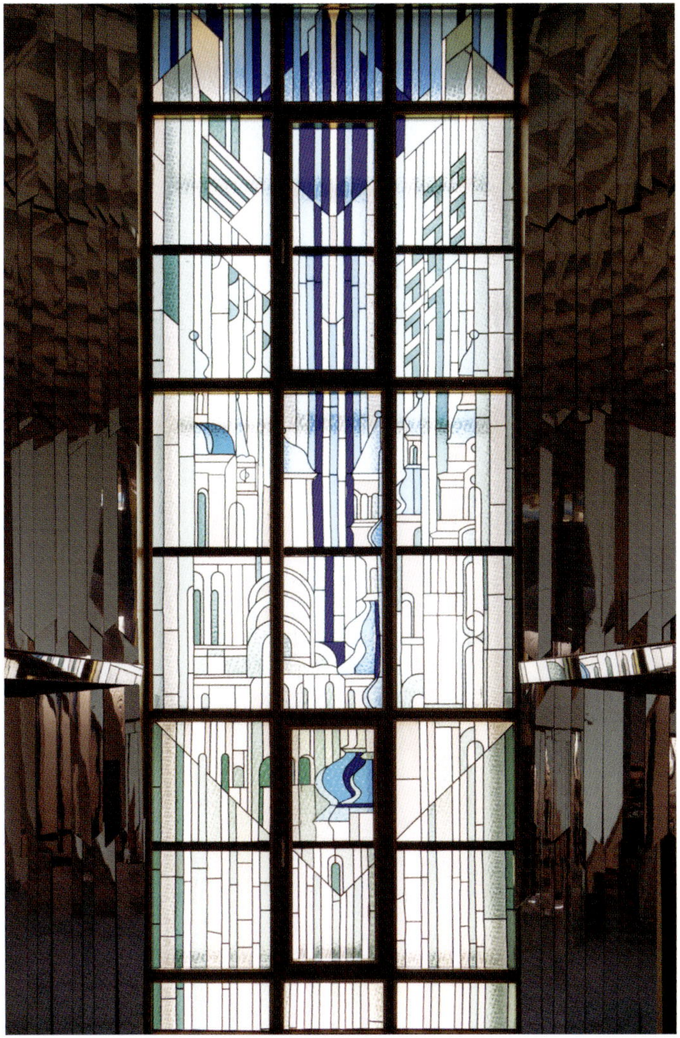

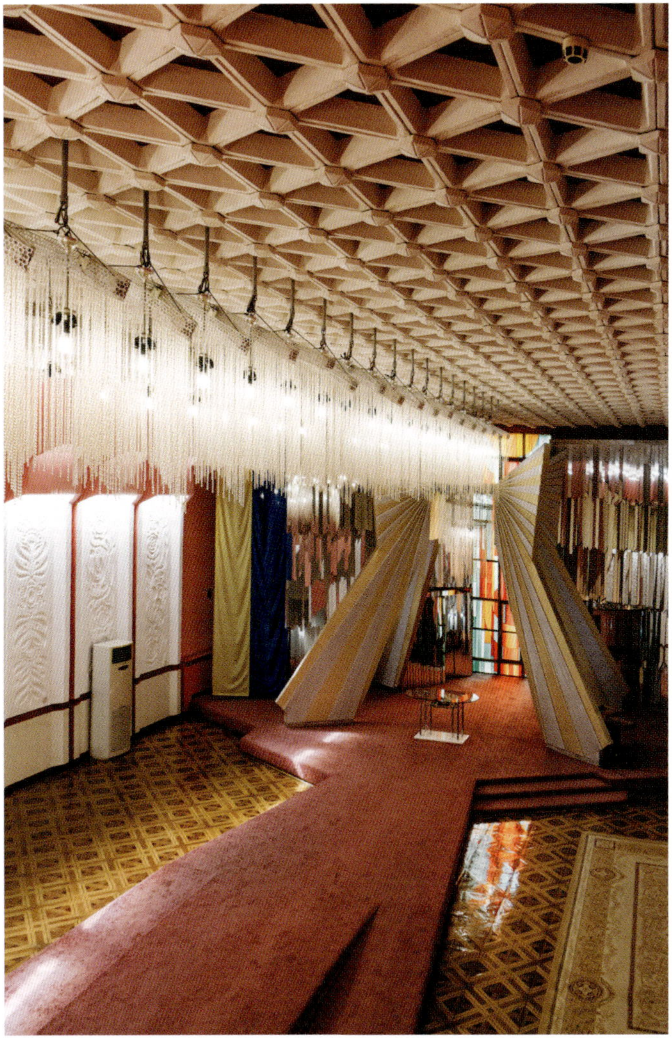

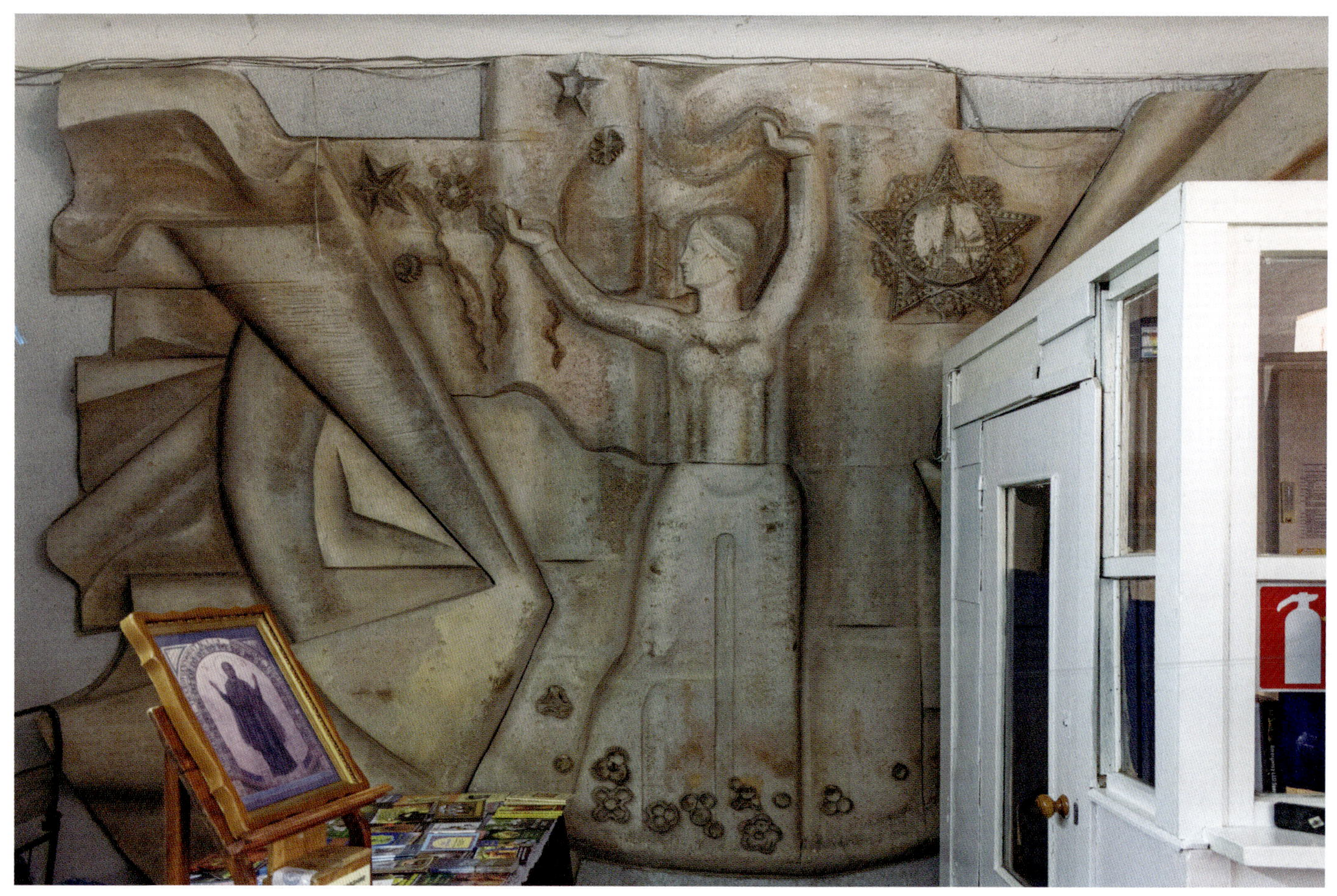

Peremoha Cinema
Chernihiv
1980s
Architects: Zinaida Travka, Viktor Chikin
Artist: Oleksii Kriukov

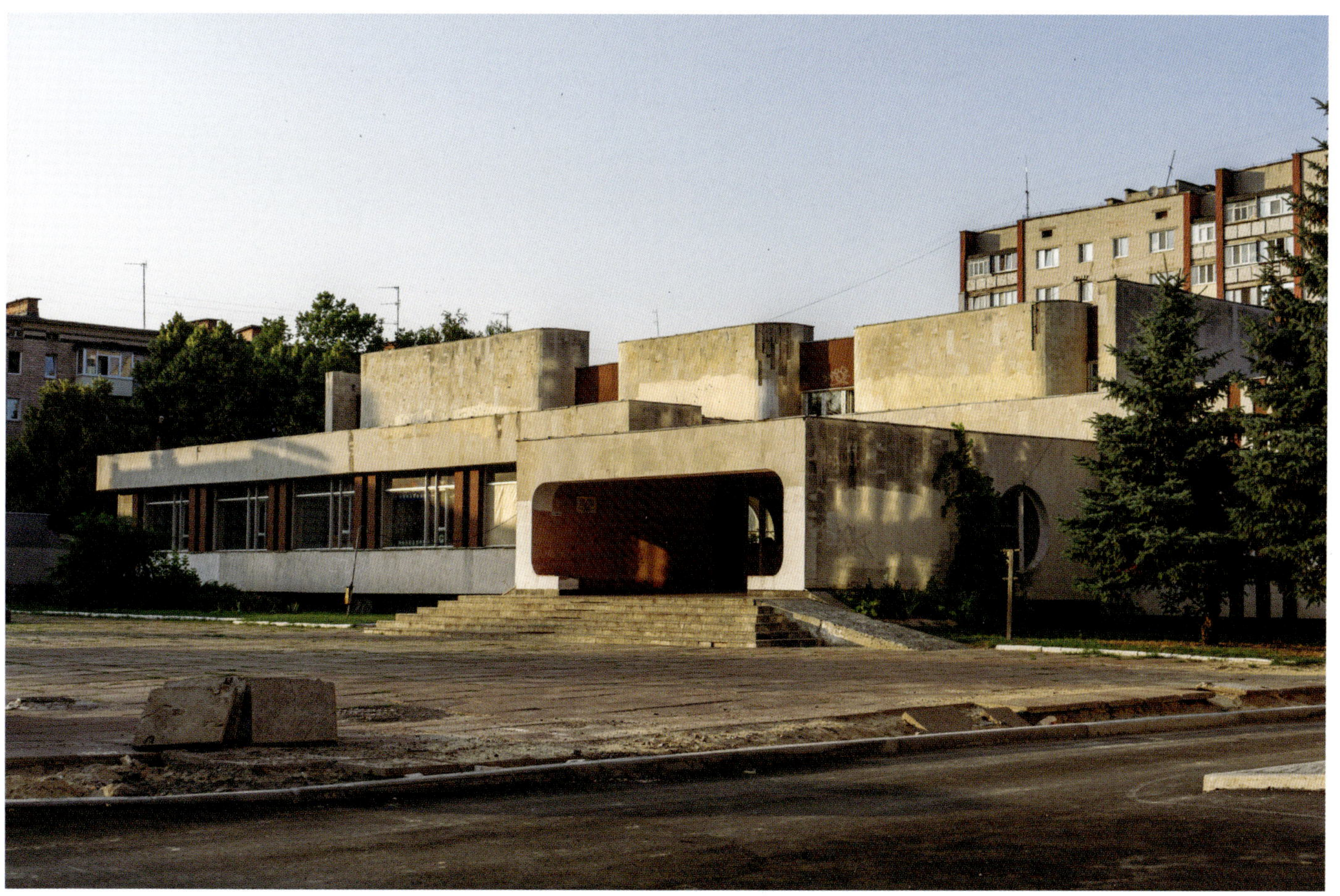

Following the collapse of the USSR, the Peremoha municipal cinema struggled to compete with the new, privately run cinemas that began to appear in popular shopping malls. The building fell into neglect, and after a period as a store selling religious goods, it stood vacant.

In 2023, students and activists revitalised the building, transforming it into a venue focused on technology and culture, renamed the Peremoha Centre. Fortunately, the original facade and the bas-relief by Oleksii Kriukov were preserved.

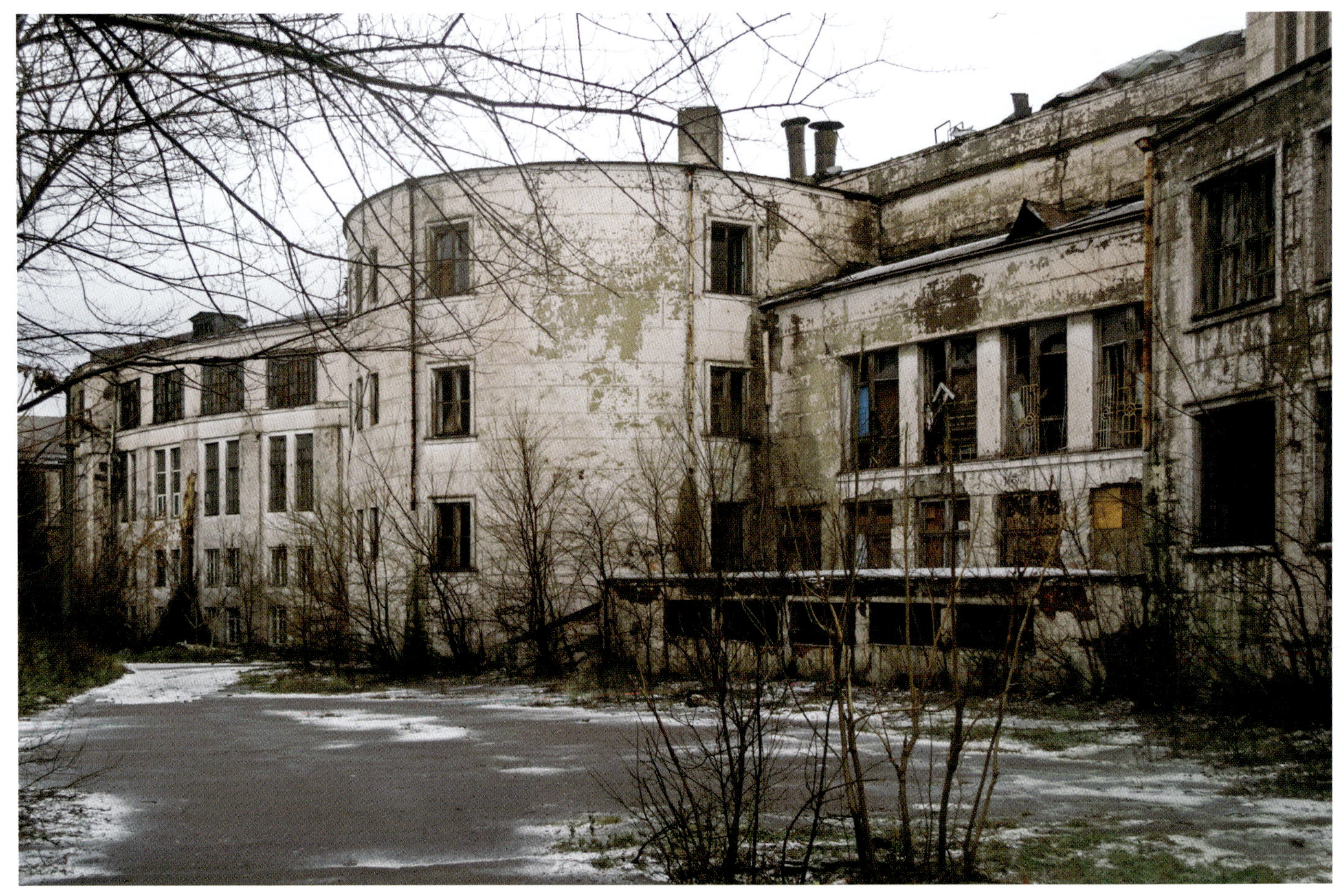

Illich Palace of Workers
Dnipro
1926–32
Architect: Oleksandr Krasnoselskyi

The building embodies Constructivism (1920s–30s), an early modernist movement from the USSR that emphasised abstract, geometric forms to express the era's industrial progress and egalitarian socialist ideals. Built for the workers of the Dnipro Metallurgical Plant, the Palace

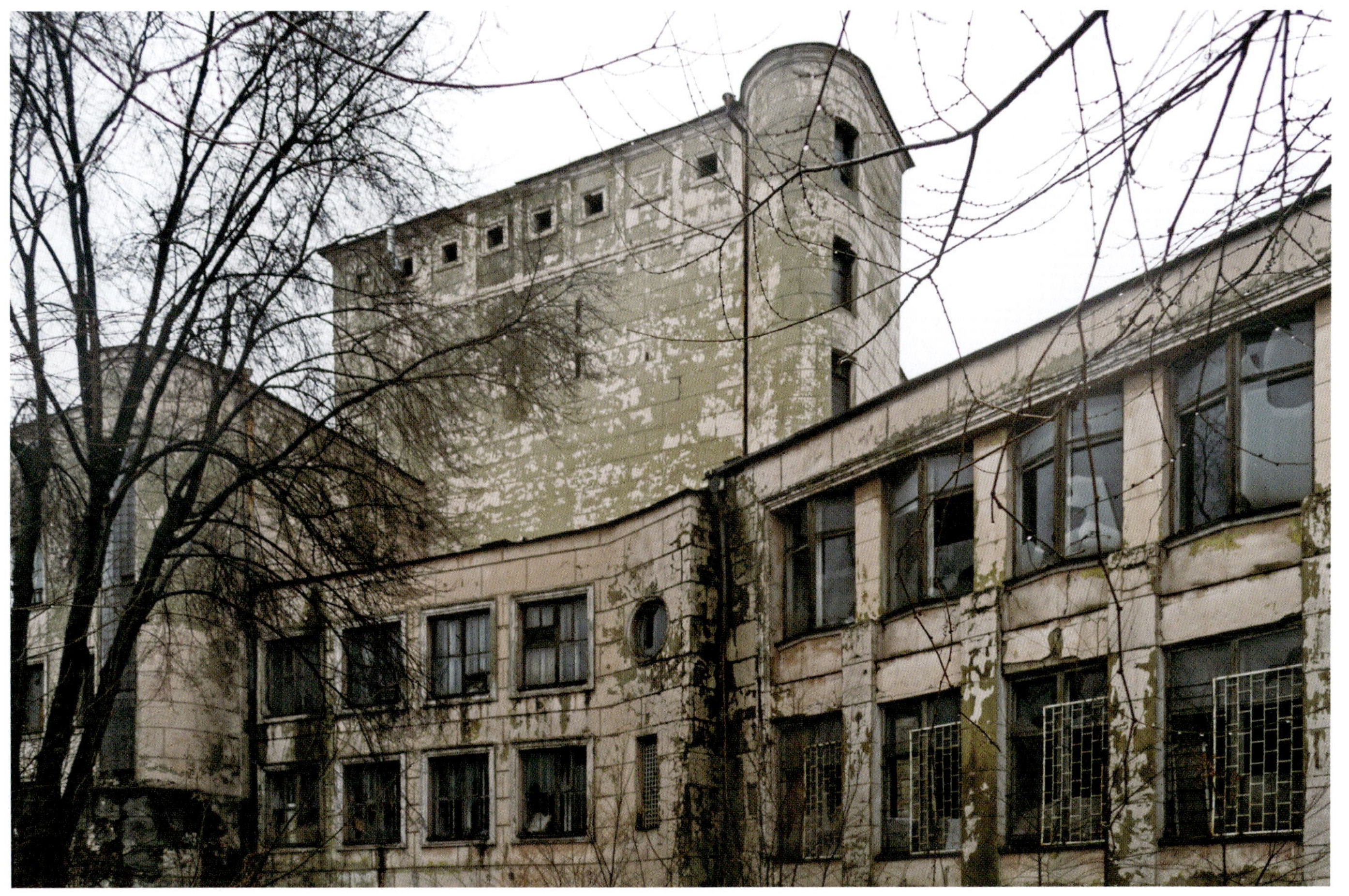

was the city's largest venue at the time of its completion, but since 1991 and the fall of the USSR, it has fallen into neglect. In 2017, the city sold the Palace for $200,000, with an agreement making explicit reference to its listed classification. However, the new owners have sought to revoke this protected status using legal action, their controversial renovations already damaging the building's authentic architecture. Despite fines, they continue to block site inspections from representatives of the Dnipro Cultural Heritage Department.

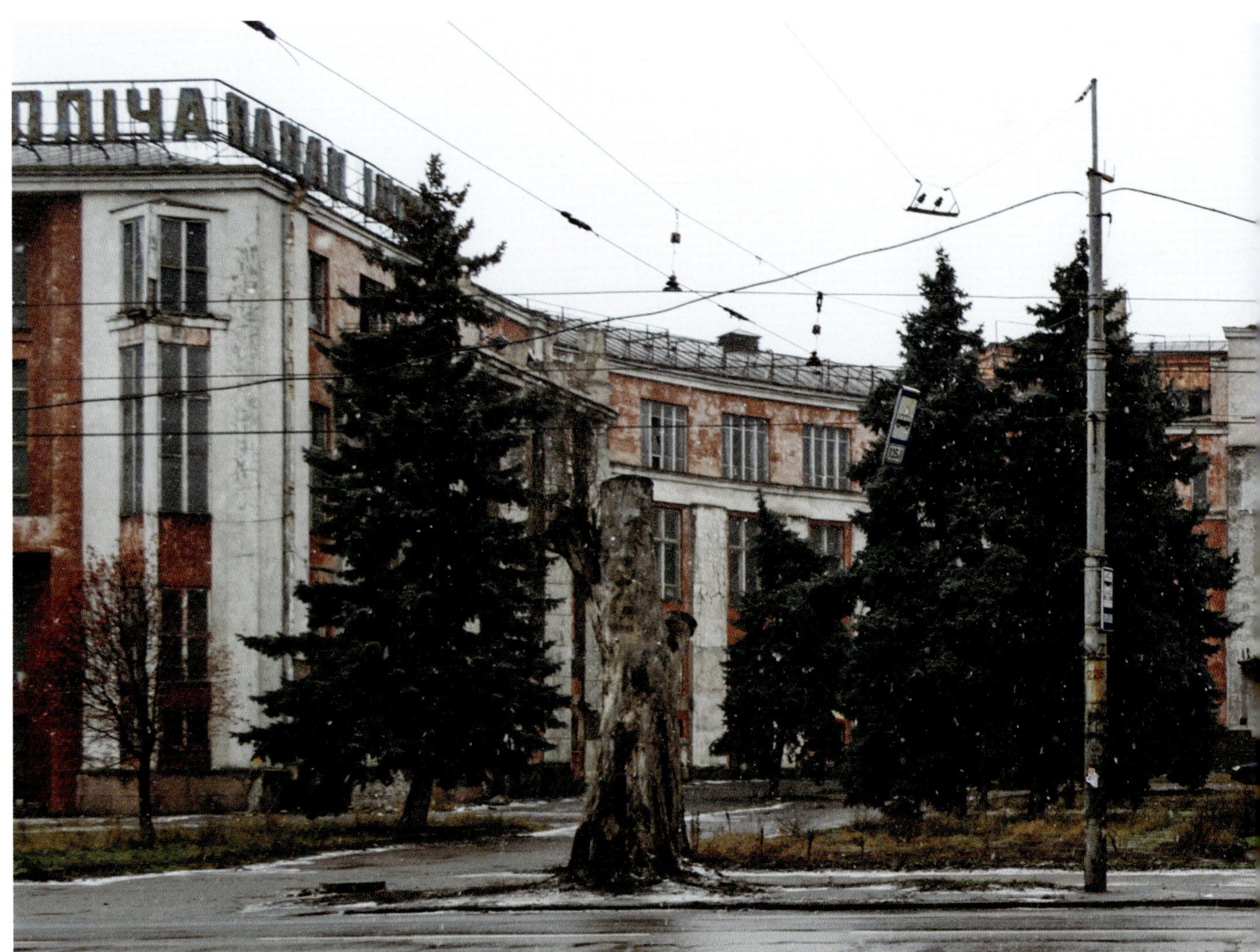

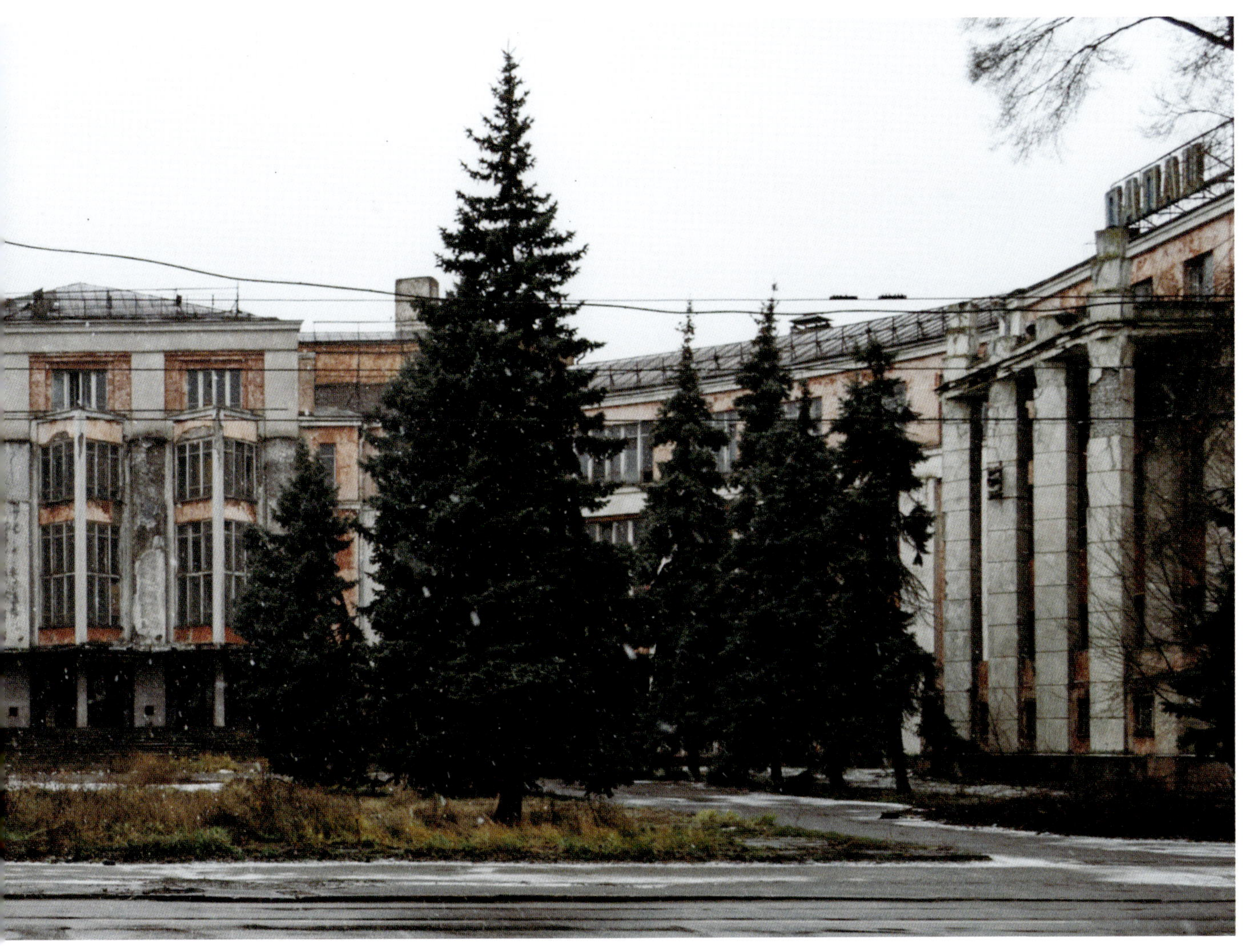

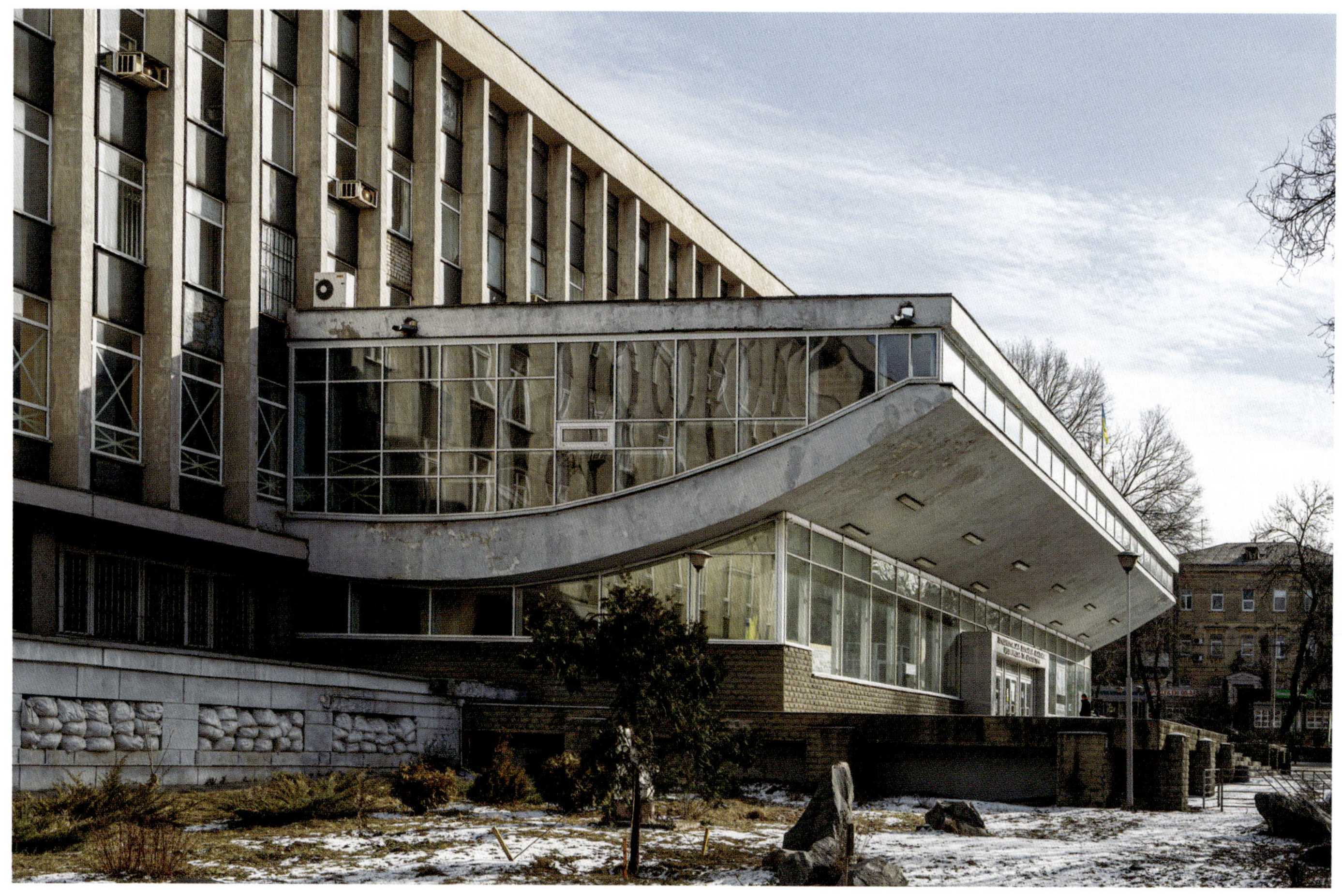

Prydniprovska State Academy of Civil Engineering and Architecture
Dnipro
above and right: 1970
Architect: Oleh Petrov

far right and overleaf: 1930s
Architect: Henrikh Shvetskyi-Vinetskyi

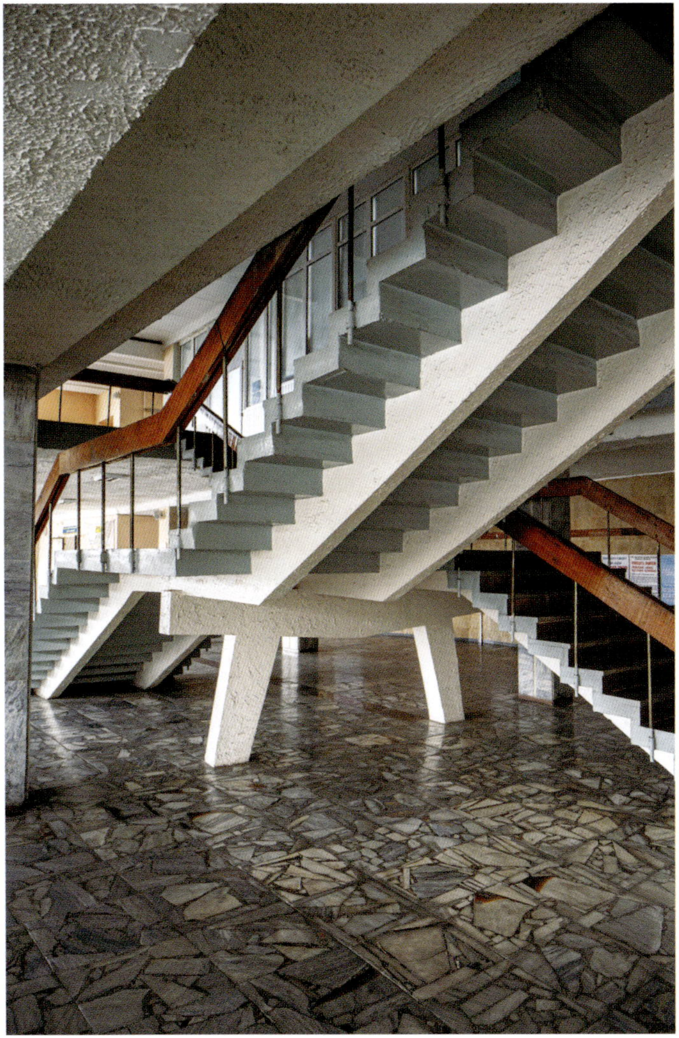

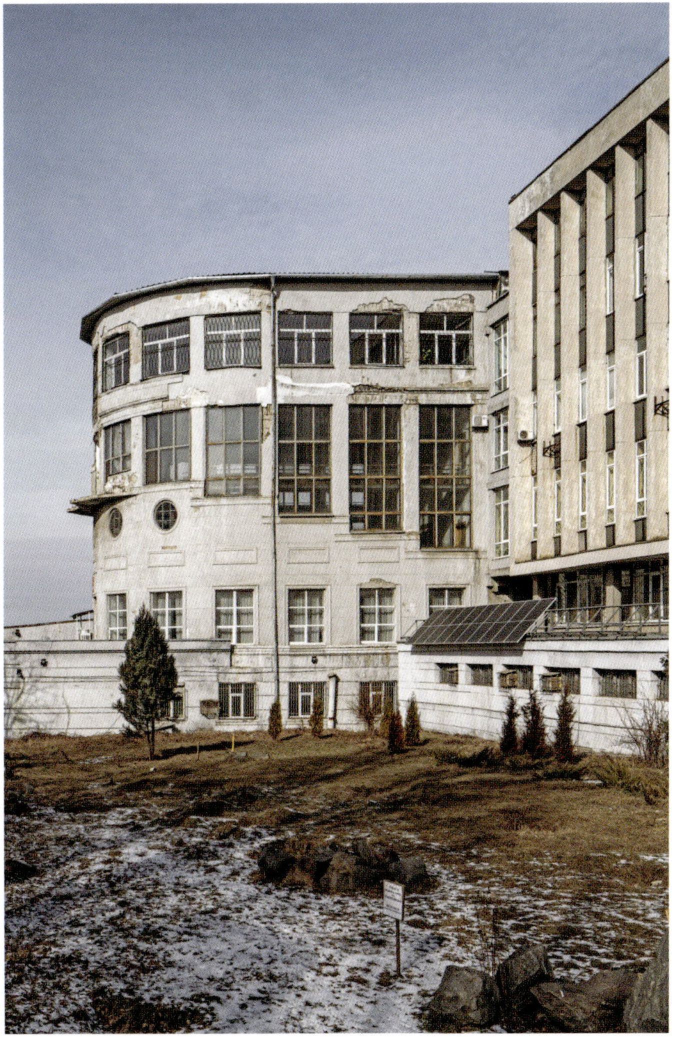

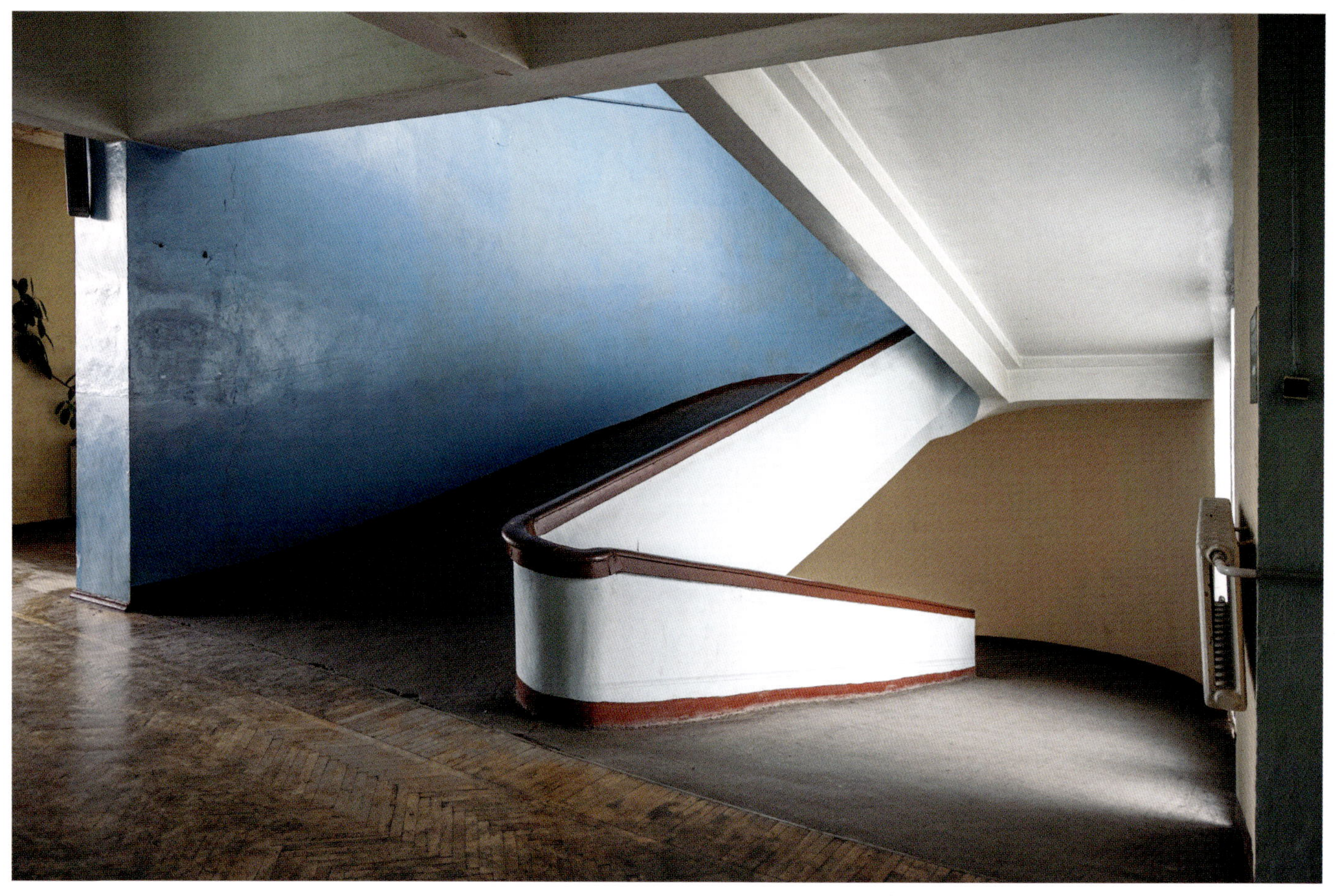

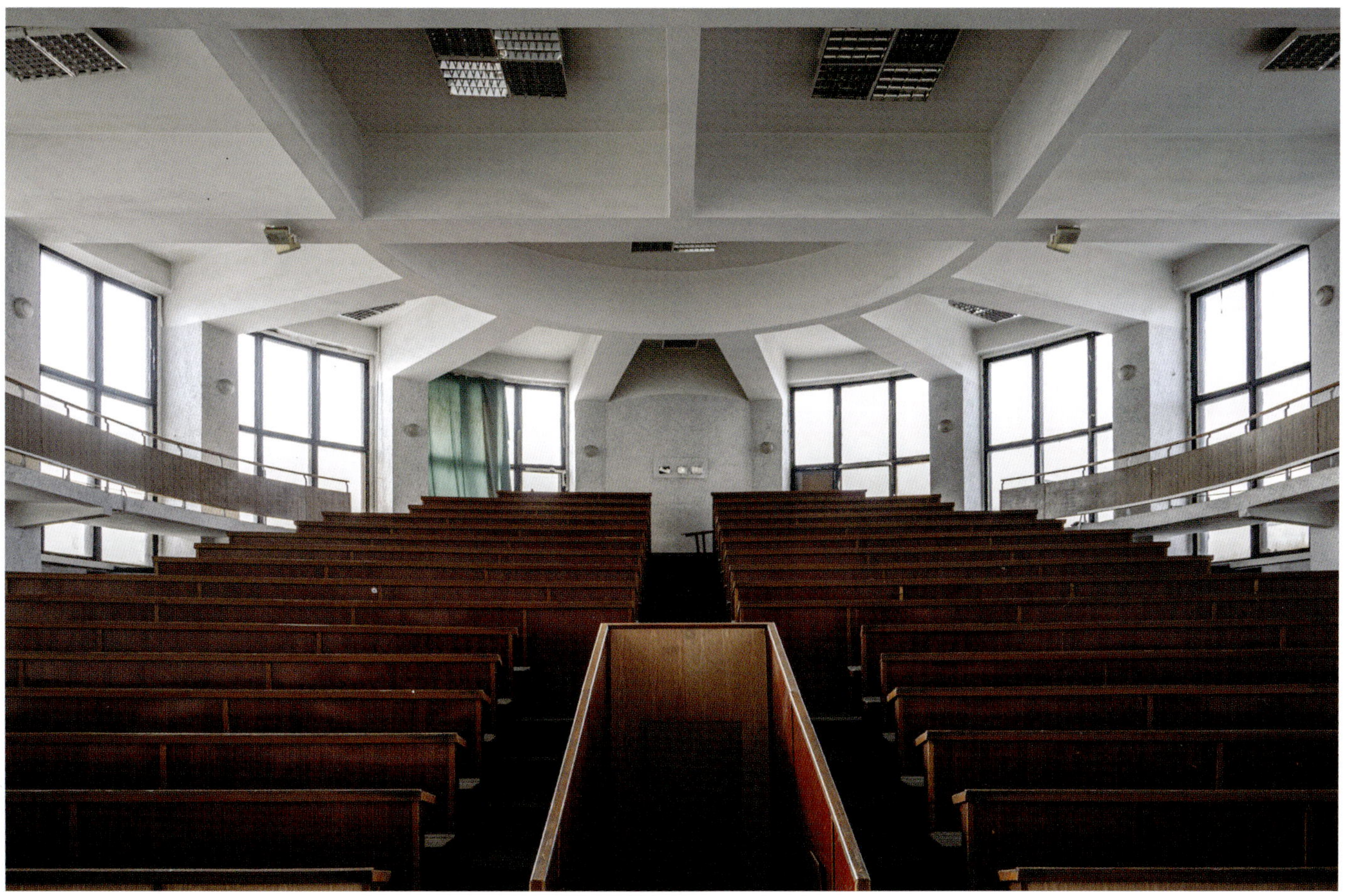

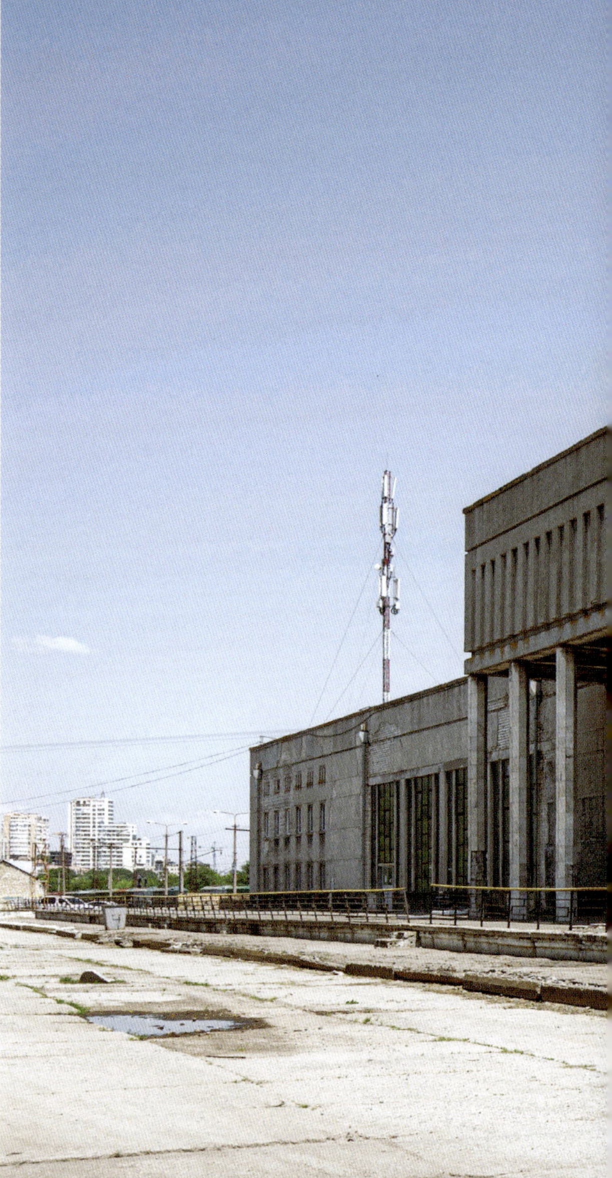

Dnipro-Lotsmanska Railway Station
(formerly Dnipropetrovsk-Pivdennyi Railway Station)
Dnipro
1975
Architect: Yevsei Sorin
Artists: Roman Shusterman, Leonid Talskyi

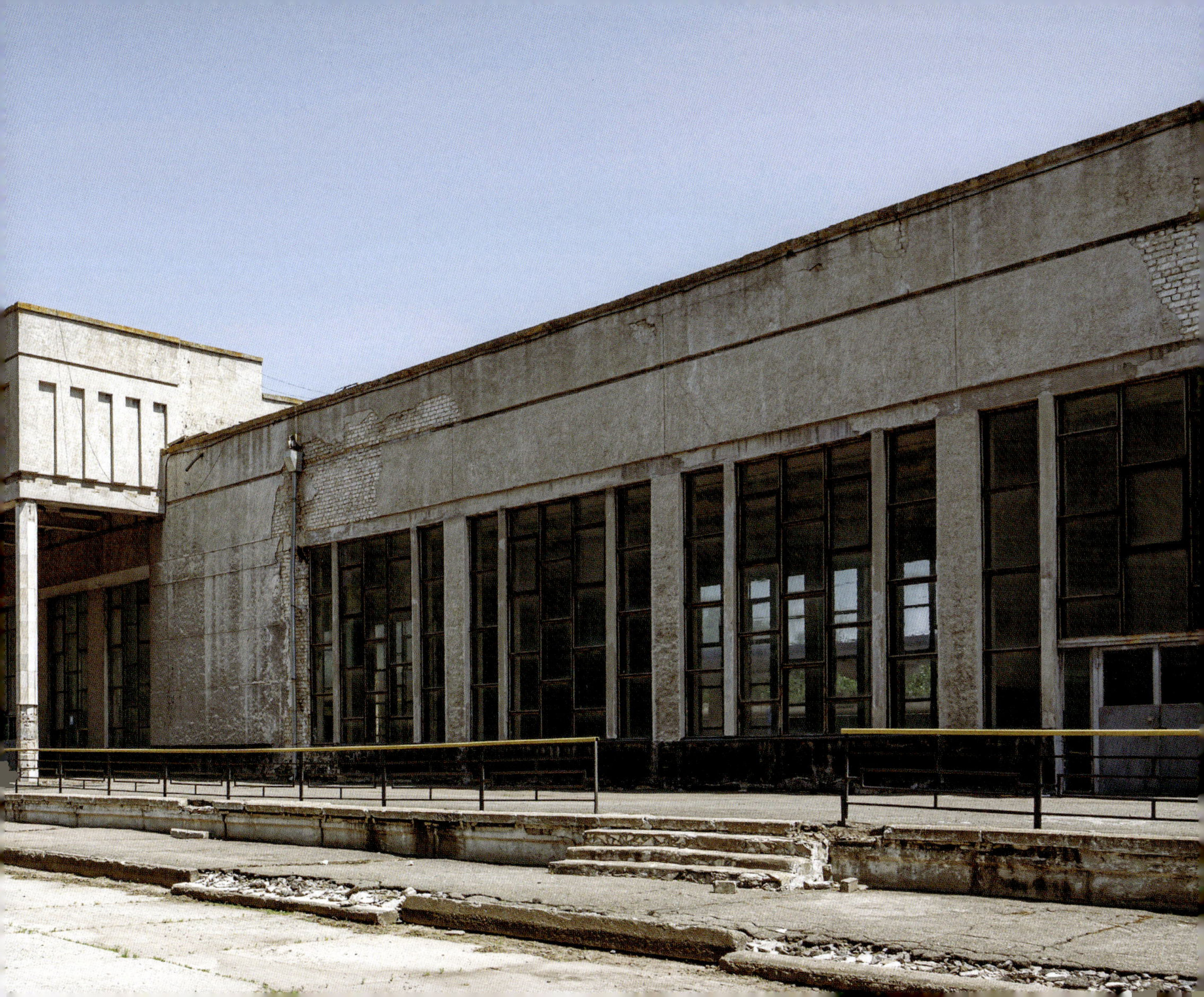

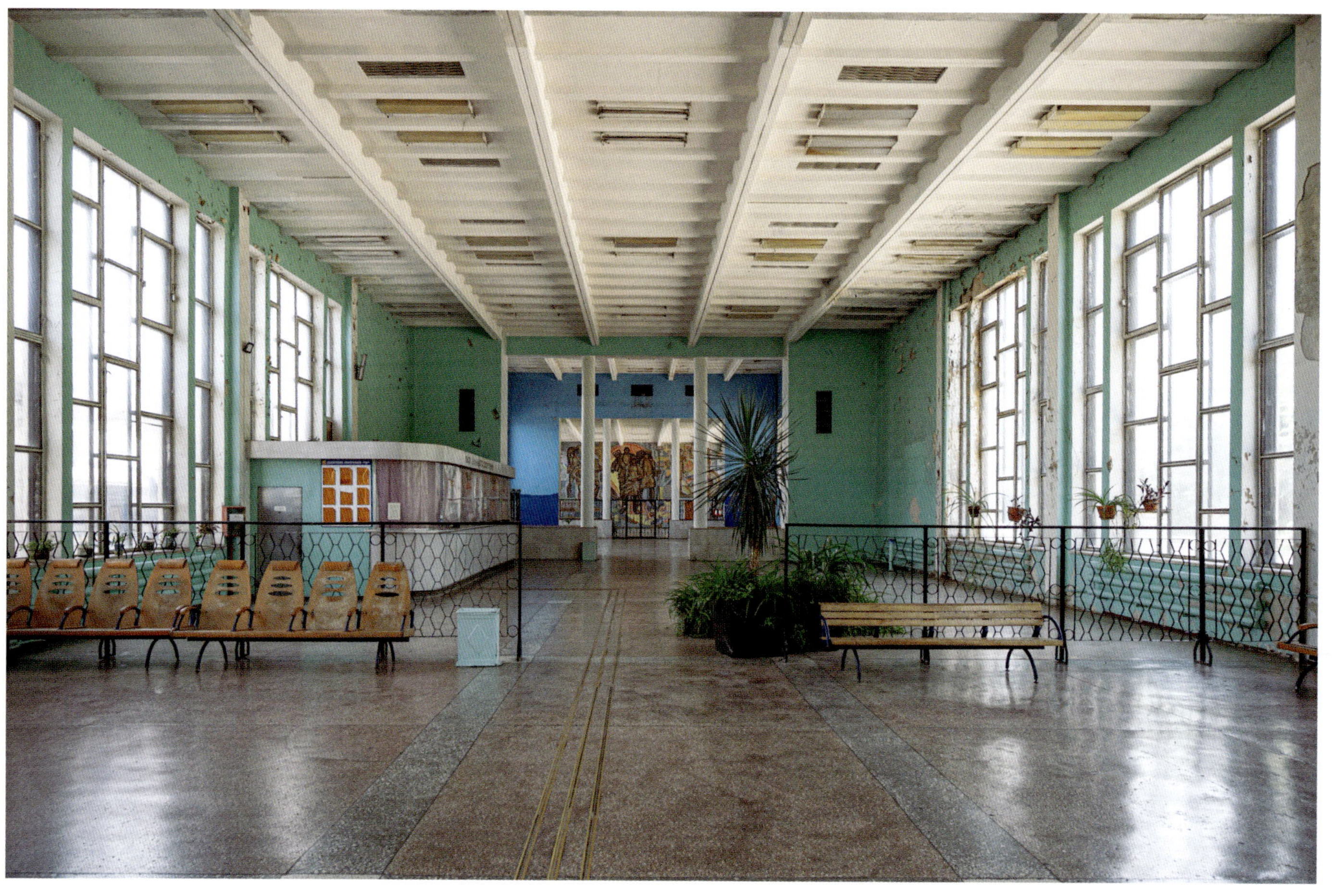

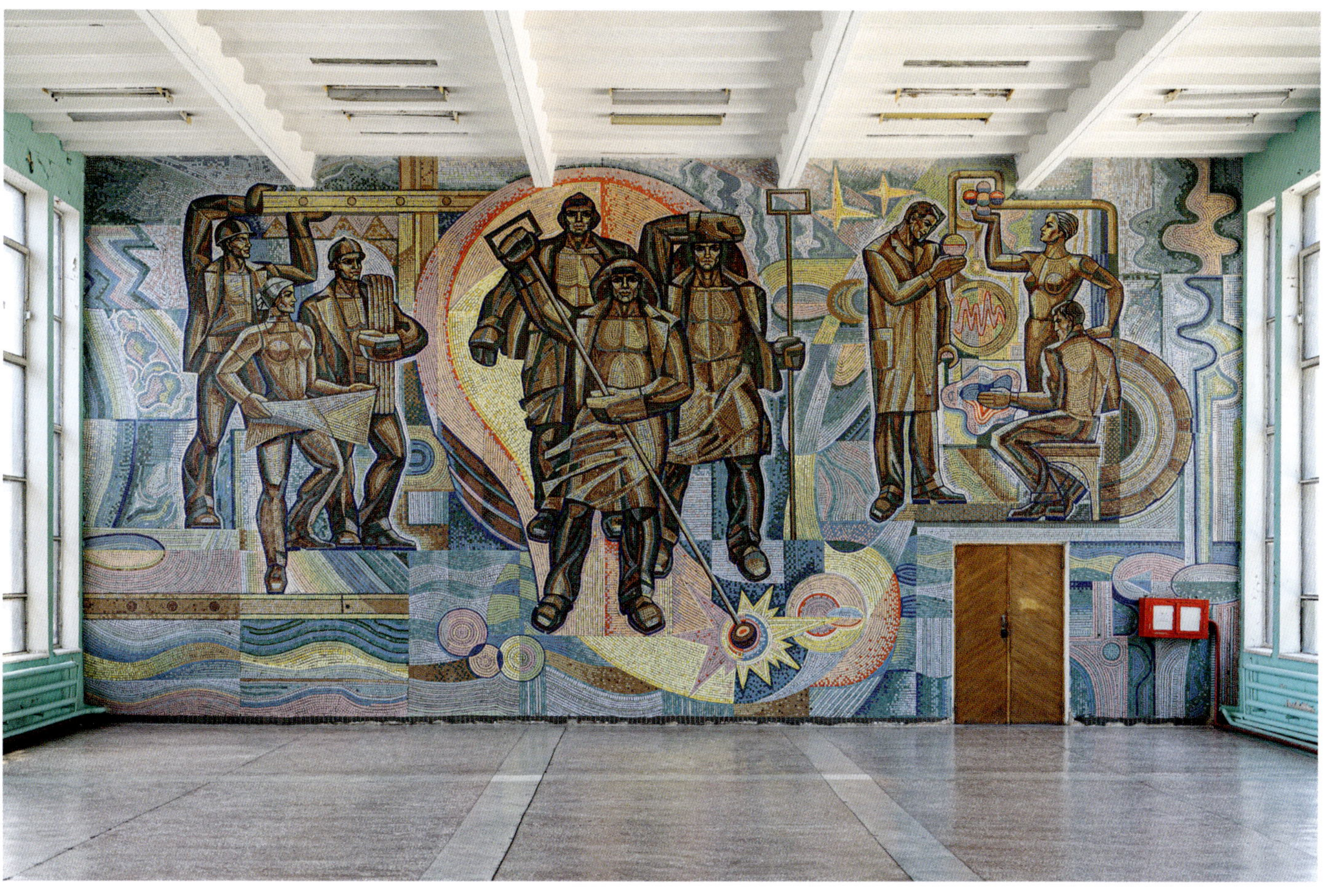

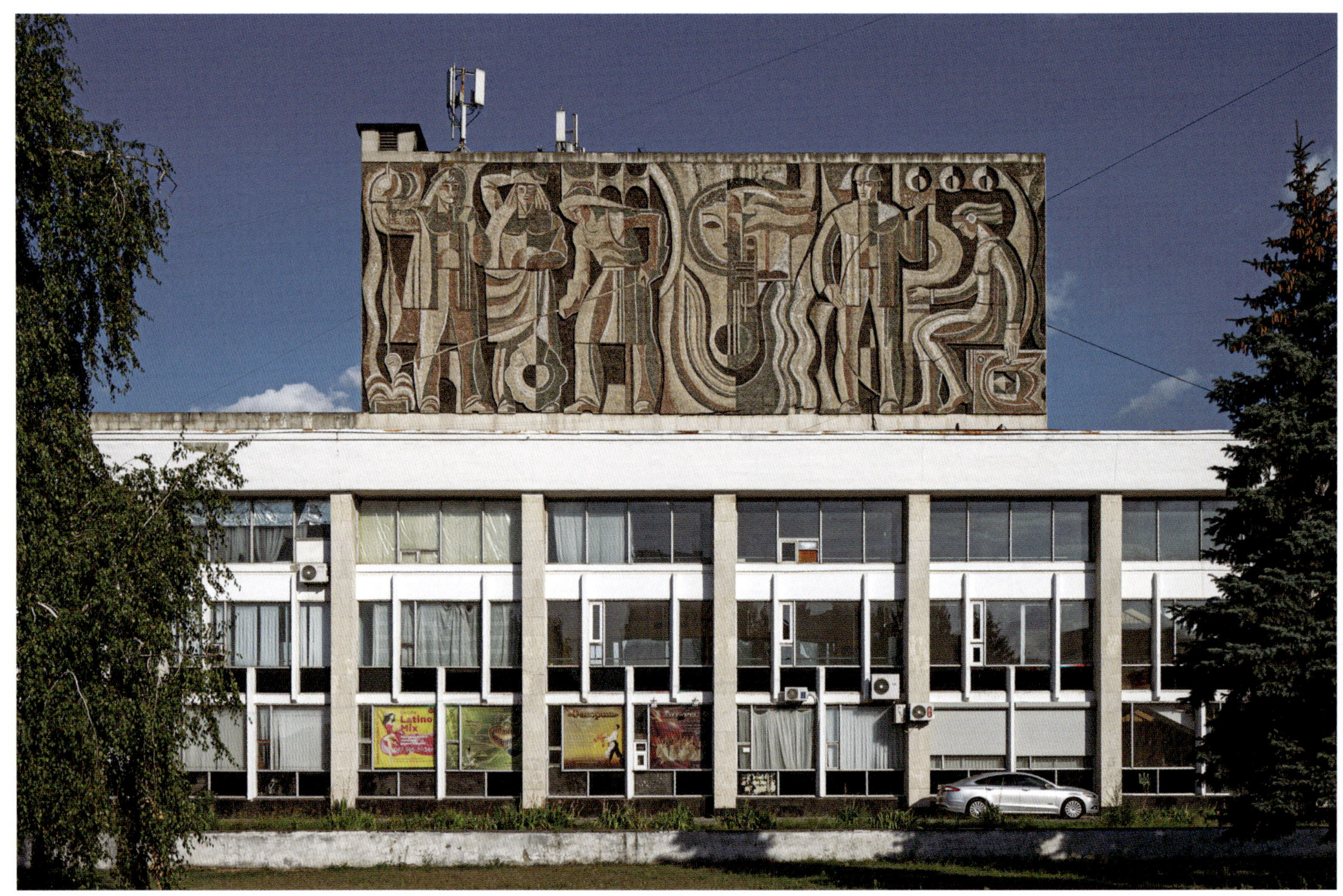

Metalurh Palace of Culture
Dnipro
1978

The Palace was built using plans for standard project No. 2C-06-6-
69, designed by the Central Research Institute for Standard and
Experimental Design of Entertainment Buildings and Sports Facilities
(TsNIIEP), while artworks were created by local artists (see also p234).

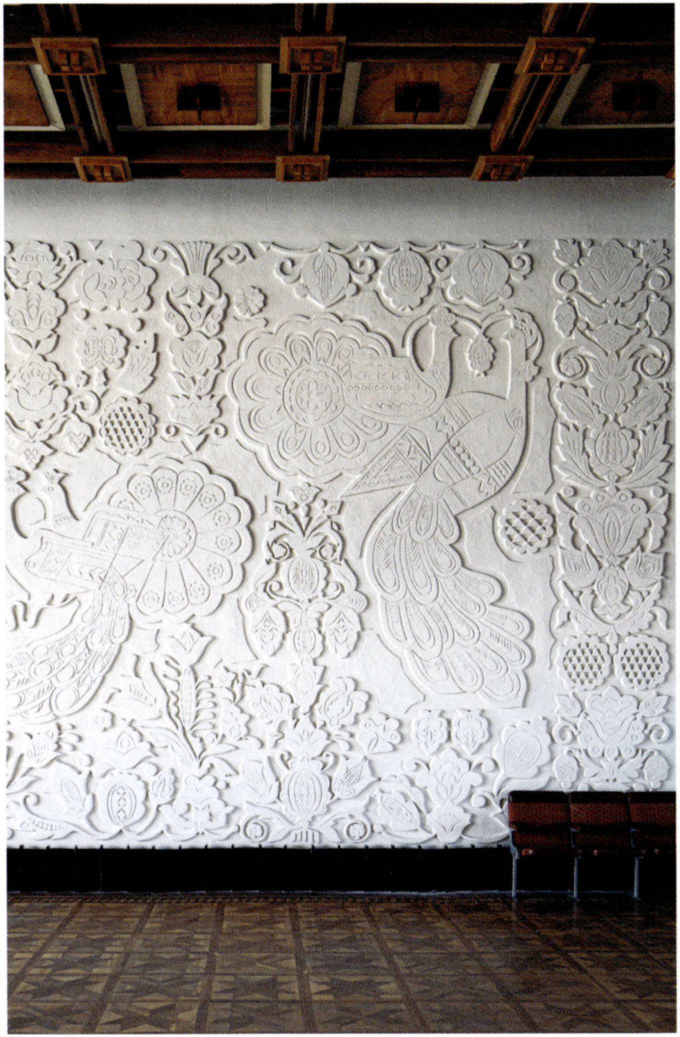

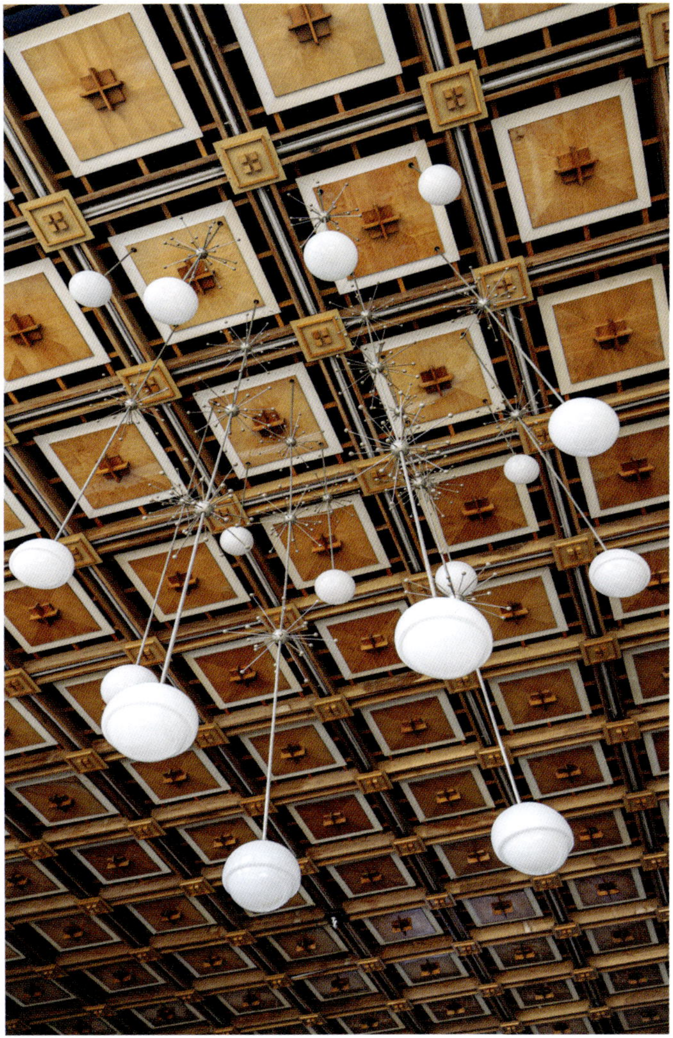

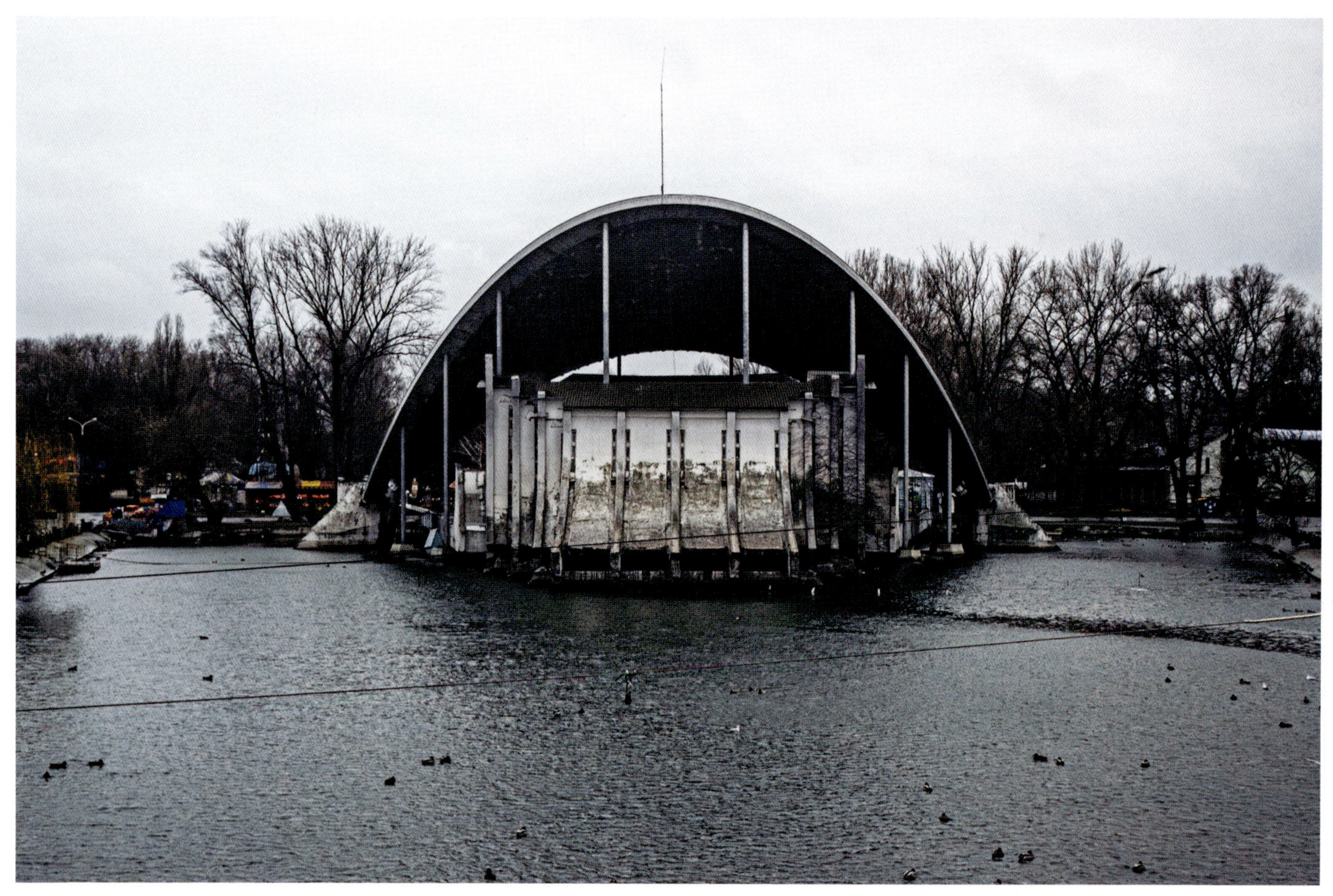

Budivelnyk Summer Theatre
Dnipro
1978
Architect: Oleh Petrov
Engineer: I. Edelshtein

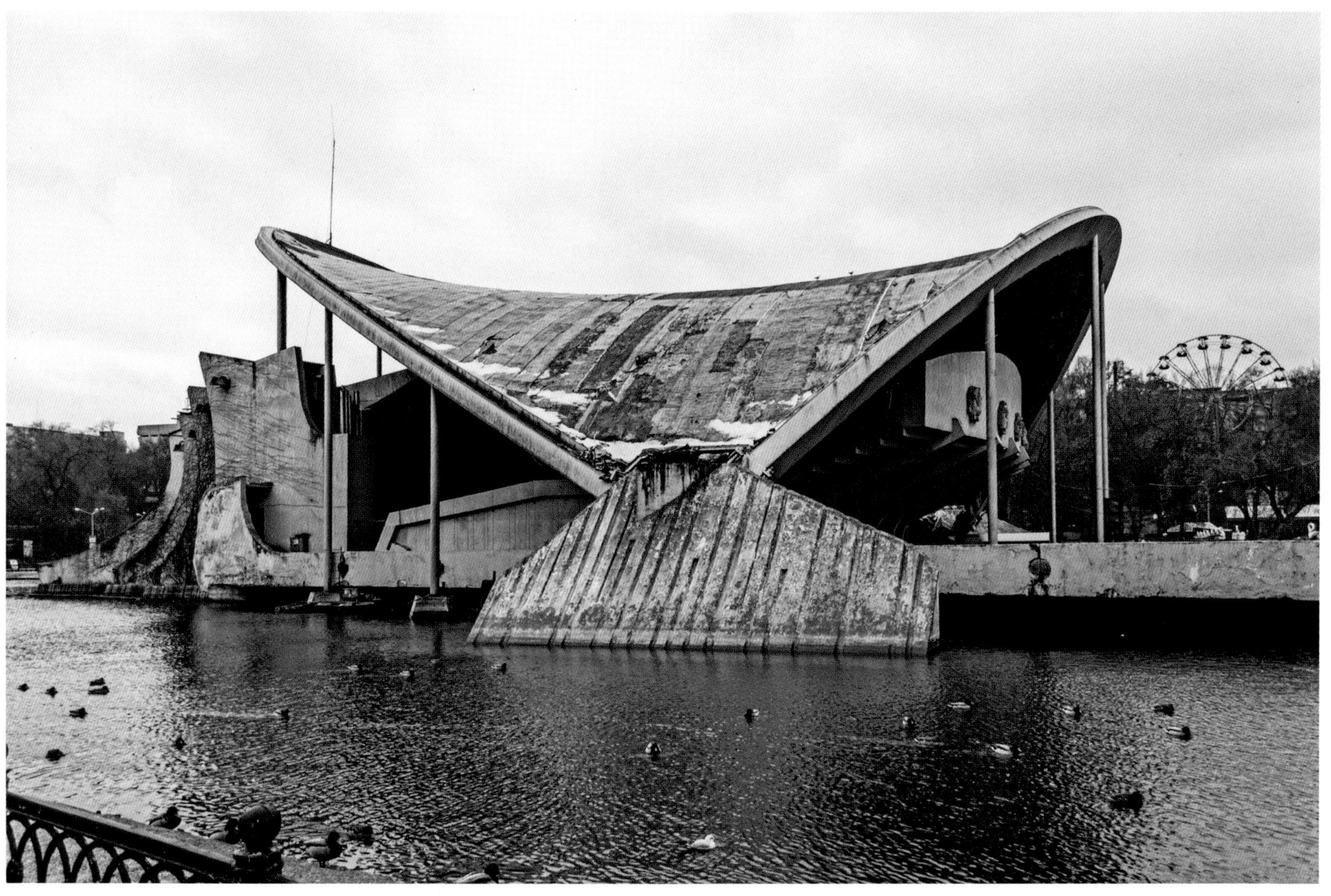

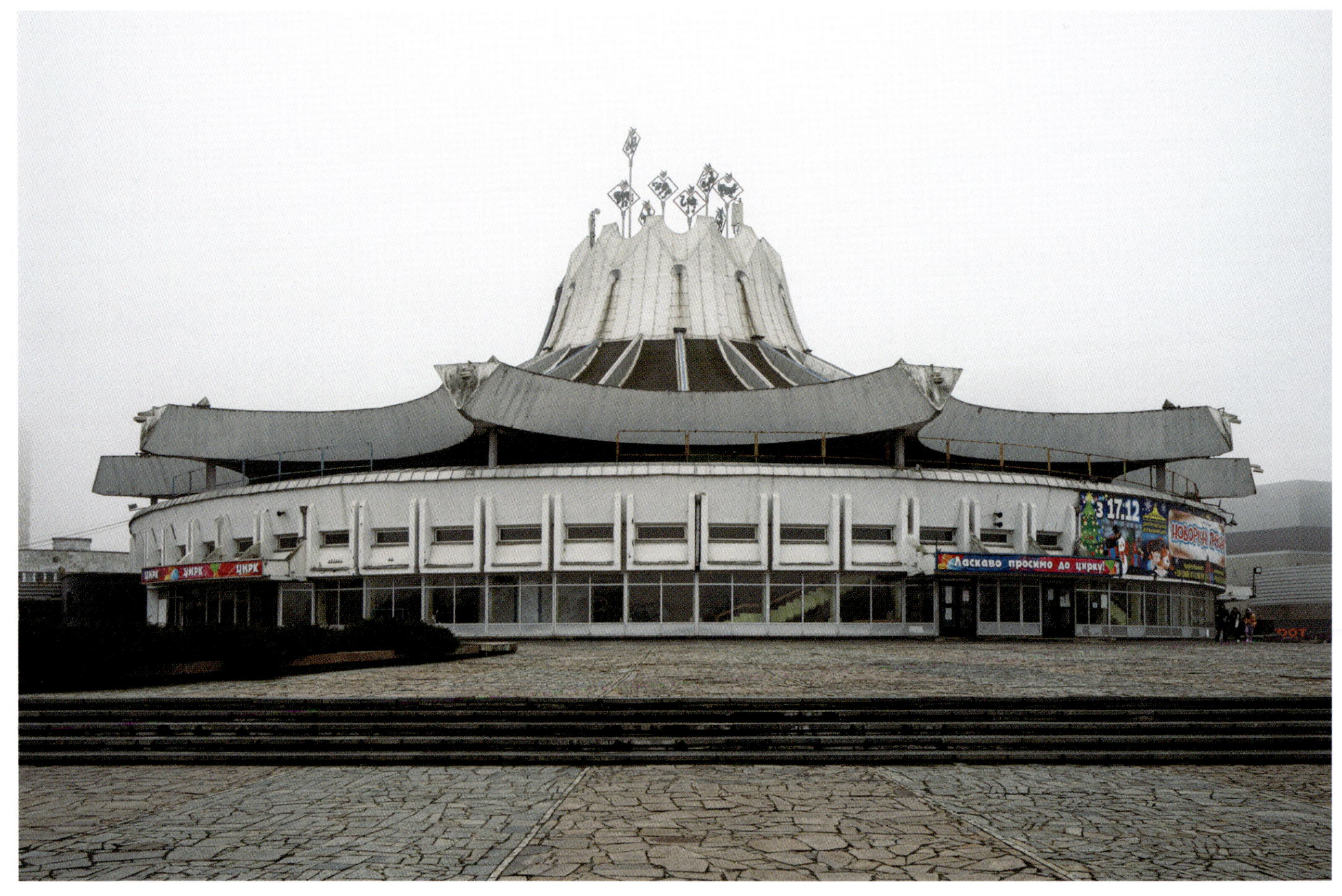

Dnipro Circus
Dnipro
1978–80
Architects: Pavlo Nirinberg, Serhii Zubariev
Engineers: V. Hopankov, A. Sihaev

right: House of Circus Artists
Dnipro
1985
Architect: Oleh Chmona

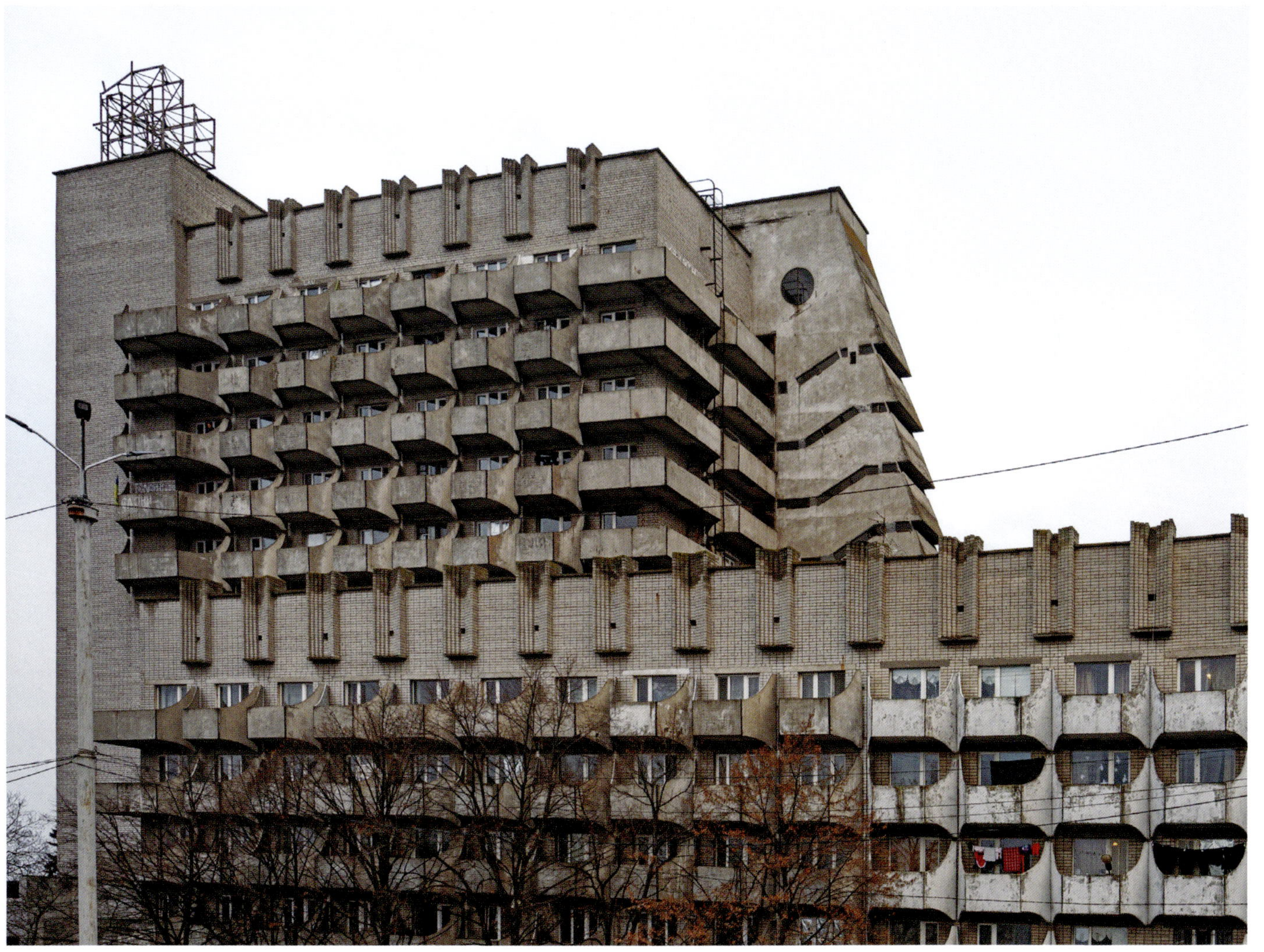

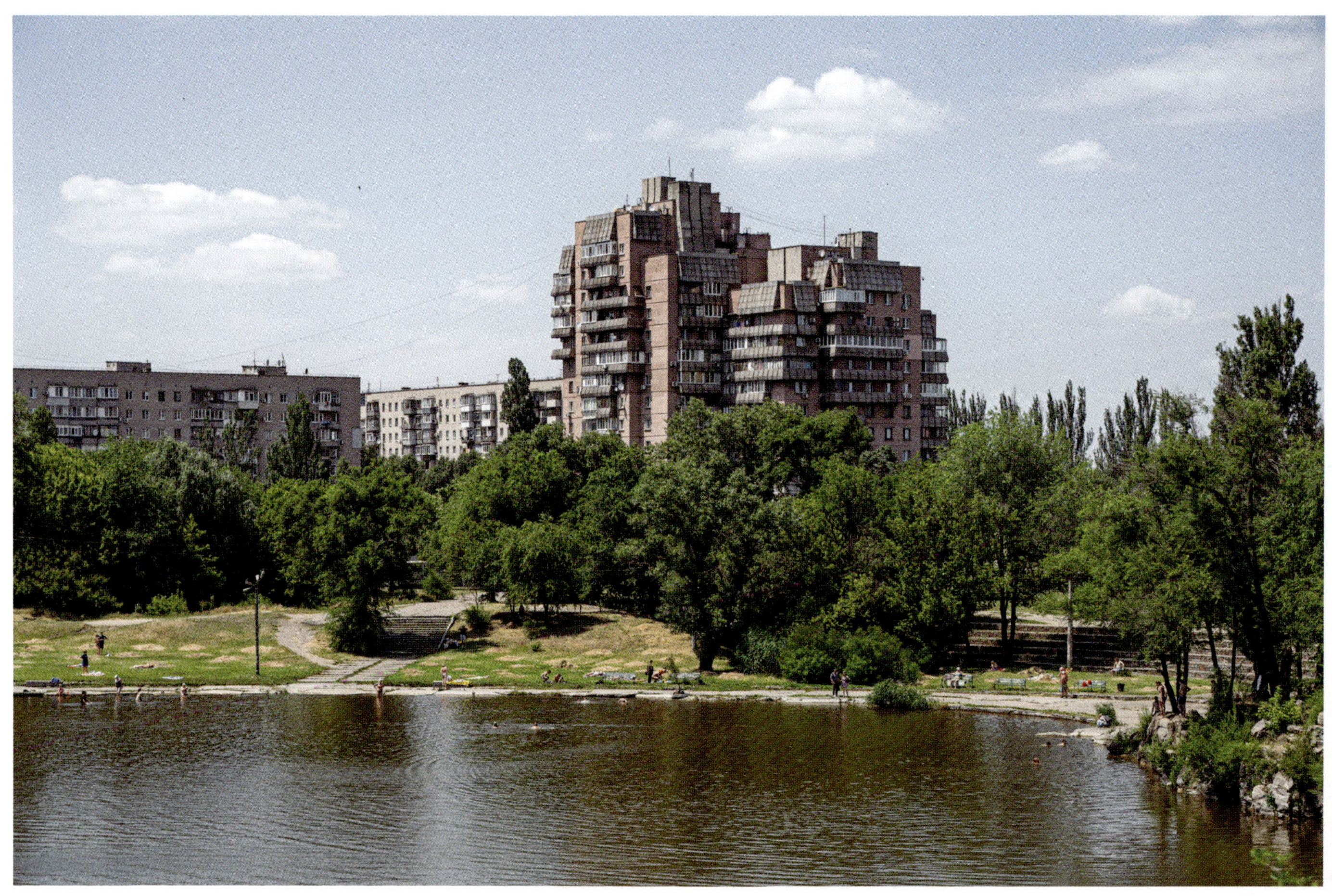

Residential building, Chervonyi Kamin microdistrict
Dnipro
1980–86
Architect: Oleh Chmona

One method used by architects to break the monotony of mass housing was to integrate high-rise buildings with unique designs. These landmarks were intended to serve as compositional focal points and to enrich the urban landscape with expressive architectural forms.

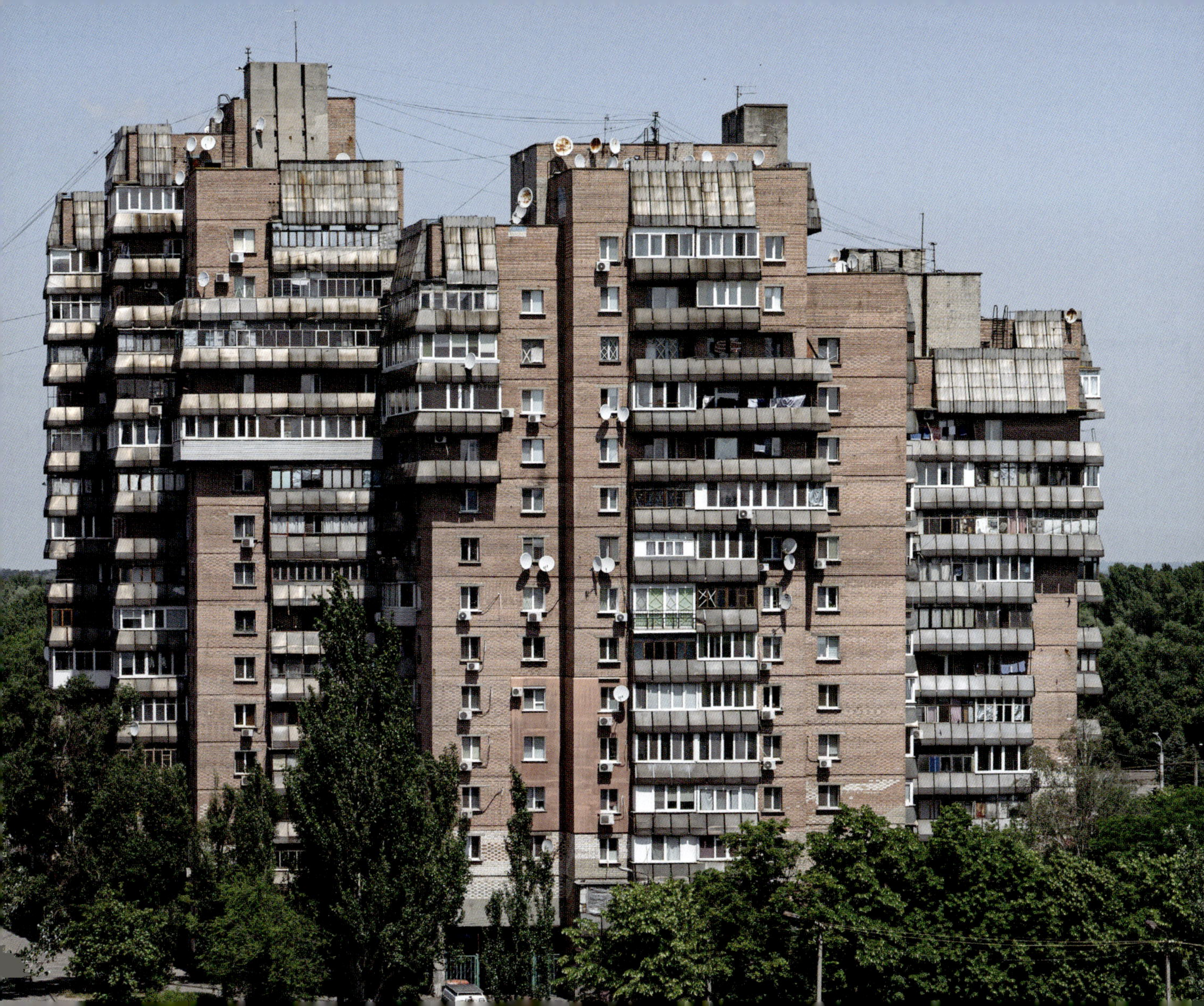

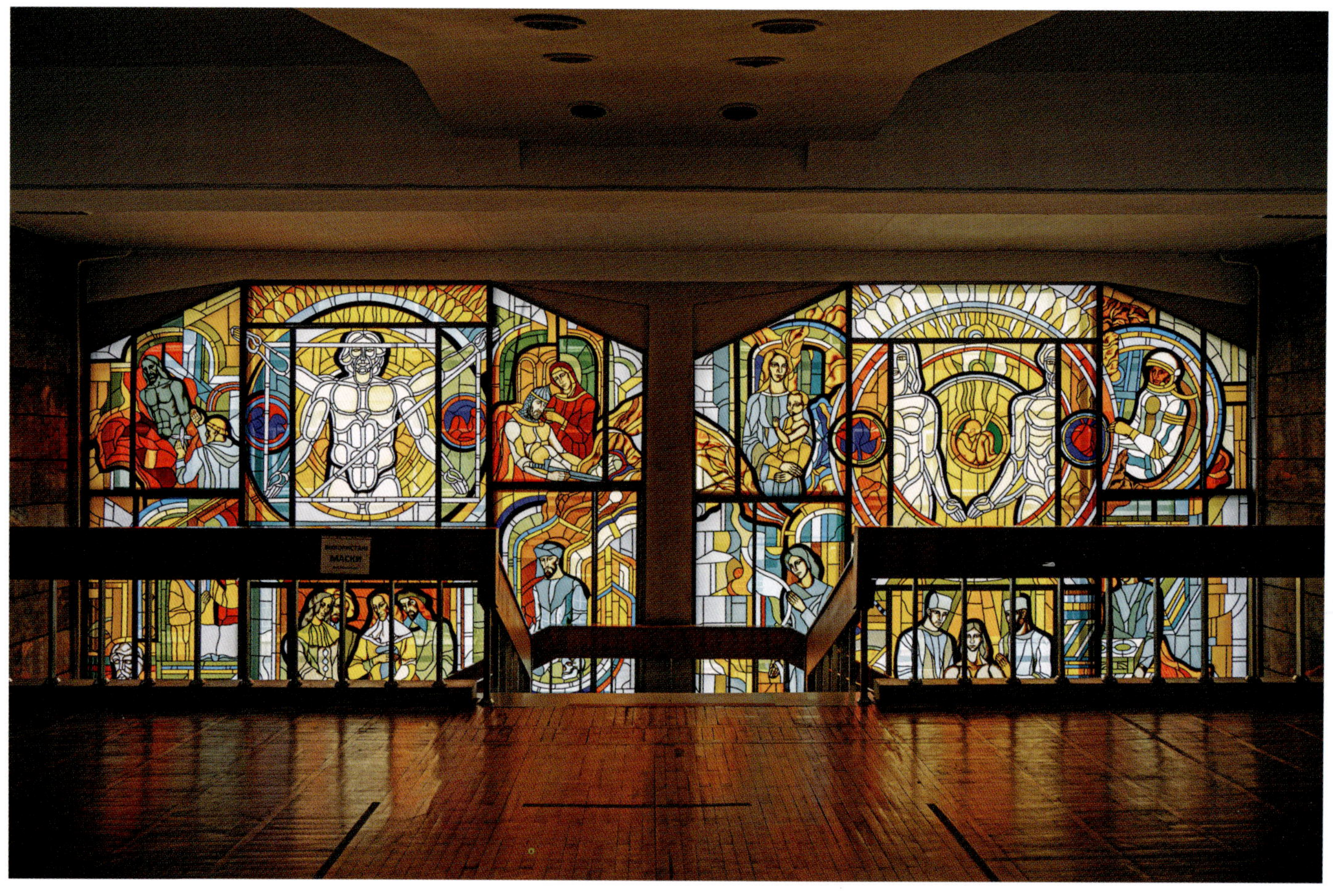

Dnipro State Medical University, Building No.3
Dnipro
1984

Architects: M. Shneierson, Y. Kryvtsov, L. Pavlenko, P. Nirinberg
Engineer: Borys Medhauz
Stained glass artist: Viacheslav Danylov

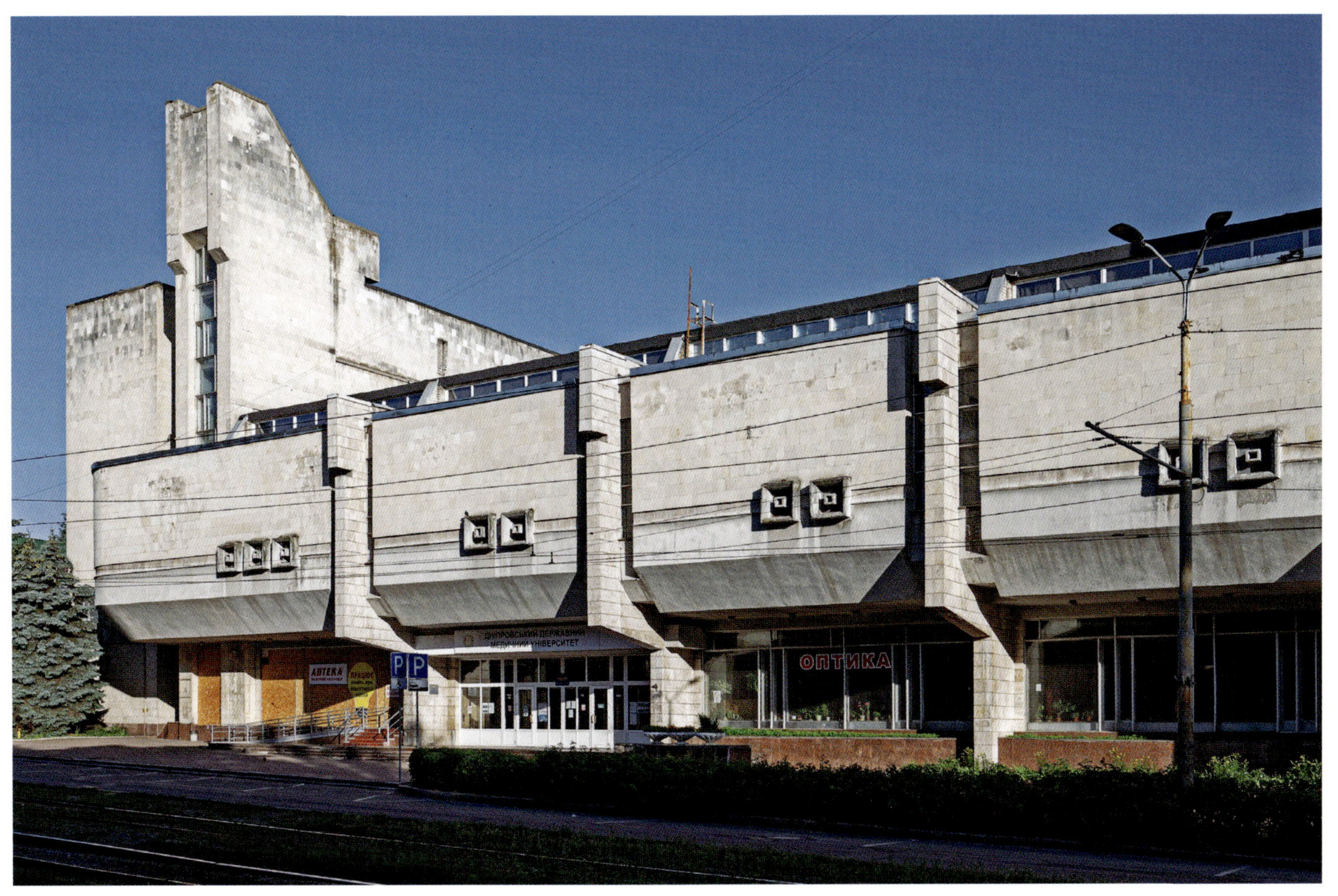
АПТЕКА
P P
Дніпровський державний
медичний університет
ОПТИКА

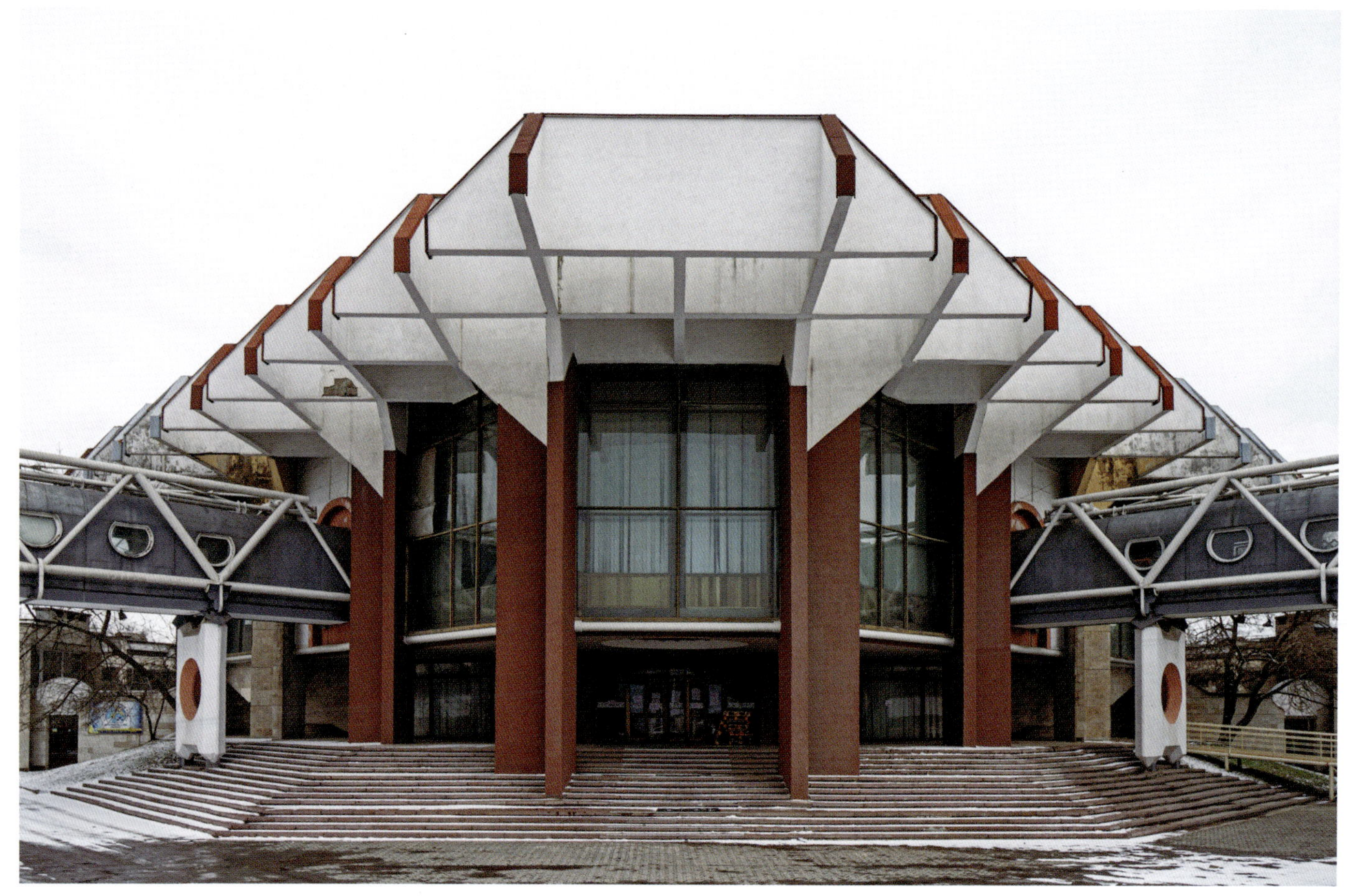

Palace of Children and Youth
(formerly the Palace of Pioneers and Schoolchildren)
Dnipro
1985–90
Architects: Yevhen Amosov, Tetiana Solodovnyk,
Viktor Garcia Ortega, A. Klever
Engineers: Anatolii Bobrovnyk, Larysa Bobrovnyk, Borys Dryk
Artists: Viacheslav Danylov, Vasyl Miroshnychenko, Serhii Isaiev, Leonid
Khaliavskyi, Tetiana Yushkova, Oleksandr Dubovyk, Oleksandr
Shabanov, A. Pertsovskyi

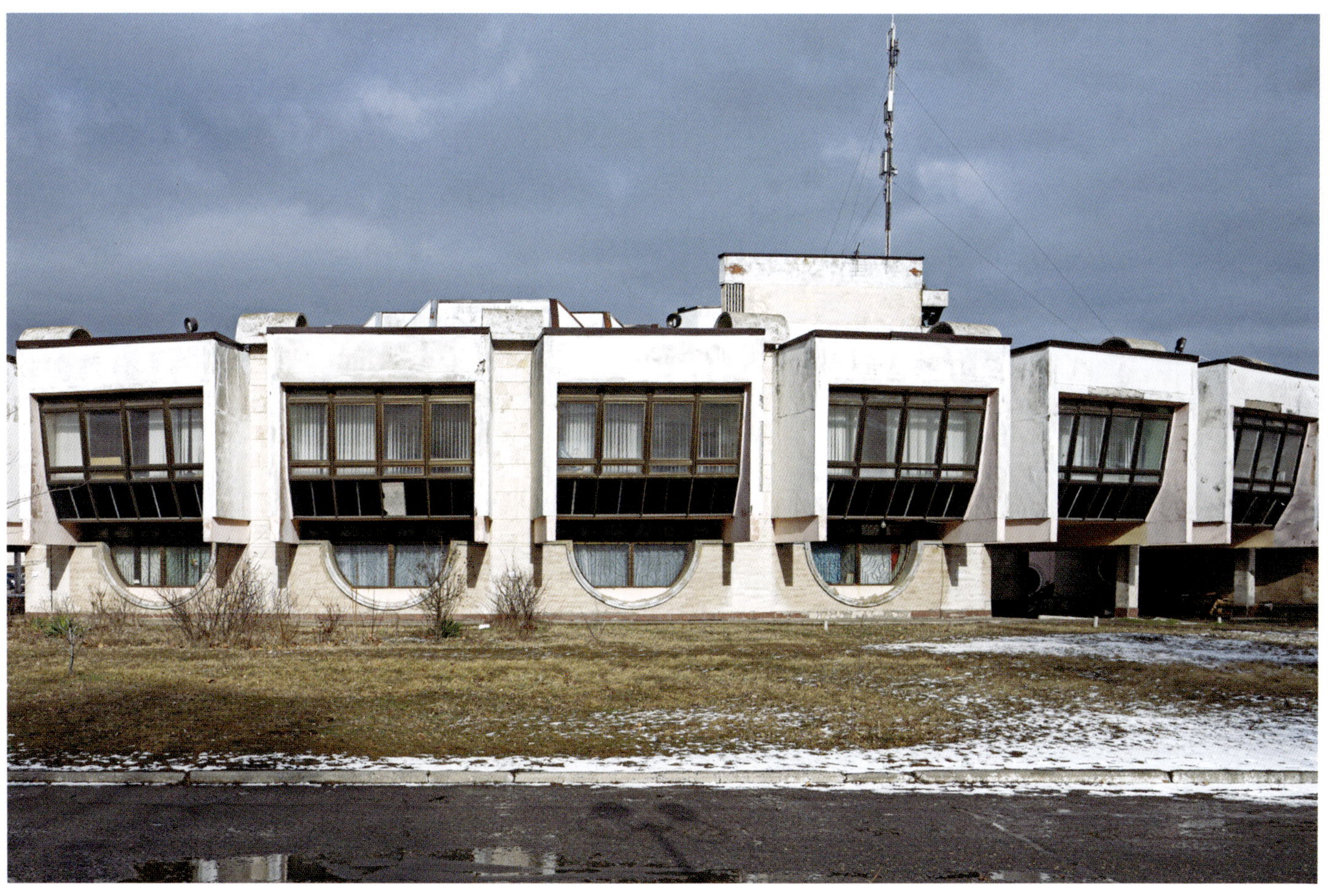

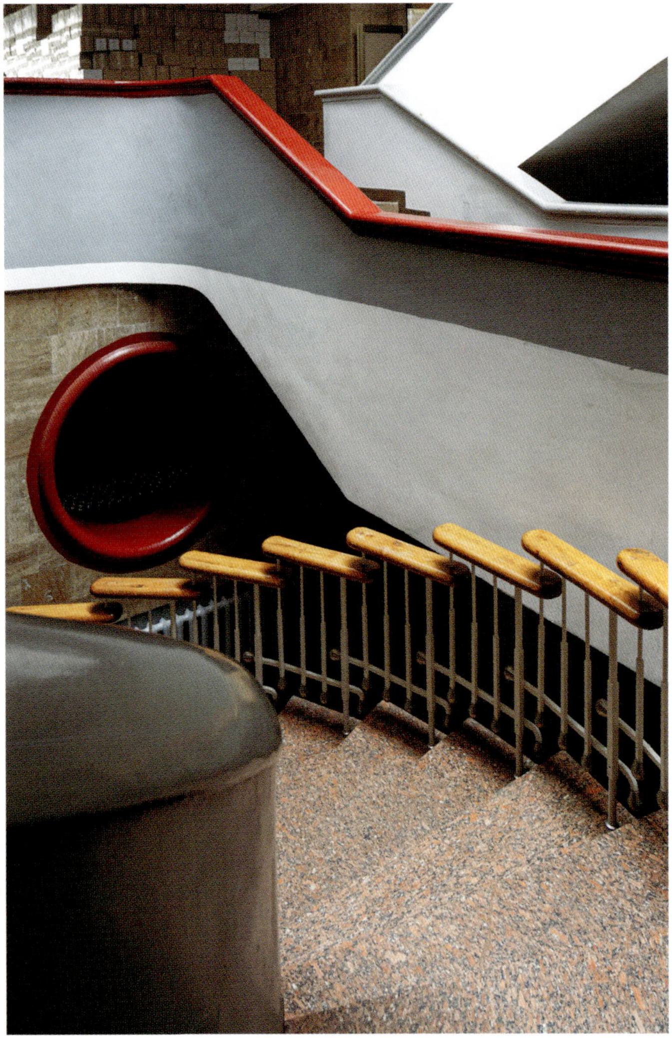

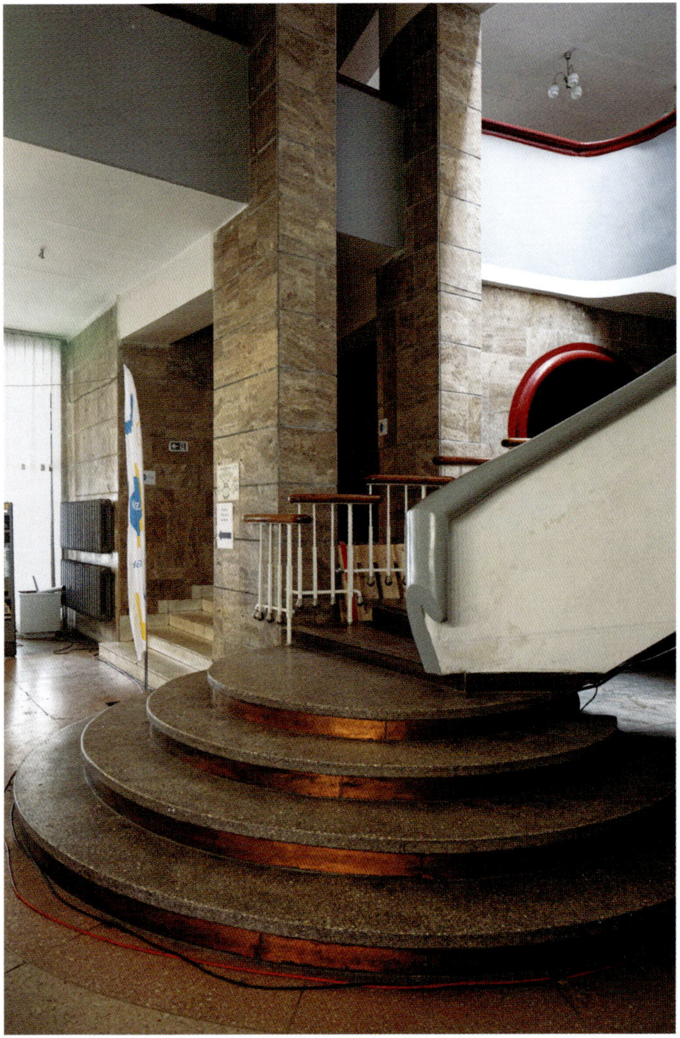

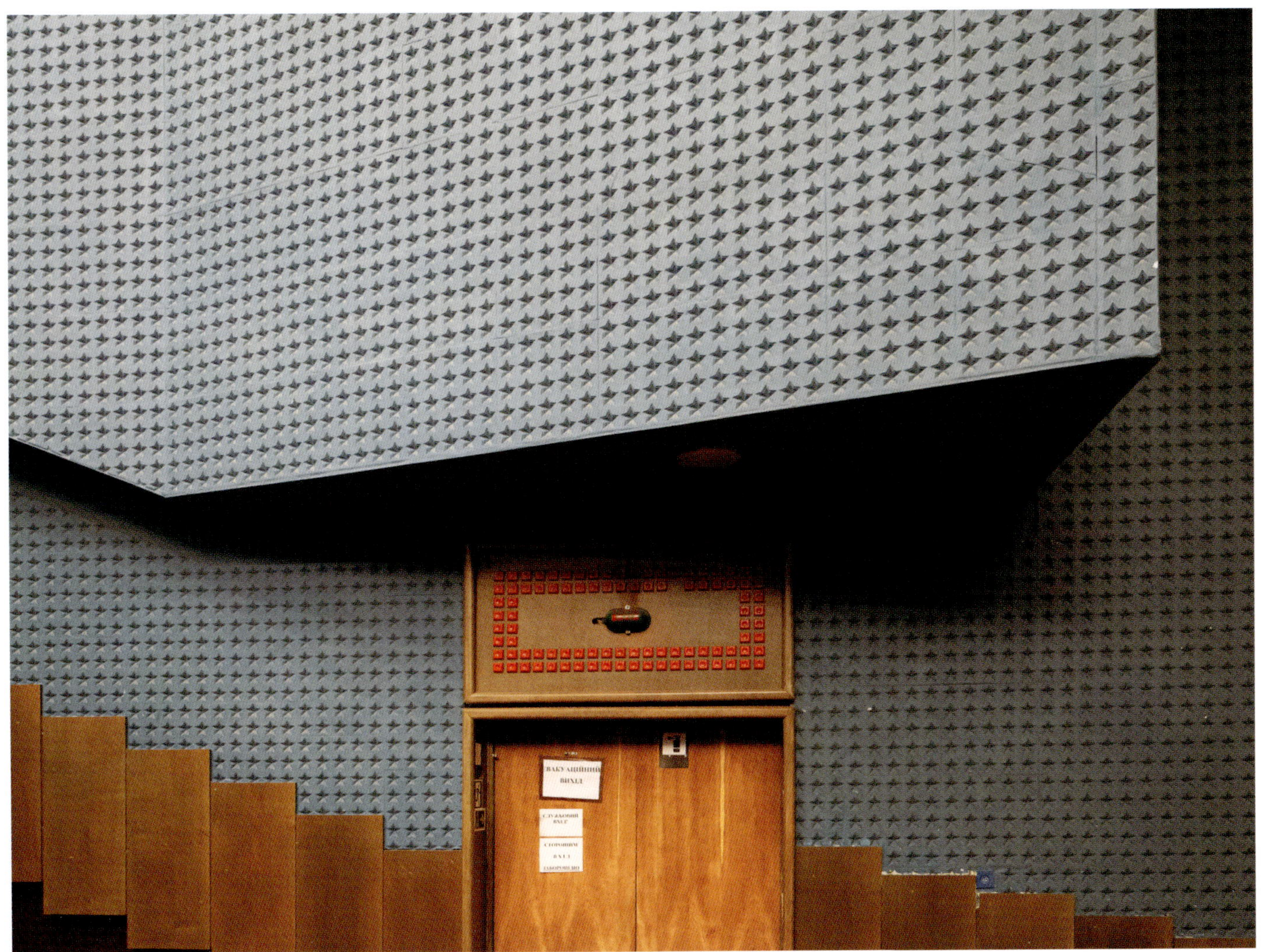
ЕВАКУАЦІЙНИЙ
ВИХІД
СЛУЖБОВИЙ
ВХІД
СТОРОННІМ
ВХІД
ЗАБОРОНЕНО

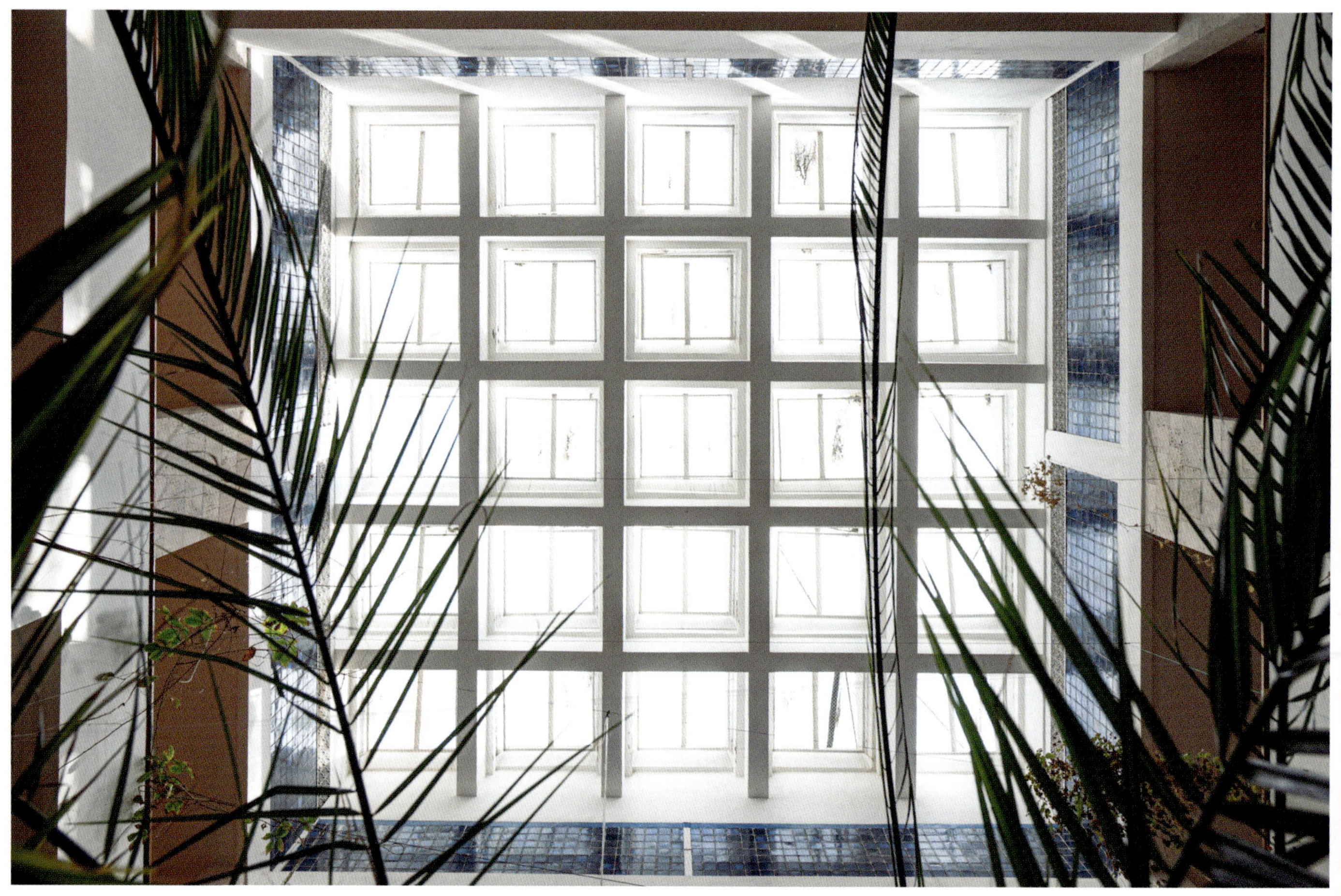

Scientific Library, Dnipro National University
Dnipro
1989
Architect: Oleksandr Novikov

Established in 1918, the scientific library moved to this purpose built
site in 1989. The building's strict geometry is reinforced by the vertical
panels of its *brise soleil*, which deflect sunlight to minimise heat gain.
Inside, a large skylight floods the winter garden atrium with light.

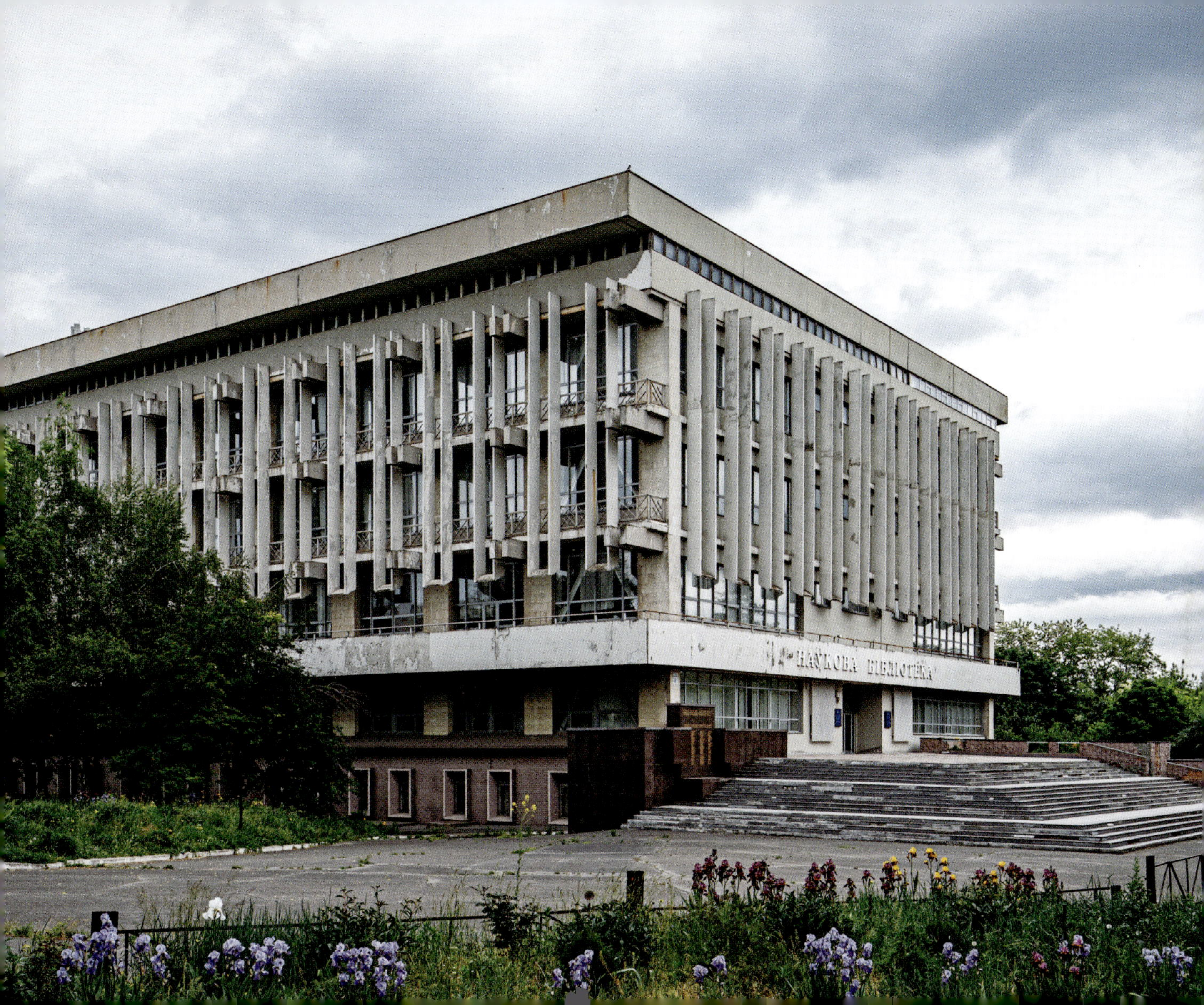

НАУКОВА БІБЛІОТЕКА

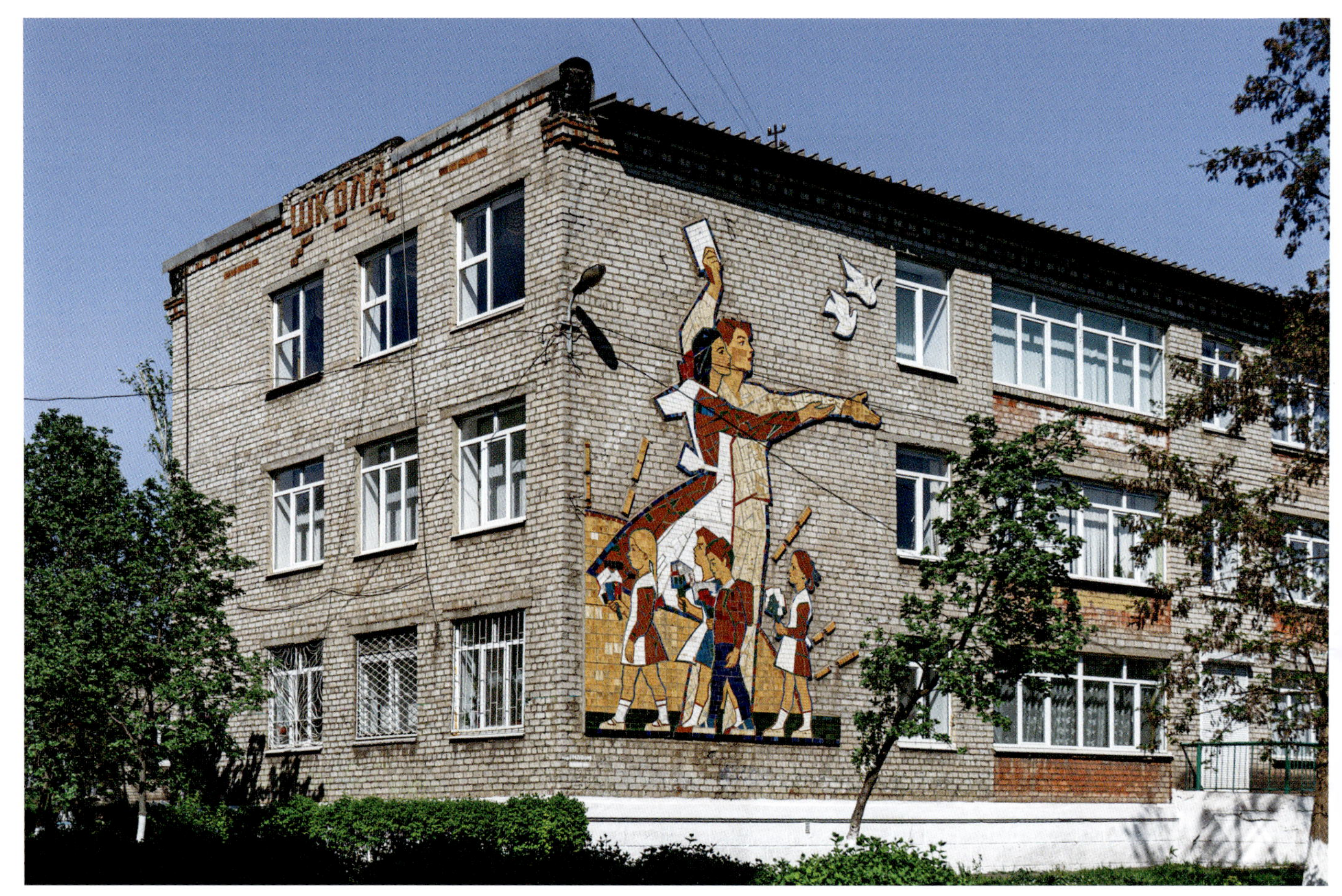

'First Graders' mosaic, School No.34,
Mariupol, Donetsk Oblast
1963
Artists: Valentyn Konstantinov, Lel Kuzminkov

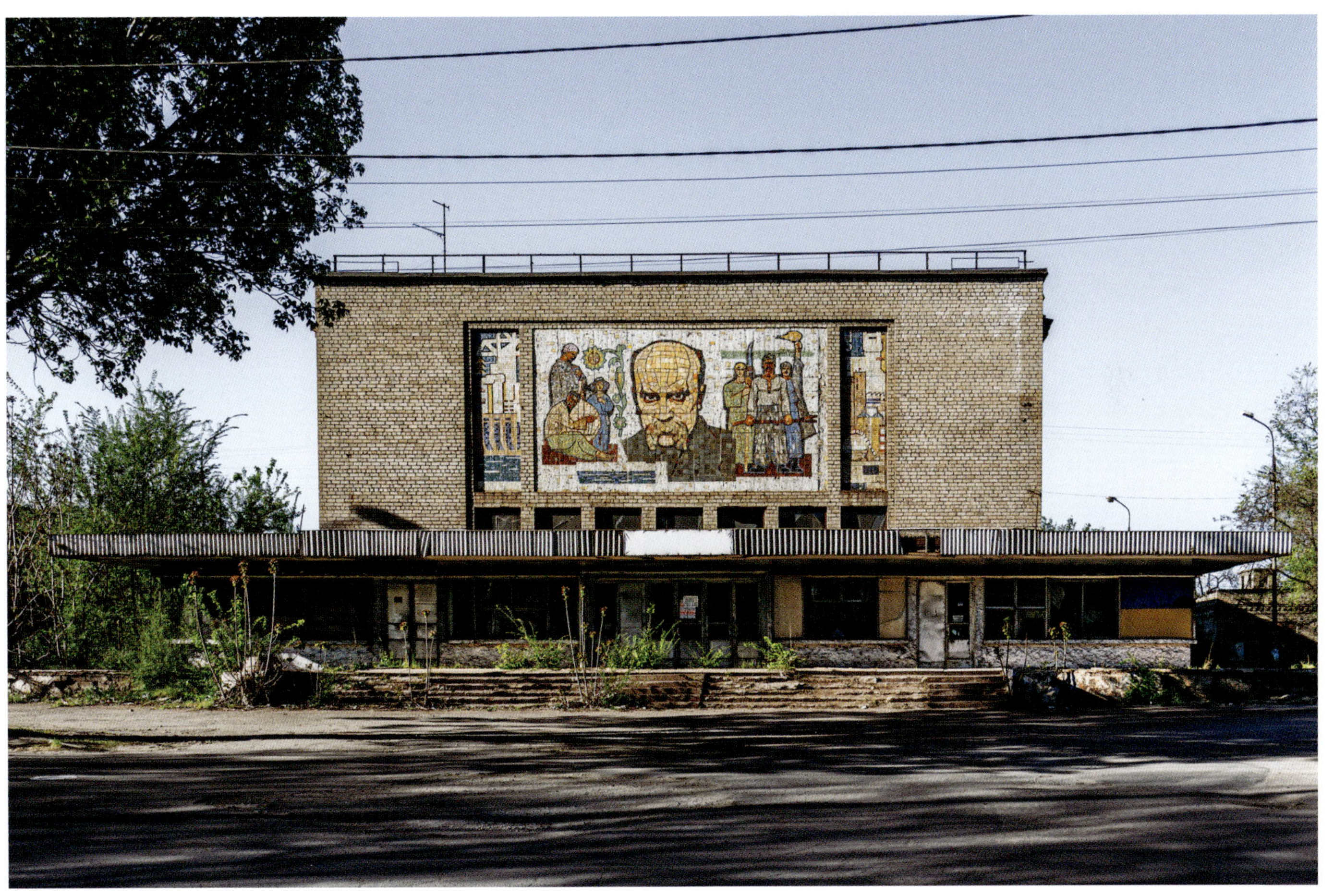

'Taras Shevchenko' mosaic, Taras Shevchenko Cinema
Mariupol, Donetsk Oblast
1965
Artists: Yakiv Raizin, Mykola Tykhonov, Oleksandr Kechedzhi

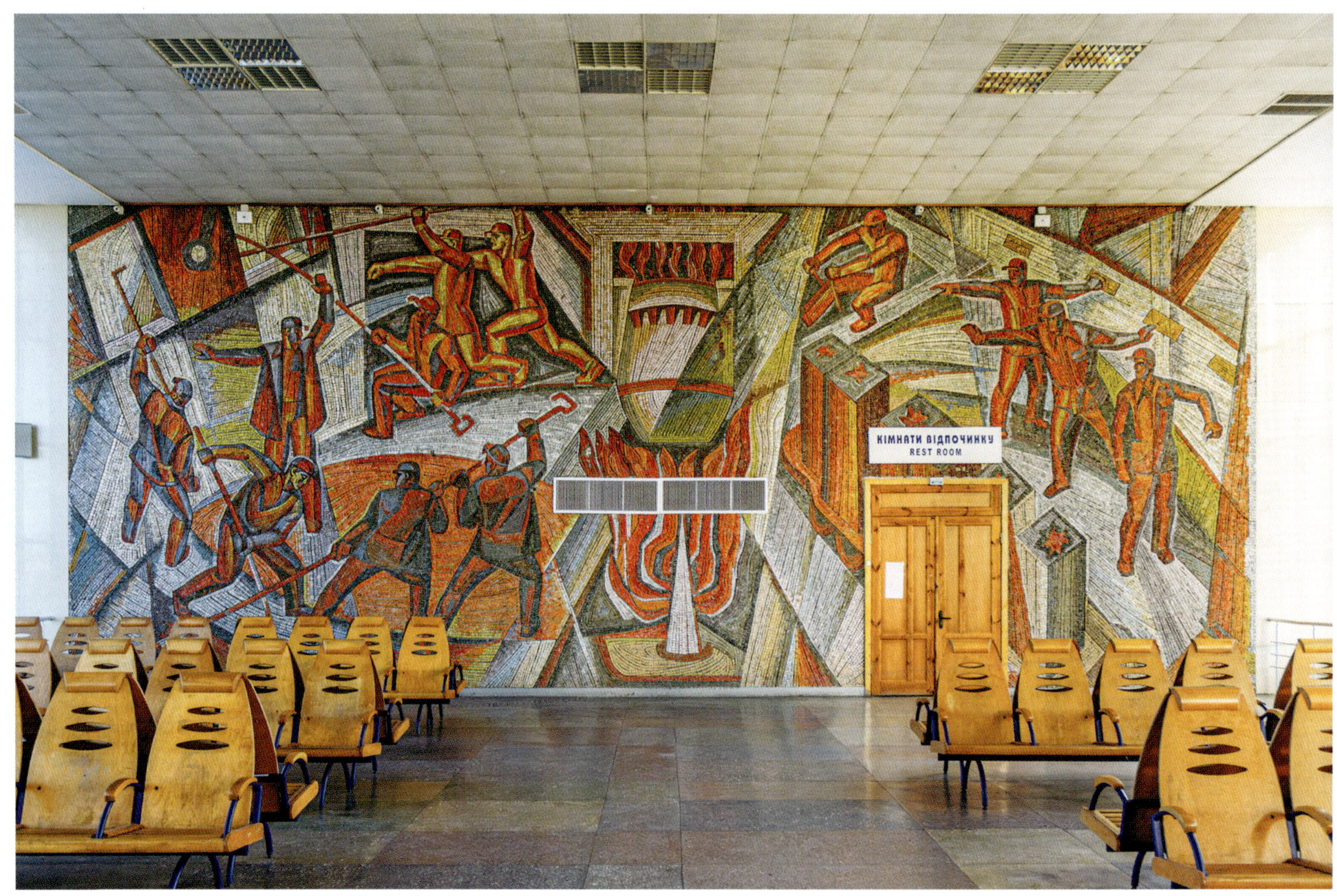

'Metallurgists' mosaic, Mariupol Train Station
Mariupol, Donetsk Oblast
1974
Artists: Valentyn Konstantinov, Lel Kuzminkov

The train station sustained heavy damage during the Siege of Mariupol (24 February–20 May 2022). However, the mosaics survived until 2023 when the Russians demolished the building, replacing it with a new structure in 2024.

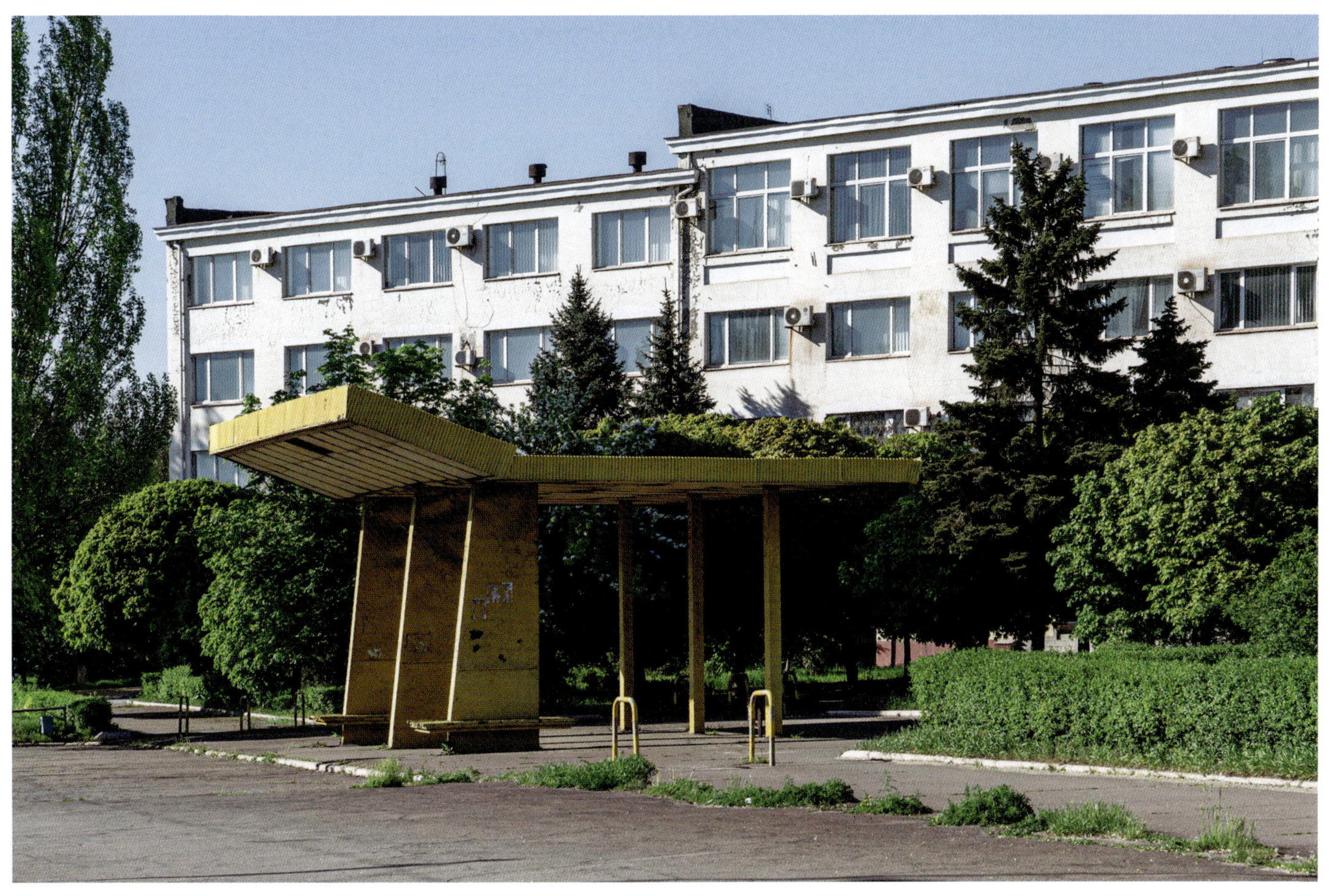

Bus stop
Mariupol, Donetsk Oblast
1980s

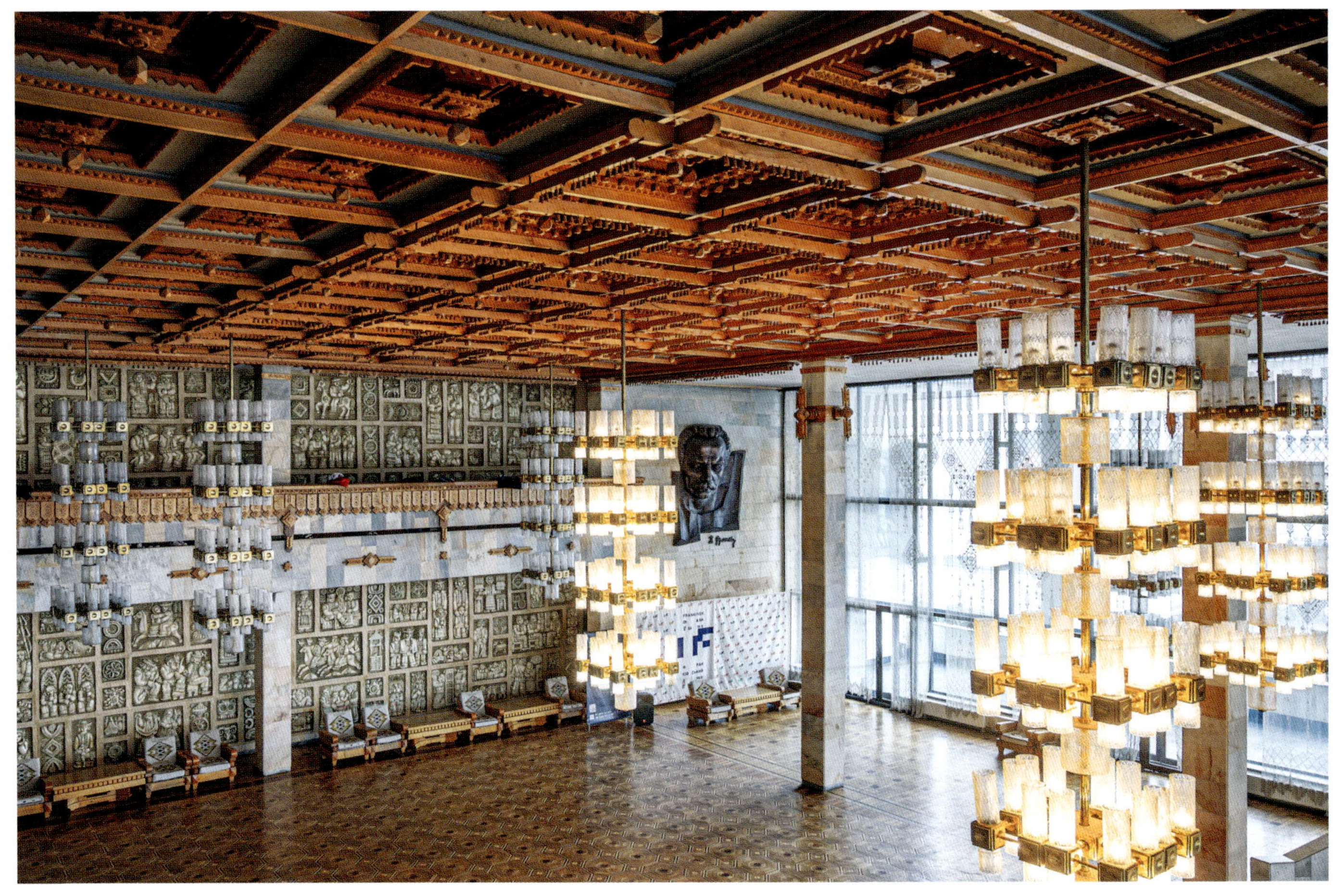

Ivano-Frankivsk Music and Drama Theatre
Ivano-Frankivsk
1967–80
Architect: Stepan Slipets

Interior architect: Dmytro Sosnovyi
Engineer: Leonid Sandler
Artists: Valentyn Danyliuk, Vasyl Vilshuk, Yosyp Kosovych, Mykhailo Murafa, Volodymyr Shevchuk, Anton Ovchar, Vasyl Lukashko

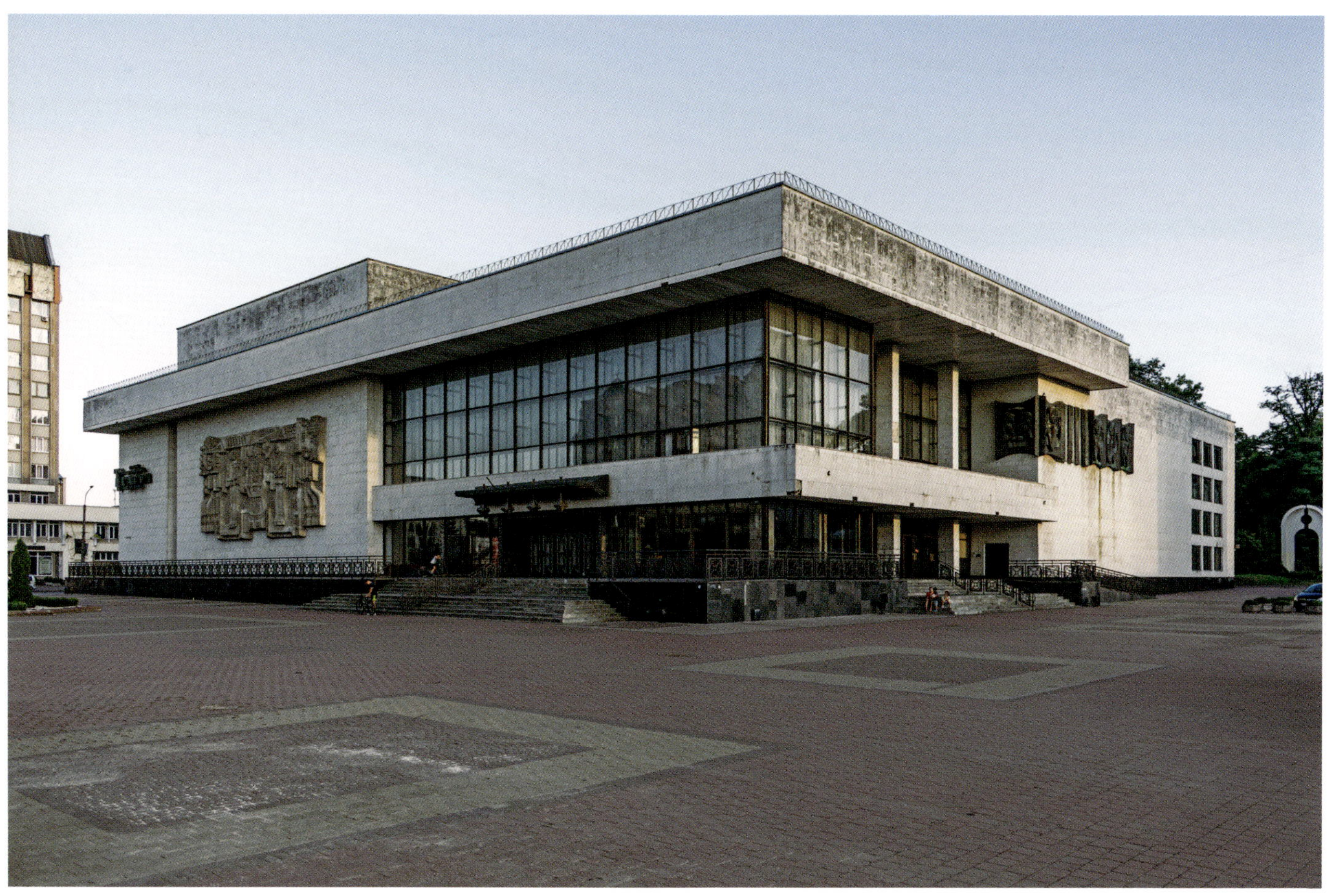

The building's modernist facade contrasts with its lavish interior that celebrates local folk traditions: carved wooden ceilings, furniture crafted by local artisans and decorated with Hutsul patterned fabrics, and a monumental ceramic panel depicting scenes from Hutsul life.

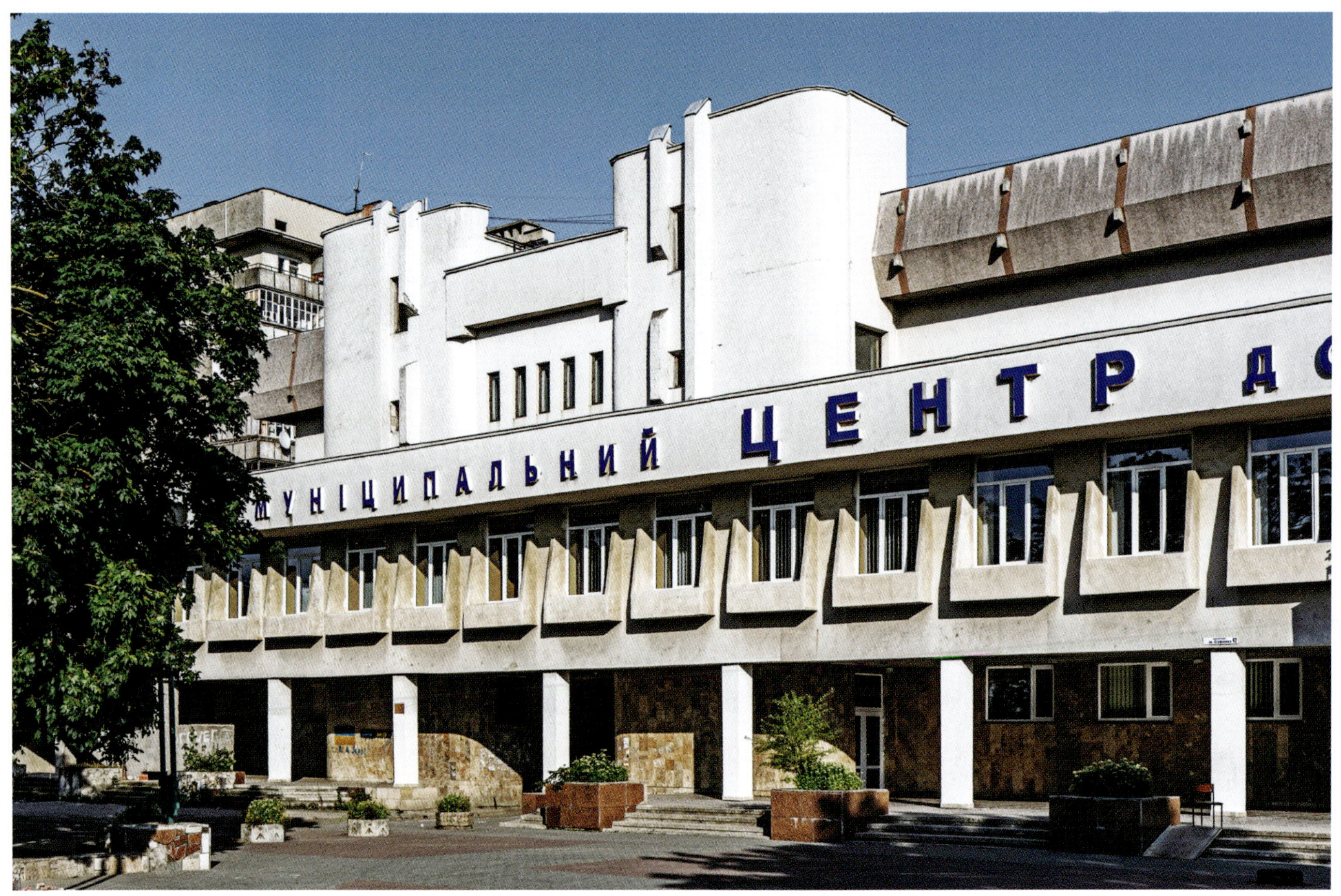

Municipal Leisure Centre
(formerly 'Budivelnyk' Culture and Sports Complex)
Ivano-Frankivsk
1989

The complex was designed by the Ivano-Frankivsk arm of DIPROMISTO, the Ukrainian State Institute of Urban Planning, part of a network of such institutes employing architects across the Soviet Union. Some, like the branch in Kyivproekt, employed a staff of up to 1,000 people.

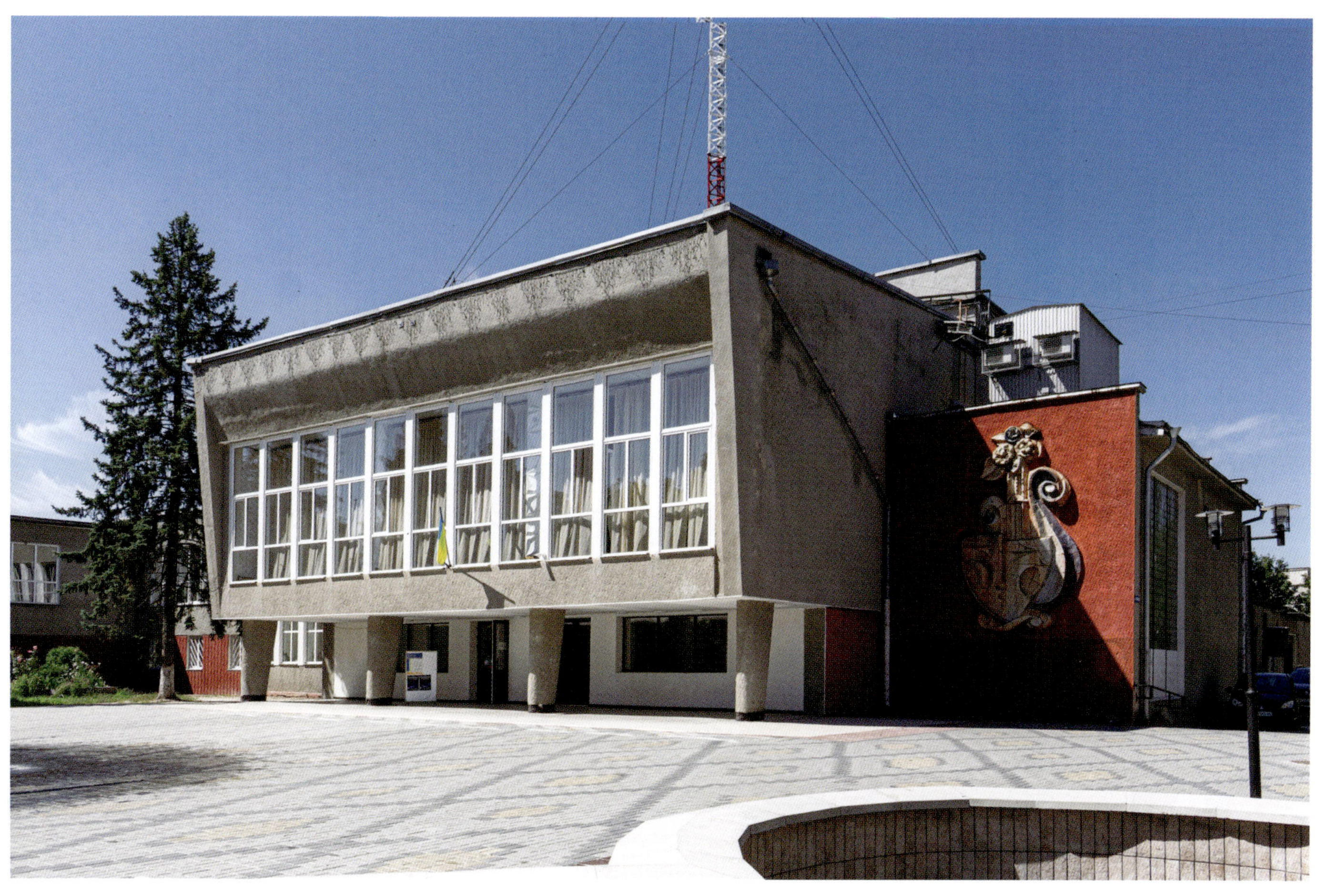

Yunist Palace of Culture
Kalush, Ivano-Frankivsk Oblast
1967

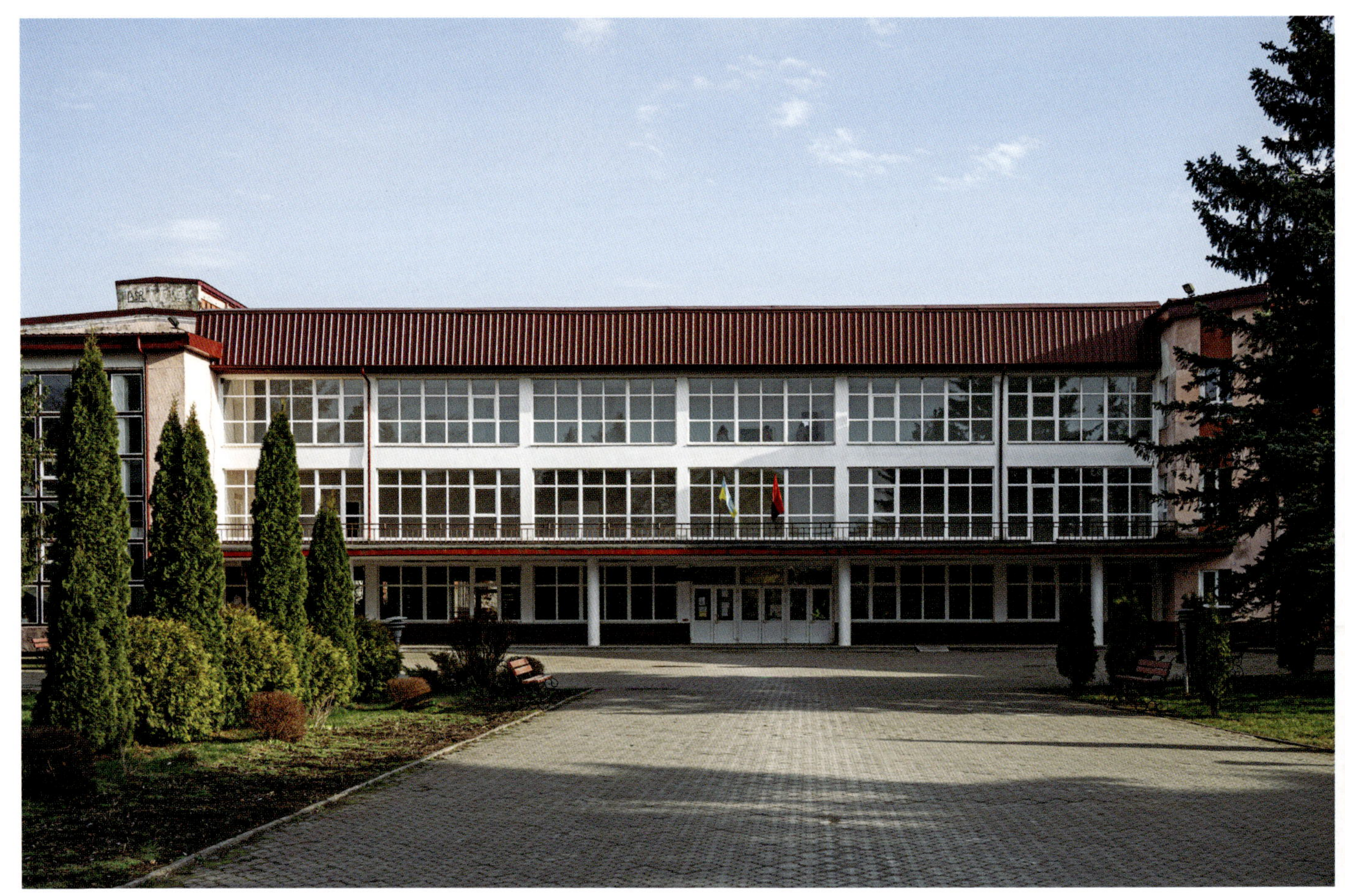

'Prometheus' Palace of Culture
Burshtyn, Ivano-Frankivsk Oblast
1971–74
Artists: Viktor Elkonin, Yurii Aleksandrov

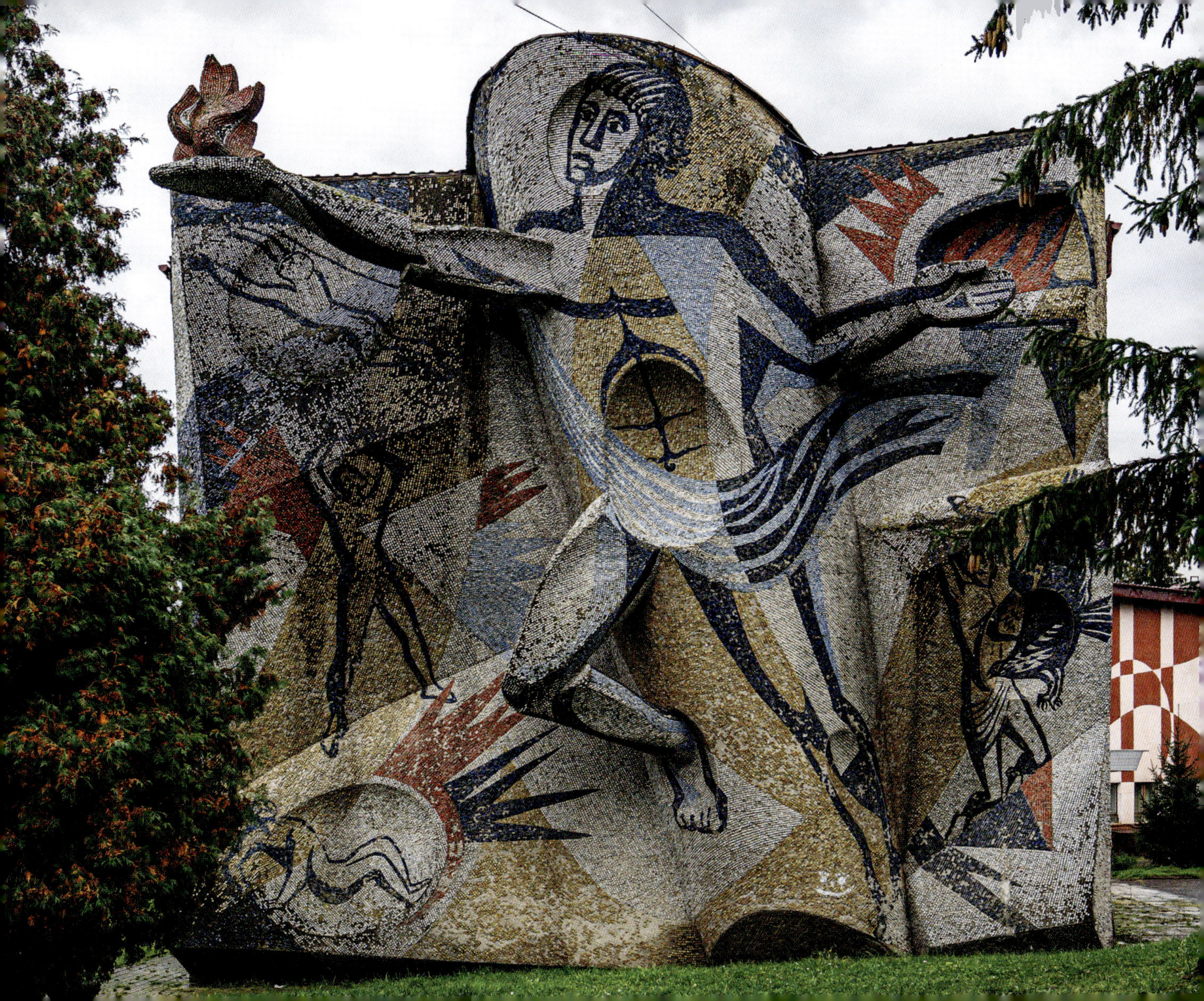

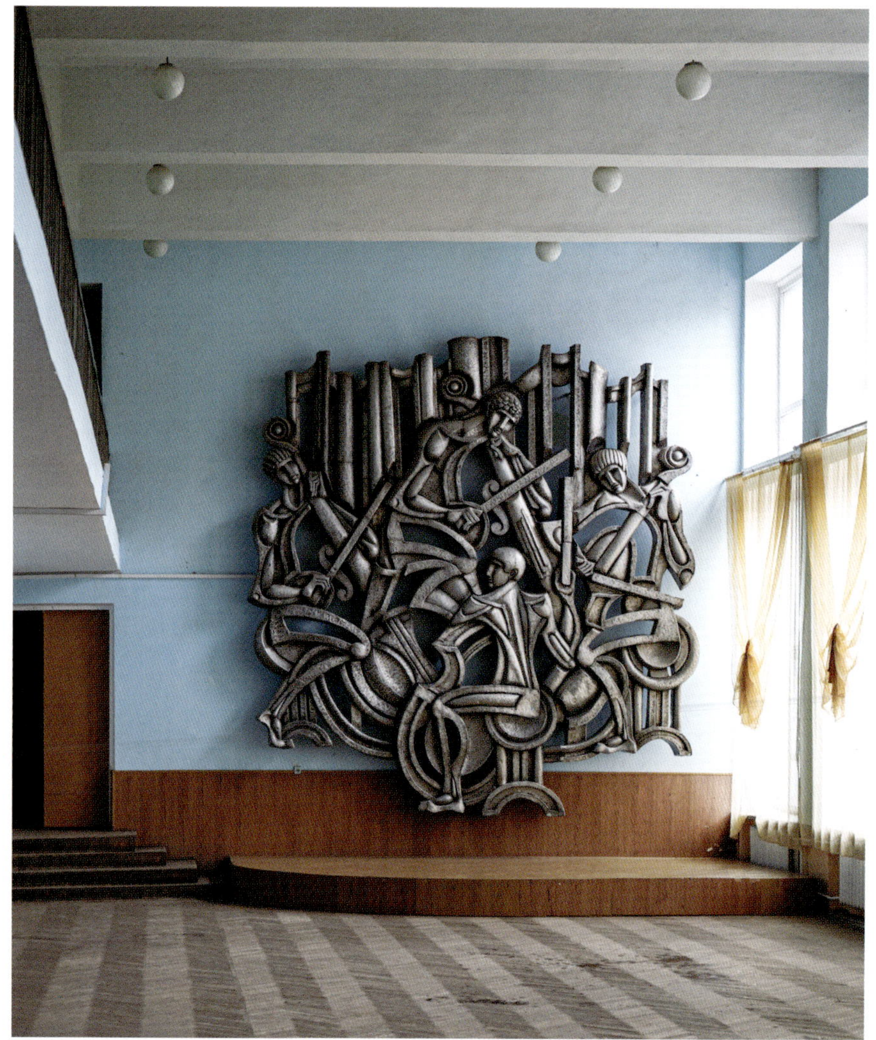

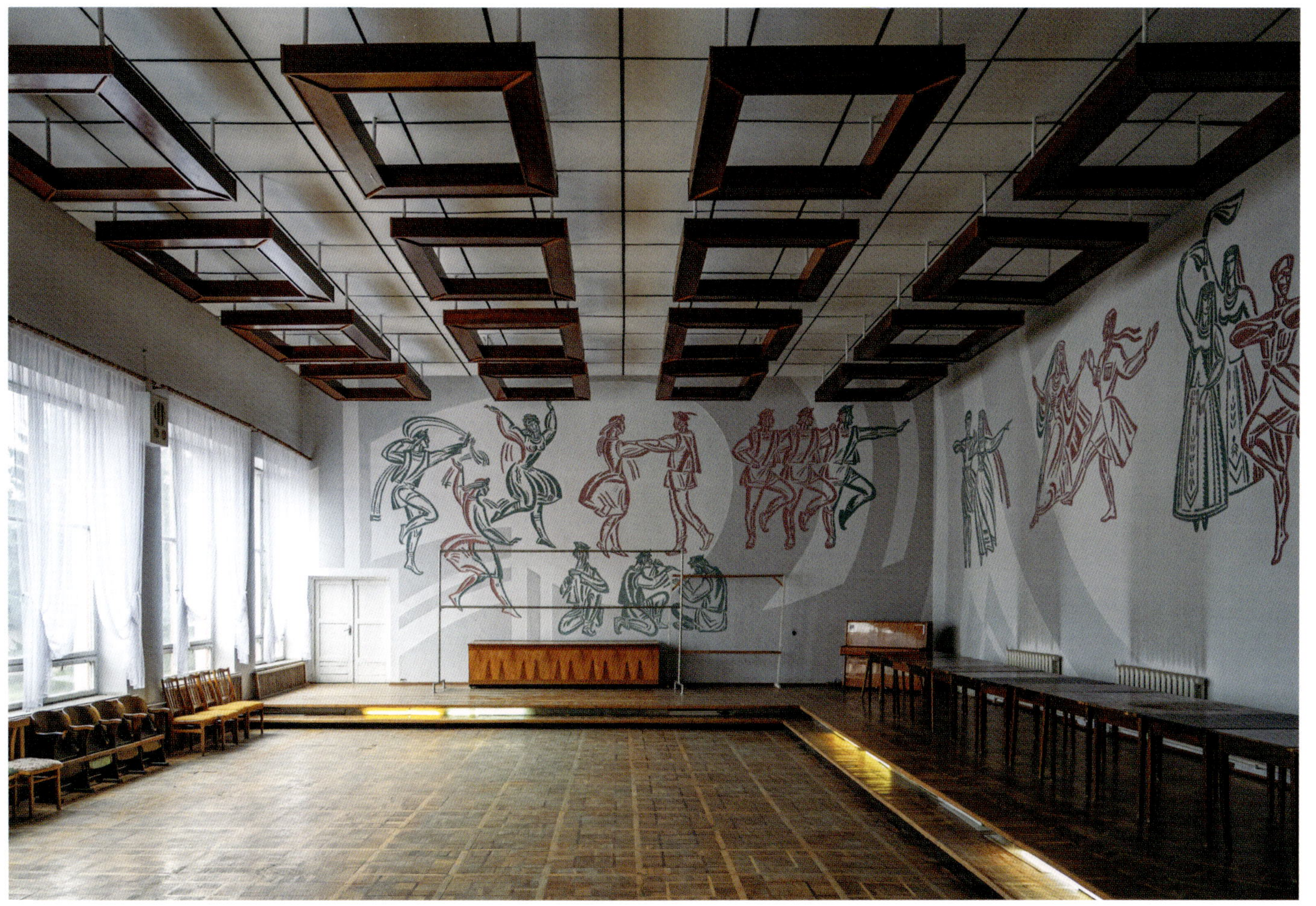

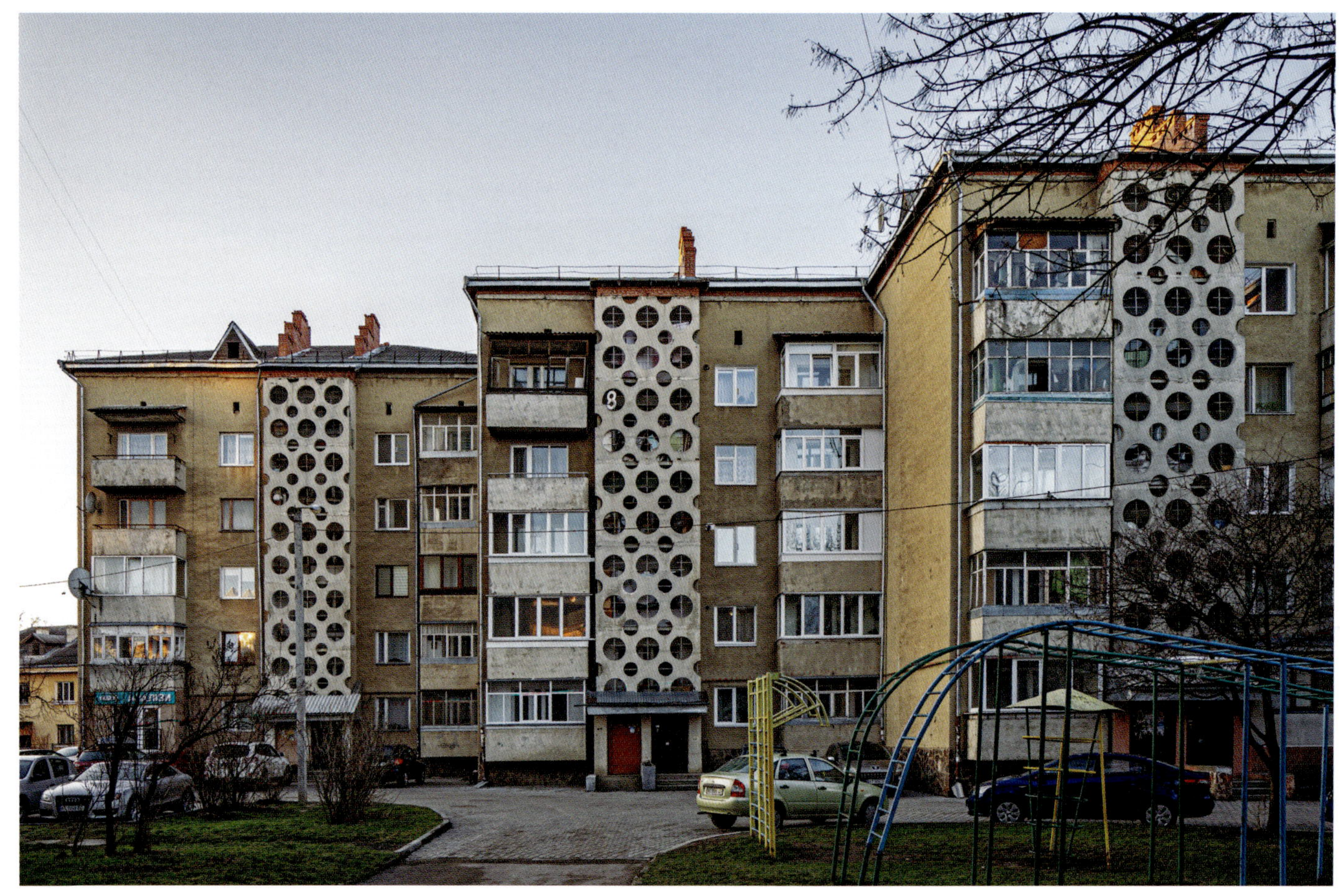

Residential buildings
Ivano-Frankivsk
1970s

right: Residential buildings with local folk motifs
Nadvirna, Ivano-Frankivsk Oblast
1970s

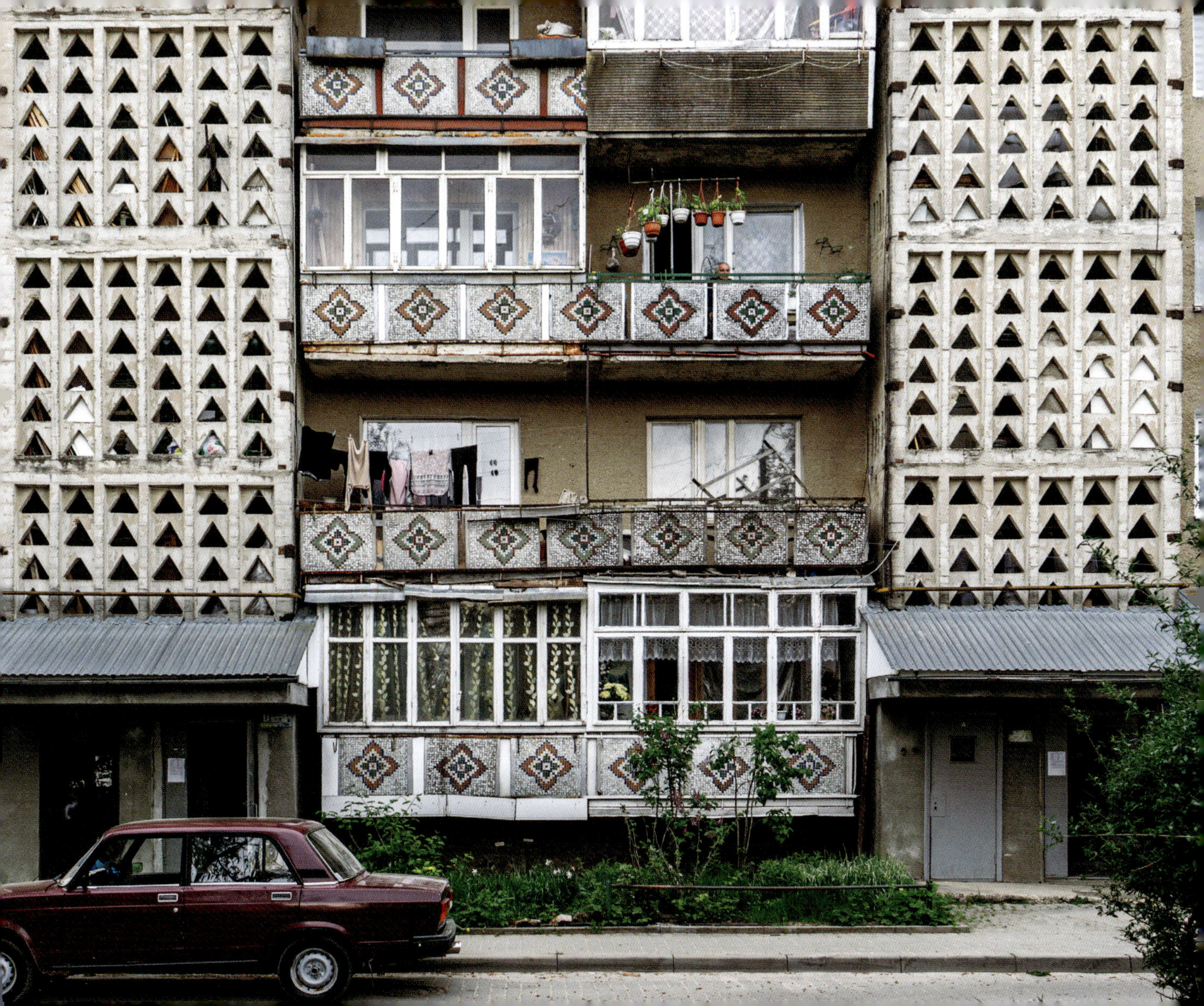

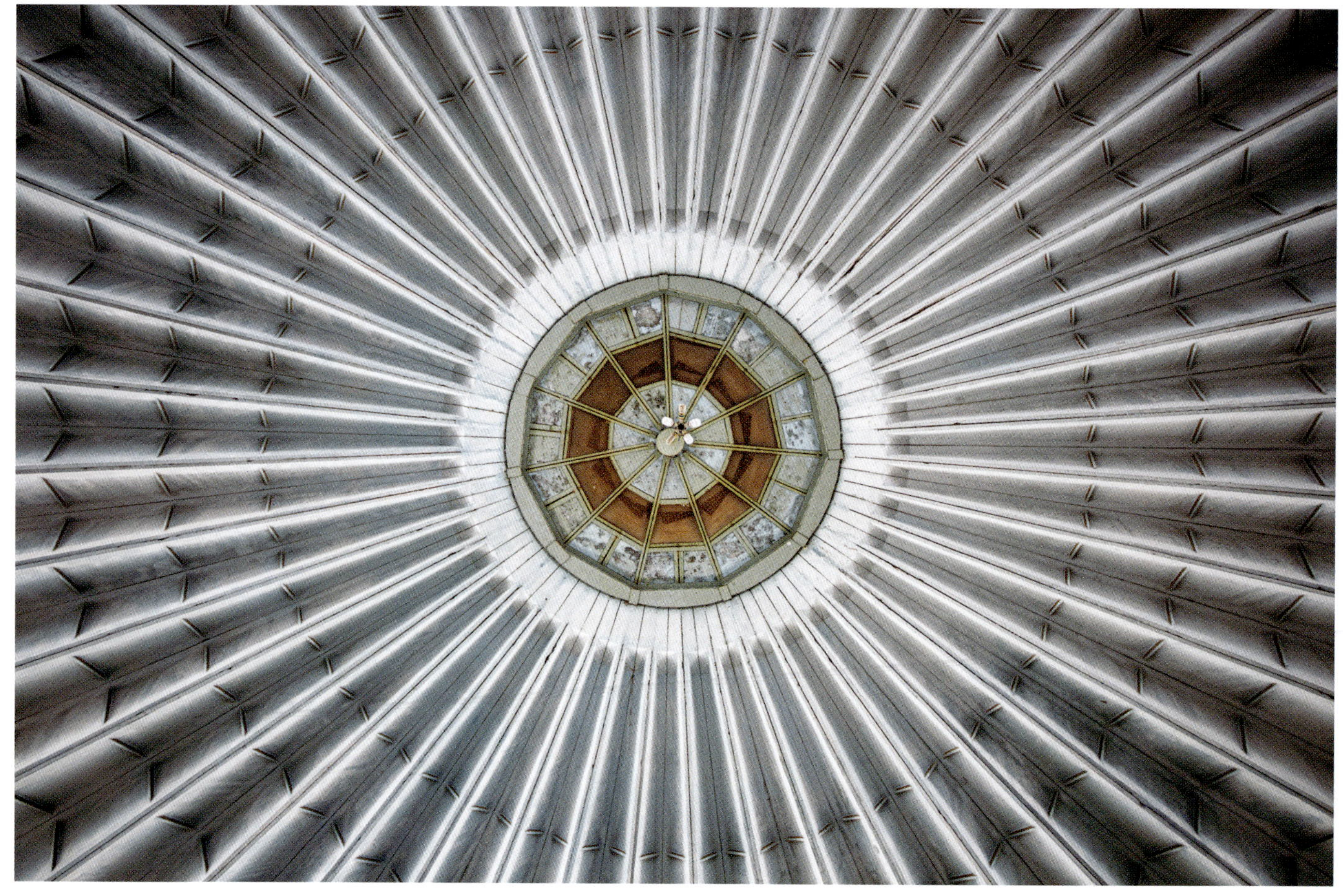

Ivano-Frankivsk Market
Ivano-Frankivsk
1989

Architect: Volodymyr Lukomskyi
Engineers: Zenovii Davydiuk, Orest Ivasyk, V. Harnaha, T. Vasylenko,
T. Vilchynska, V. Kuznietsova

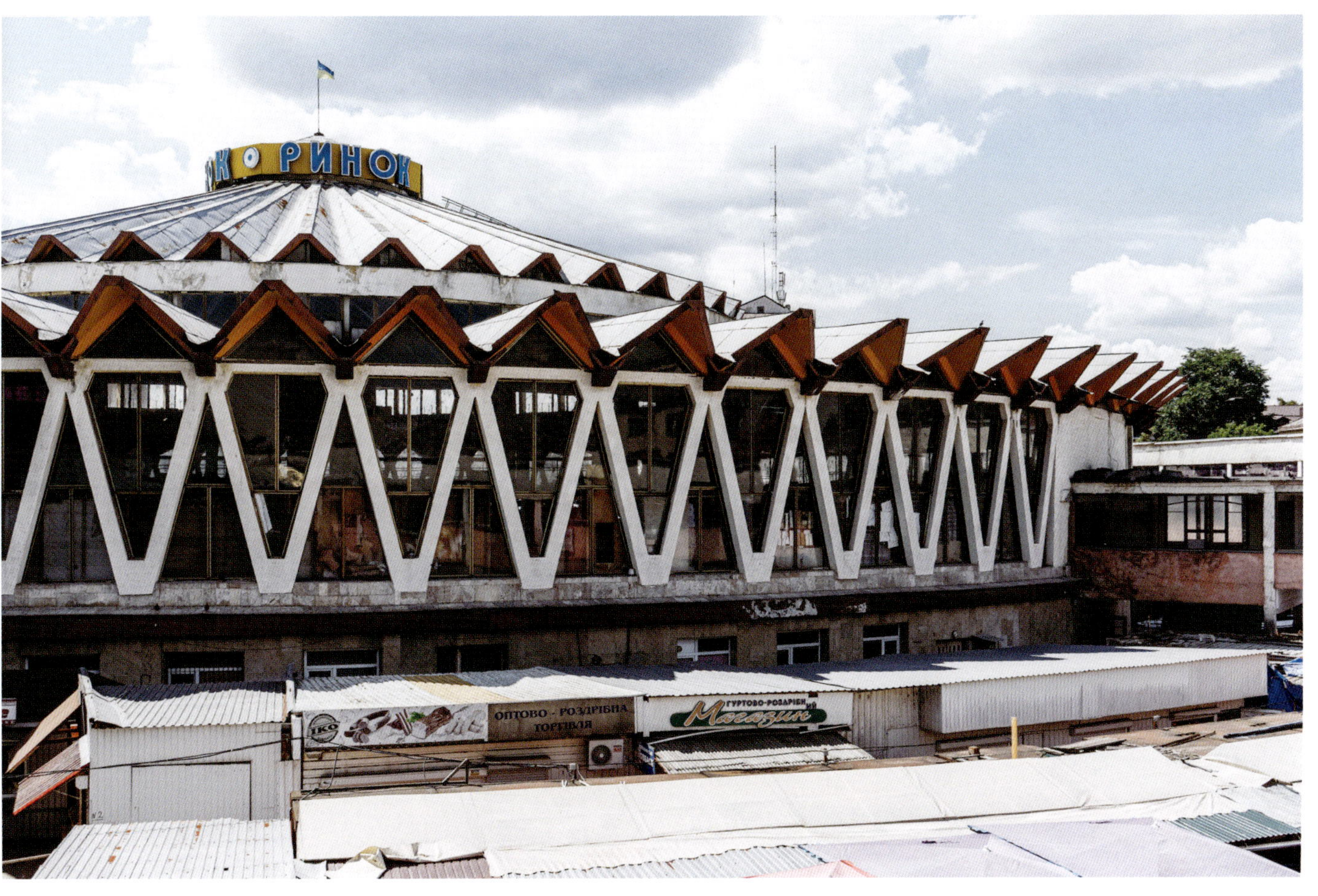
КО РИНОК
ОПТОВО - РОЗДРІБНА
ТОРГІВЛЯ
ГУРТОВО-РОЗДРІБНИЙ
Магазин

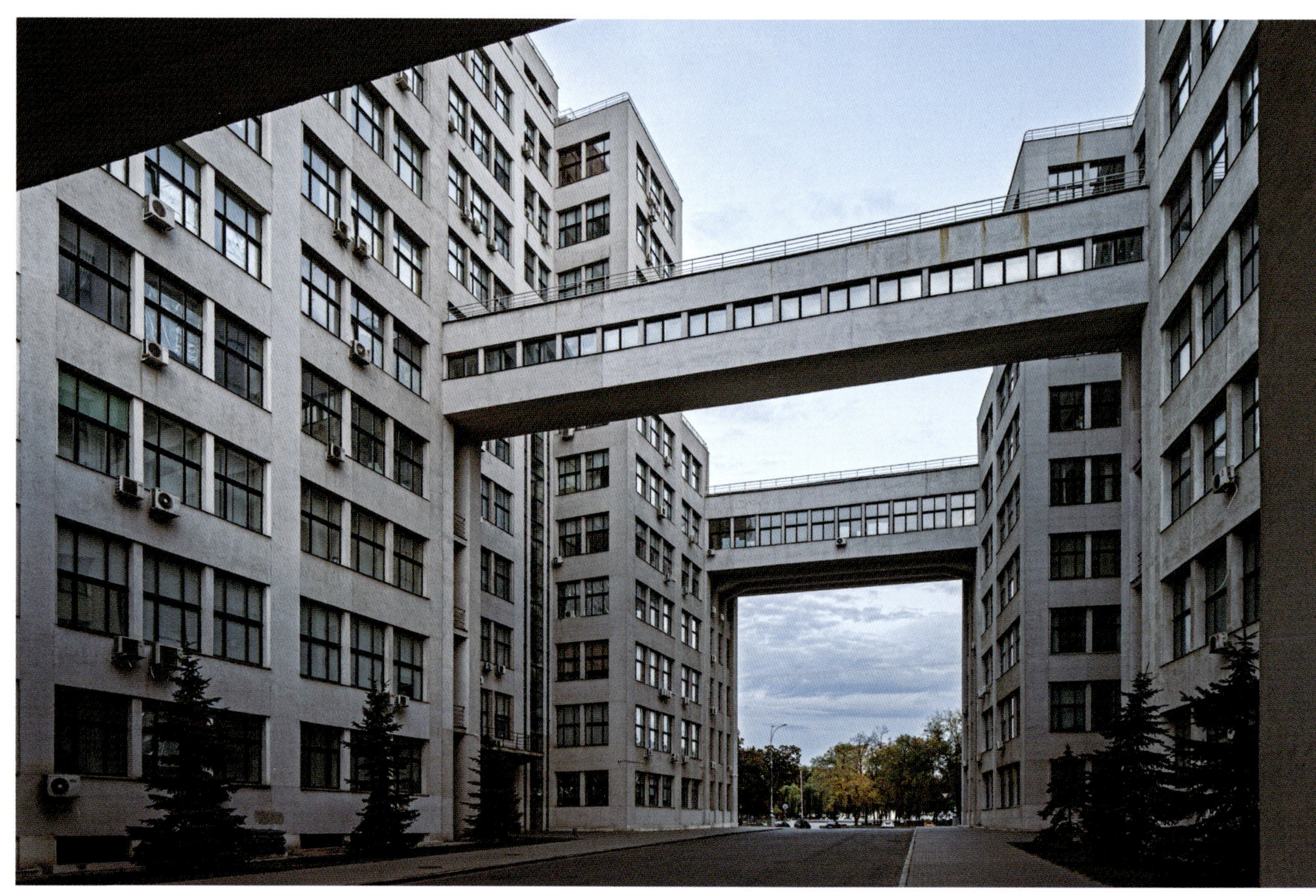

Derzhprom (The State Industry Building)
Kharkiv
1925–29
Architects: Serhii Serafimov, Samuil Kravets, Mark Felher
Engineer: Pavlo Rotert

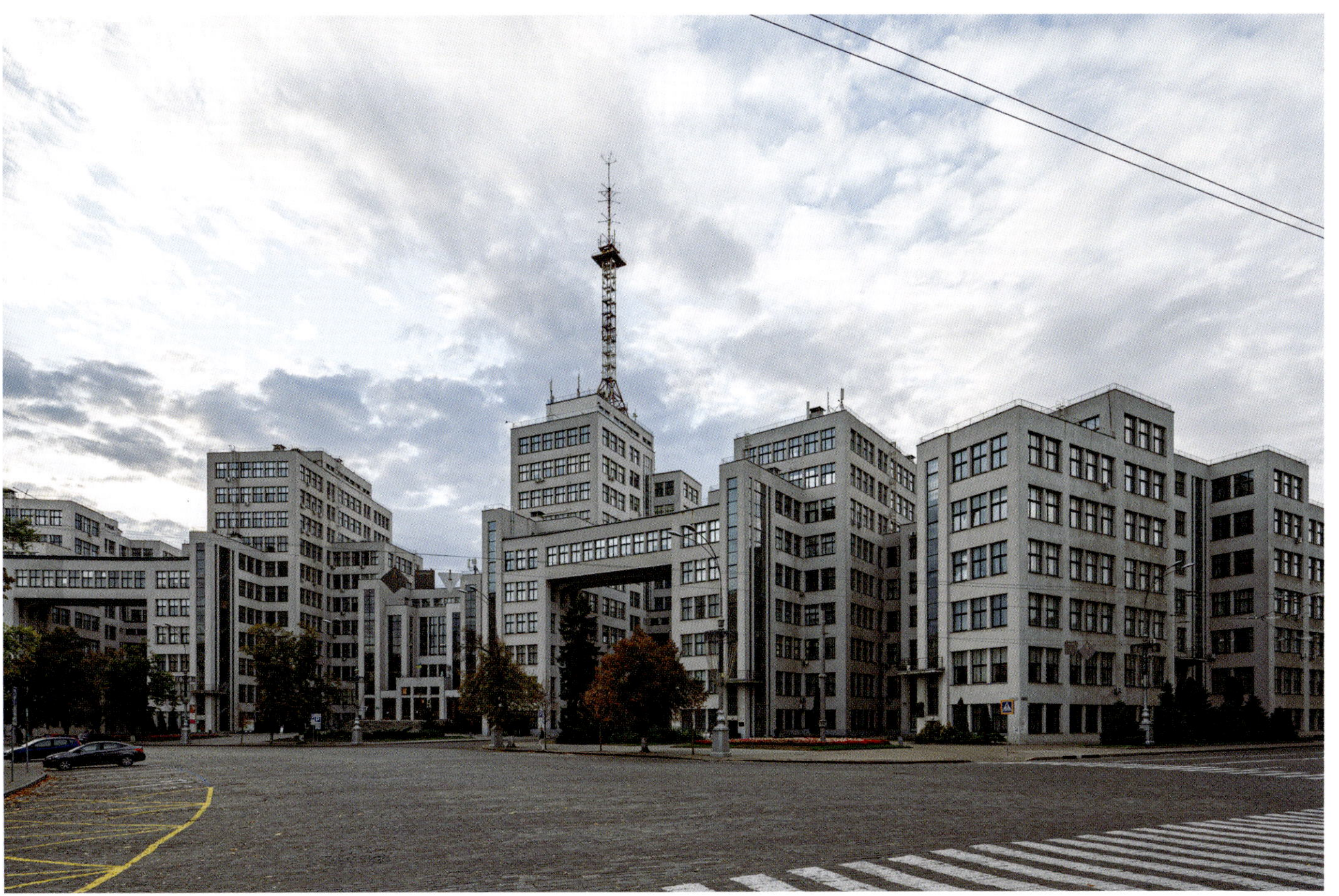

The first modern skyscraper to be built in the Soviet Union, Derzhprom is a world-renowned icon of the Constructivist era (1920s–30s). It is one of the few buildings in Kharkiv from that period to have survived World War II without being reconstructed in the Stalinist Empire style of the 1940s. In 2017 Derzhprom was added to UNESCO's Tentative World Heritage List and in 2022 placed under provisional enhanced protection. By 2024, the building had survived three Russian bomb strikes. It continues to function as a governmental office.

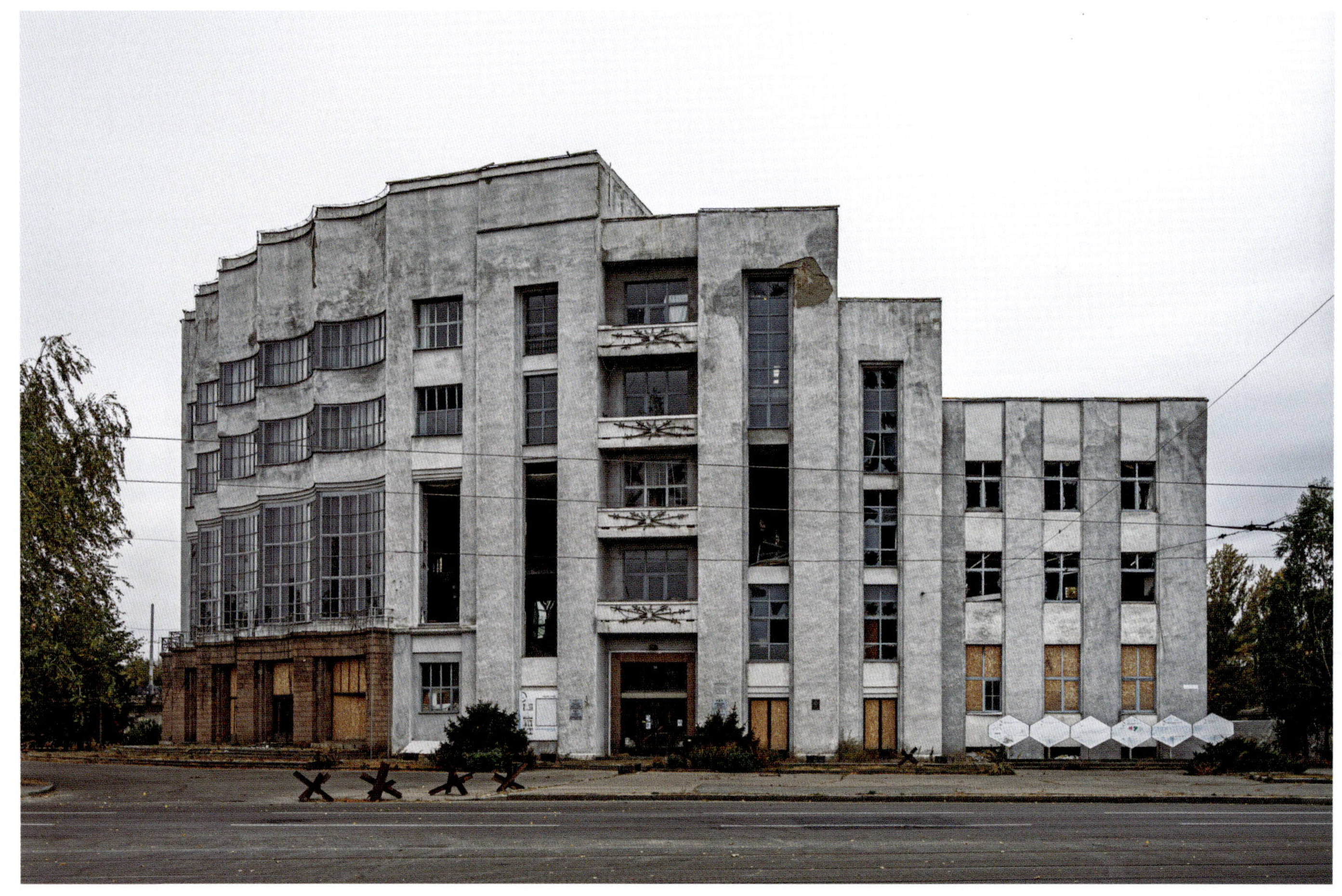

'Zaliznychnyk' Railroad Workers Palace of Culture
Kharkiv
1928–32
Architect: Oleksandr Dmytriiev
Artist: Eugene Lanceray

A direct Russian missile hit in 2022, followed by a 24-hour fire, caused extensive damage to this Constructivist landmark. The fate of the interior paintings by Eugene Lanceray, rare examples of Soviet public art from the 1930s, remains unknown.

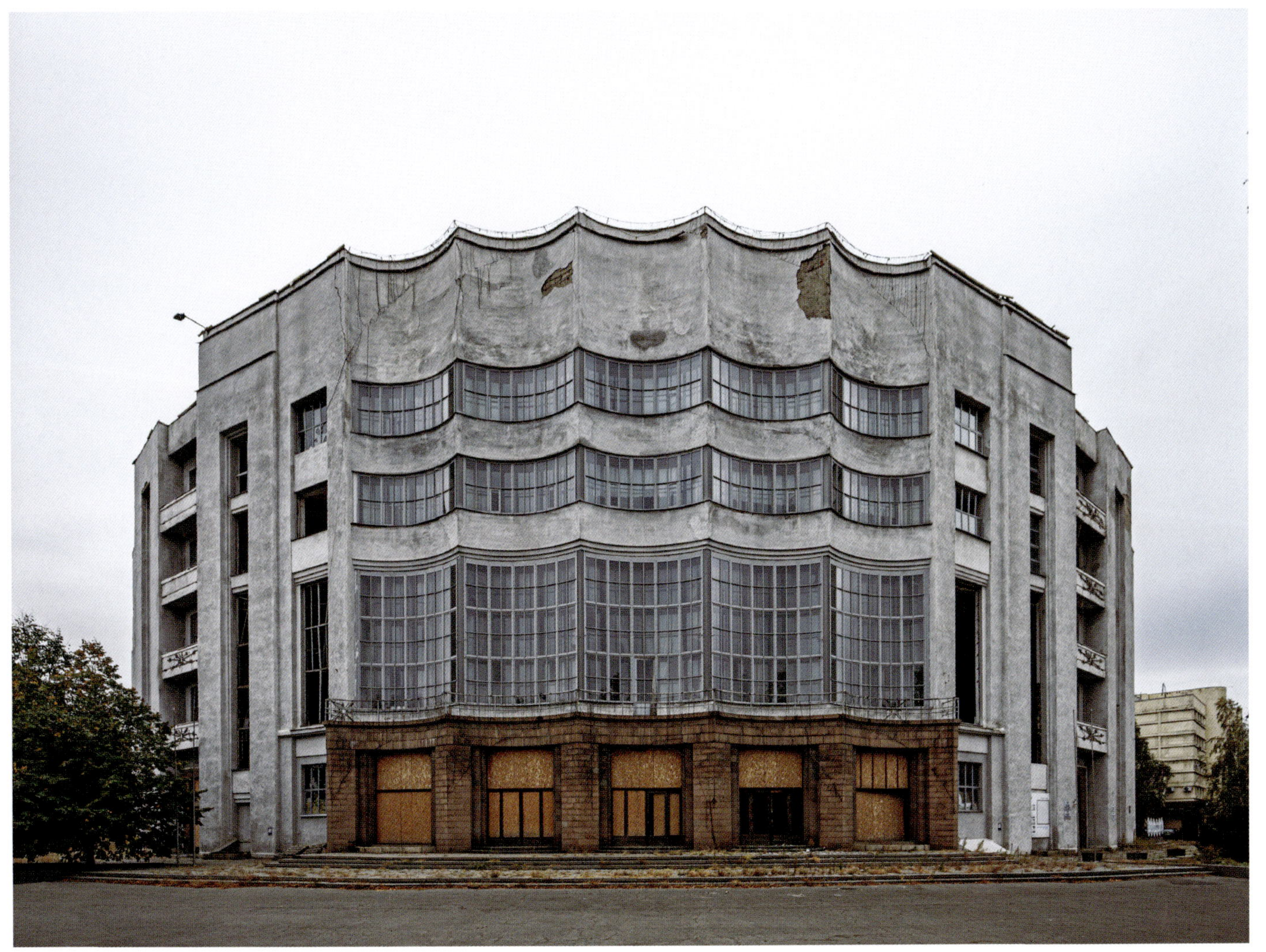

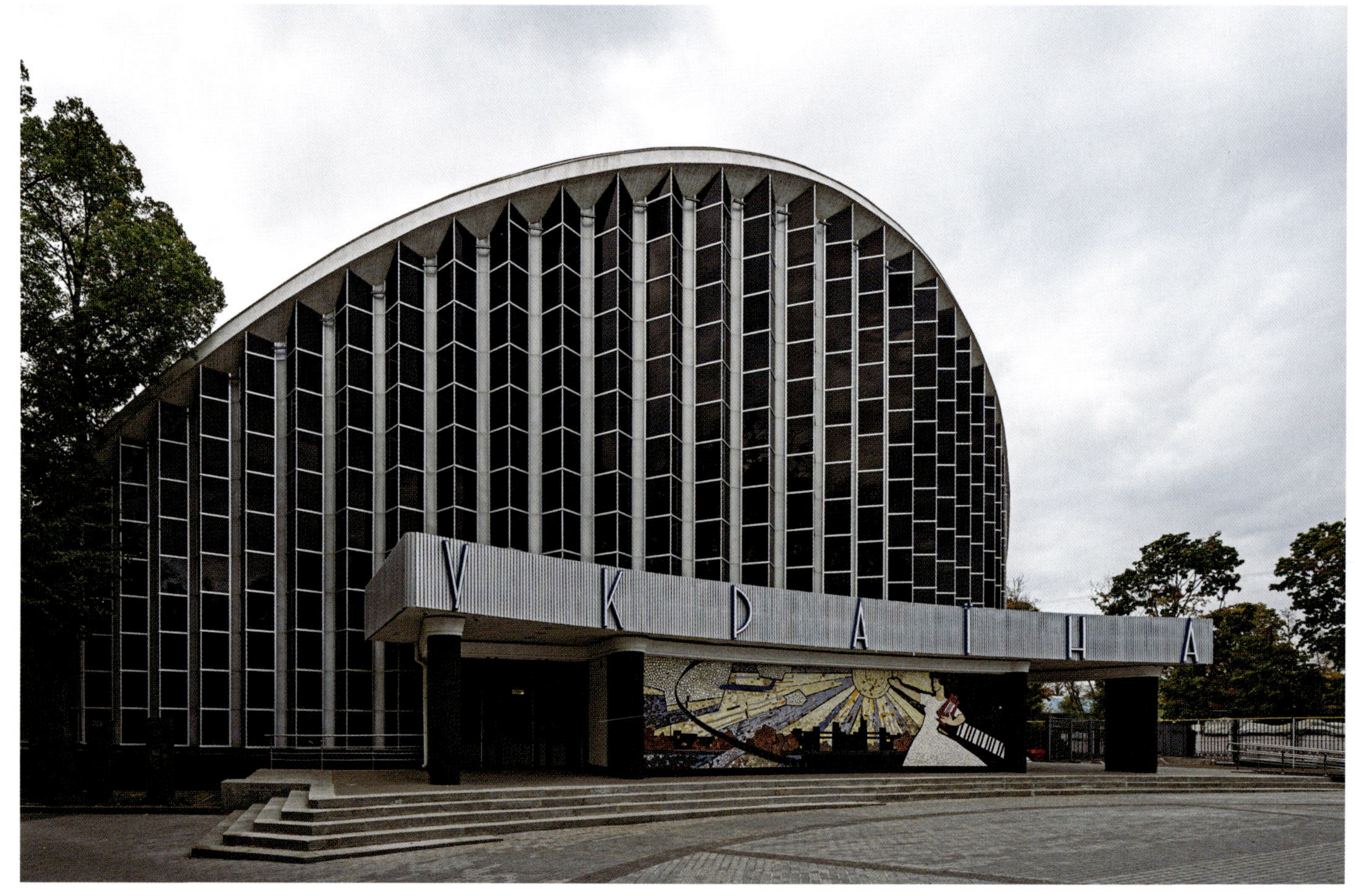

'Ukraina' Concert and Cinema Hall
Kharkiv
1960–63

Architects: Vadym Vasyliev, Yurii Plaksiev, Volodymyr Rieusov
Engineer: Lev Fridhan
Artists: E. Rohanova, Vadym Vasyliev

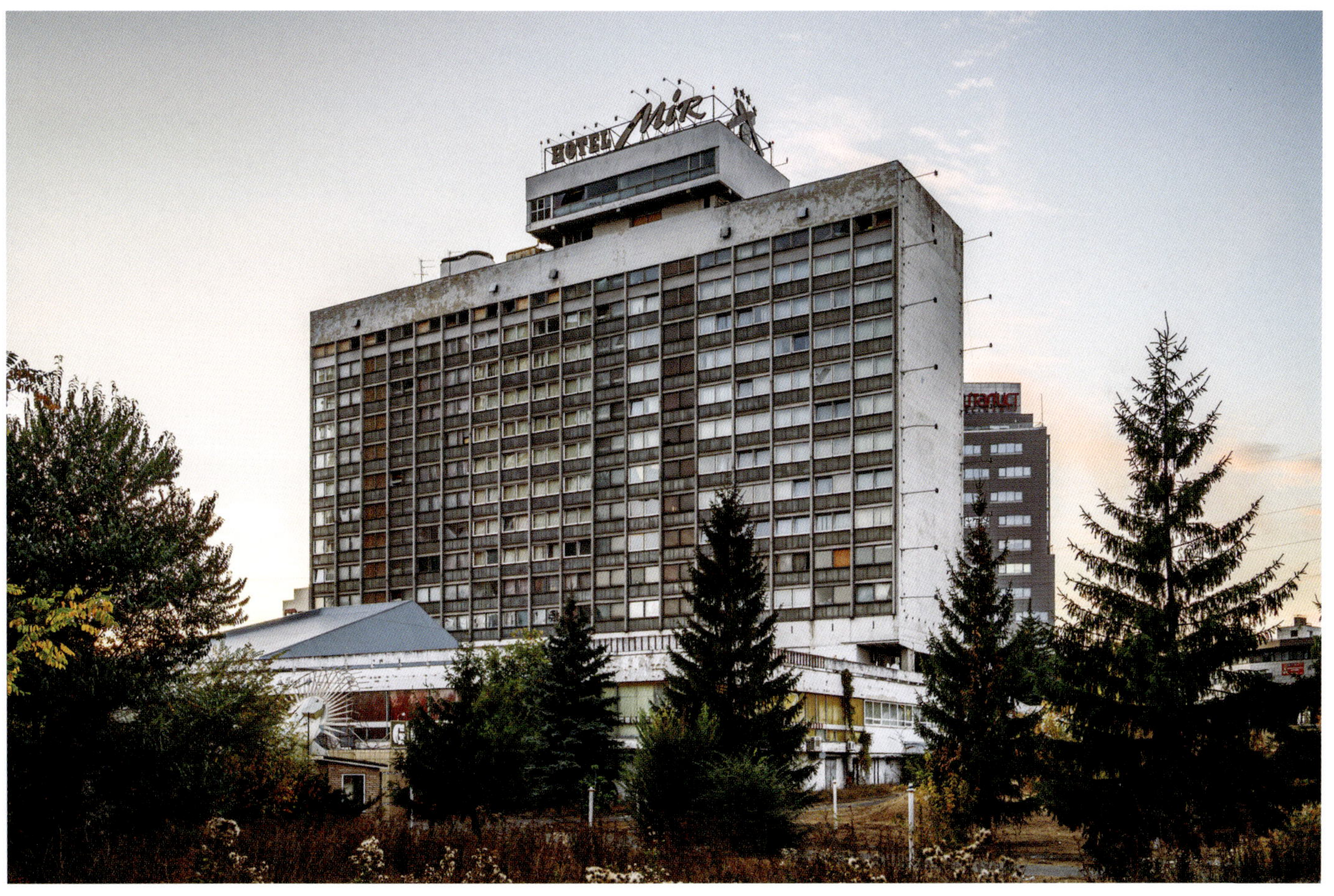

'Mir' Hotel
Kharkiv
1977–79

Architects: Serhii Myrhorodskyi, Roman-Enrique Hupalo, Ihor Ivanov,
Viktor Savchenko, N. Didenko
Engineer: V. Kuziakiv
Artist: Viacheslav Klokov

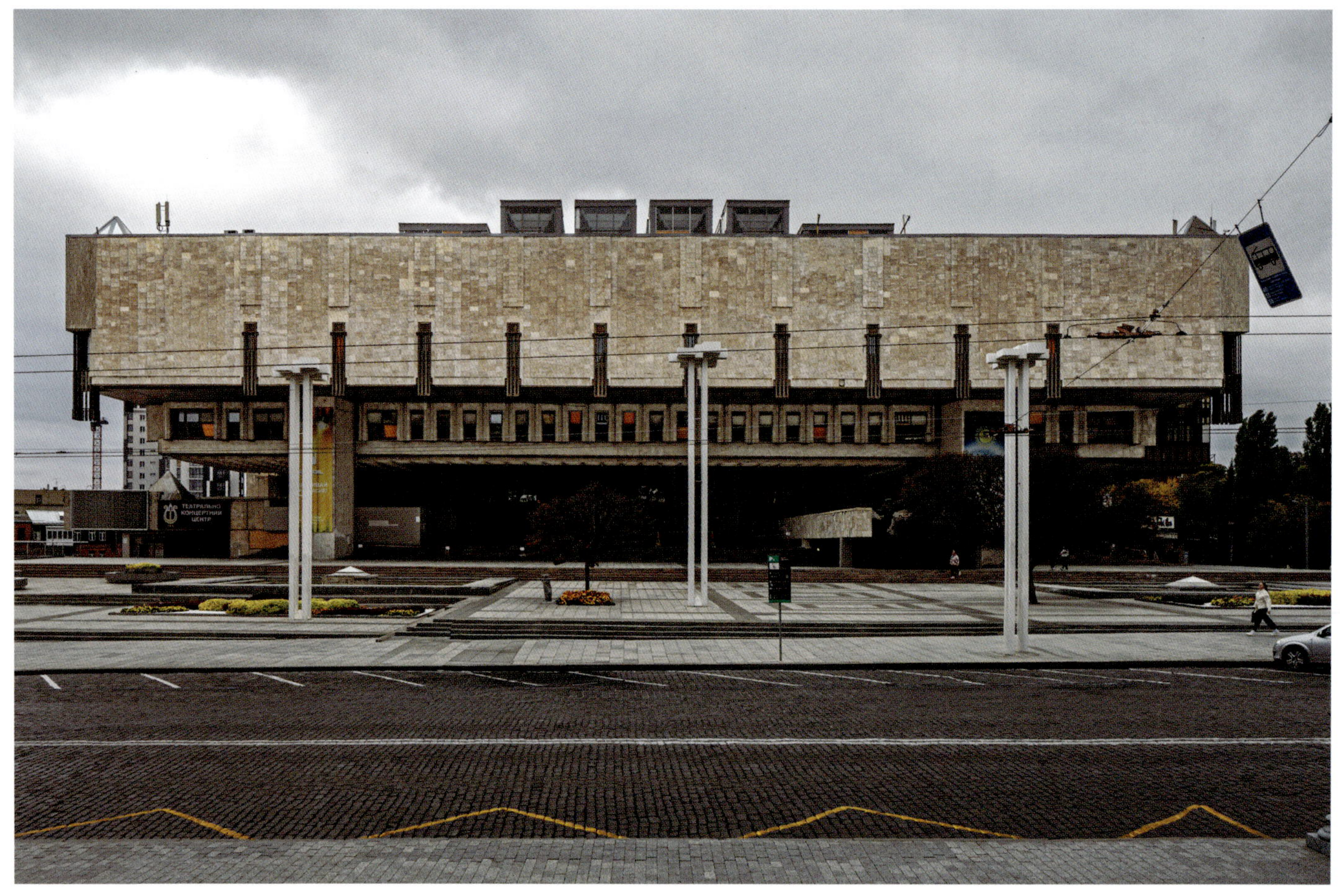

Kharkiv National Academic Opera and Ballet Theatre
Kharkiv
1970–90

Architects: Serhii Myrhorodskyi, Viktor Yelizarov, Roman-Enrique Hupalo, N. Chuprina, A. Zybin
Artist: Serhii Yastrebov

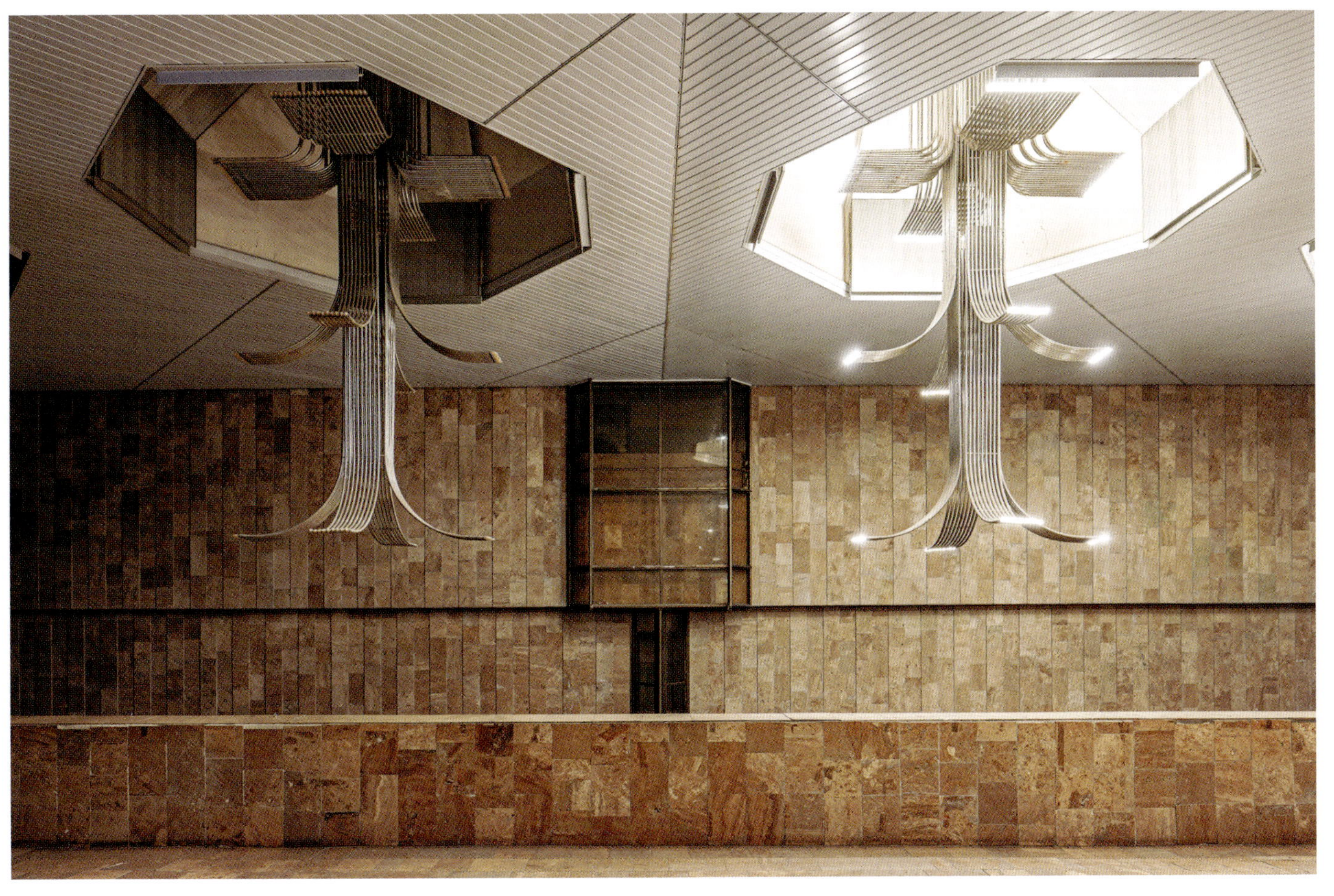

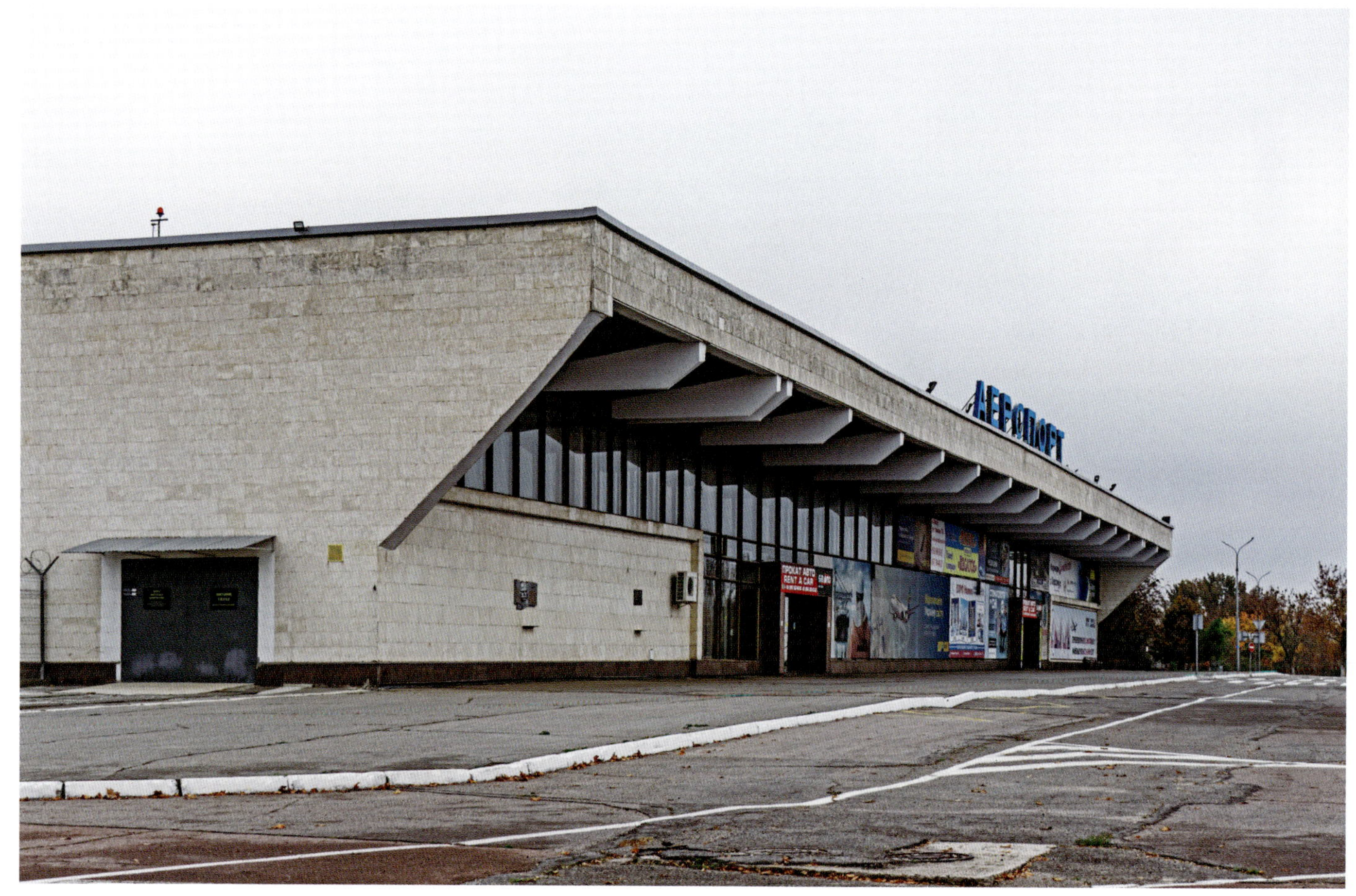

Kherson Airport Terminal
Kherson
1984

Architect: V. Khan
Engineer: M. Maremukha

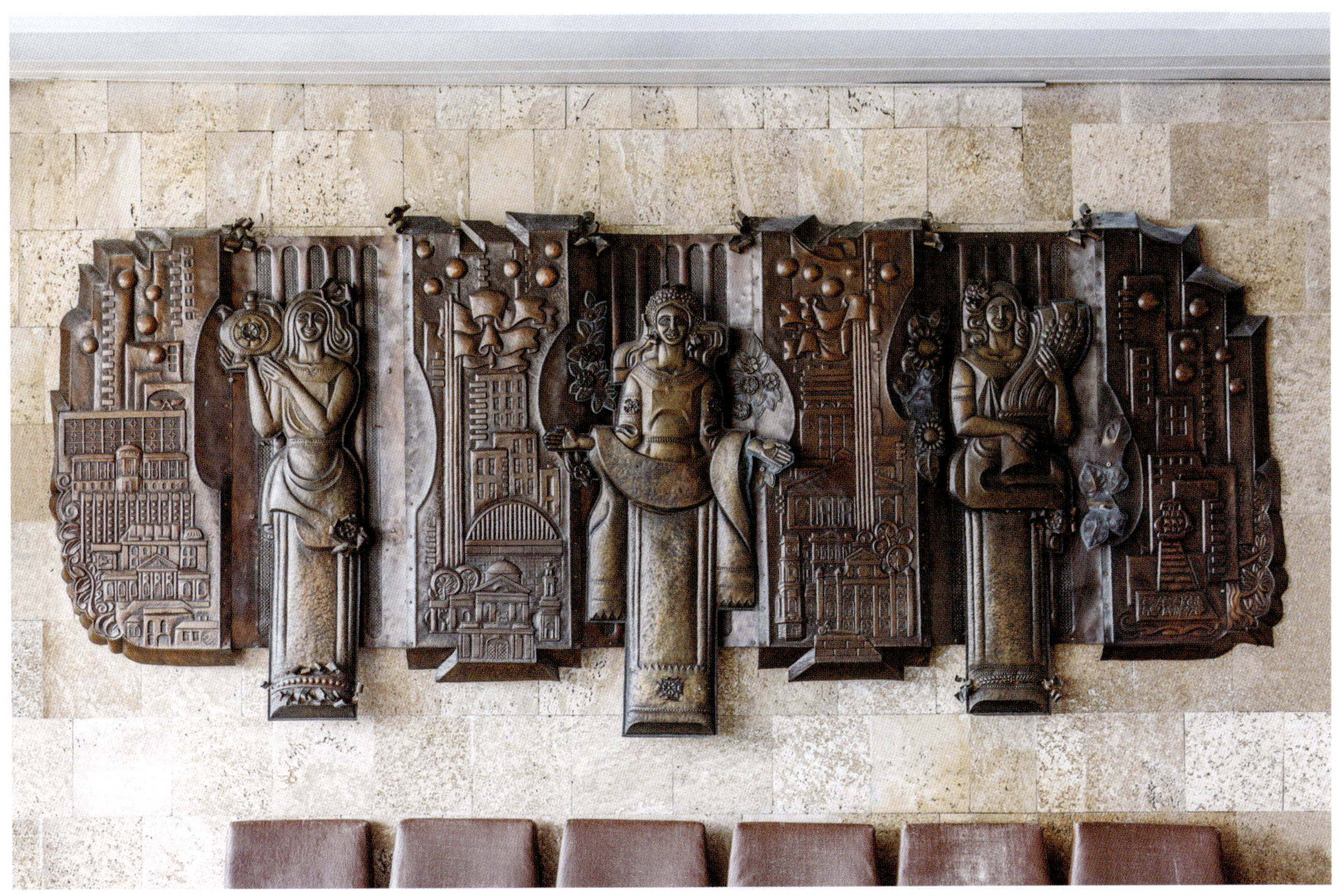

In the Soviet era, airports were built in every regional centre across Ukraine as part of a strategy to enhance transportation networks and foster regional economic development. Affordable ticket prices were part of the Soviet state's non-profit approach to transportation, reflecting an ideological commitment to mobility for all citizens regardless of income. Some airports closed after 1991, but most remained operational until 2022. Following military action during the Russian occupation of the city in 2022, Kherson Airport was destroyed.

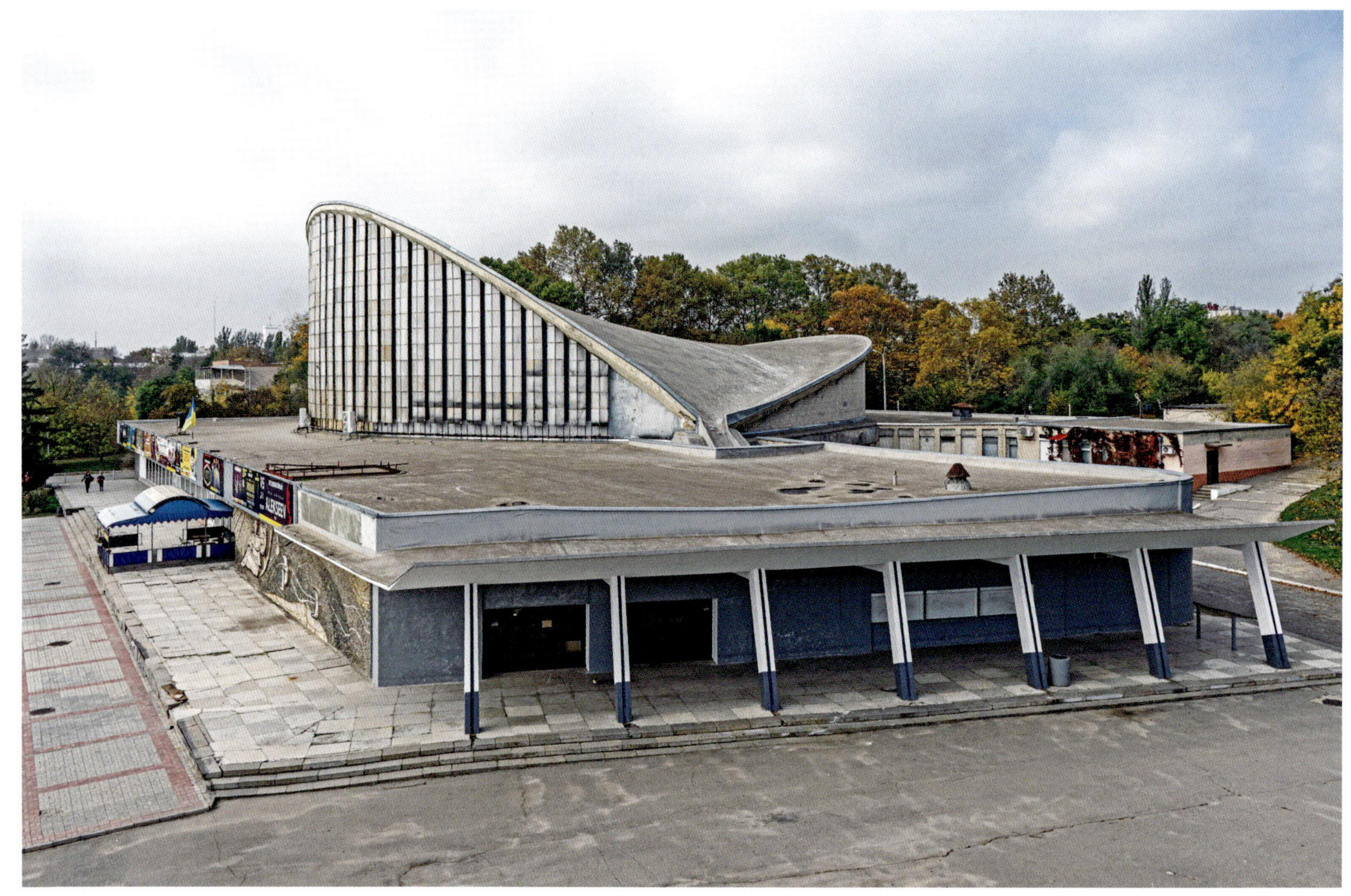

'Yuvileinyi' Cinema and Concert Hall
Kherson
1970
Architects: Vadym Vasyliev, Hryhorii Sokolovskyi,
Halyna Skrypchenko

This building, constructed on the former site of the Kherson fortress, was damaged by the Russian air raid in 2023. It is an adaptation of an earlier project by Vasyliev (the 'Ukraina' Cinema and Concert Hall, Kharkiv, 1963).

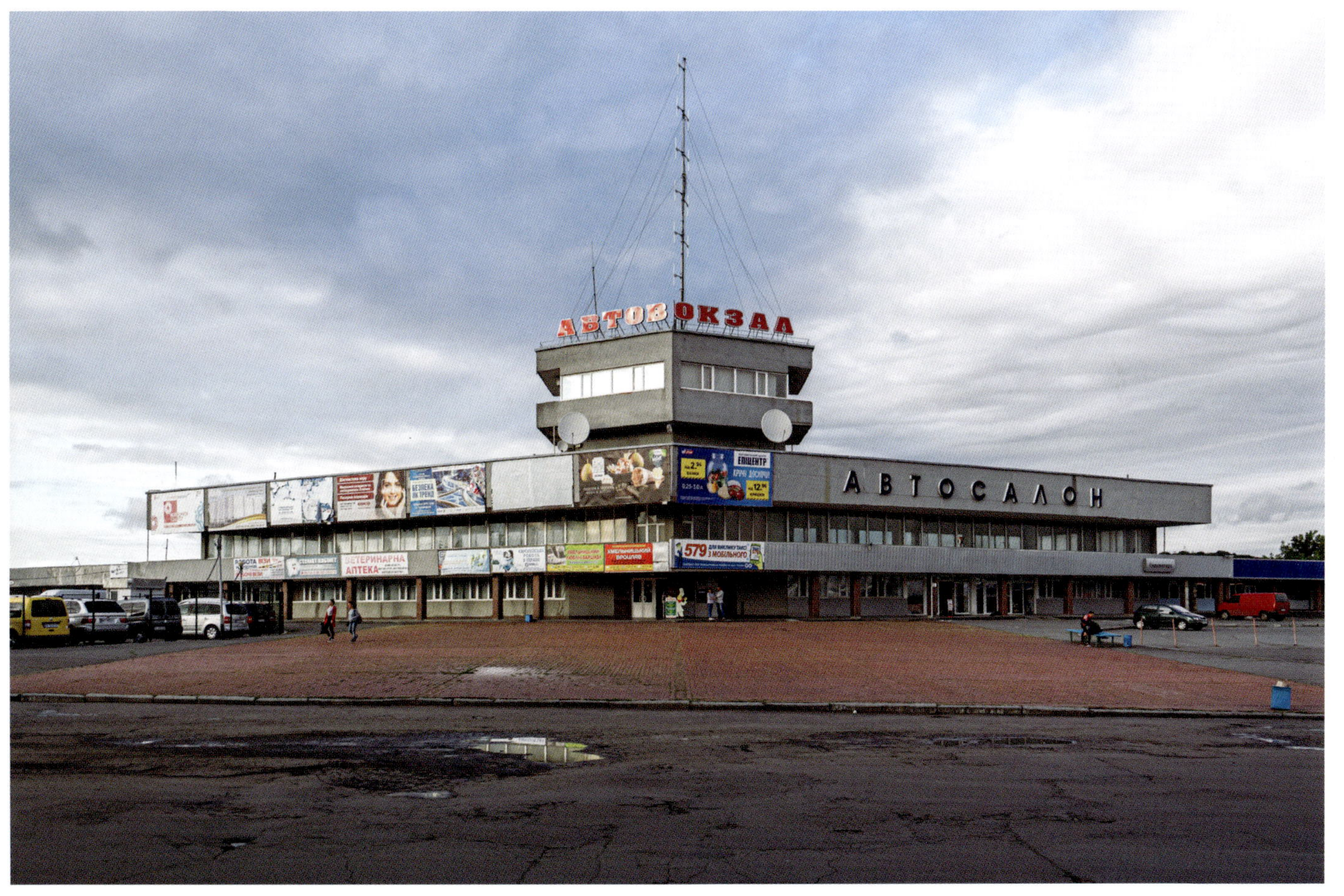

Khmelnytskyi Bus Station
Khmelnytskyi
1989
Architects: Andrii Laba, V. Demetskyi, V. Sheliuh
Engineer: E. Shraibman

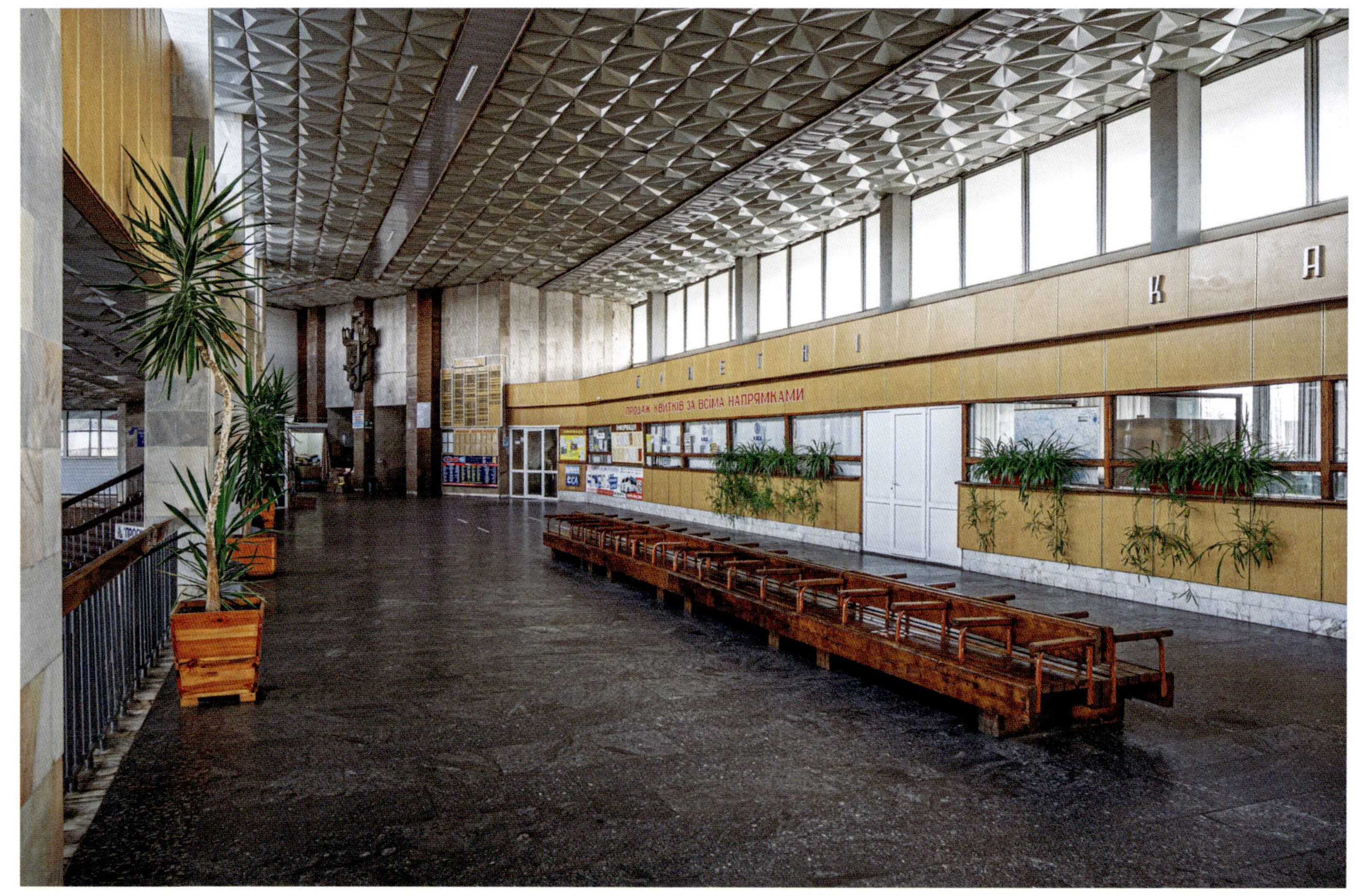
КАСИ
ПРОДАЖ КВИТКІВ ЗА ВСІМА НАПРЯМКАМИ

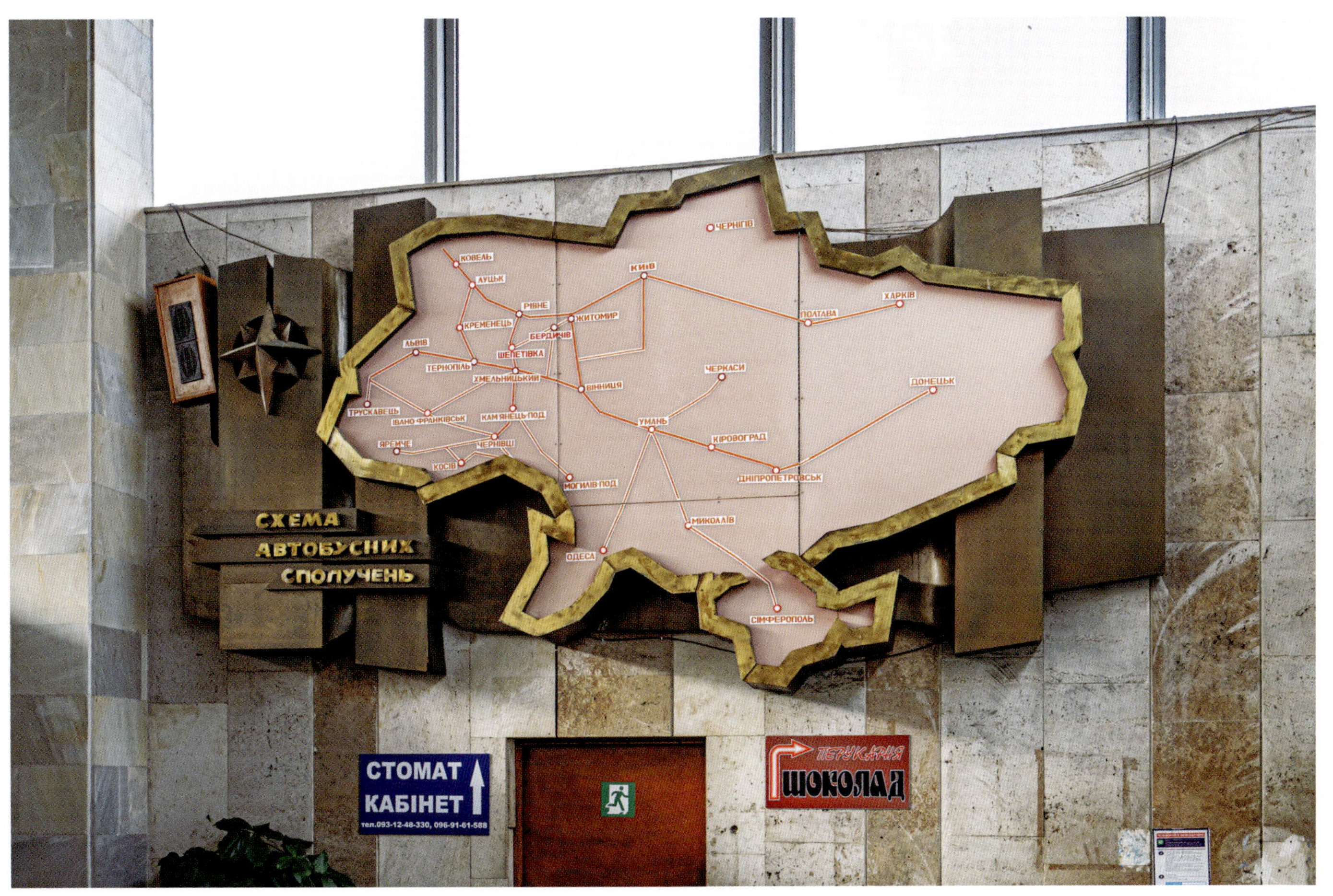
СХЕМА
АВТОБУСНИХ
СПОЛУЧЕНЬ
ЧЕРНІГІВ
КОВЕЛЬ
ЛУЦЬК
КИЇВ
РІВНЕ
ХАРКІВ
КРЕМЕНЕЦЬ
ЖИТОМИР
ПОЛТАВА
БЕРДИЧІВ
ЛЬВІВ
ШЕПЕТІВКА
ТЕРНОПІЛЬ
ЧЕРКАСИ
ХМЕЛЬНИЦЬКИЙ
ВІННИЦЯ
ДОНЕЦЬК
ТРУСКАВЕЦЬ
ІВАНО-ФРАНКІВСЬК
КАМ'ЯНЕЦЬ ПОД.
УМАНЬ
КІРОВОГРАД
ЯРЕМЧЕ
ЧЕРНІВЦІ
КОСІВ
ДНІПРОПЕТРОВСЬК
МОГИЛІВ ПОД.
МИКОЛАЇВ
ОДЕСА
СІМФЕРОПОЛЬ
СТОМАТ
КАБІНЕТ
тел.093-12-48-330, 096-91-61-588
ПЕРУКАРНЯ
ШОКОЛАД

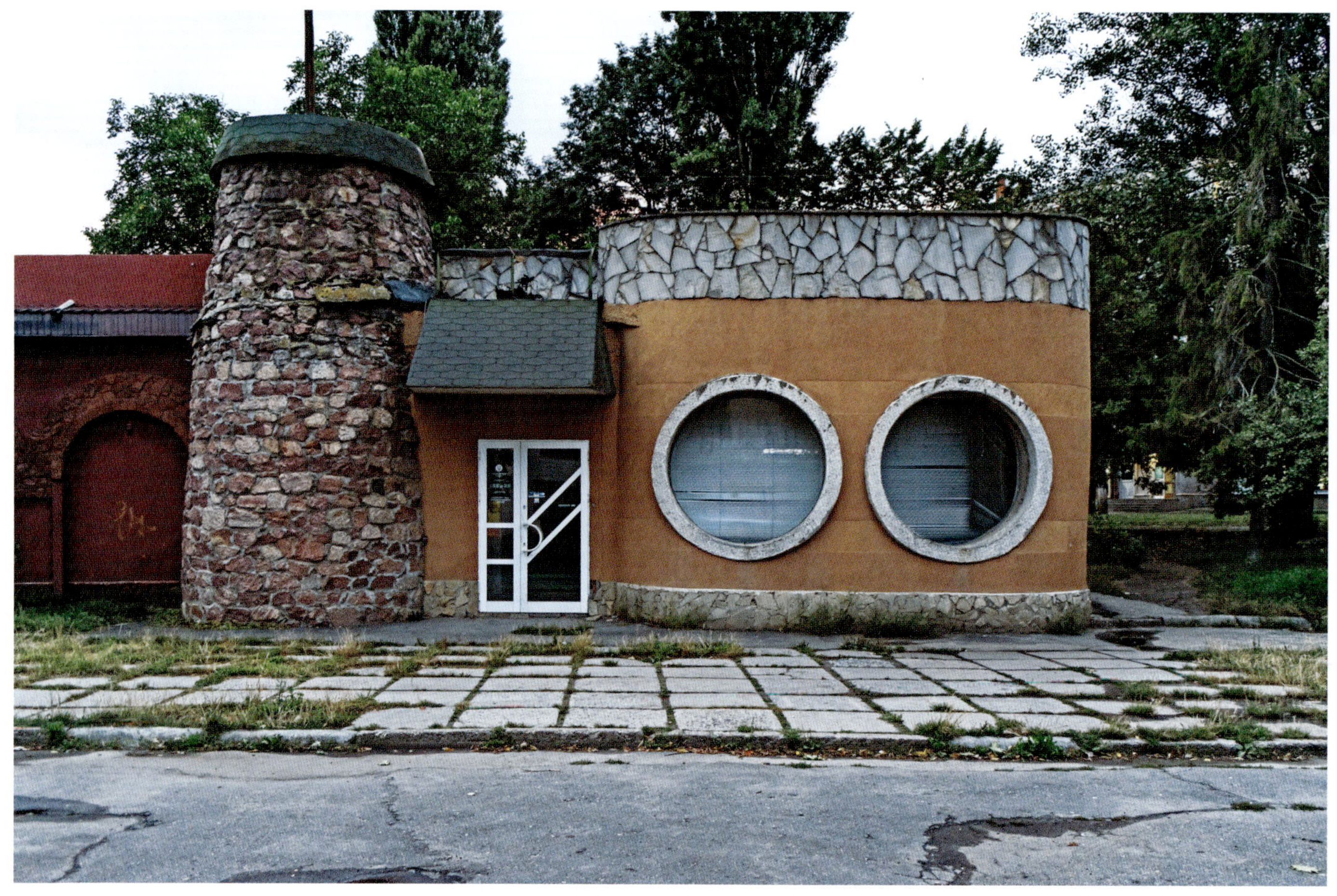

'Tourist' Restaurant
Khmelnytskyi
1970s

The stylised stone-clad walls and tower alluded to the city's medieval history, while the brutalist use of block material anchored the design in modernity. After undergoing alterations in the 2000s, the building was ultimately demolished in 2021 to make way for a mall.

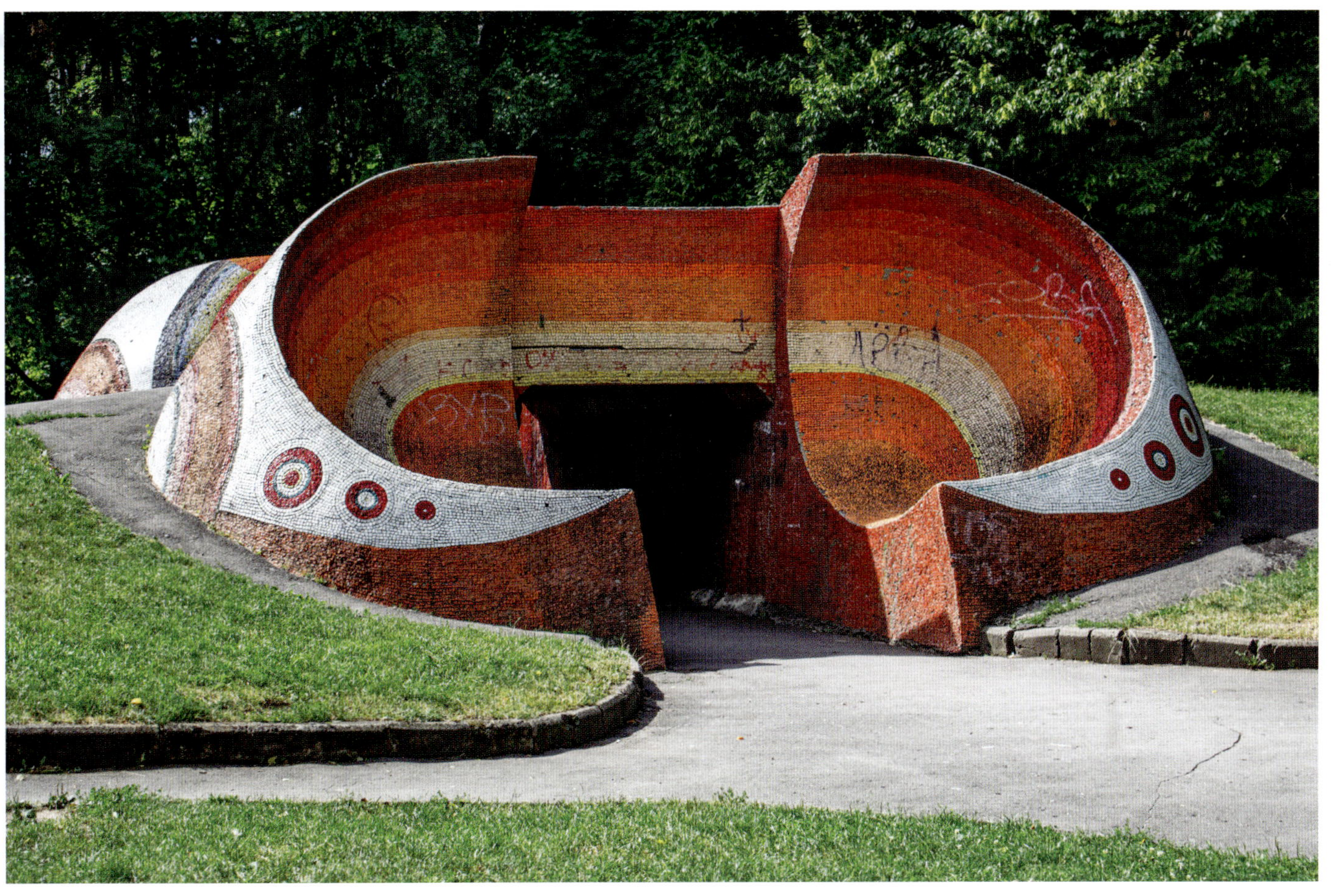

Mosaic Overpass at the Children's Mini Car Track
Khmelnytskyi
1982
Artist: Mykola Mazur

During the 1980s and 1990s, the artist Mykola Mazur created dozens of artworks in parks and public buildings throughout Khmelnytskyi Oblast. Most were made from scrap metal, while this overpass in Chekman Park was crafted from concrete and smalt.

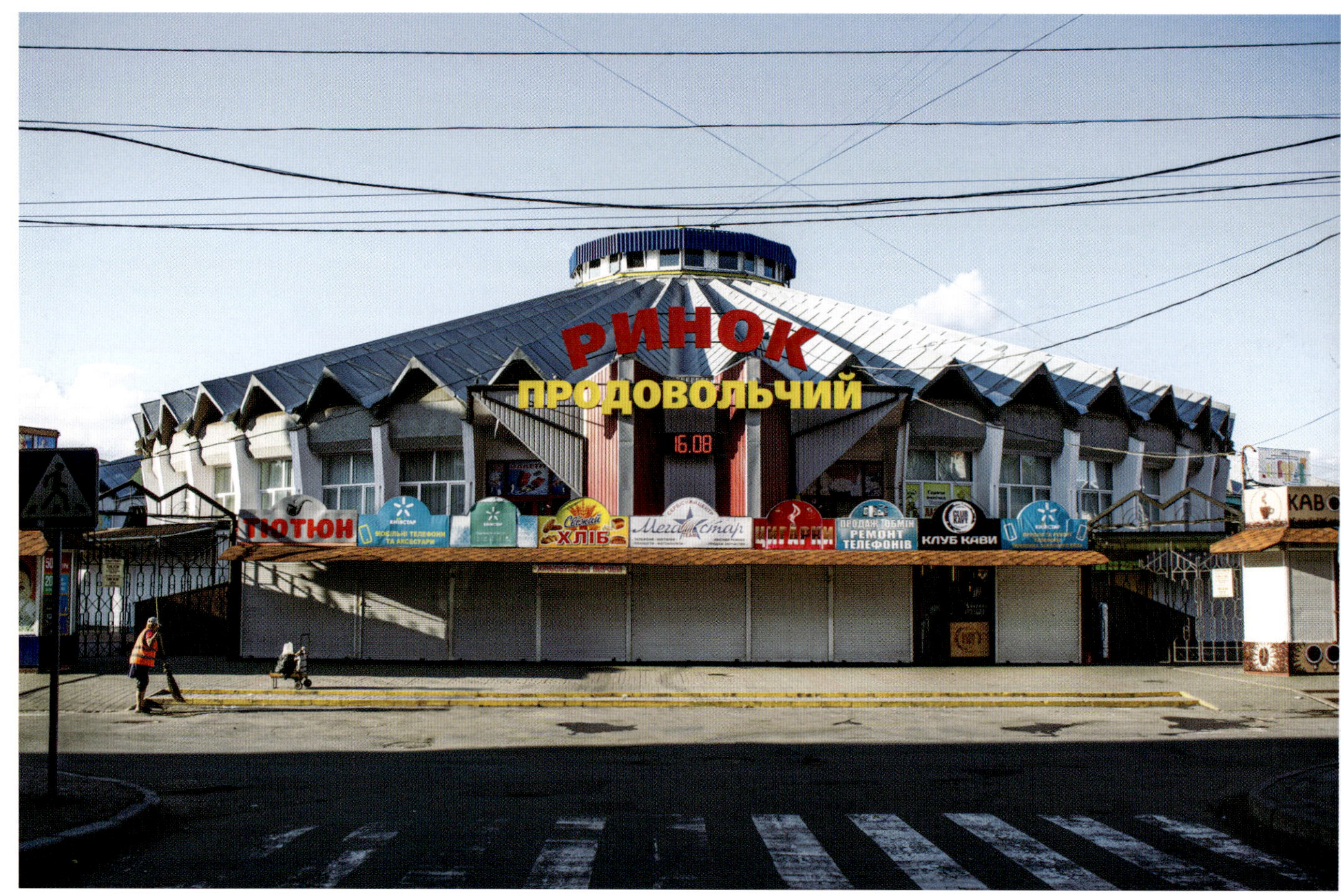

Khmelnytskyi Market
Khmelnytskyi
1989
Architect: Hlynyk, Ukrdiprotorh Institute
(Ukrainian State Institute for Design of Public Trade Enterprises)

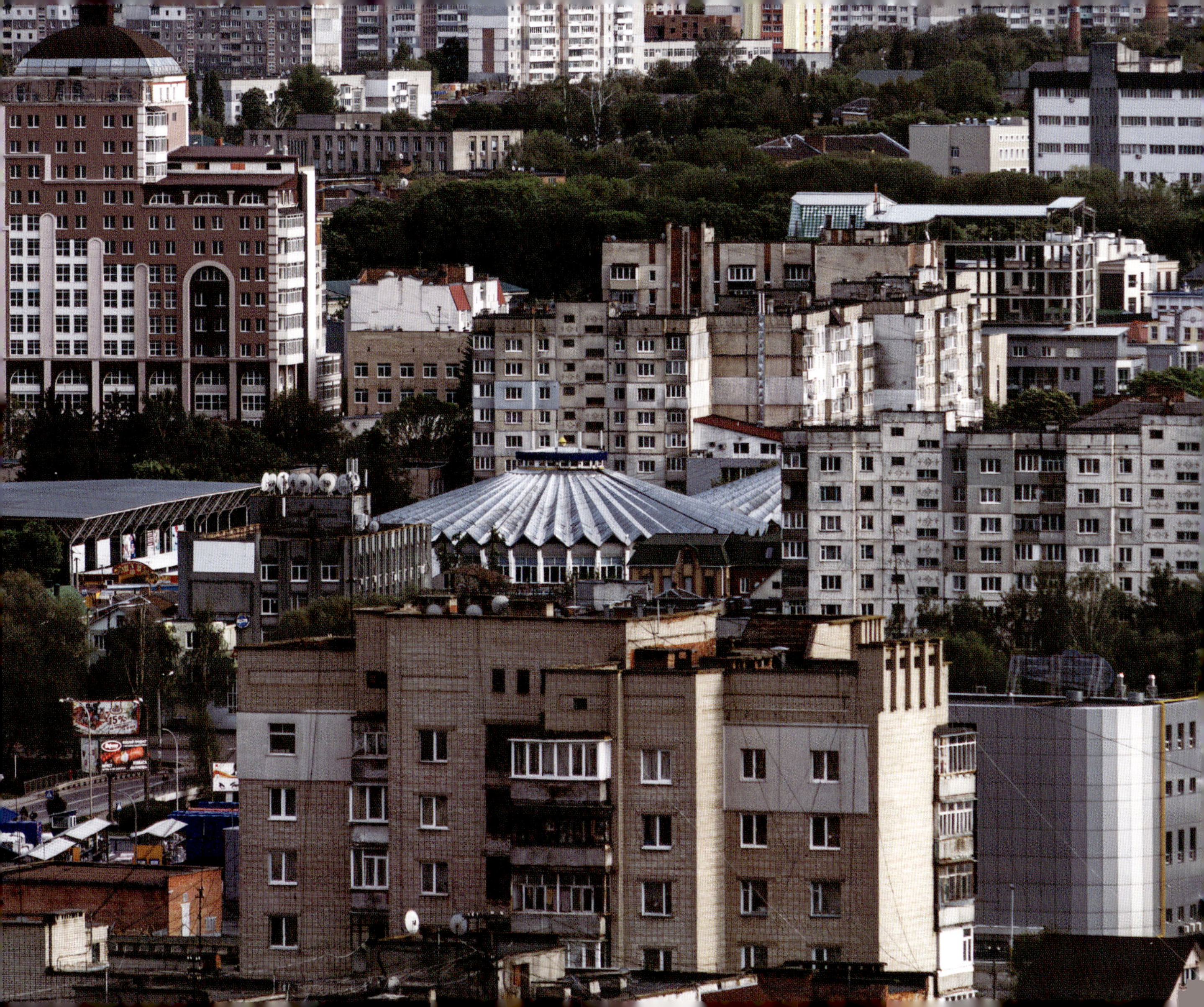

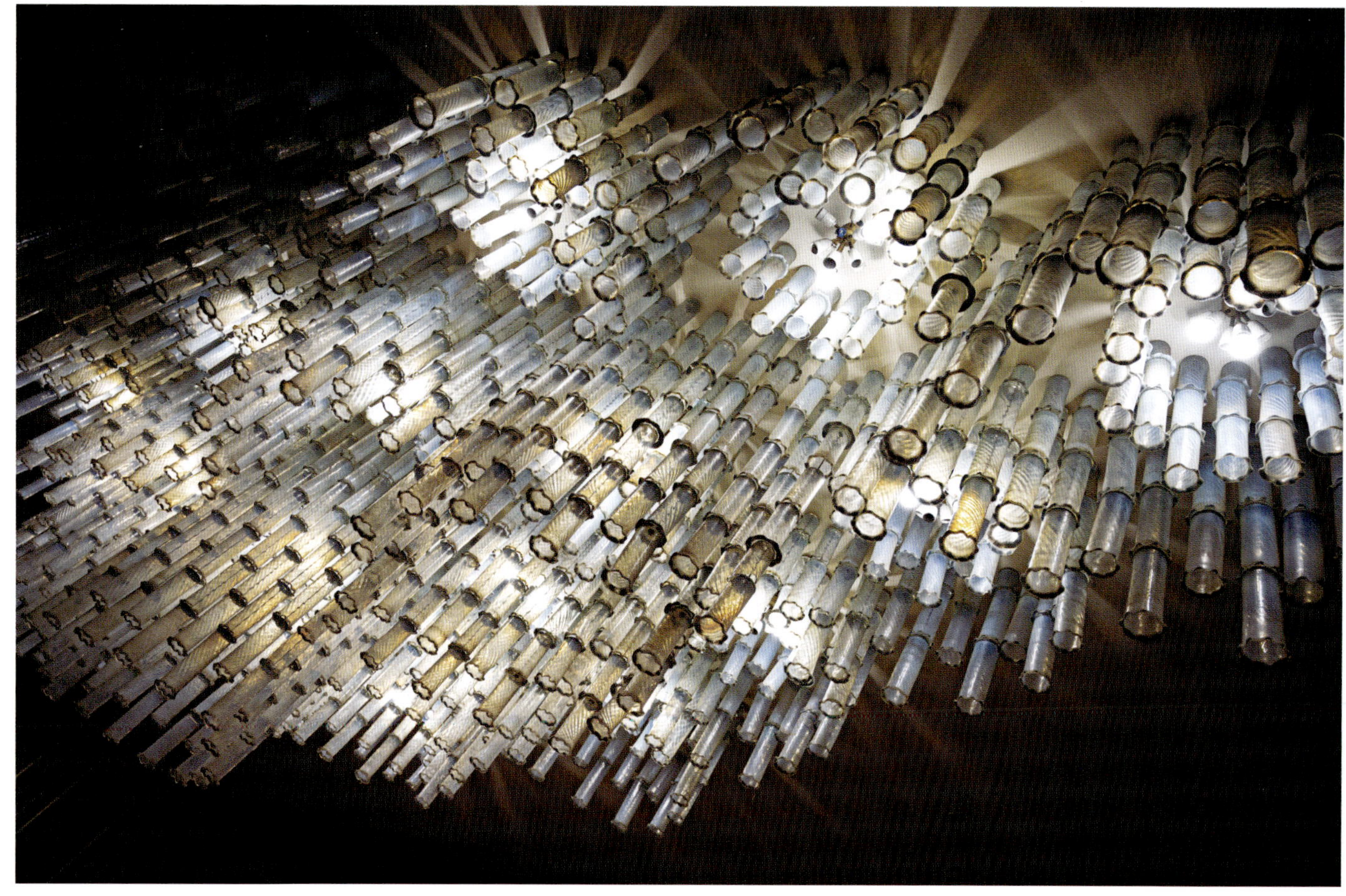

Khmelnytskyi Music and Drama Theatre
Khmelnytskyi
1973–82
Architects: Klavdiia Yurovska, Roza Karazina, V. Zorina

Engineers: T. Kappel, T. Fedorenko
Glass artists: Andrii Bokotei, Zenovii Flinta, Frants Cherniak,
Vasyl Drachuk, Sviatoslav Martyniuk

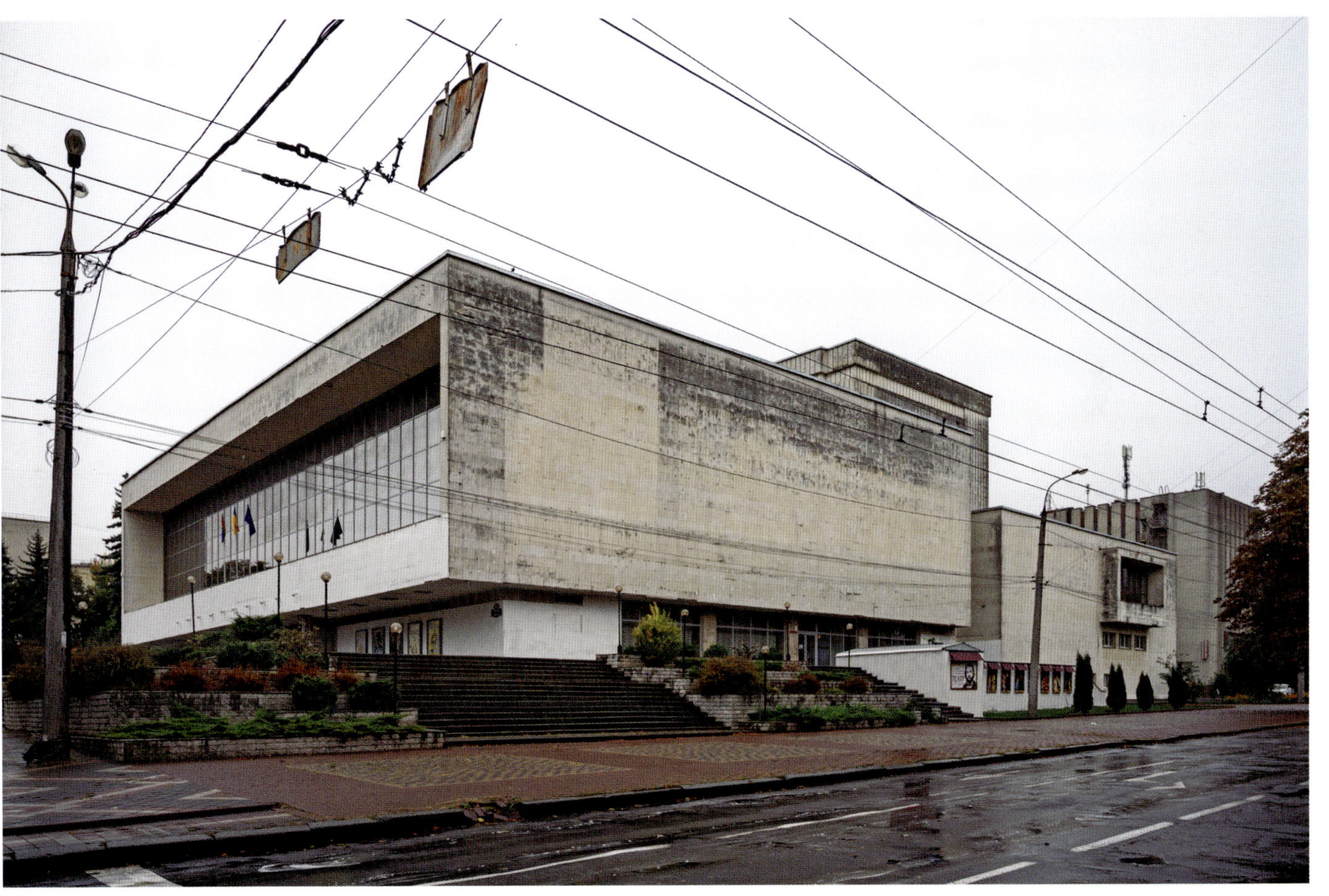

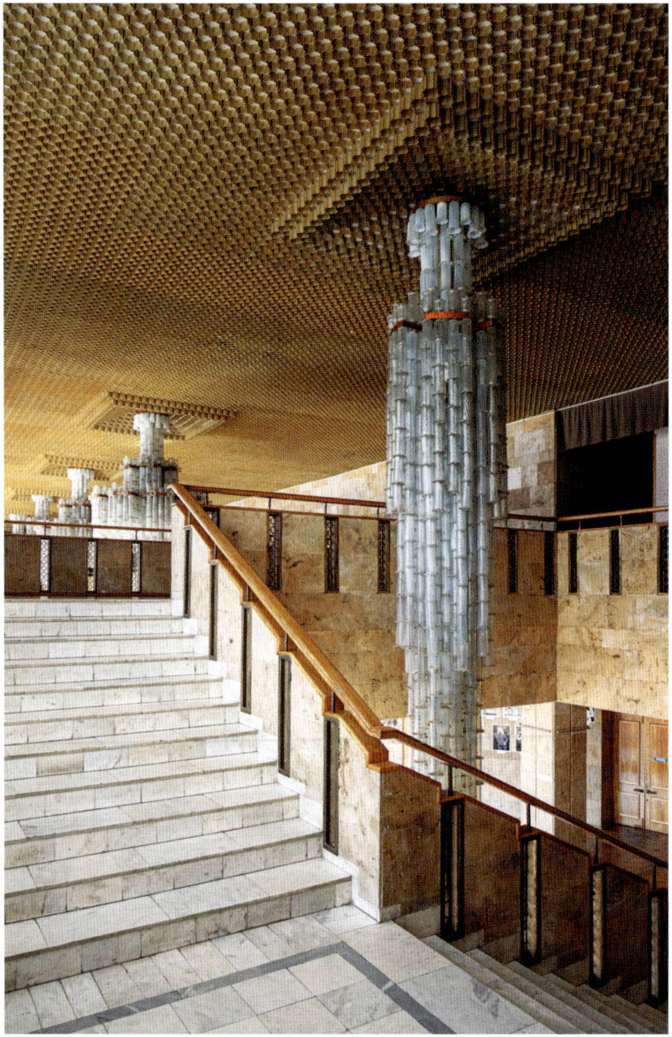

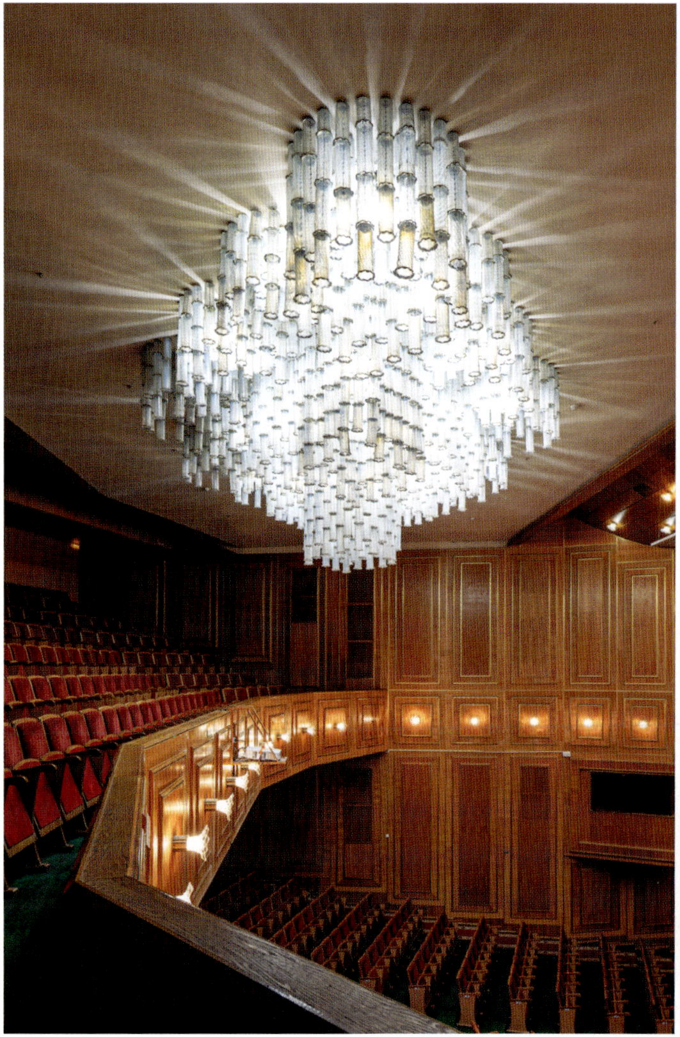

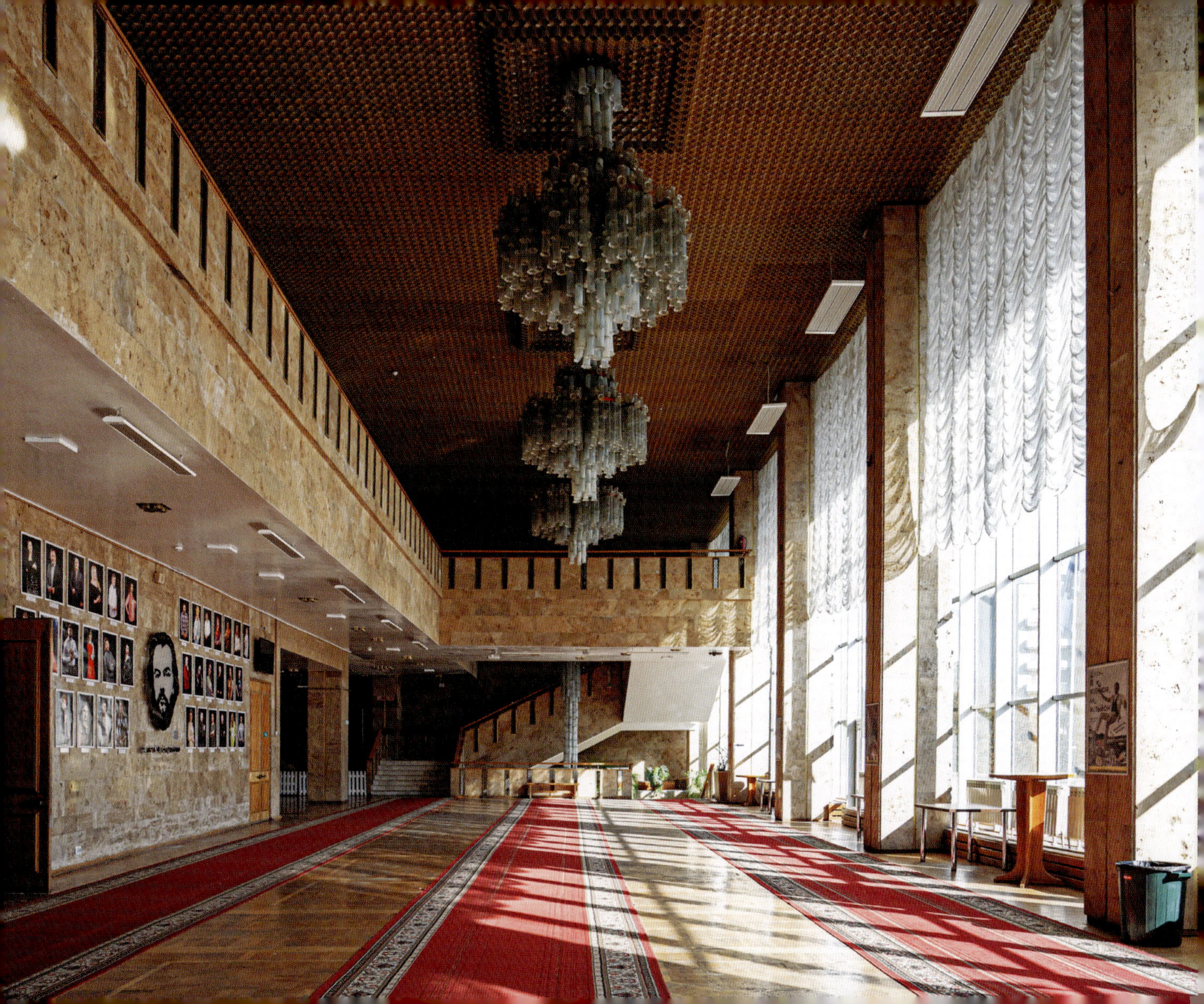

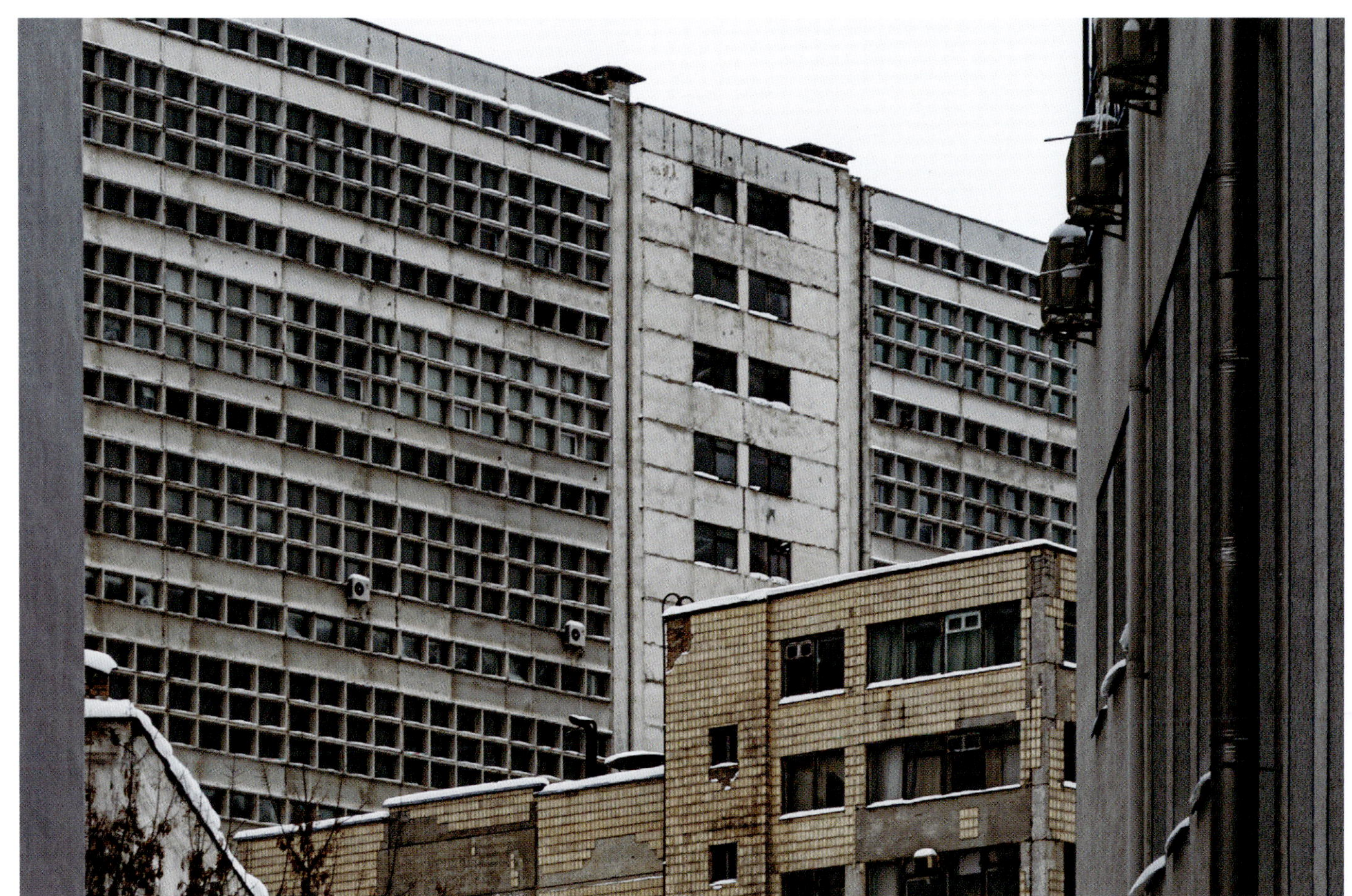

Arsenal Factory
Kyiv
With its history spanning over two centuries, the Arsenal Factory
expanded in the 1980s with these towering production facilities.

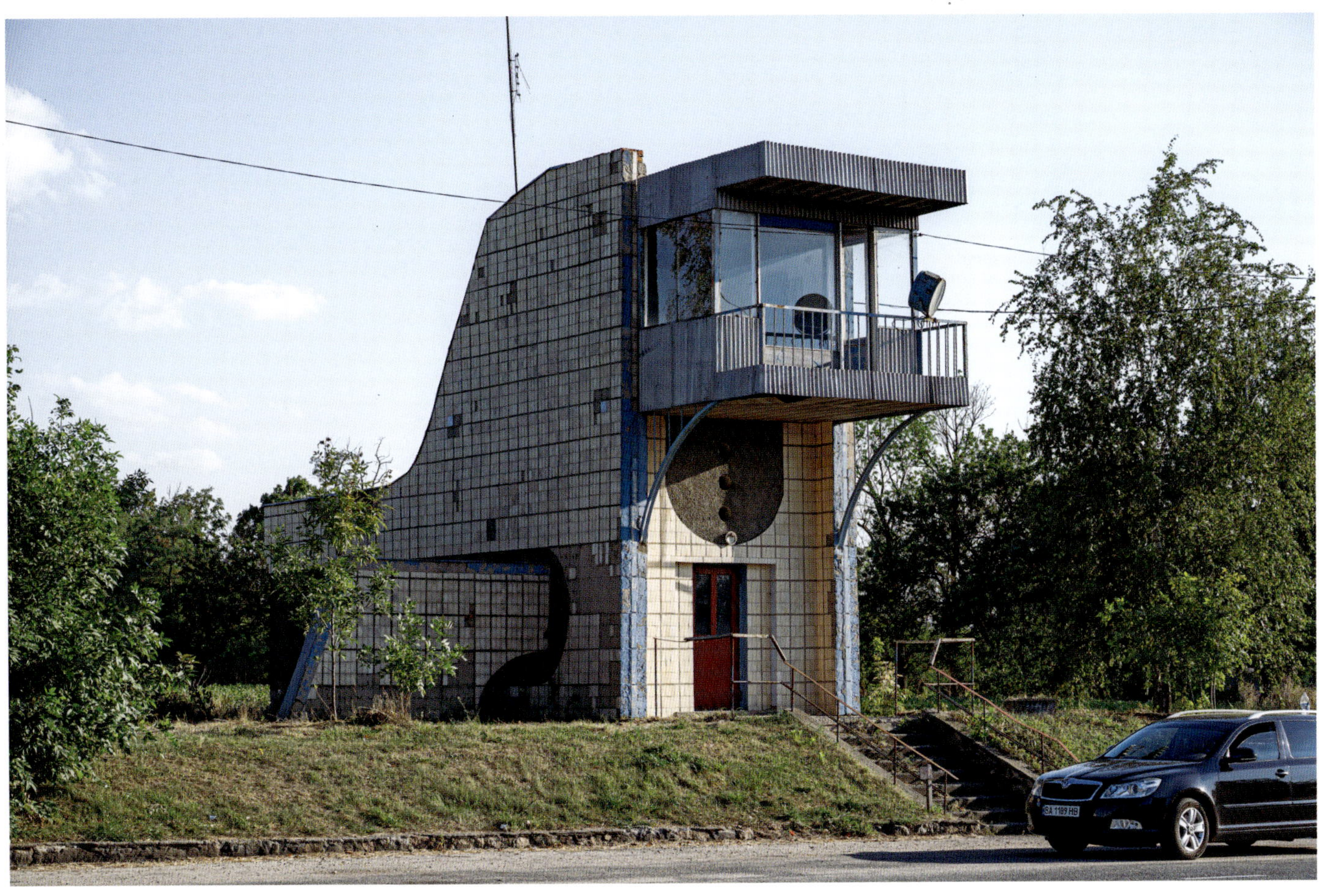

Novoarkhanhelsk Police Station
Kirovohrad Oblast
1960s

In the 1950s, the growing number of road vehicles led to traffic control booths being built in Soviet cities, alongside larger, permanent versions on motorways. The city booths were scrapped in the 2000s, but many of the motorway stations are still manned by police today.

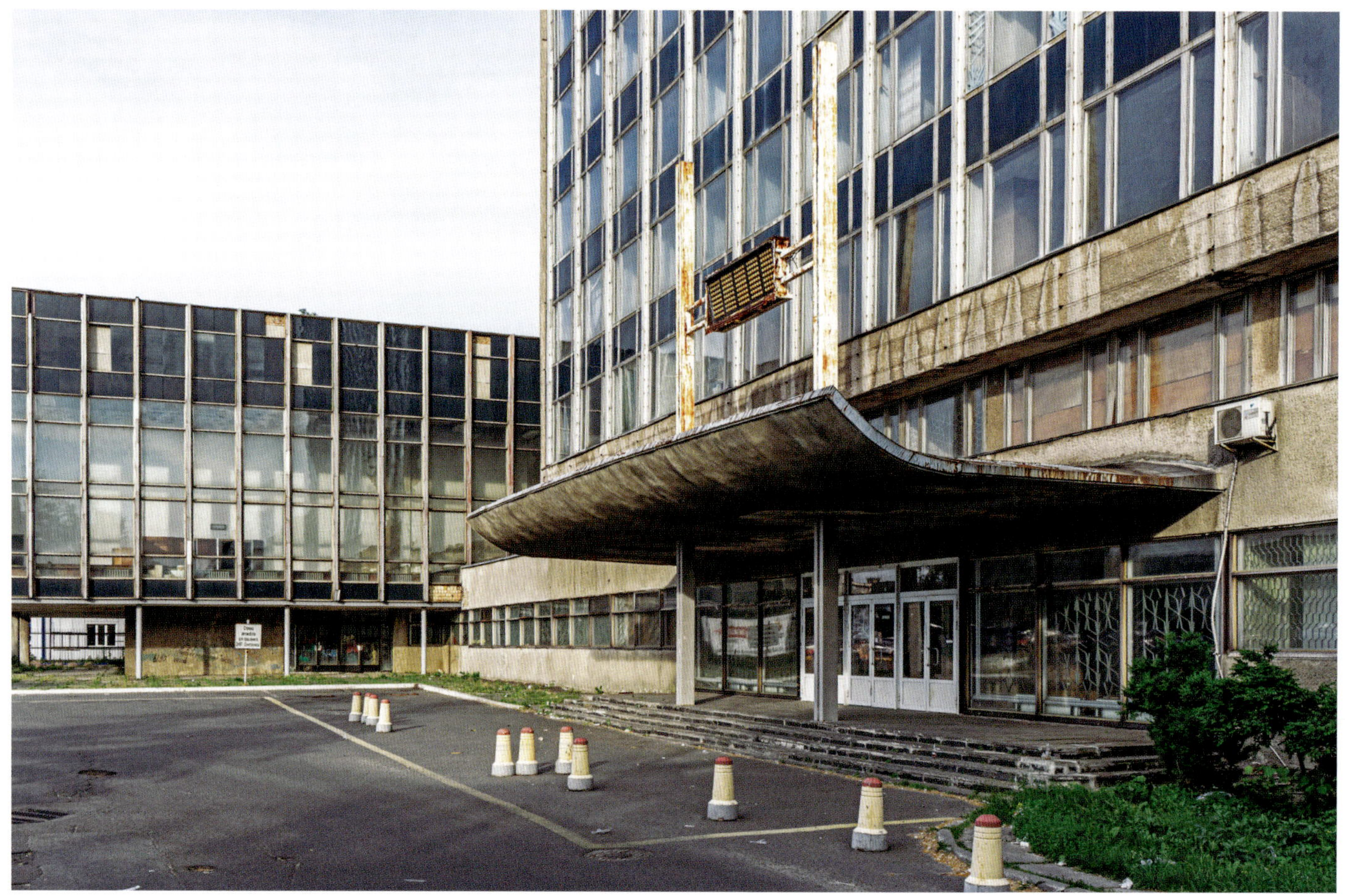

Electronmash Factory Complex
Kyiv
1970s–80s

In its prime, the sprawling Electronmash Factory comprised production facilities, a high-rise building housing their design offices, a Palace of Culture, and a massive two-storey canteen. In line with the Soviet government's emphasis on worker welfare, specially produced artworks

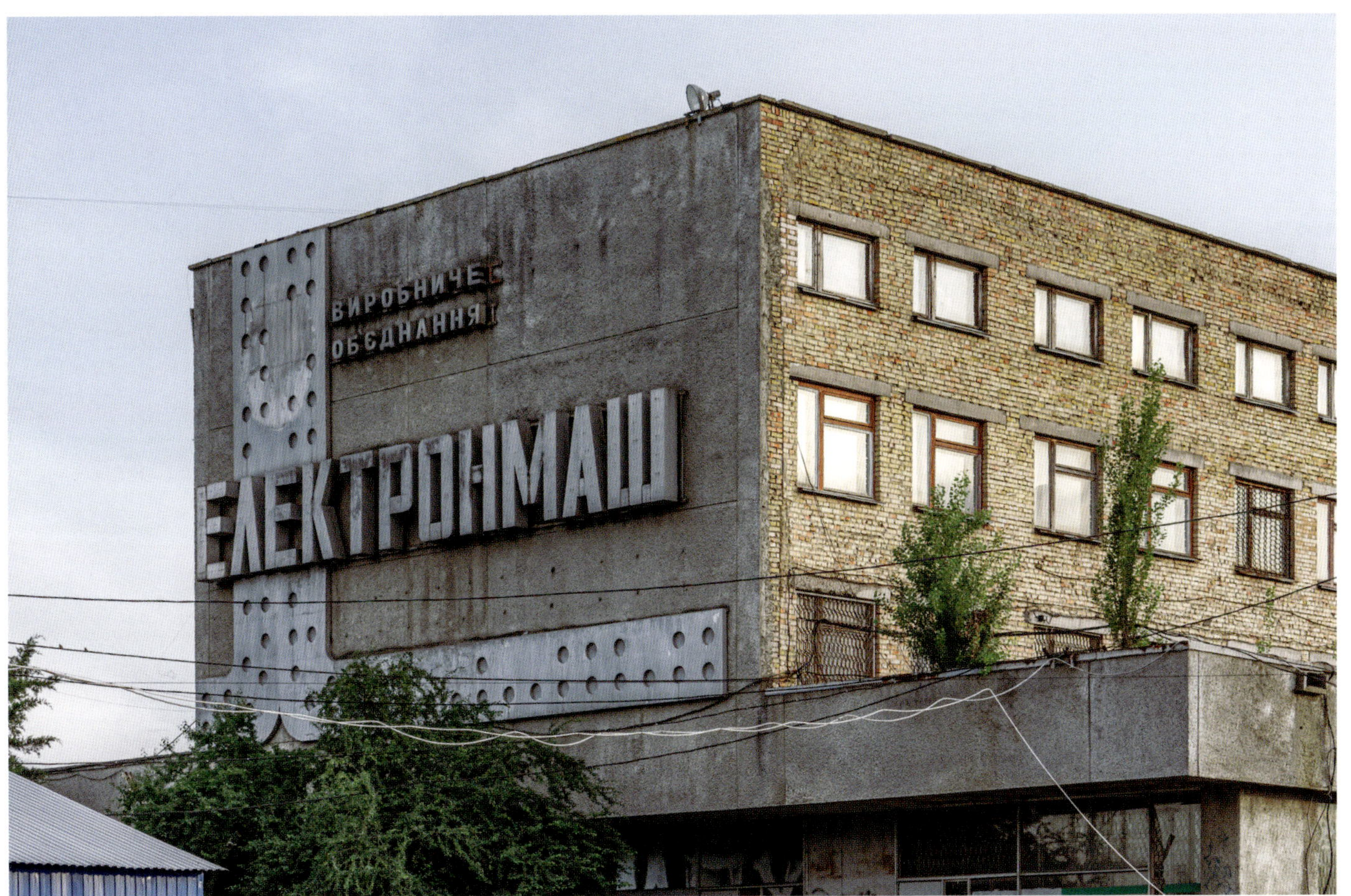

were incorporated into every part of the Electronmash complex. However, like many Soviet industrial giants, the company struggled to adapt to the market economy following the collapse of the USSR and over time, the state sold the facilities off piece by piece. In 2009 the production buildings were replaced by a shopping mall. In 2021, despite public protests, the unique Palace of Culture was demolished. The canteen and high-rise have also been looted, leaving much of their unique interiors in ruins.

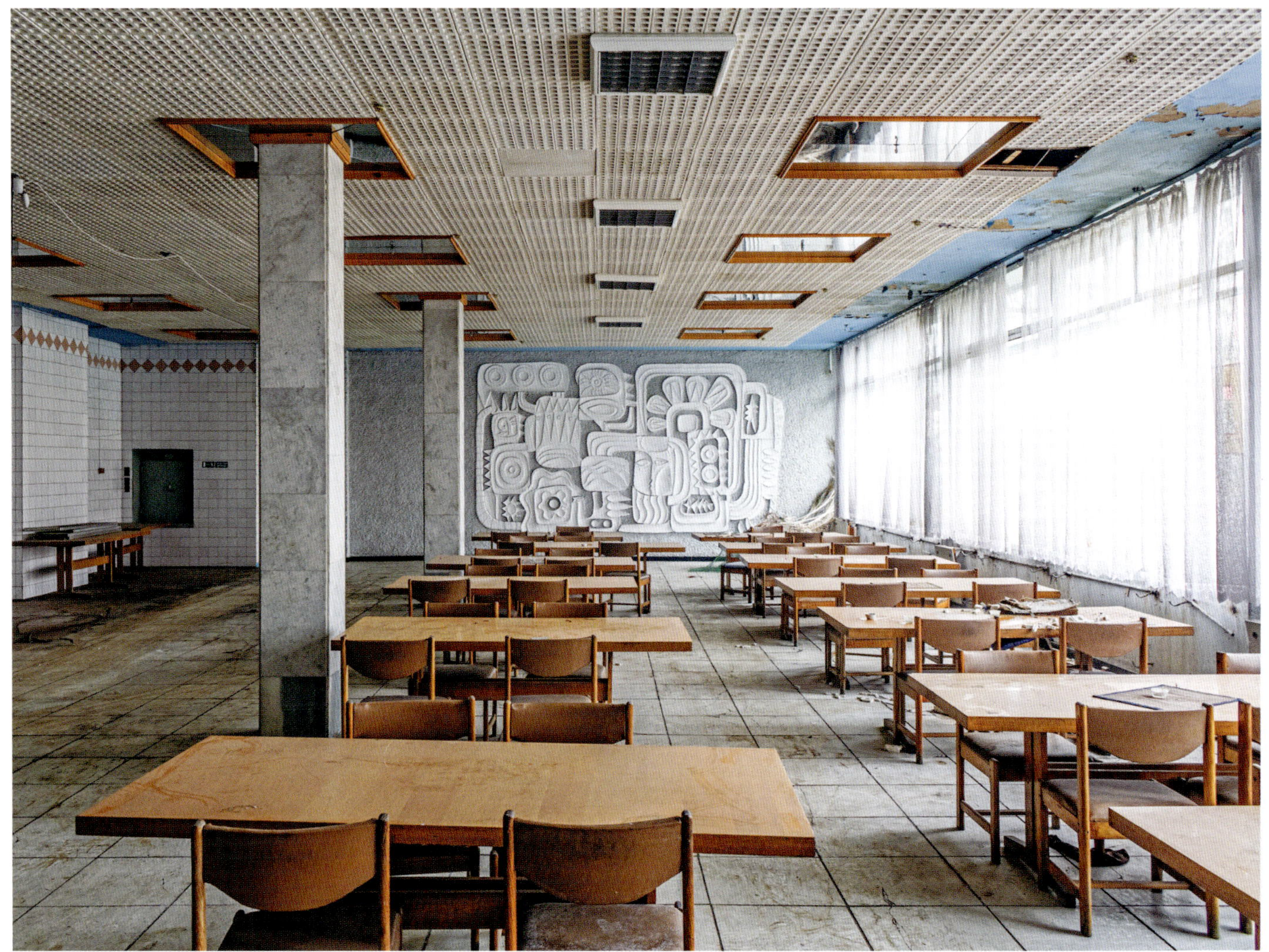

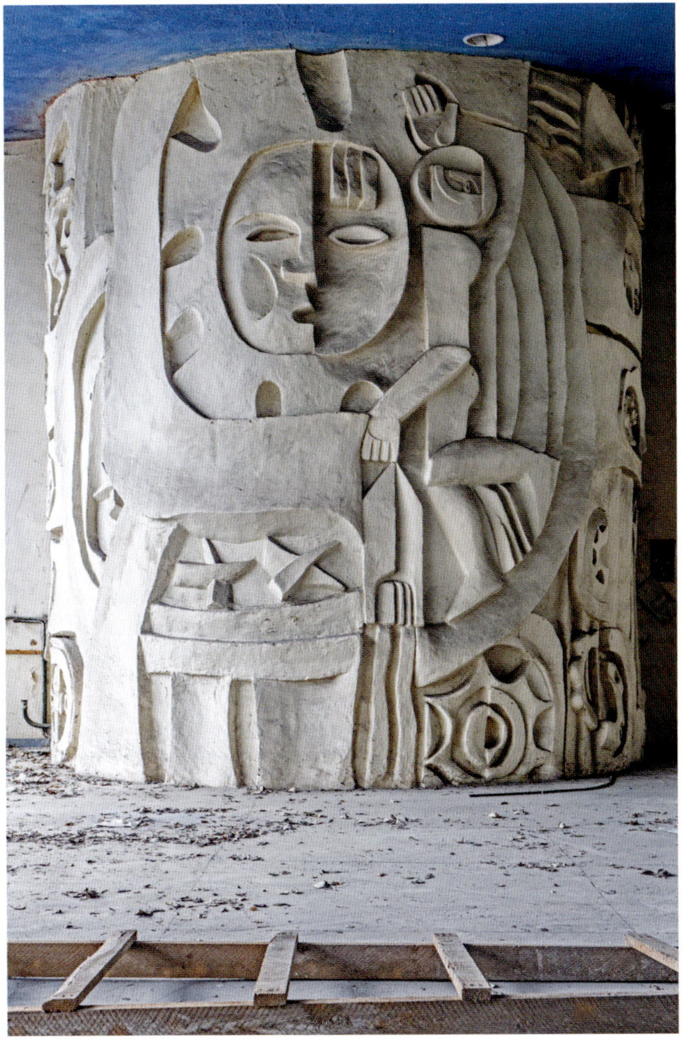

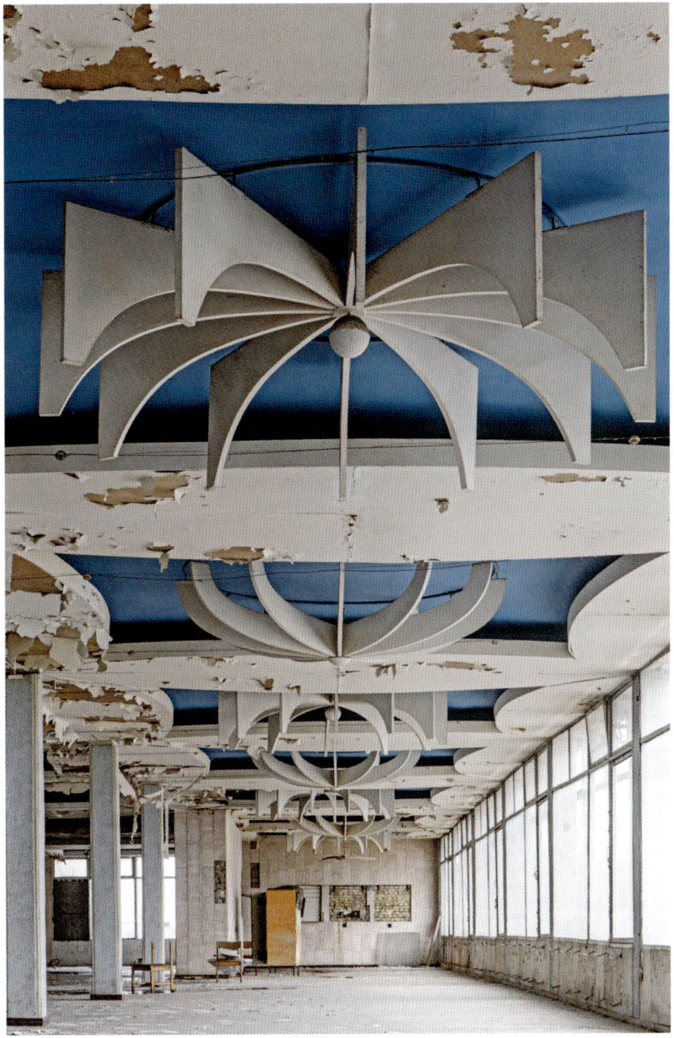

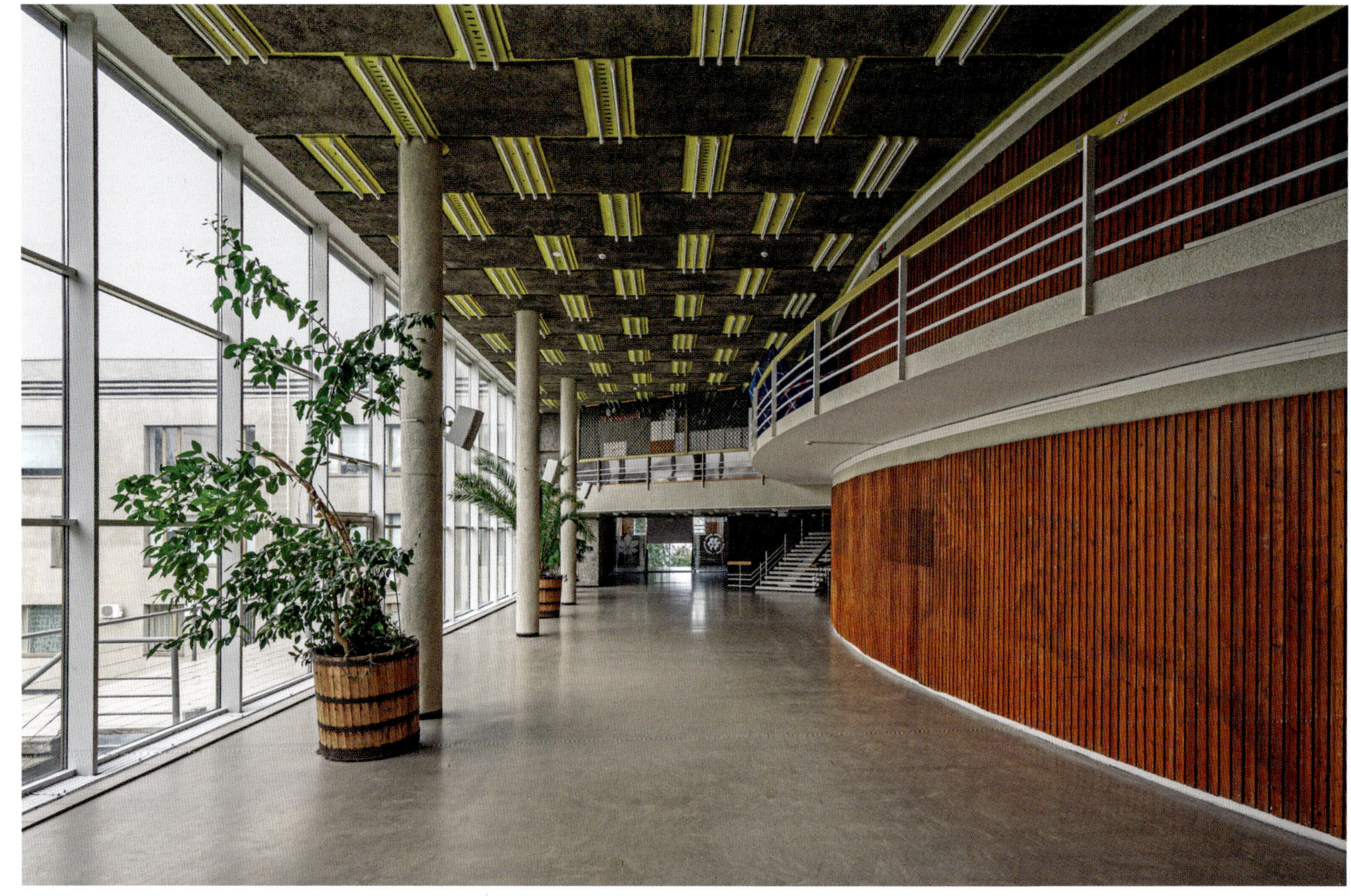

Palace of Children and Youth
(formerly Palace of Pioneers and Schoolchildren)
Kyiv
1962–65

Architects: Avraam Miletskyi, Eduard Bilskyi
Engineers: Leonid Linovych, Oleksii Pechenov
Artists: Ada Rybachuk, Volodymyr Melnichenko, Vasyl Borodai,
Valentyn Seliber

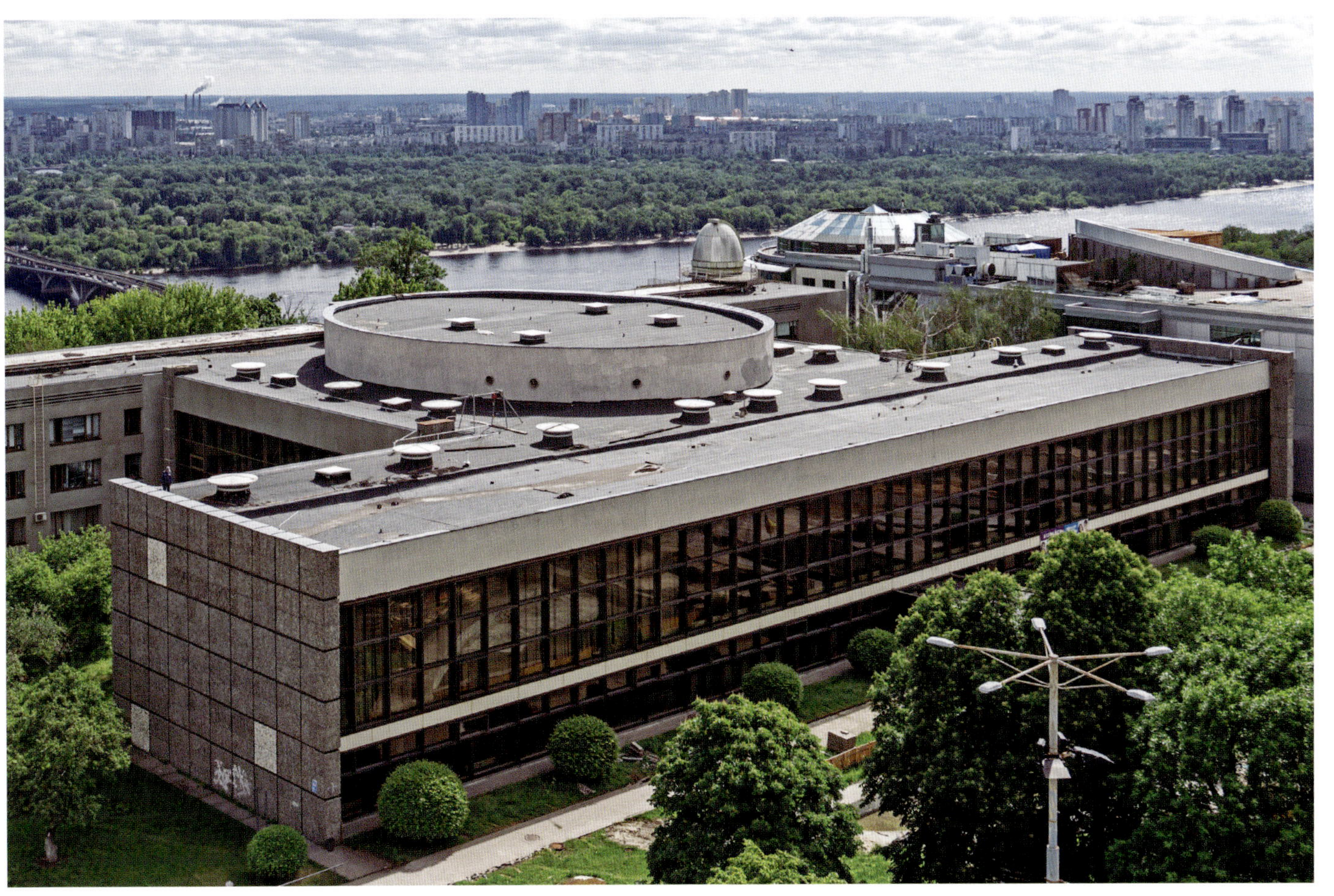

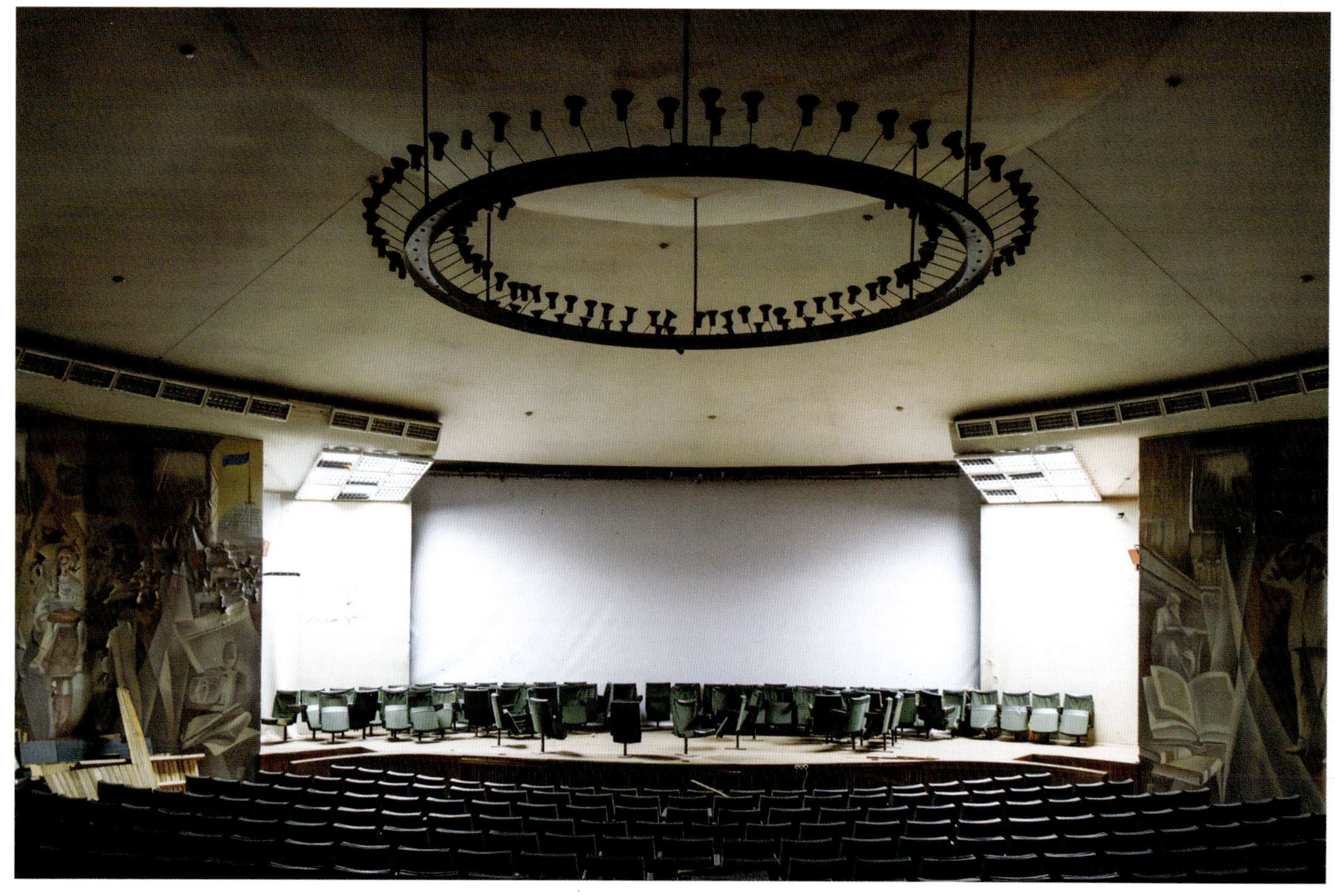

Ukrainian Institute of Scientific and Technical Expertise
and Information (known as the 'Flying Saucer')
Kyiv
1965–71

Architects: Florian Yuriev, Lev Novykov
Engineers: Oleksii Pechenov, V. Koval, L. Kovtun, N. Kofman
Artist: Borys Dovhan

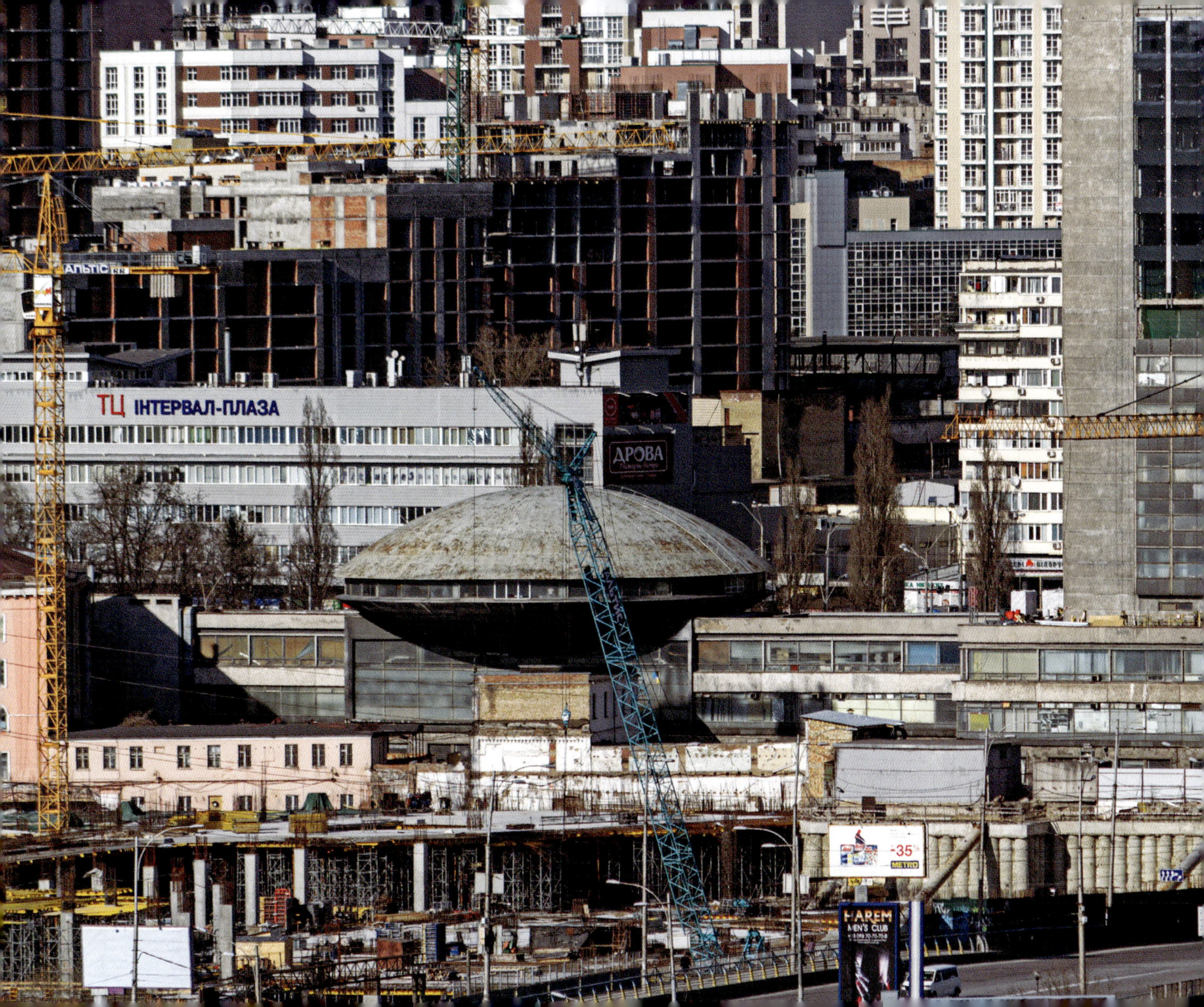
АльтІС KB
ТЦ ІНТЕРВАЛ-ПЛАЗА
ДРОВА
HAREM
MEN'S CUB
METRO
-35%

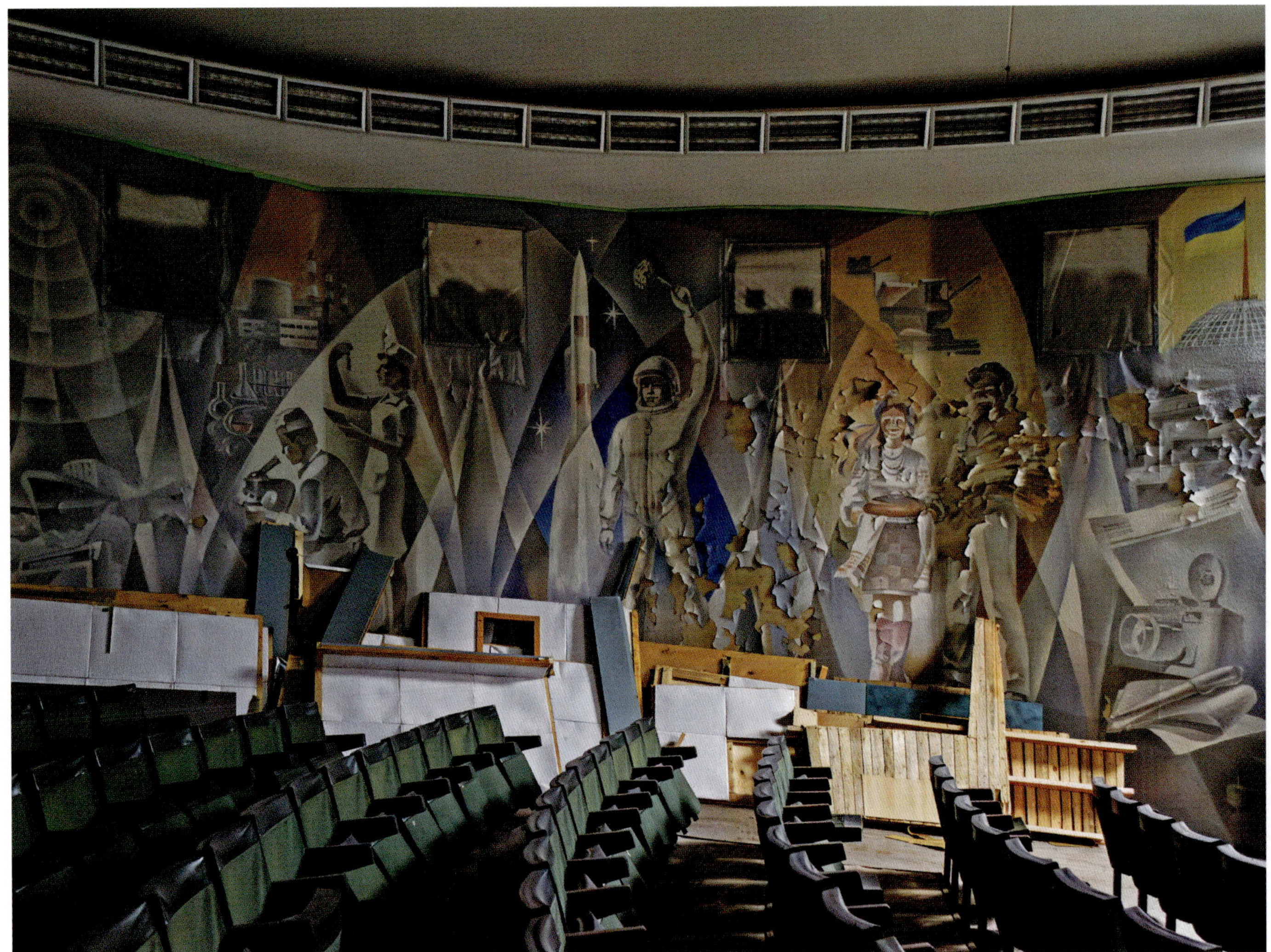

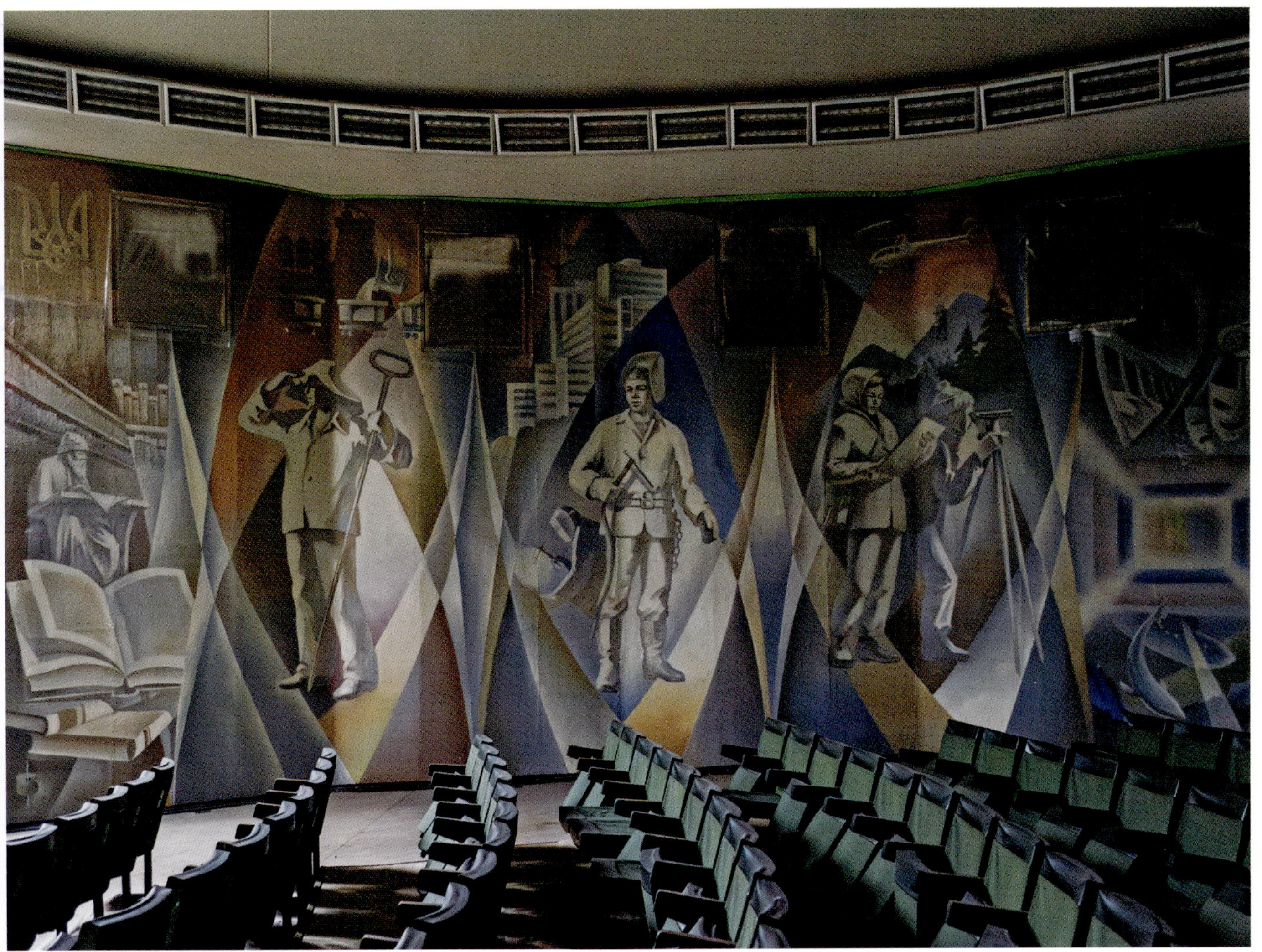

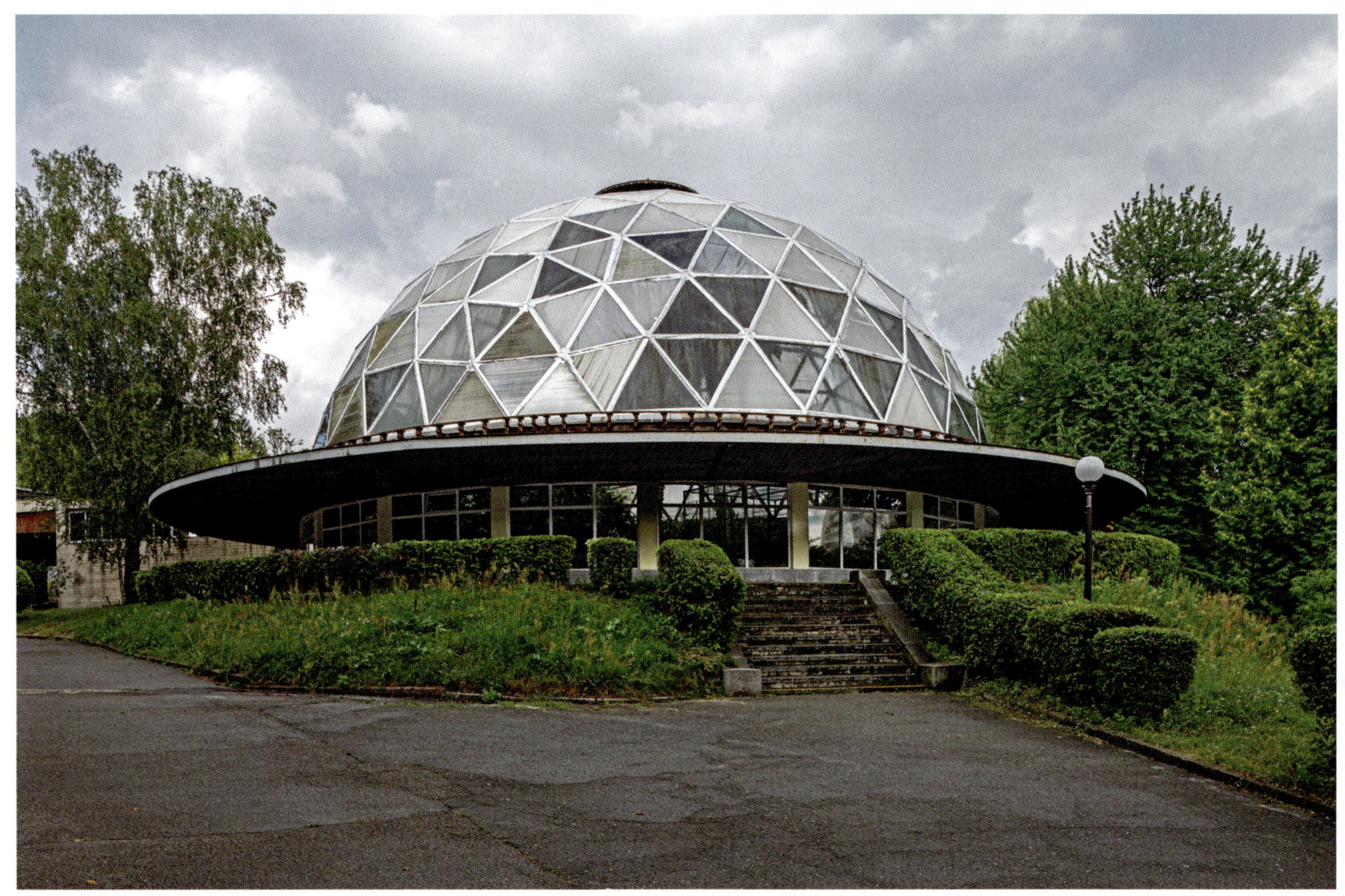

Bird Pavilion, Kyiv Zoo
Kyiv
1966
Architect: V. Mykhailov
Engineer: H. Hontskevych, H. Murashov

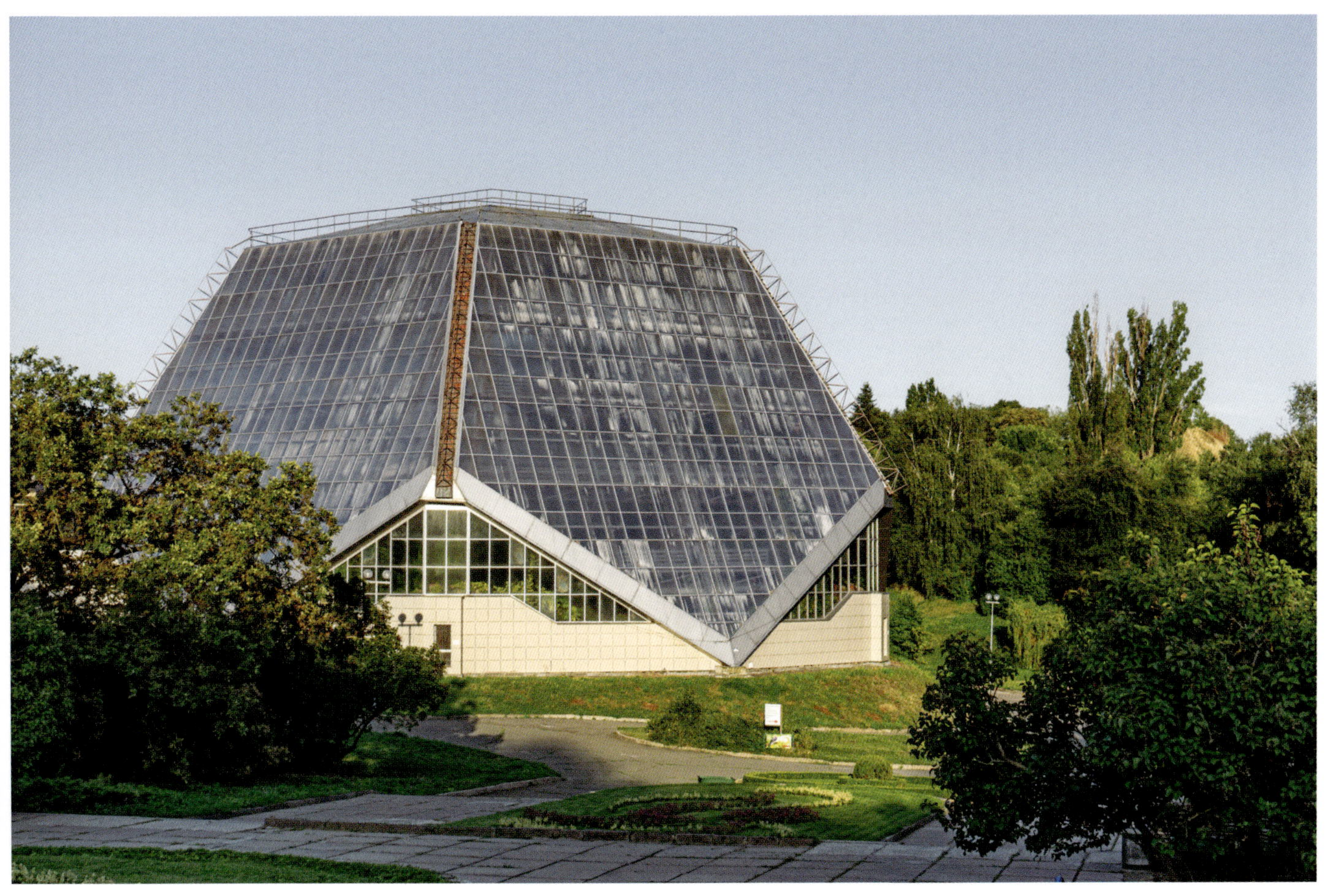

Palm House, Hryshko National Botanical Garden
Kyiv
1980s

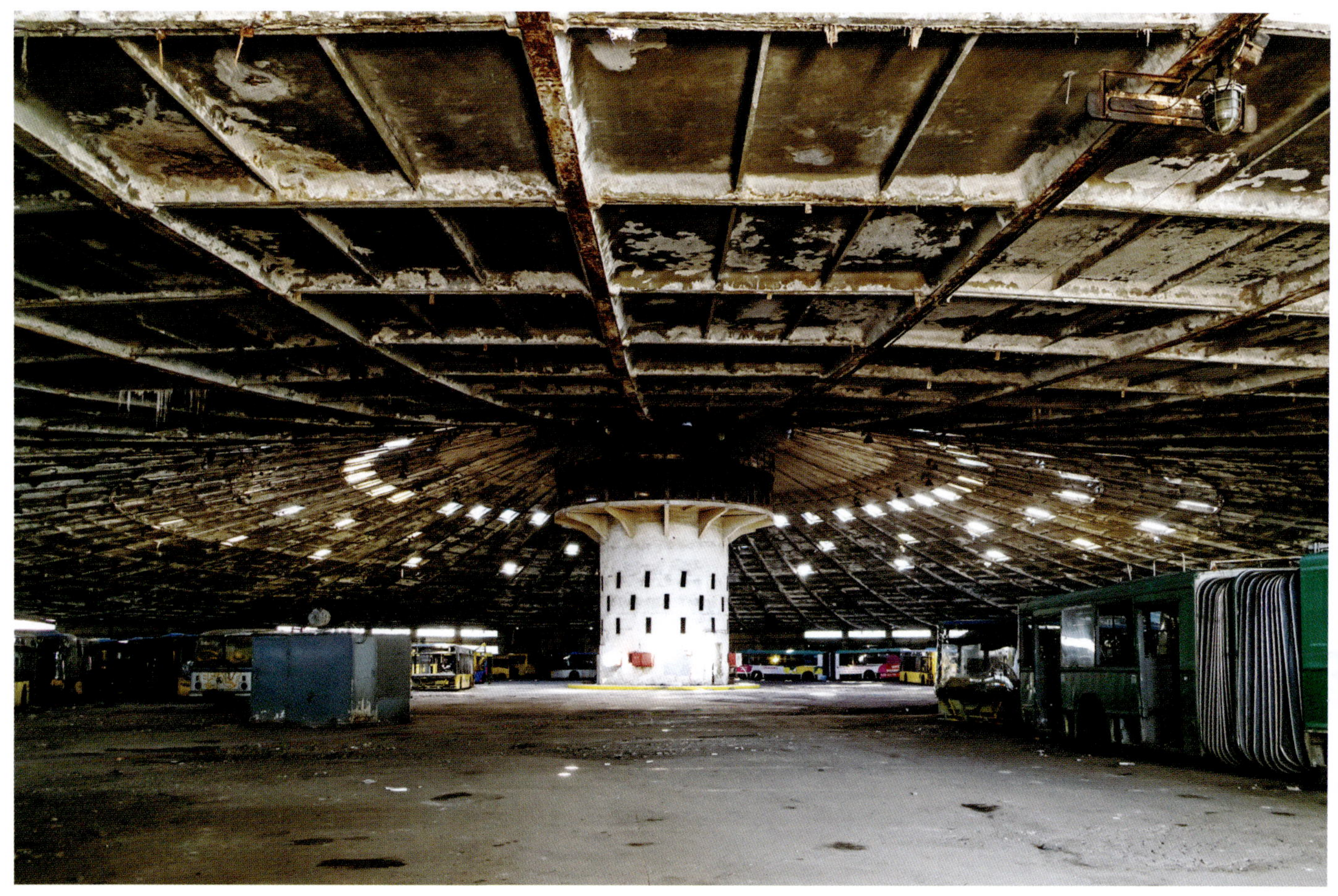

Bus Depot
Kyiv
1973–74
Architect: V. Zinkevych
Engineers: V. Kozlov, E. Volovyk, V. Marchuk

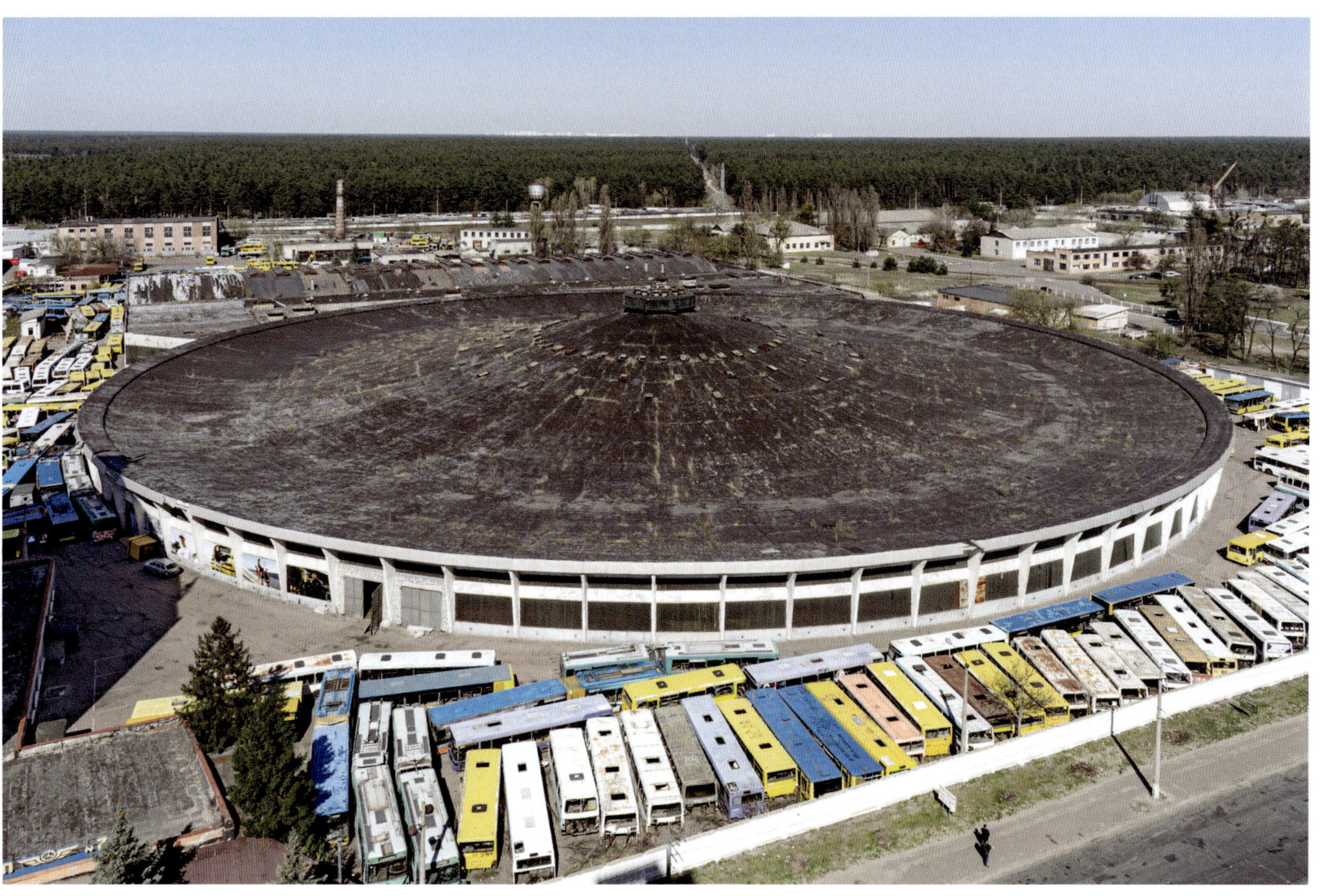

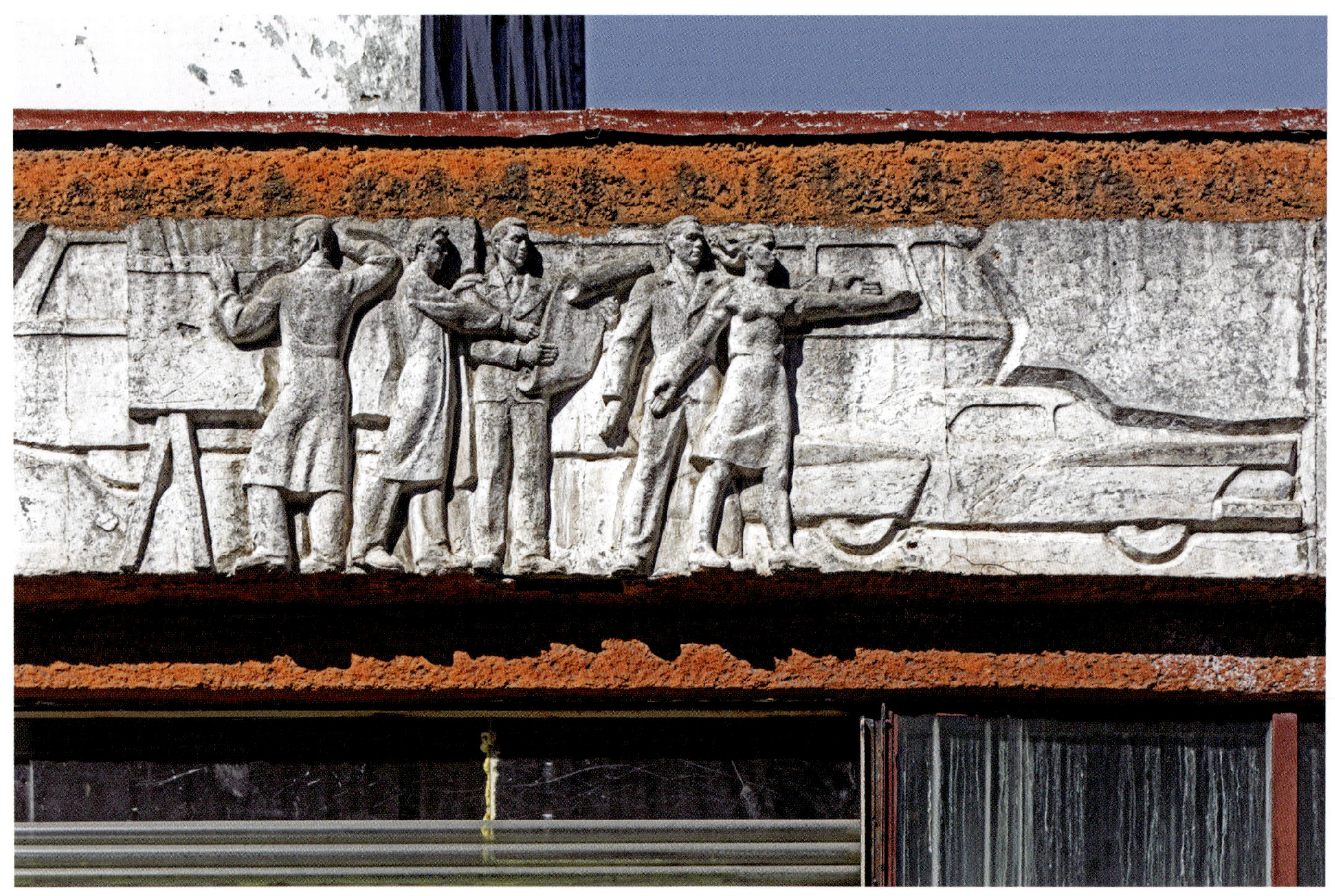

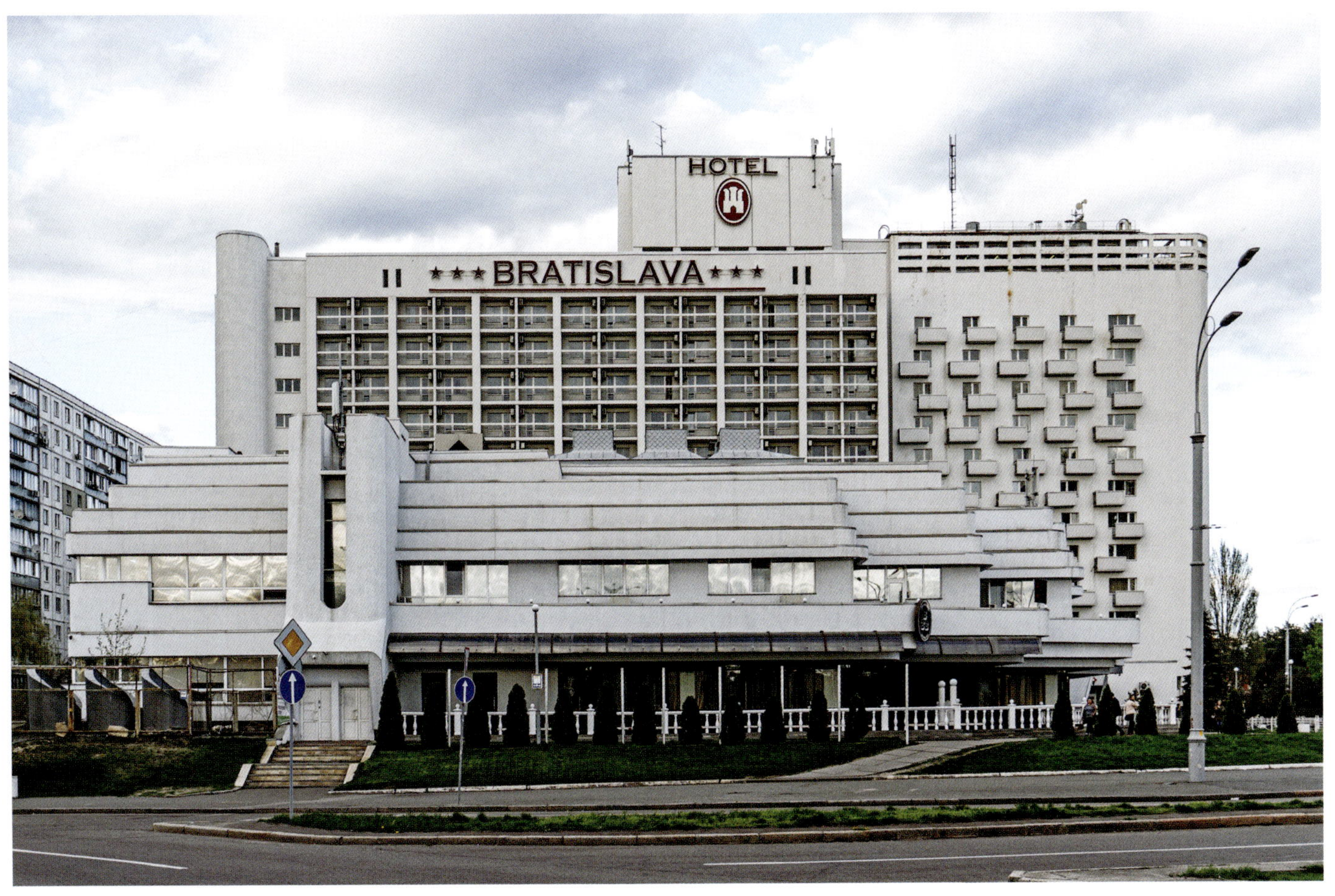

Bratislava Hotel
Kyiv
1975–80
Architects: Oleksandr Dumchev, Oleksandr Zbarskyi, Tetiana Gnezdilova

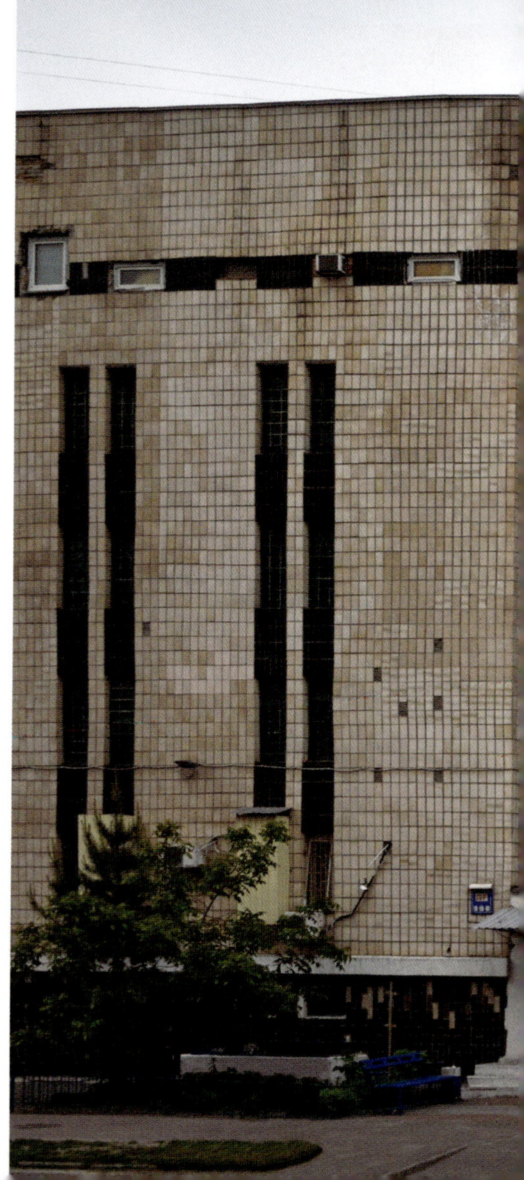

Multi-Storey Car Park
Borys Hmyria Street, Kyiv
1990s

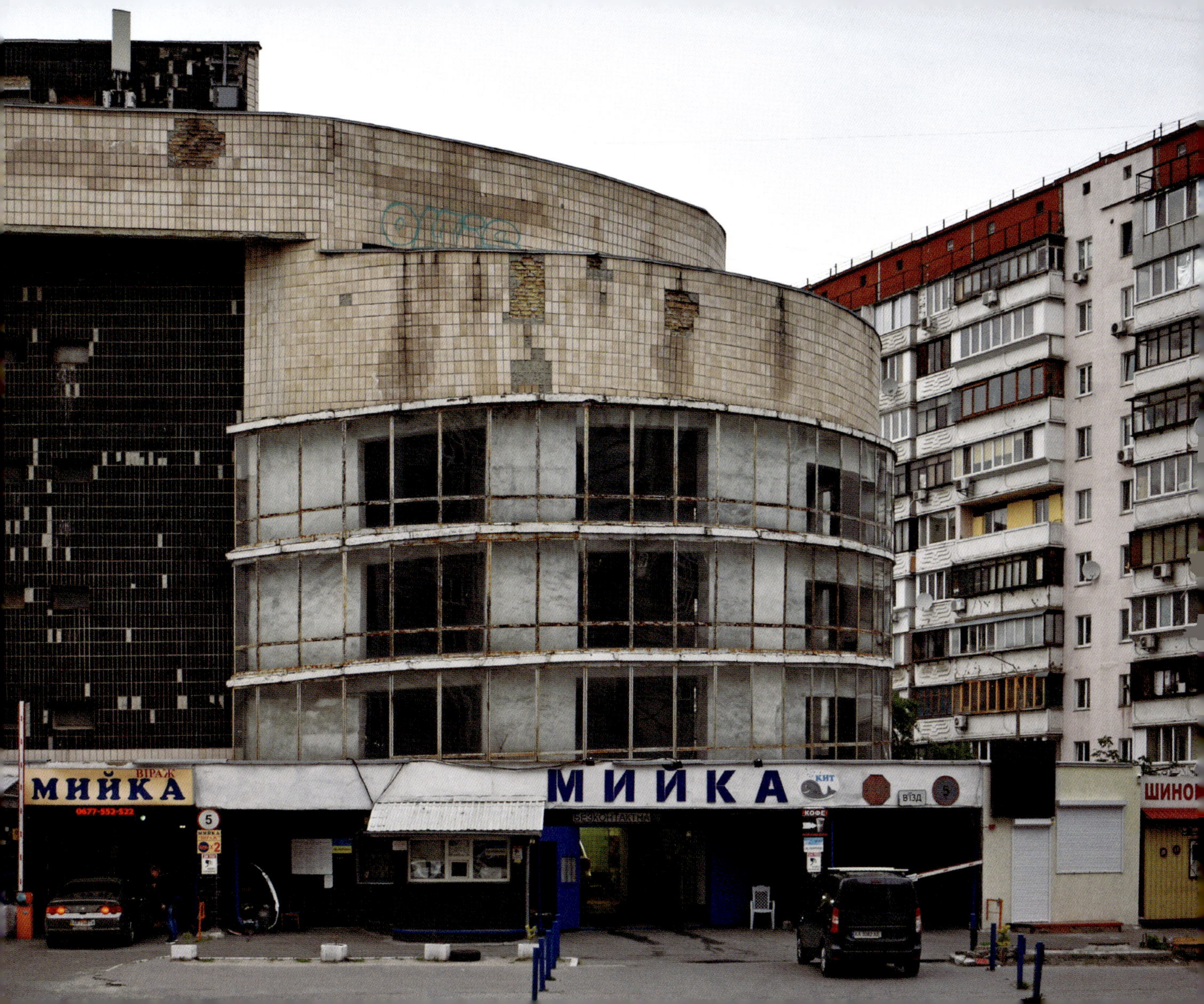
МИЙКА
ВІРАЖ
0677-552-522
5
МИЙКА
КИТ
БЕЗКОНТАКТНА
КОФЕ
ВЇЗД
5
ШИНО

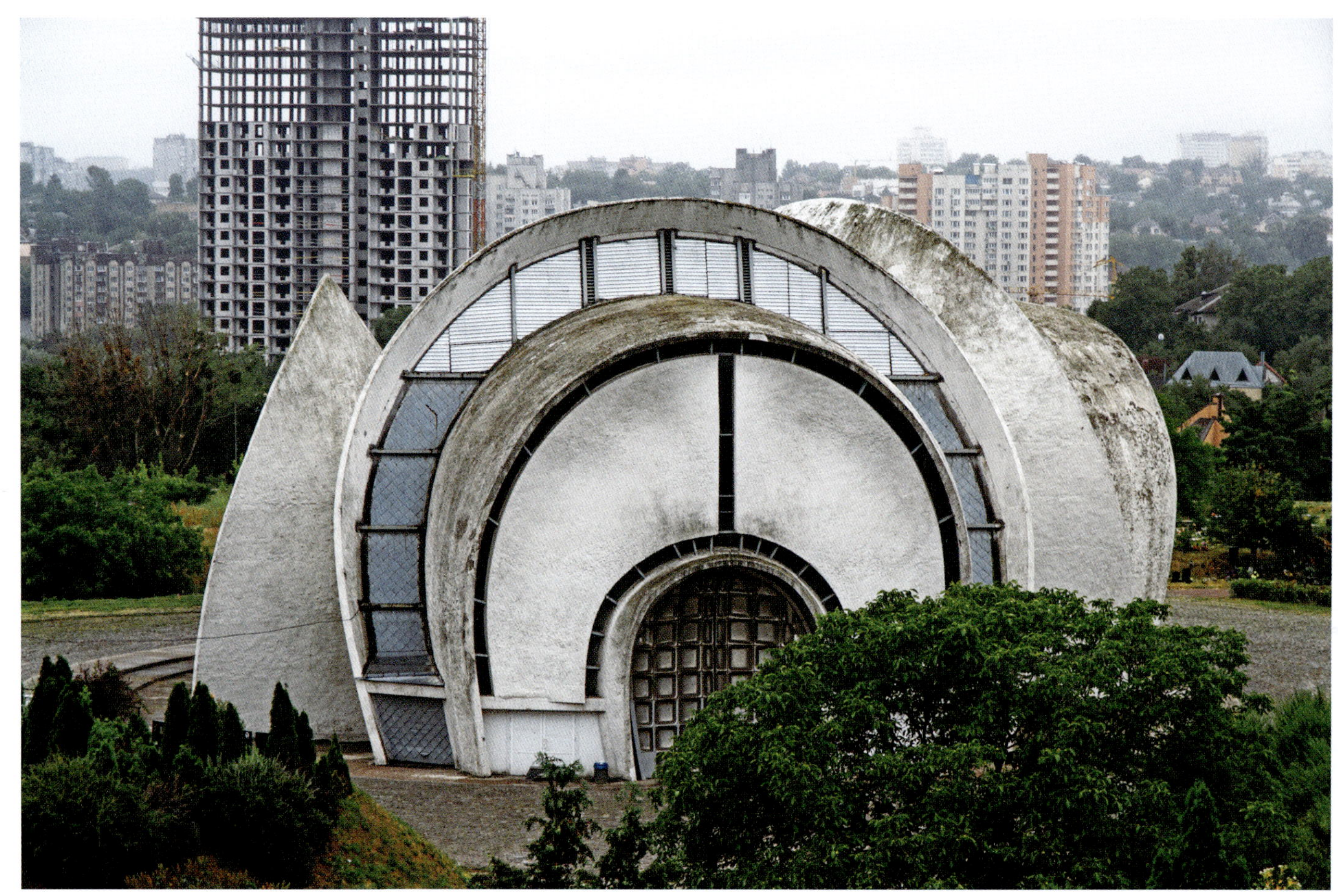

Halls of Farewell, Kyiv Crematorium
Kyiv
1970–75
Architects: Avraam Miletskyi, Ada Rybachuk, Volodymyr Melnichenko

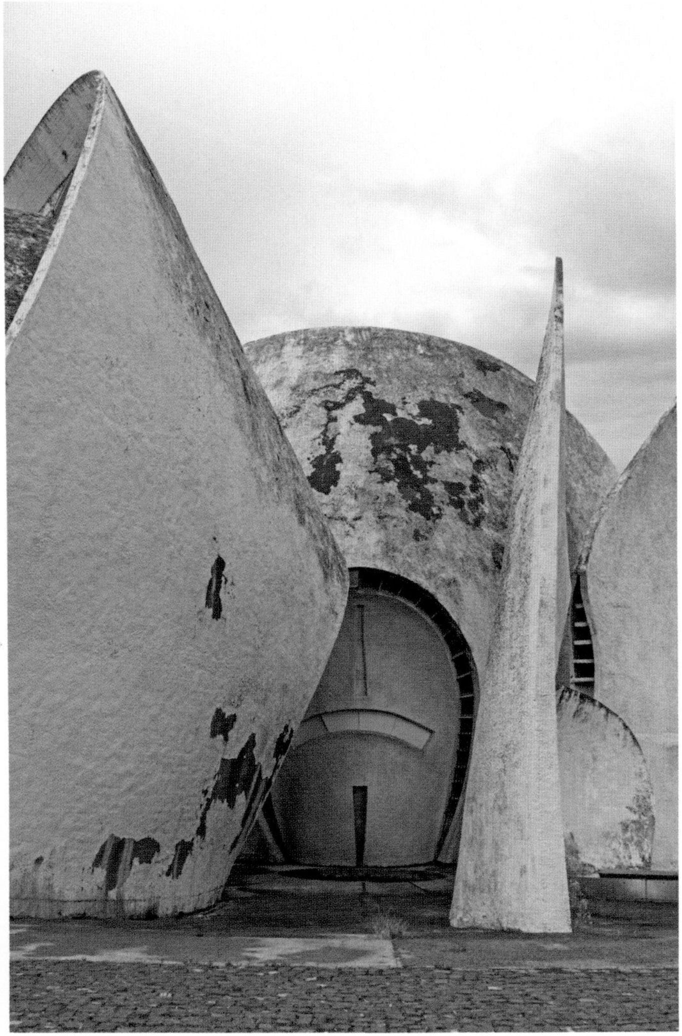

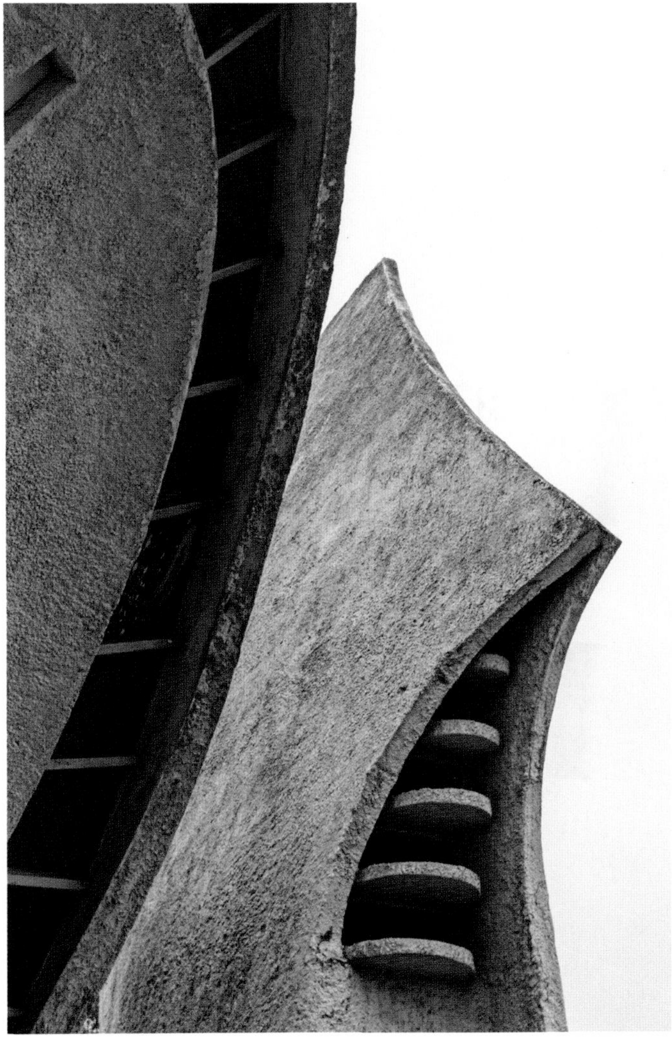

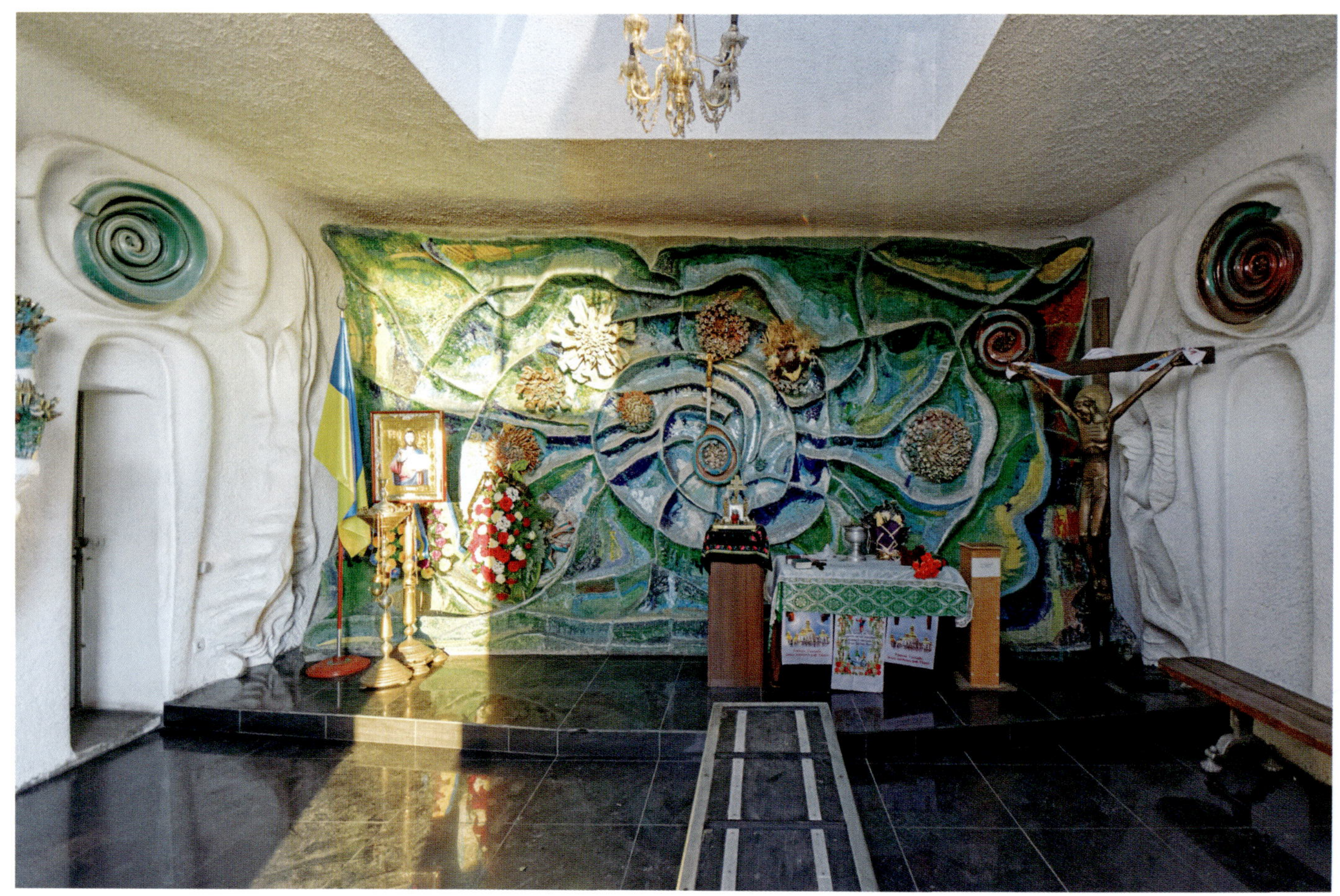

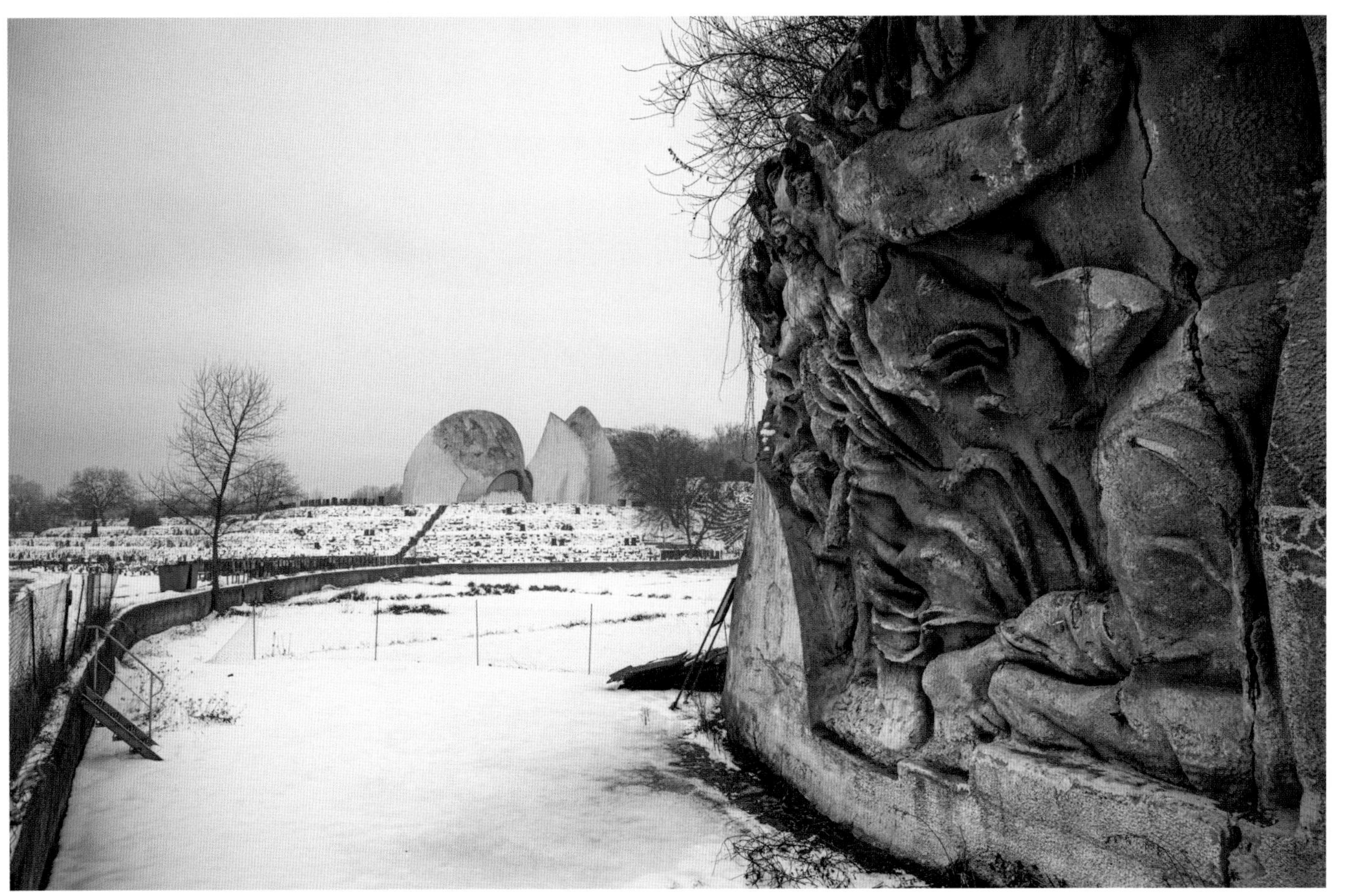

Wall of Memory, Kyiv Crematorium
Kyiv
1974–81
Artists: Ada Rybachuk, Volodymyr Melnichenko

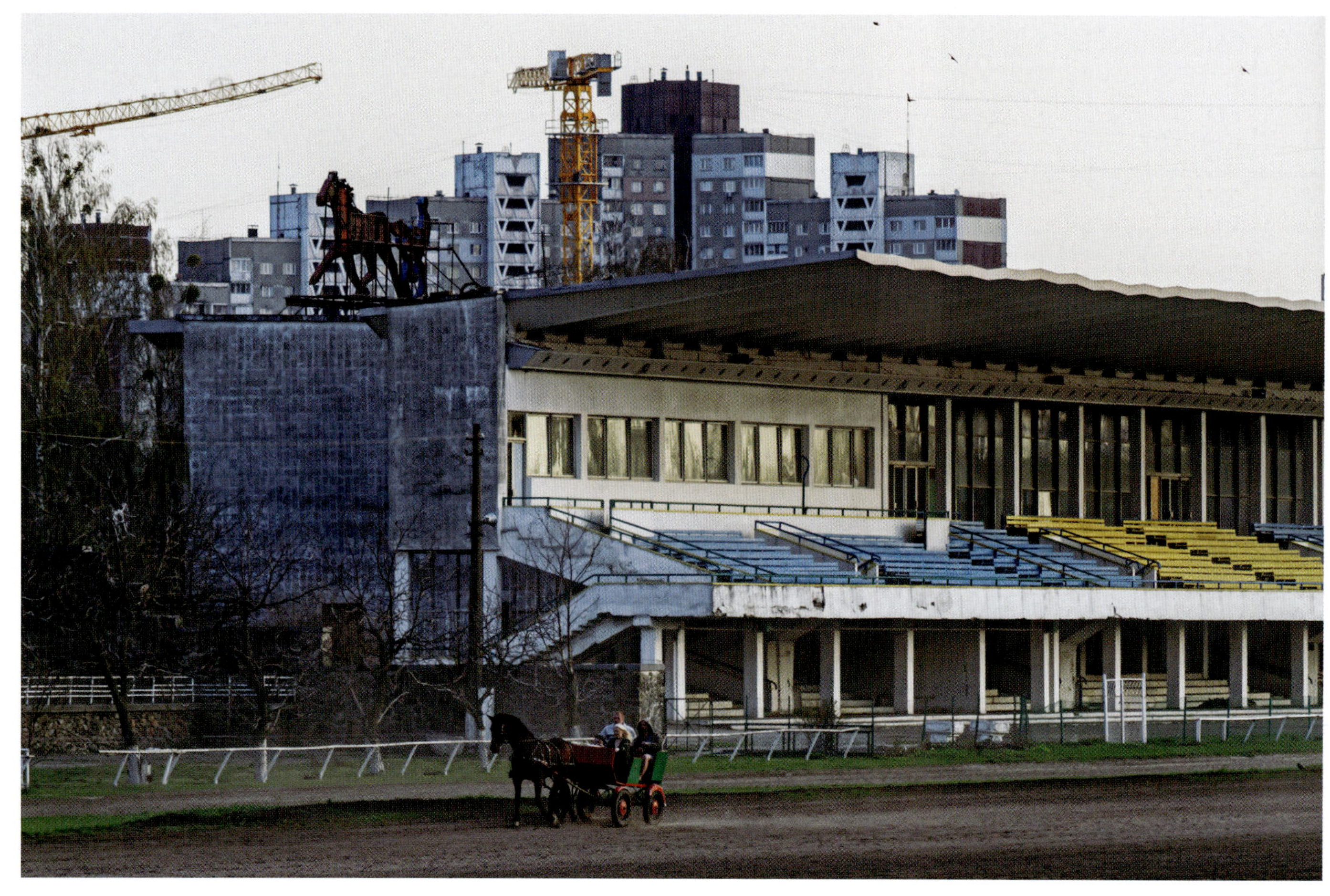

Kyiv Hippodrome
Kyiv
1962–69

Architects: V. Sherman, H. Markytian, N. Piskunenko, S. Teliuk
Engineers: V. Kobkin, H. Abrosymov
Artist: Volodymyr Lobanov

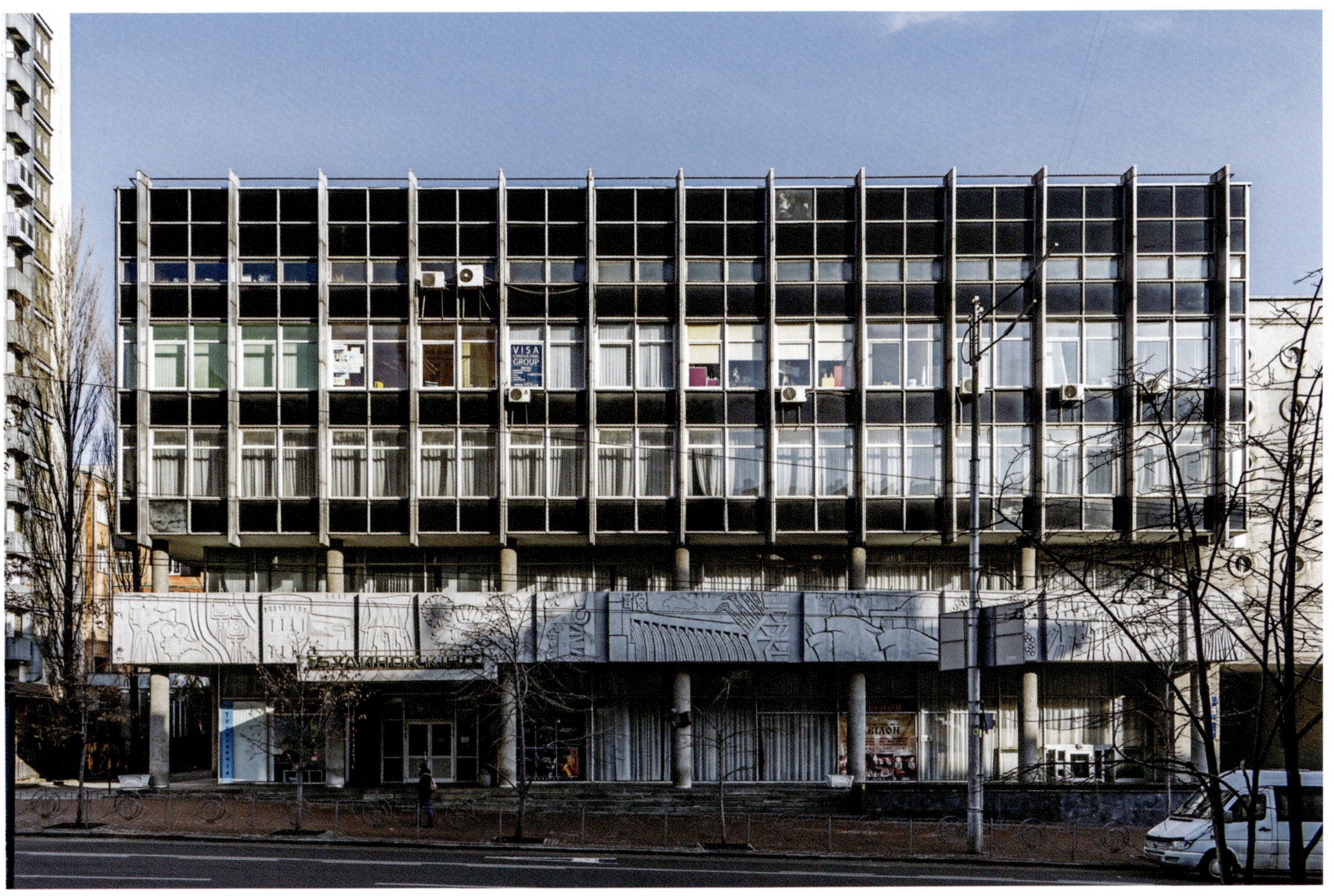

House of Cinema
Kyiv
1974
Architects: Zynovii Chechyk, Fedir Borovyk, S. Khodyk,
E. Sendziuk

Engineer: I. Onishchenko
Artists: Liudmyla Mieshkova, Nina Fedorova, Hanna Sharai, Yakiv
Padalka, Halyna Sevruk, Olena Vladimirova, Hryhorii Husid, Inna
Kolomiiets, B. Liubych

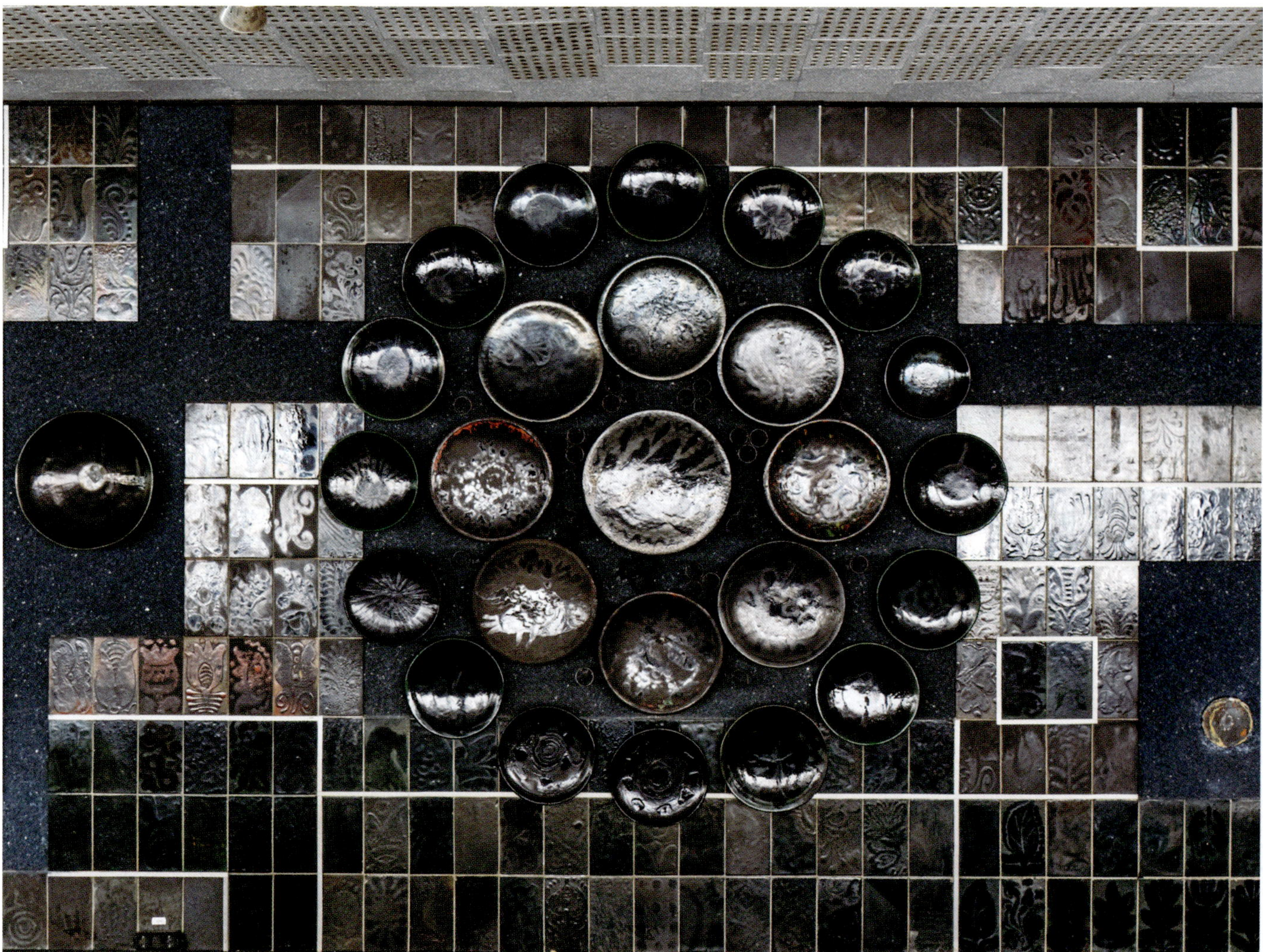

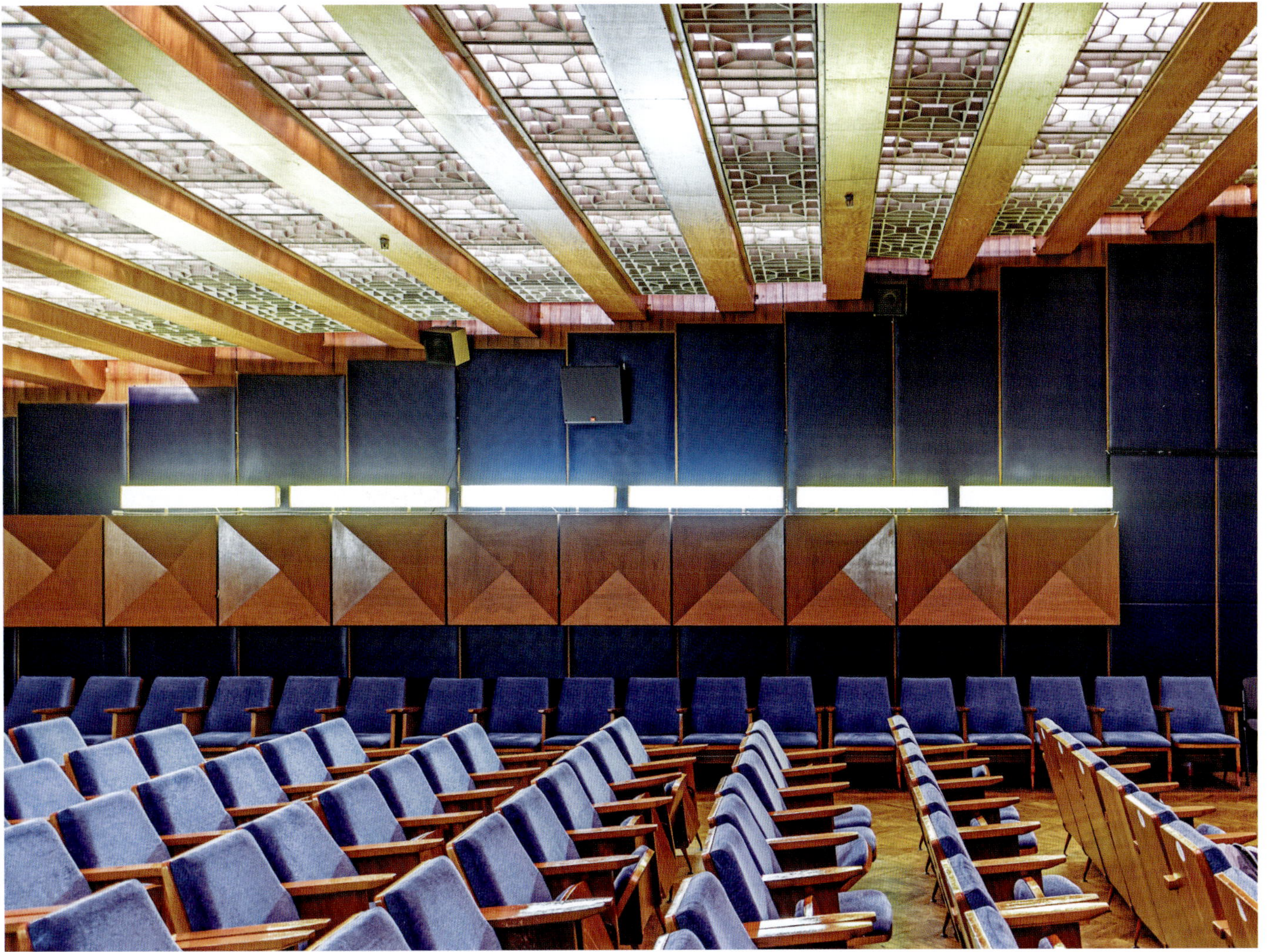

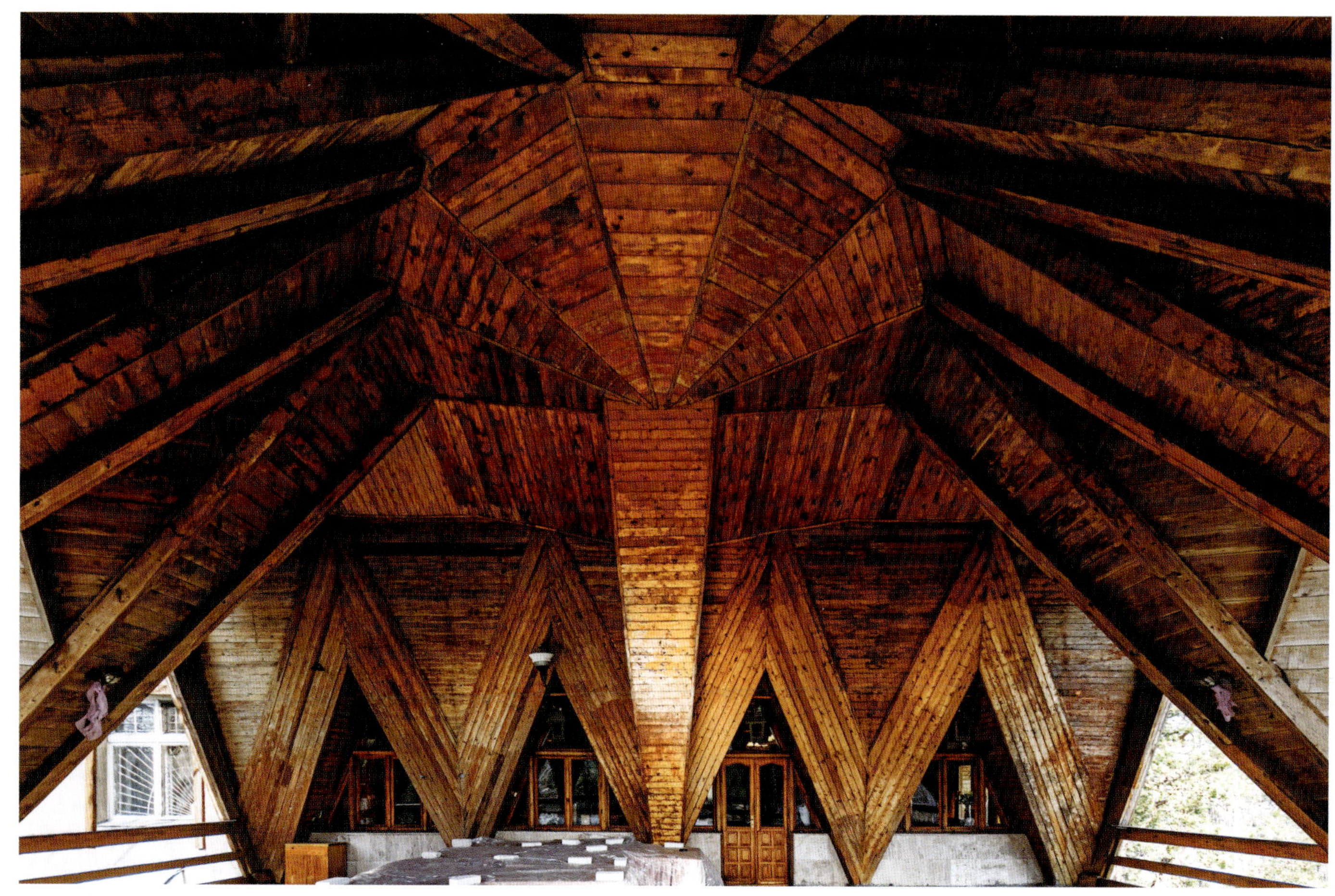

Strumok Restaurant
Kozyn, Kyiv Oblast
1971

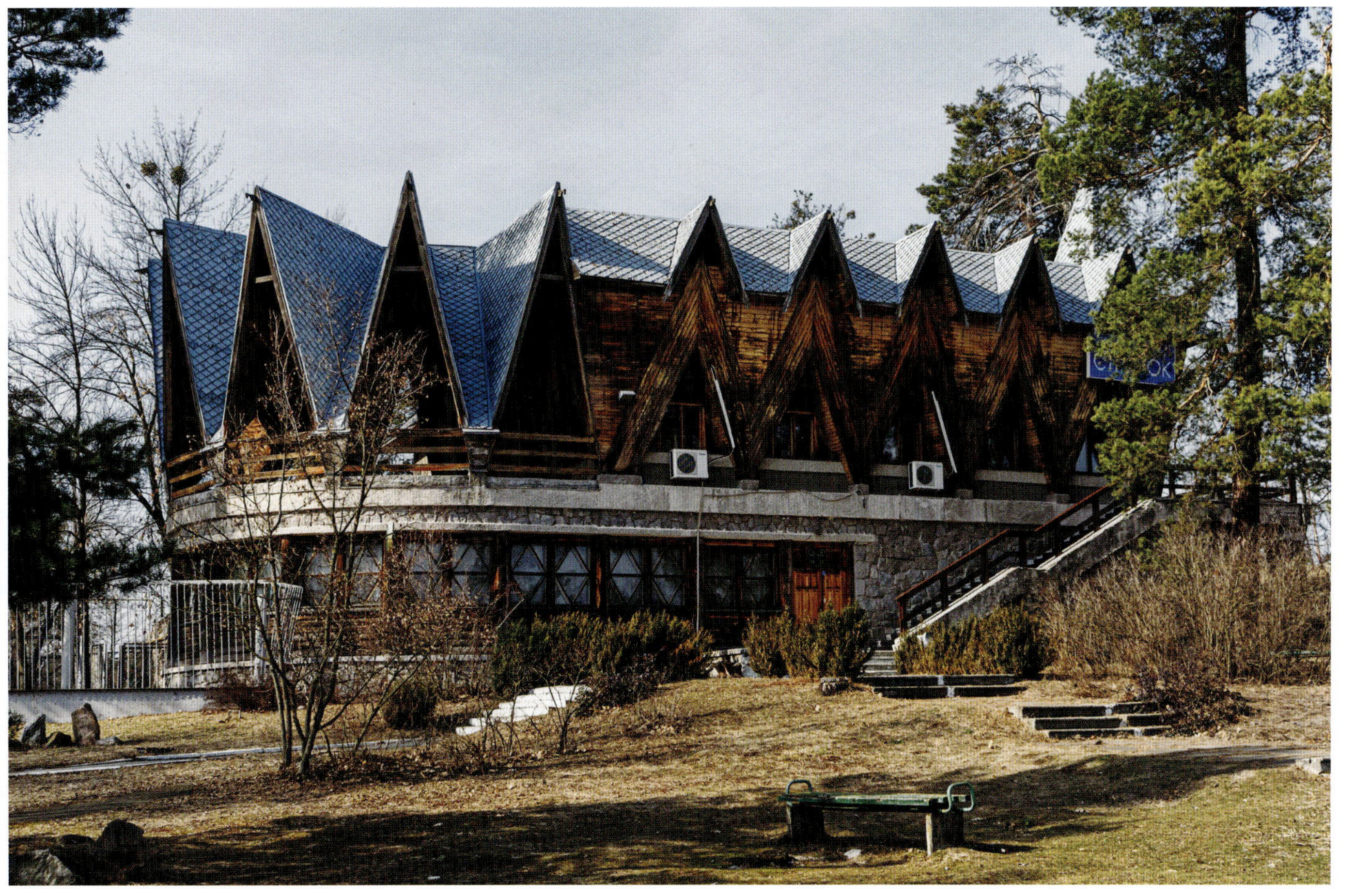

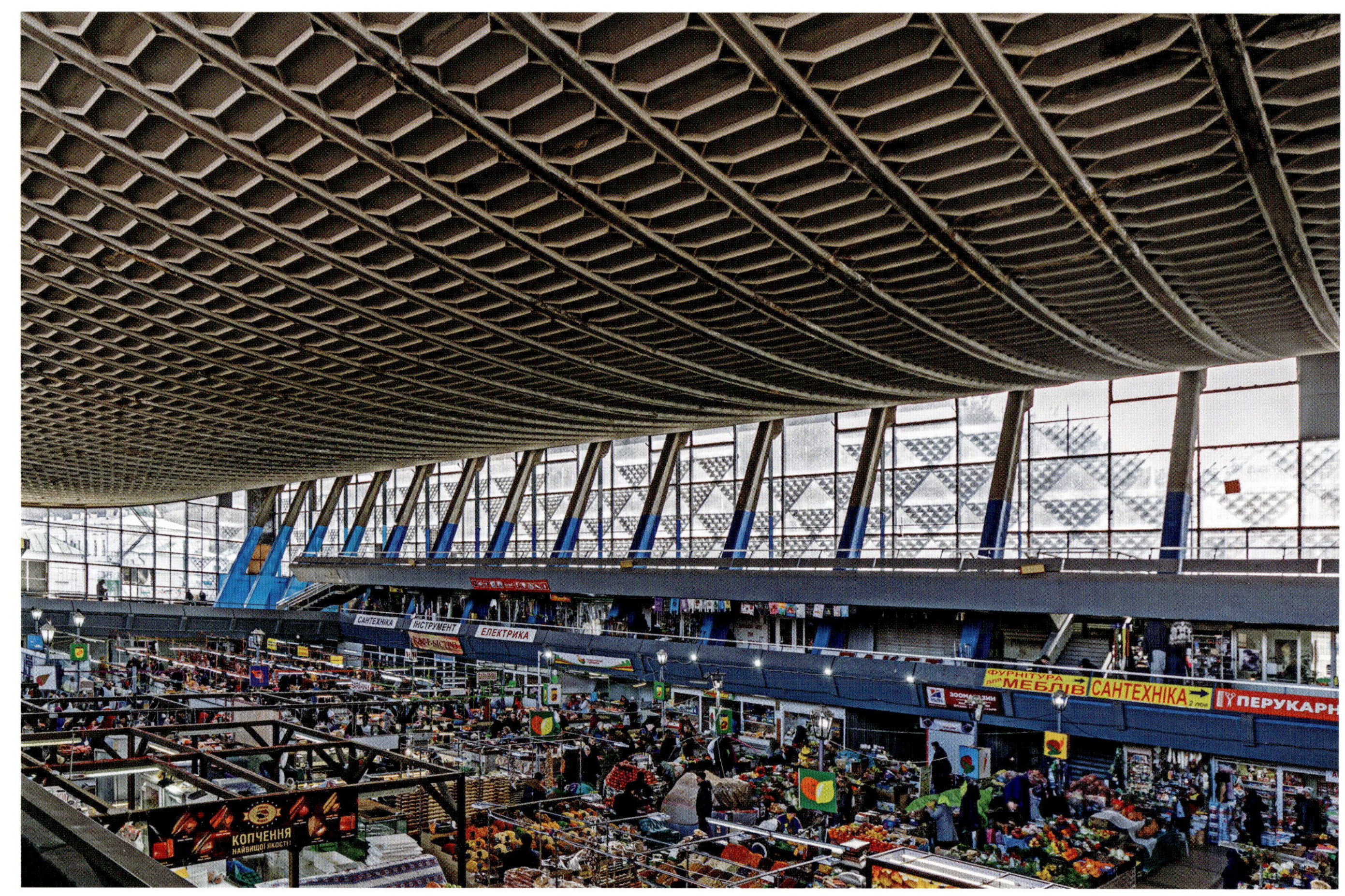

Zhytnii Market
Kyiv
1974–80
Architects: Olha Monina, Valentyn Shtolko
Engineer: Borys Bednarskyi

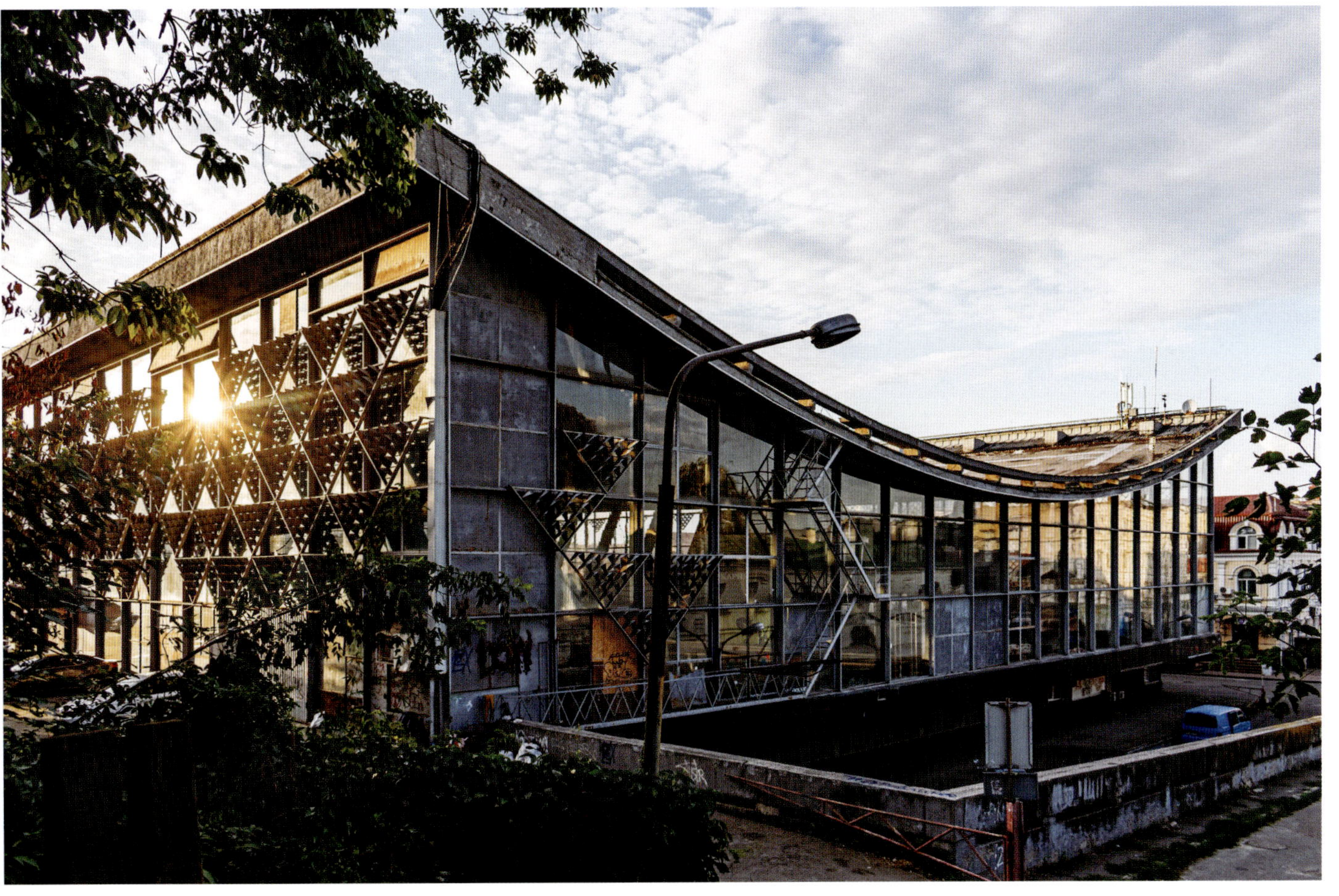

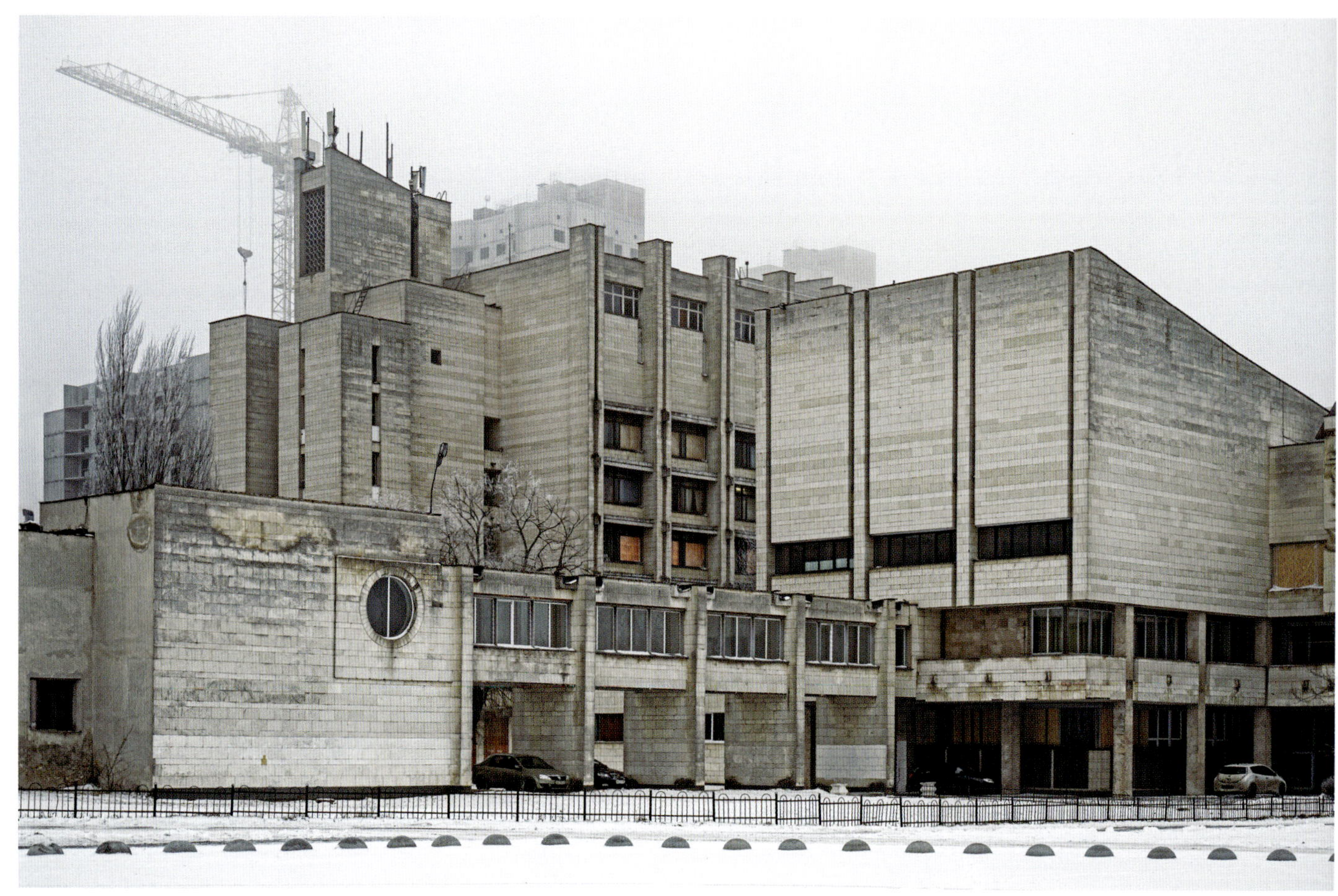

Taras Shevchenko National University of Kyiv
Kyiv
Architects: V. Ladnyi, M. Budilovskyi, V. Katsyn, L. Kolomiiets, V. Morozov
Engineers: V. Drizo, I. Shapiro

Vadym Ladnyi and Mykhailo Budilovskyi's ambitious plan for the new campus of the National University envisioned numerous buildings (lecture halls, laboratories, a library, an event hall and a shopping centre) spread across a 102.8-hectare site. Works were carried out in

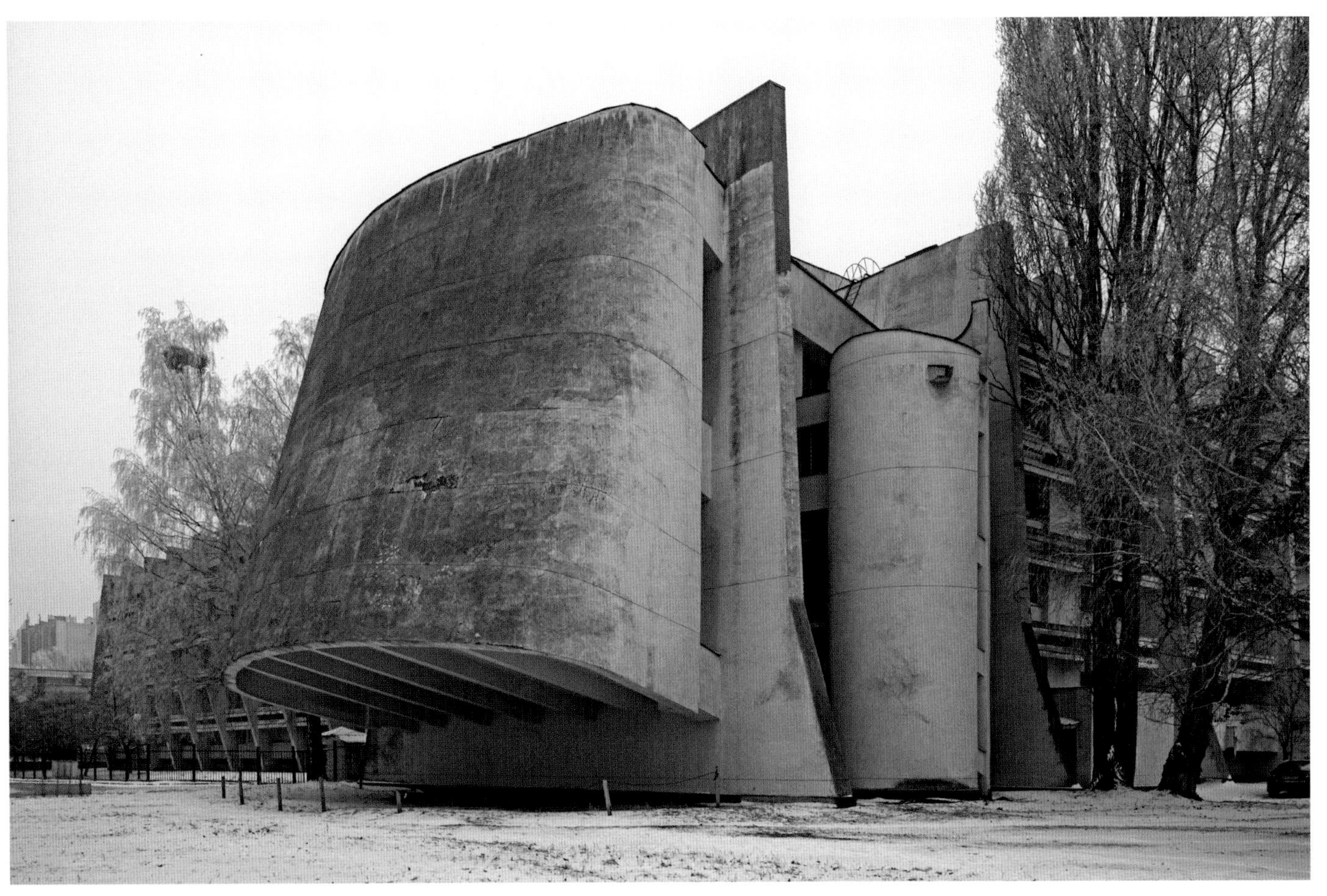

stages, with various faculty buildings finished in 1973, 1975, 1979, 1980 and 1989. However, the plan overestimated Soviet economic growth, and as a result much remained unbuilt. During the construction of the Faculty of Geography, the USSR collapsed, and the building was not completed until 2005. In the 2000s, the remaining land designated for campus expansion was controversially transferred for commercial development by the rector. Today, this modernist ensemble is surrounded and obscured by contemporary residential high-rises.

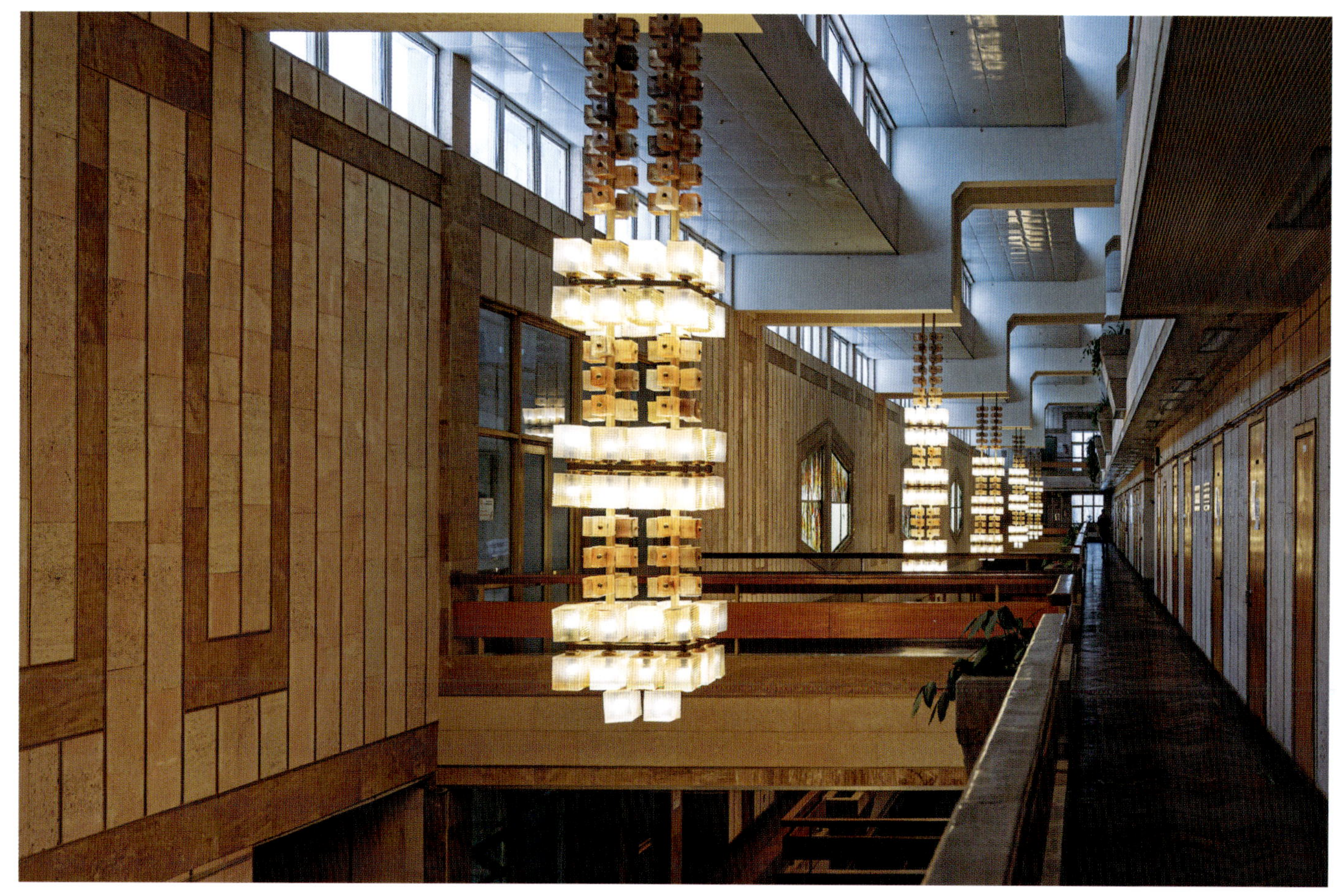

Faculty of Biology, Taras Shevchenko National University of Kyiv
1989

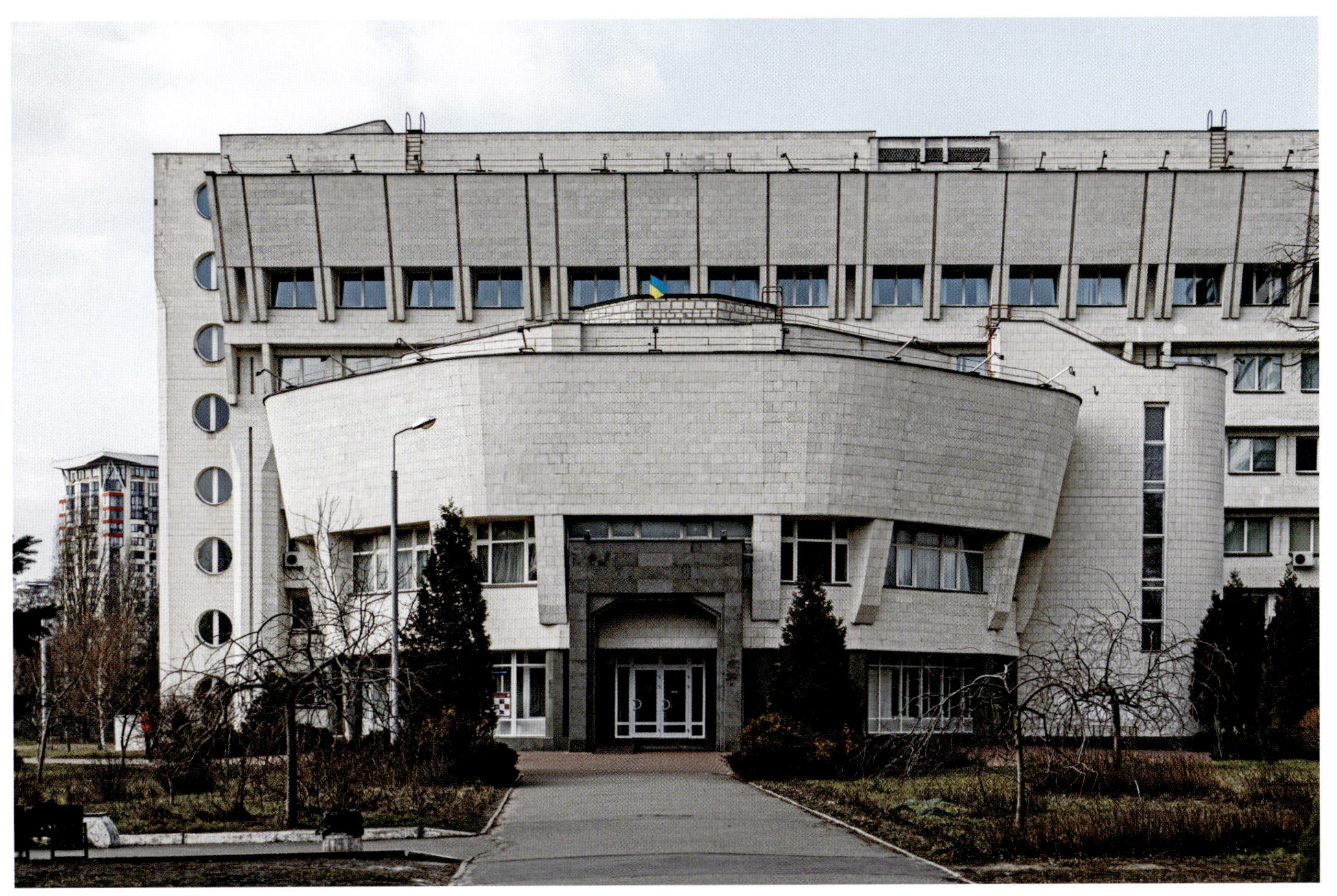

Faculty of Geography, Taras Shevchenko National University of Kyiv
2005

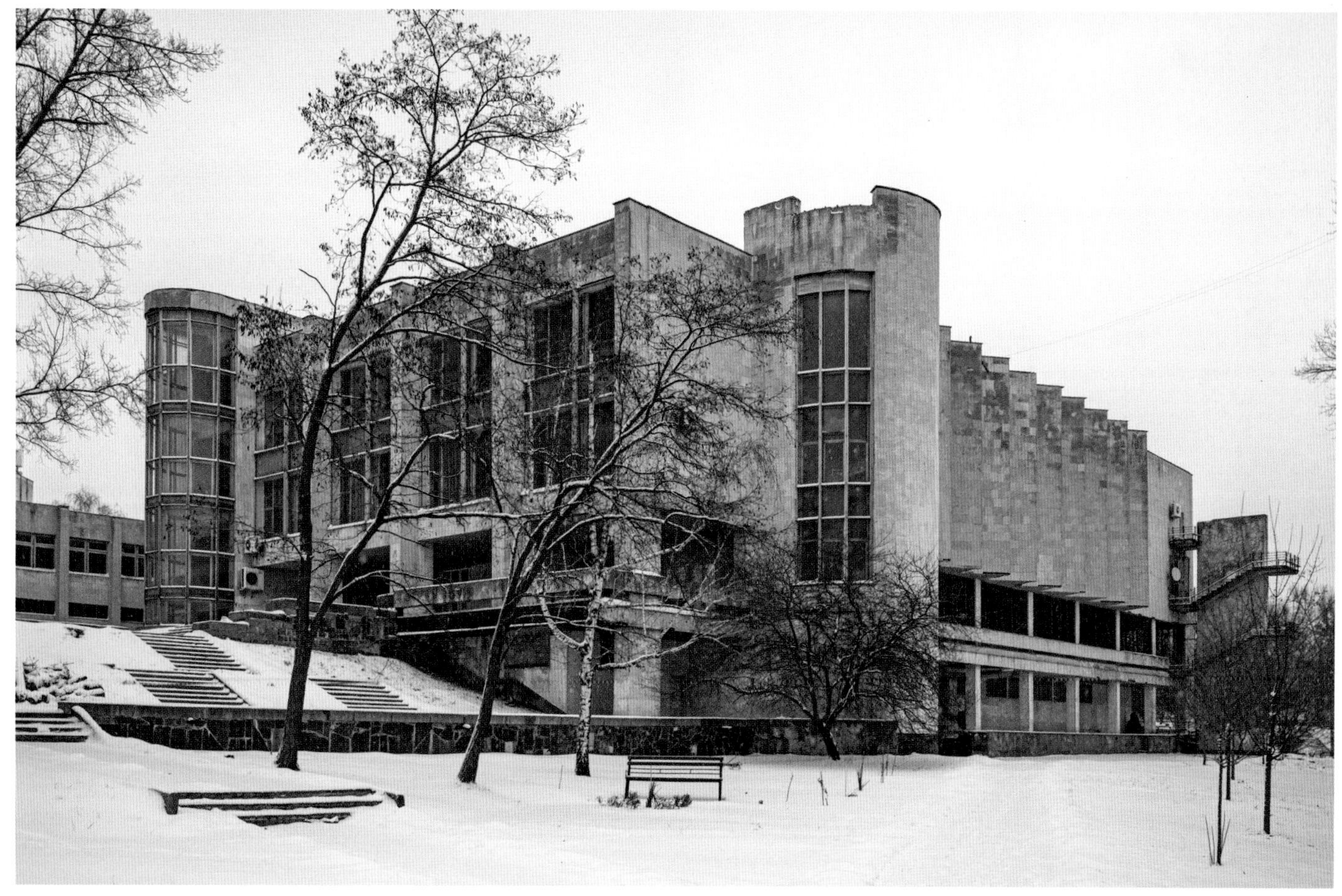

Igor Sikorsky Kyiv Polytechnic Institute
Kyiv
1975–85

Architects: Volodymyr Lykhovodov, Viktor Dovhaliuk, Oleksandr Dumchev, Viktor Sydorenko, Vladyslav Kriuchkov, et al.
Engineers: Eduard Nazarenko, Larysa Vovk, V. Nahornyi, E. Kunda, D. Hanelin, G. Alekseieva, V. Martynenko

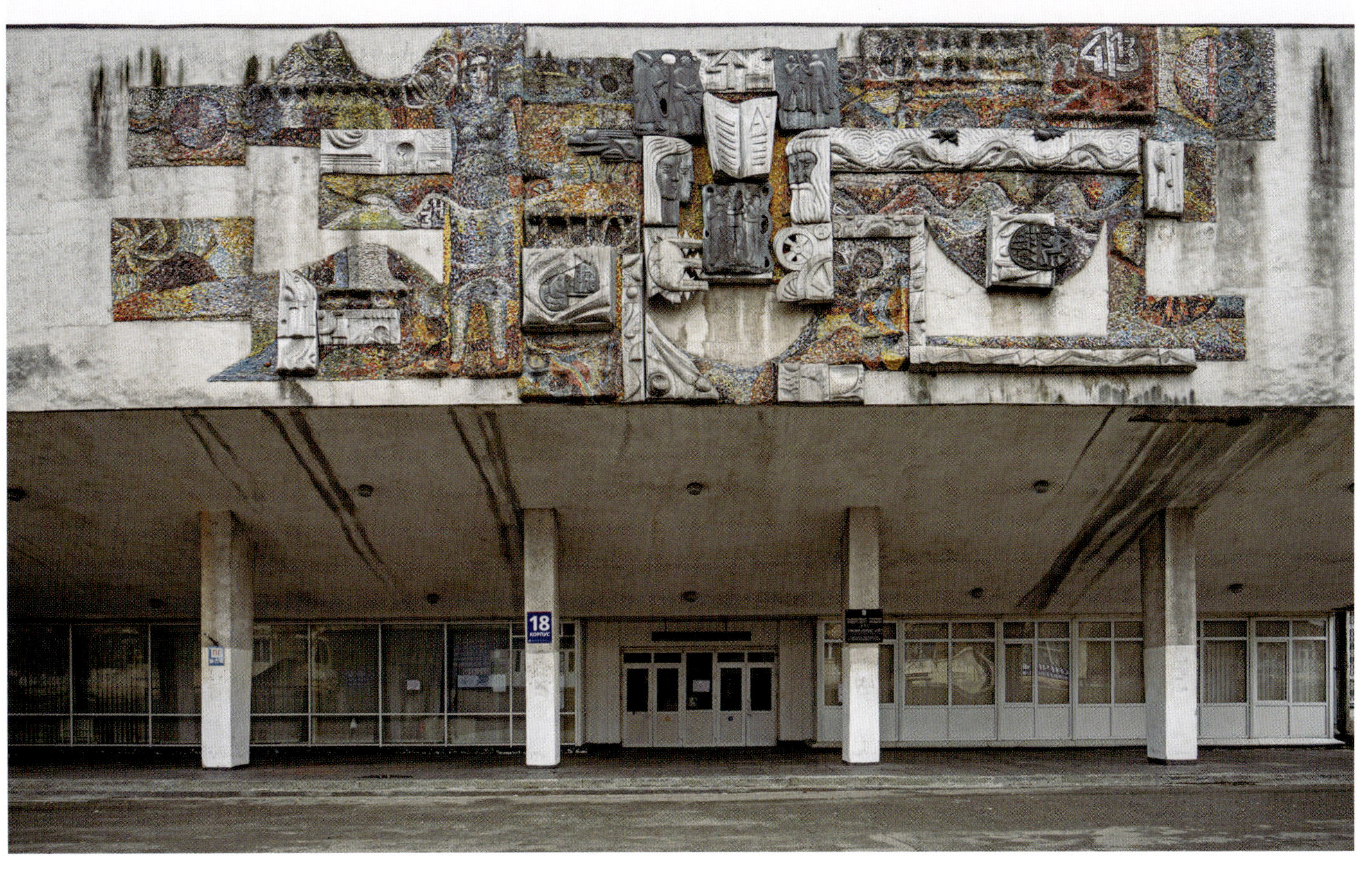

left: Canteen, Igor Sikorsky Kyiv Polytechnic Institute
1985
overleaf: Palace of Culture, Igor Sikorsky Kyiv Polytechnic Institute
1984

above: Building No.18, Igor Sikorsky Kyiv Polytechnic Institute
1980
Artist: Fedir Tetianych

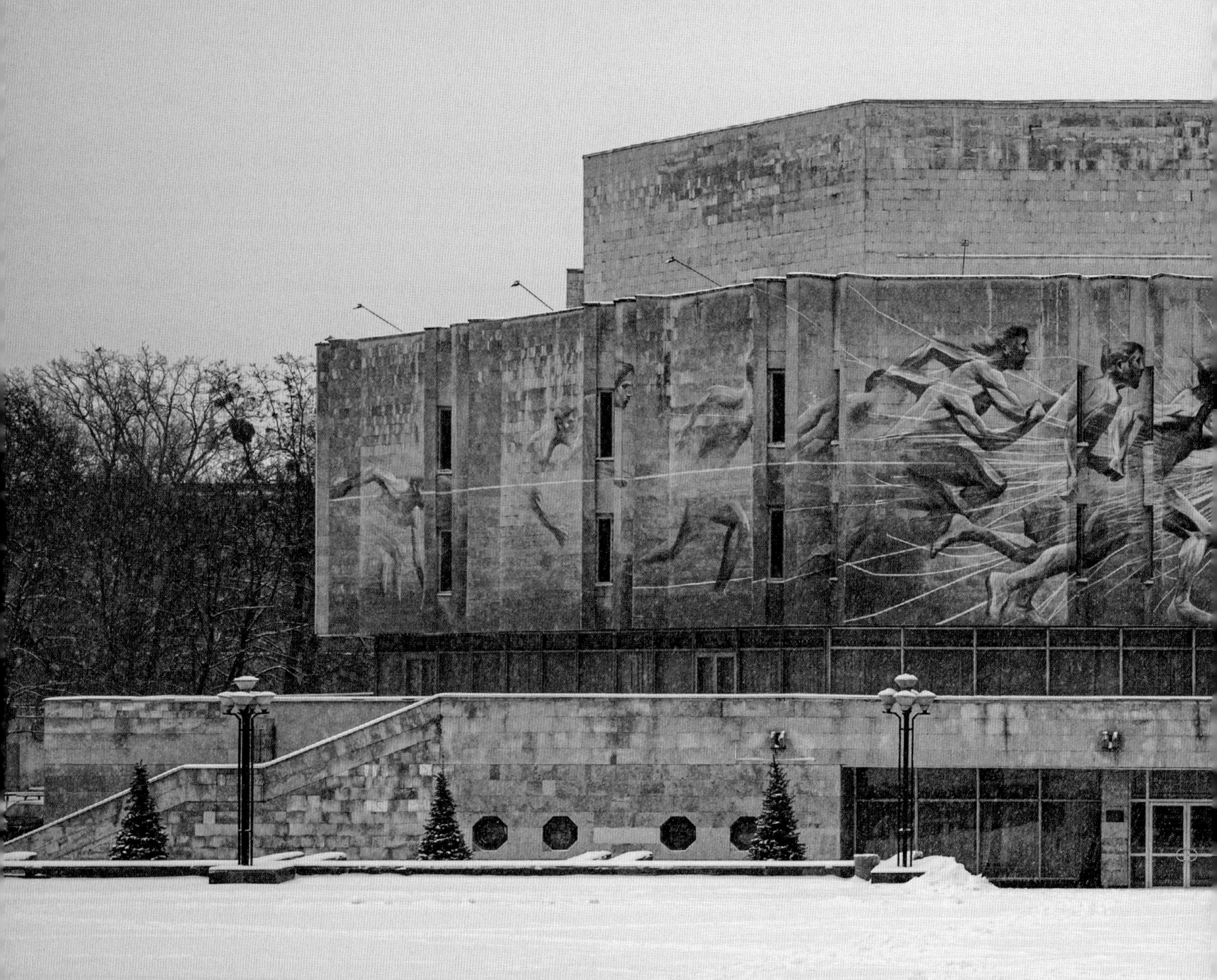

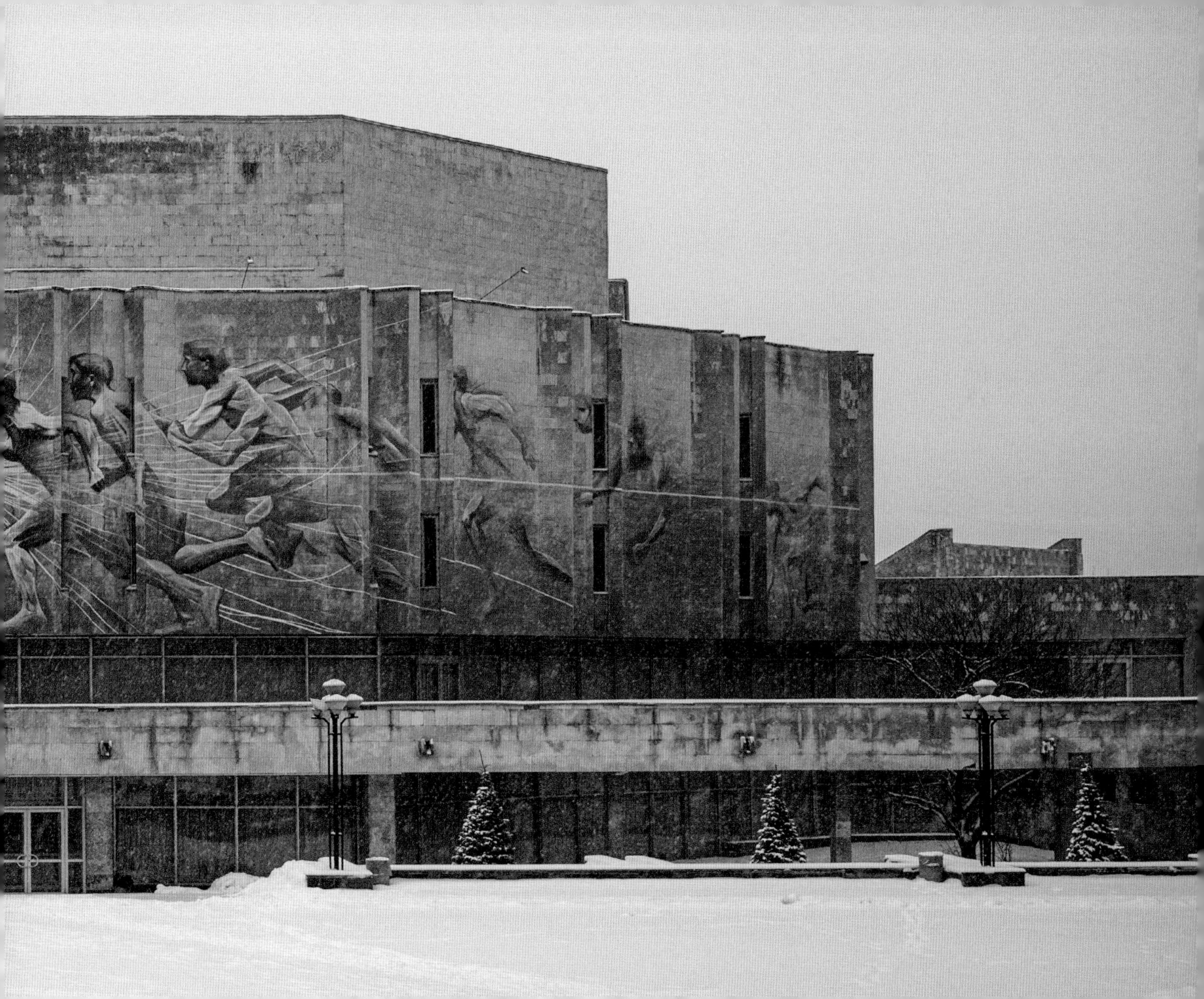

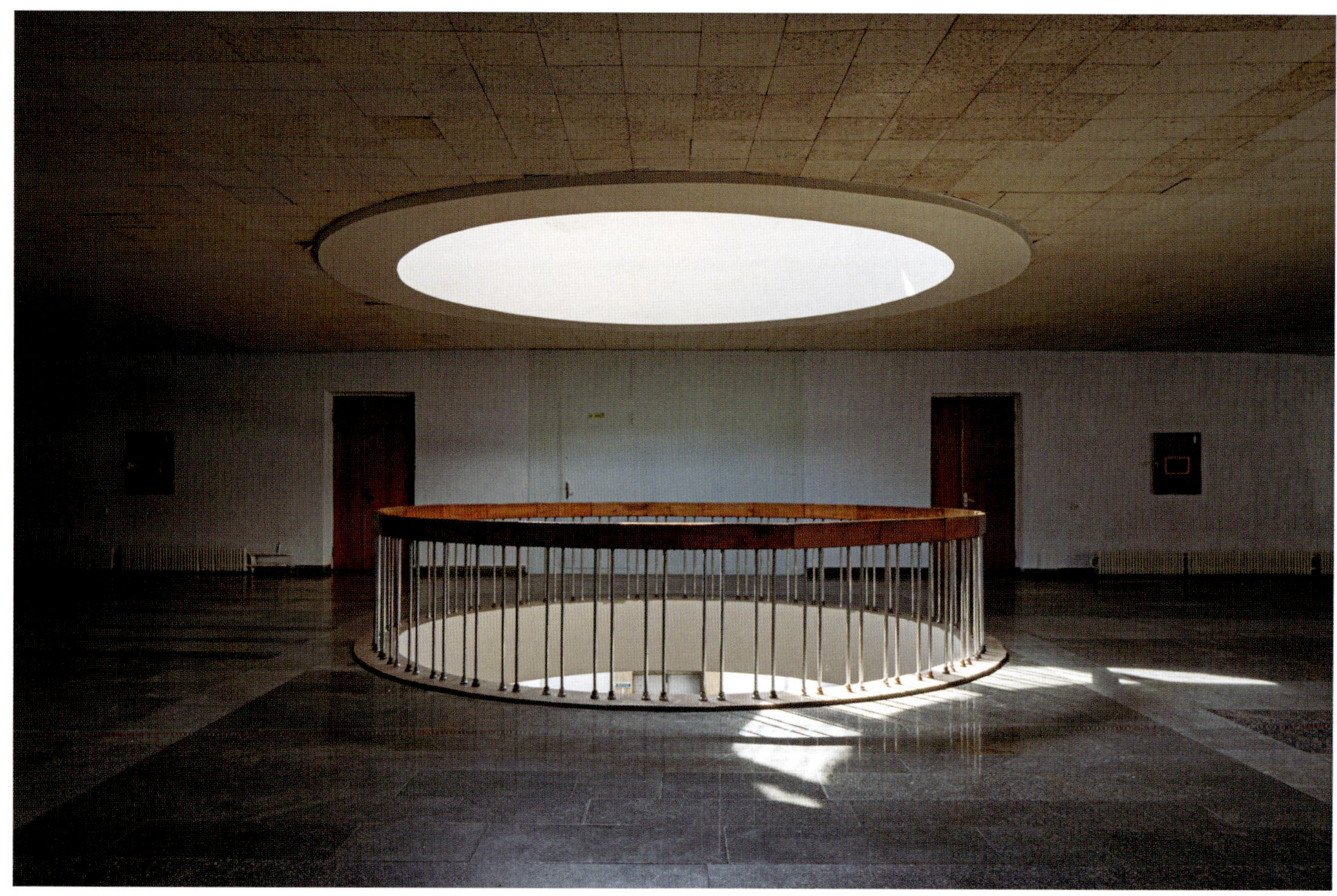

Building No.20, Igor Sikorsky Kyiv Polytechnic Institute
1978–80

Designed to meet the growing needs of one of Ukraine's leading technical universities, the new campus buildings were constructed according to a 1974 masterplan. Arranged in compositional units, they created a cohesive modernist ensemble, the largest of its kind in Kyiv.

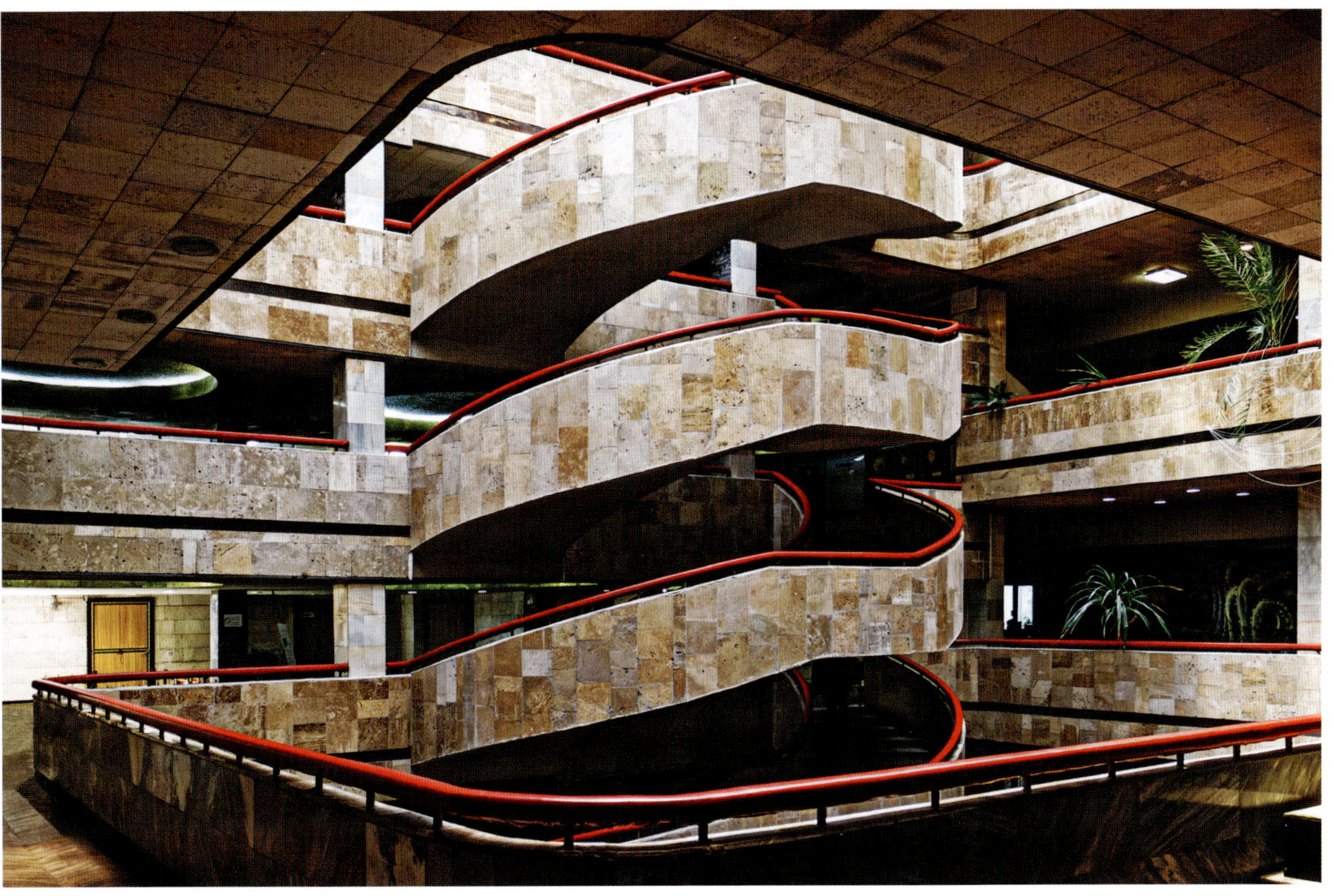

Library, Igor Sikorsky Kyiv Polytechnic Institute
1980

In recent years, many of the buildings have been used as locations for contemporary murals, including the Palace of Culture, a practice that compromises the integrity of the architectural ensemble that earned the Ukrainian State Prize for Architecture in 1988.

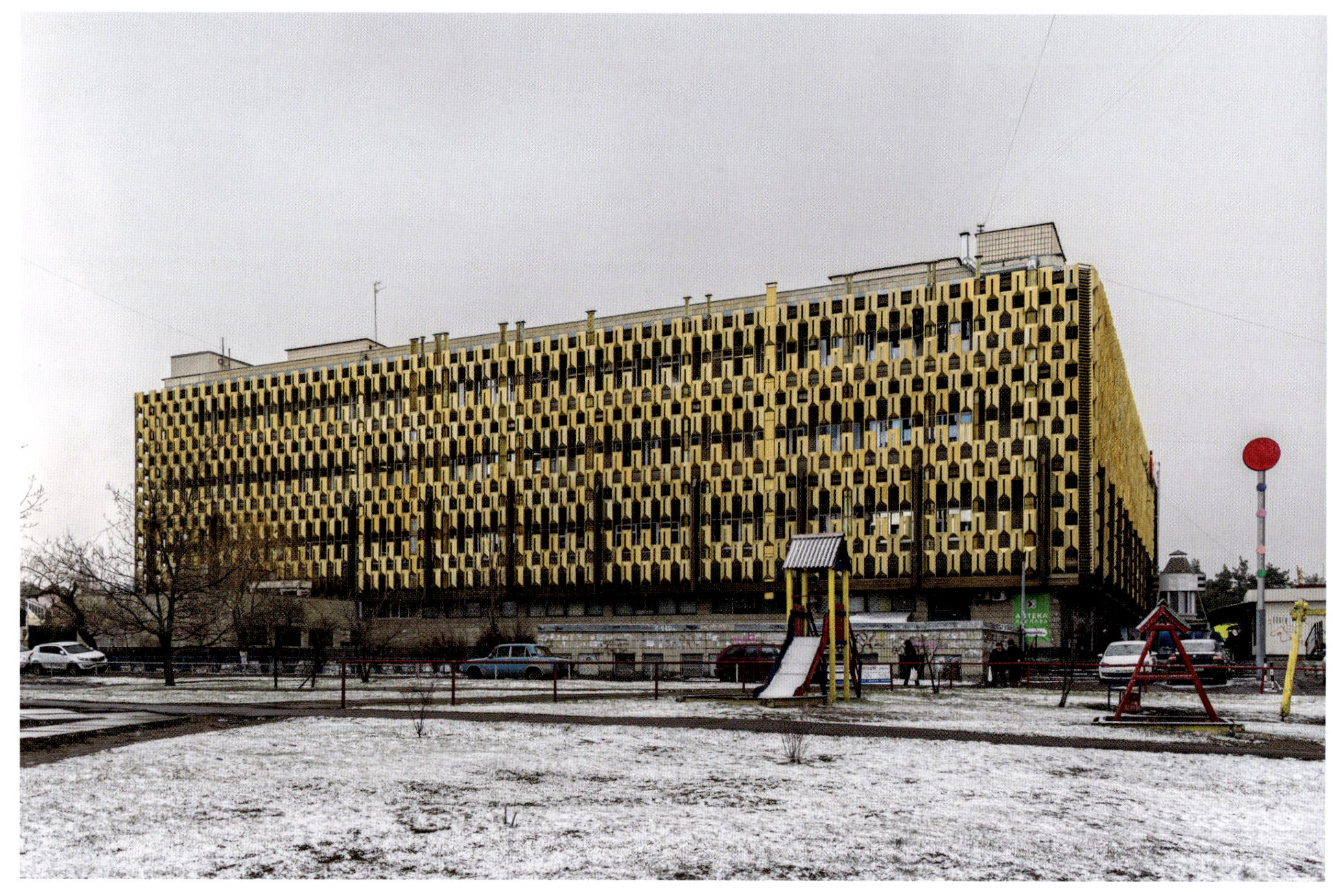

Children's World
Kyiv
1976–87
Architects: Volodymyr Zalutskyi, Yurii Borodkin
Engineer: V. Kuziakiv

Children's World was a famous Soviet chain of department stores. In 1987, its Kyiv branch opened in this new building, notable for its hinged facade made from gilded and perforated aluminium panels. In the 1990s, it was privatised and converted into a typical mall.

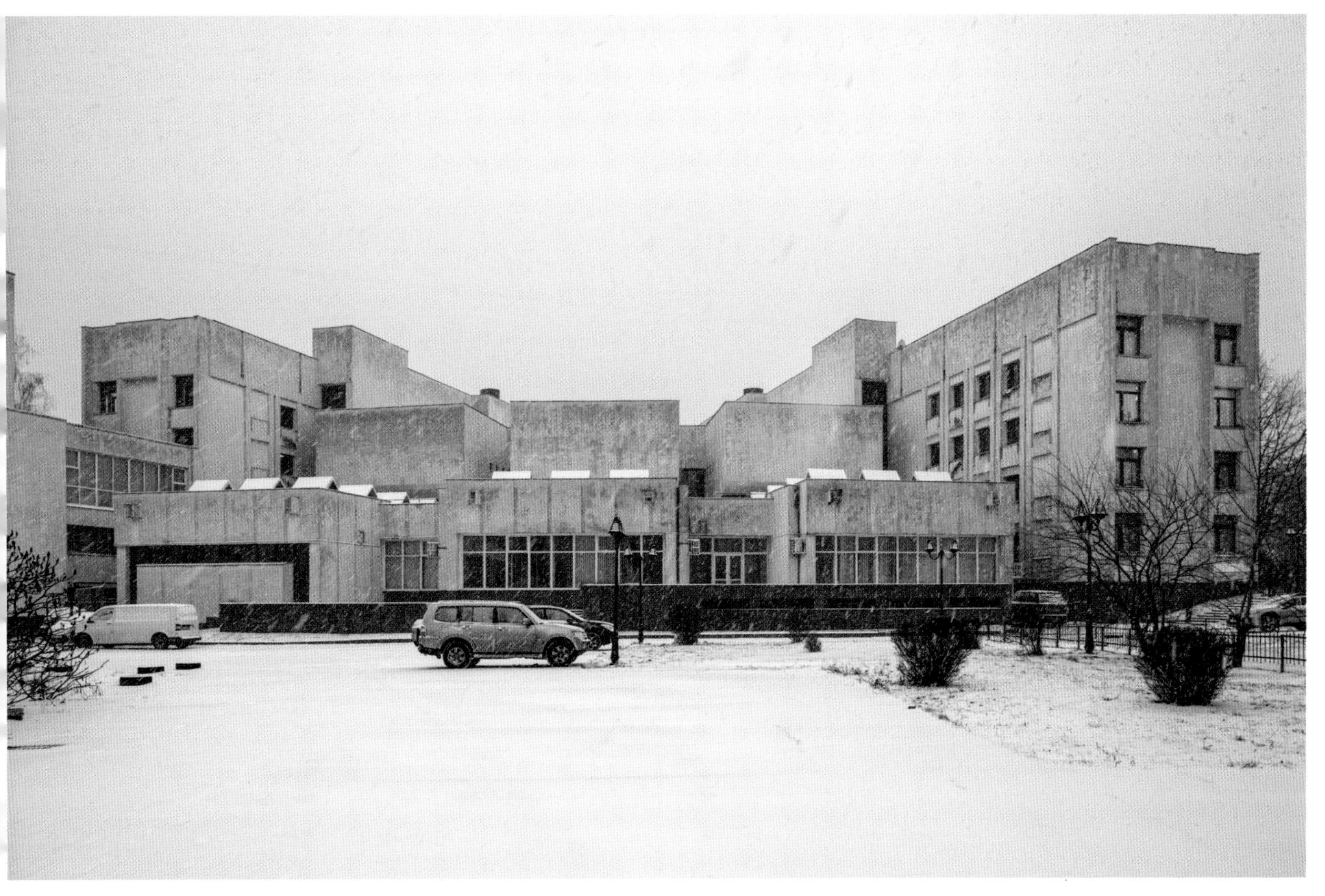

Institute of International Relations and Institute of Journalism,
Taras Shevchenko National University of Kyiv
(formerly the Kyiv Higher Party School)
Kyiv
1979–86

Architects: Ihor Shpara, Yanos Vigh, Heorhii Dukhovychnyi,
Oleksandr Nosenko, Oleksandr Tamarov, Oleksandr Klishchuk
Engineer: Ivan Onufrienko

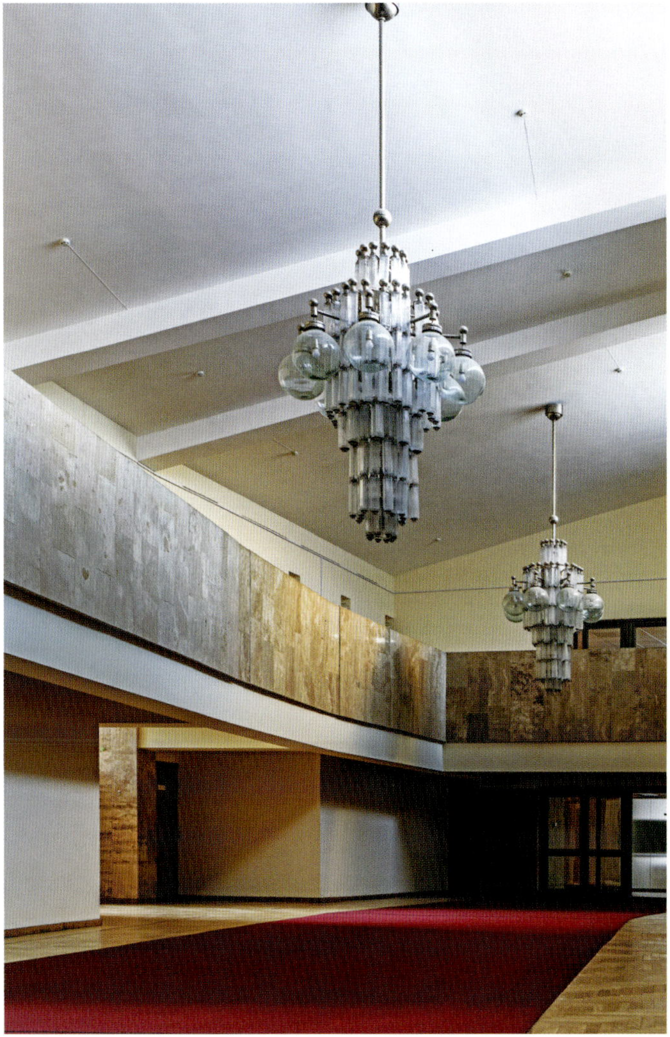

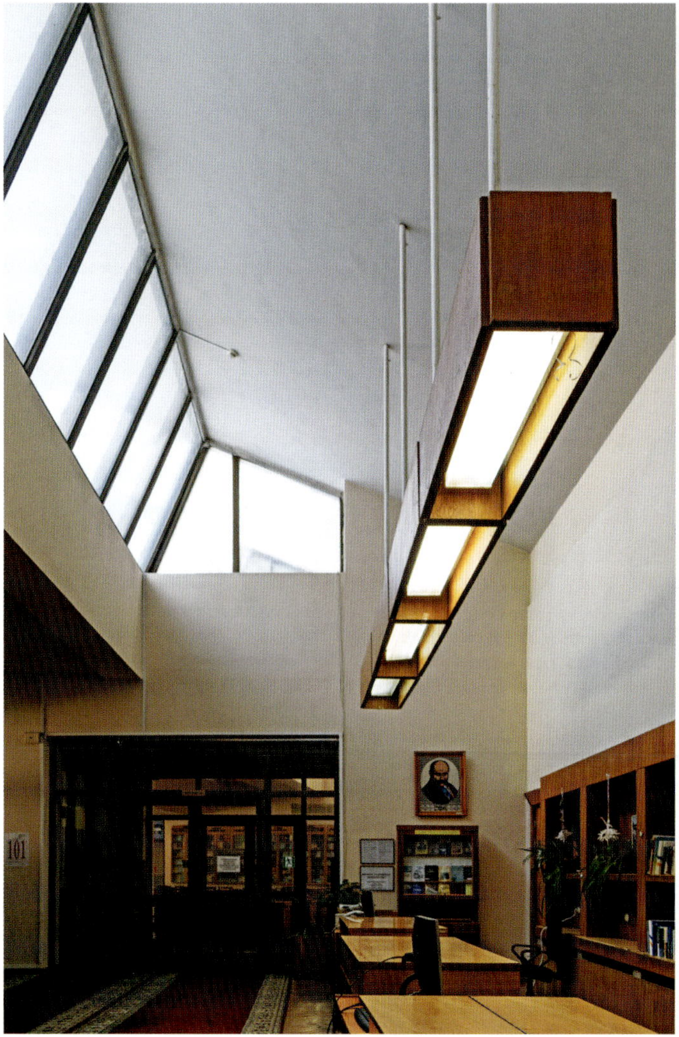

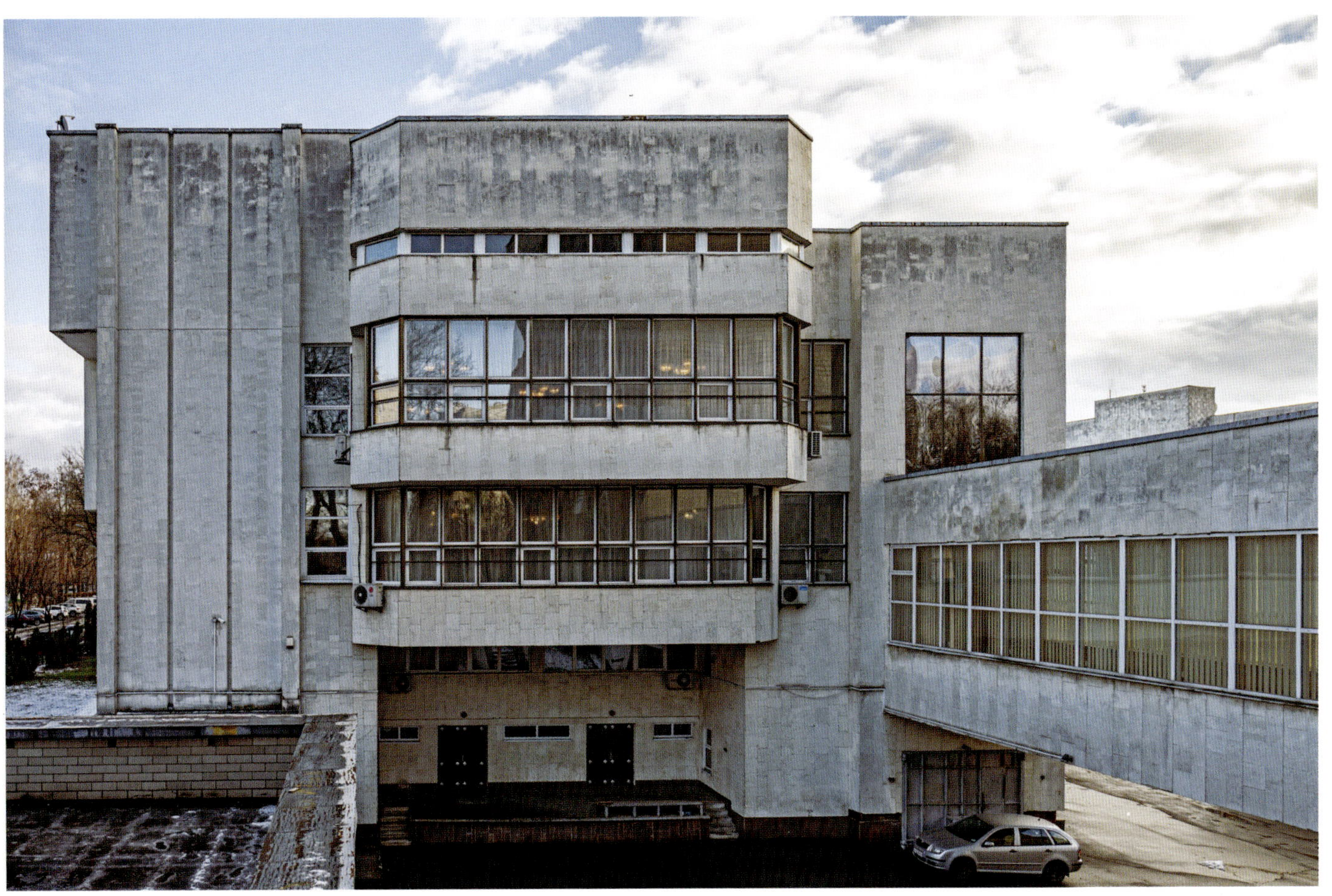

The Higher Party School was a higher educational institution of the USSR originally founded in 1946, and used for the training of leading trade-union and party officials. The complex included lecture halls, a library and a dining hall, connected to the adjacent dormitory by a covered overhead walkway. The facade, clad in white Crimean limestone, gave the monumental structure an elegant appearance. In 1991, the complex became part of the Taras Shevchenko National University of Kyiv.

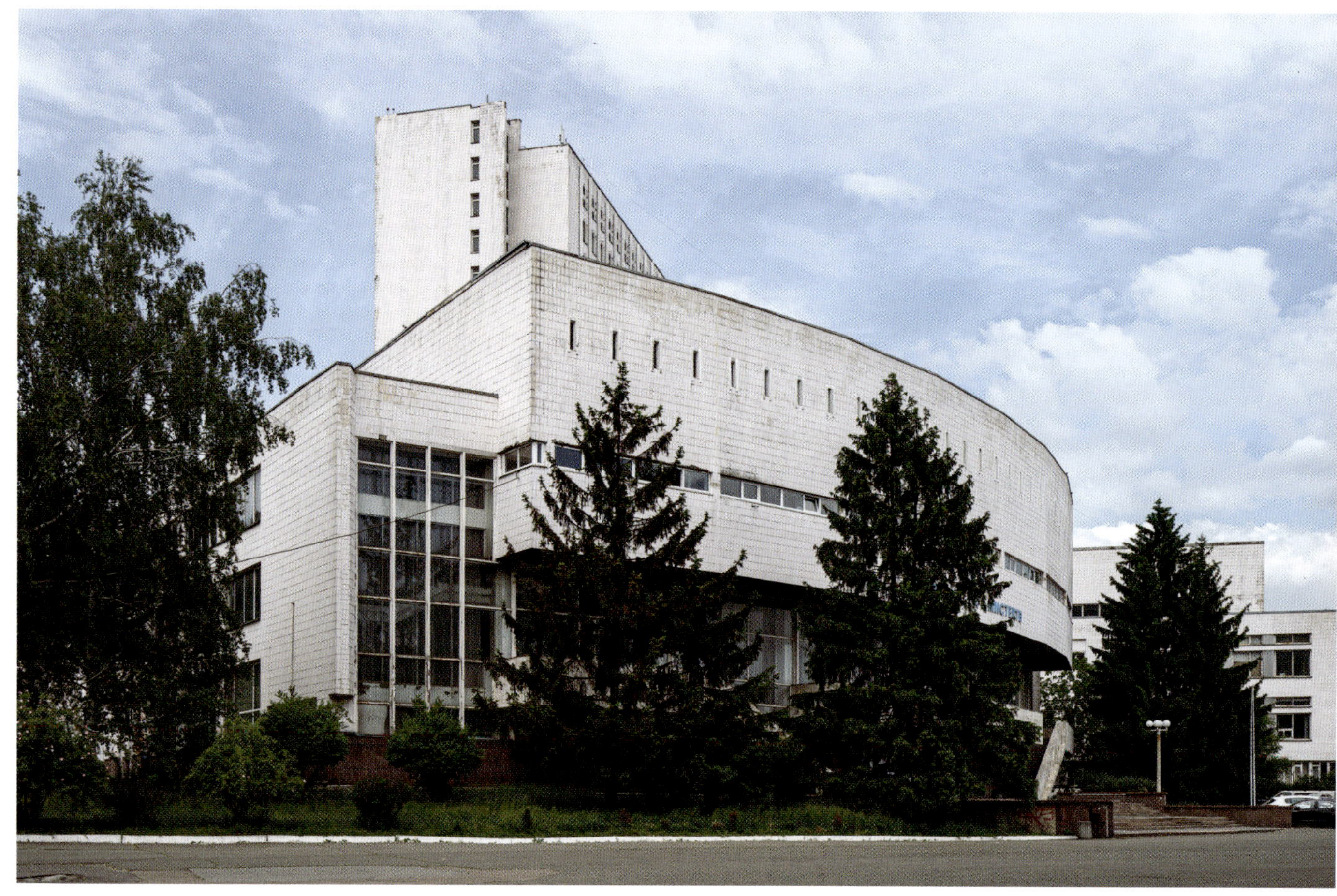

Palace of Culture, Kyiv Aviation Institute
Kyiv
1979

Architects and artists incorporated numerous artworks into the Institute buildings, employing a variety of techniques and materials. The campus features paintings, mosaics, bas-reliefs, and panels made from metal, wood, concrete, smalto, ceramics and leatherette.

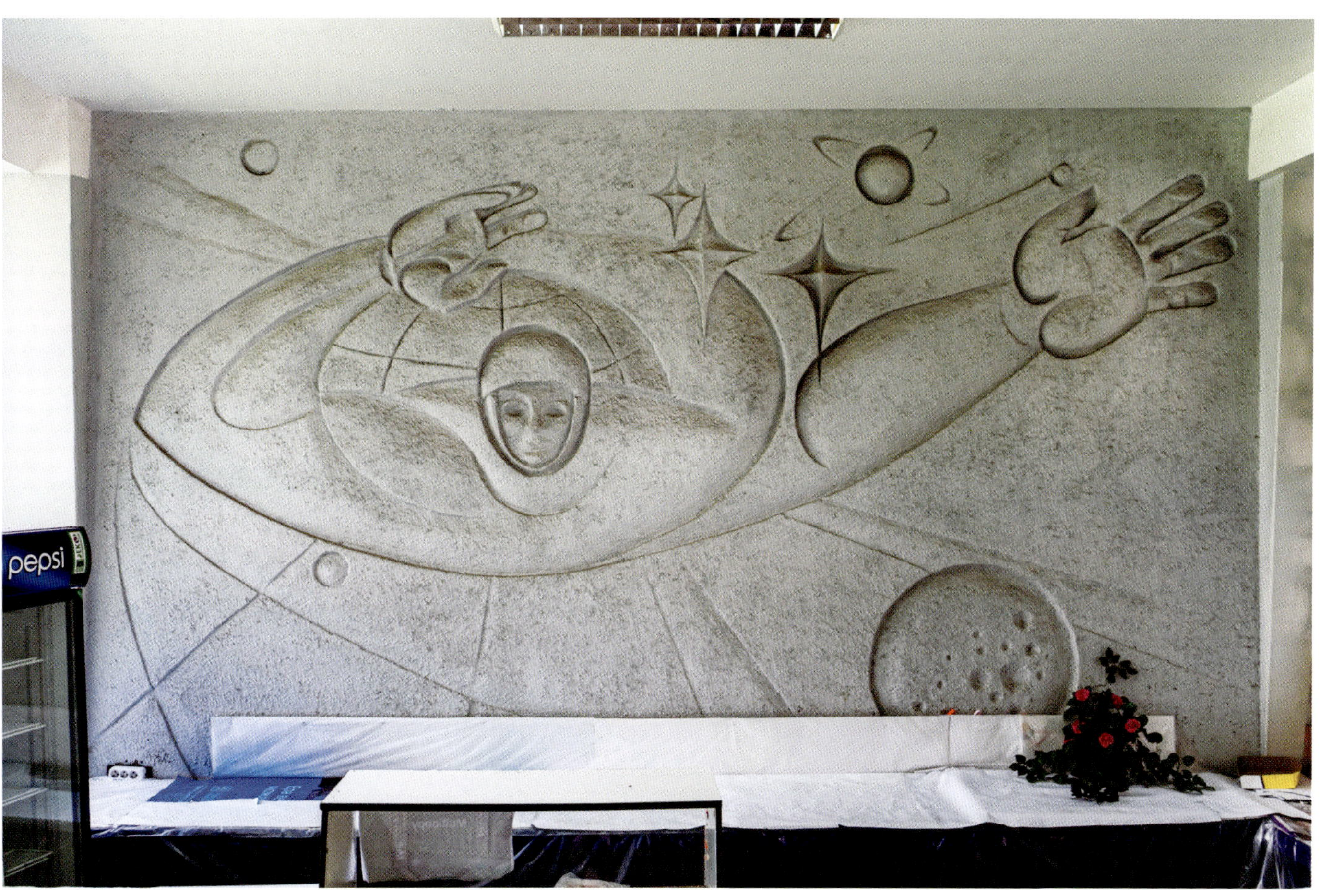

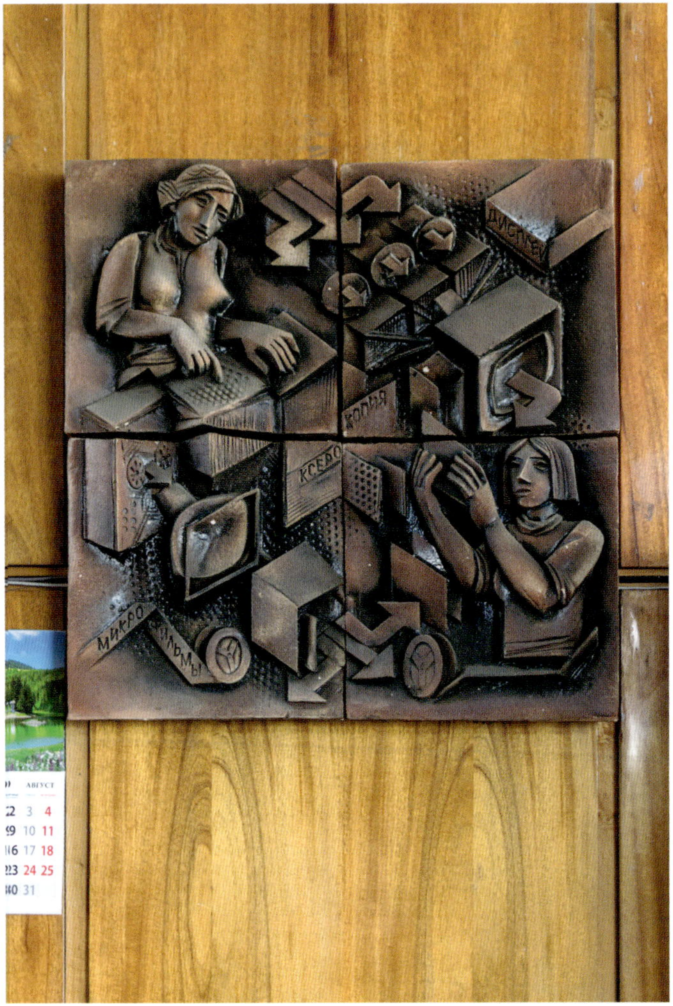

МИКРО
ФИЛЬМЫ
КСЕРО
КОПИЯ

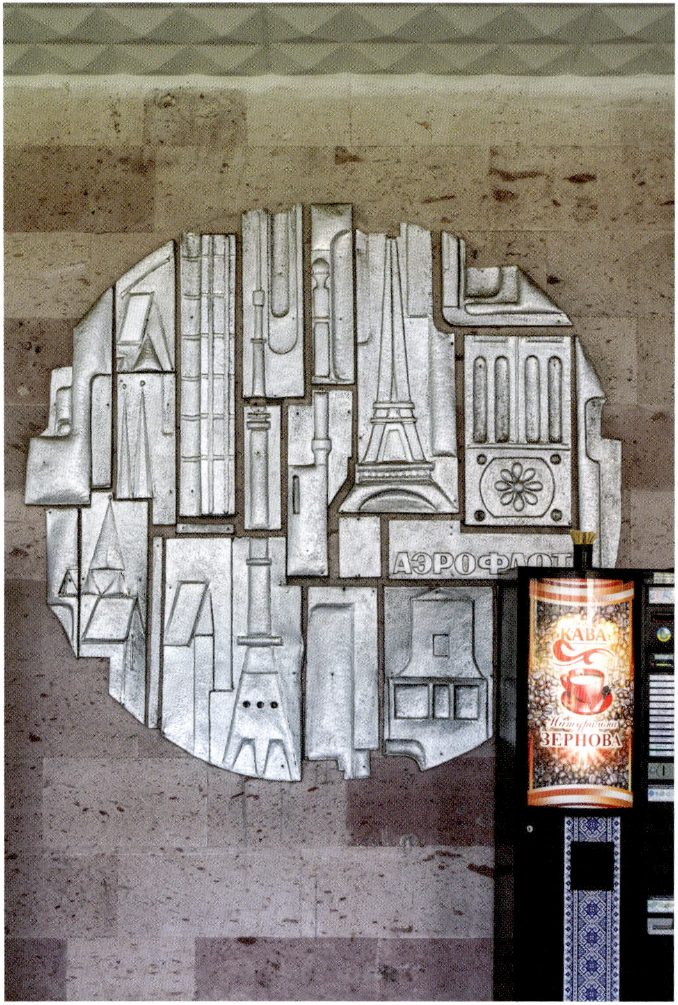

АЭРОФЛОТ
КАВА
Натуральна
ЗЕРНОВА

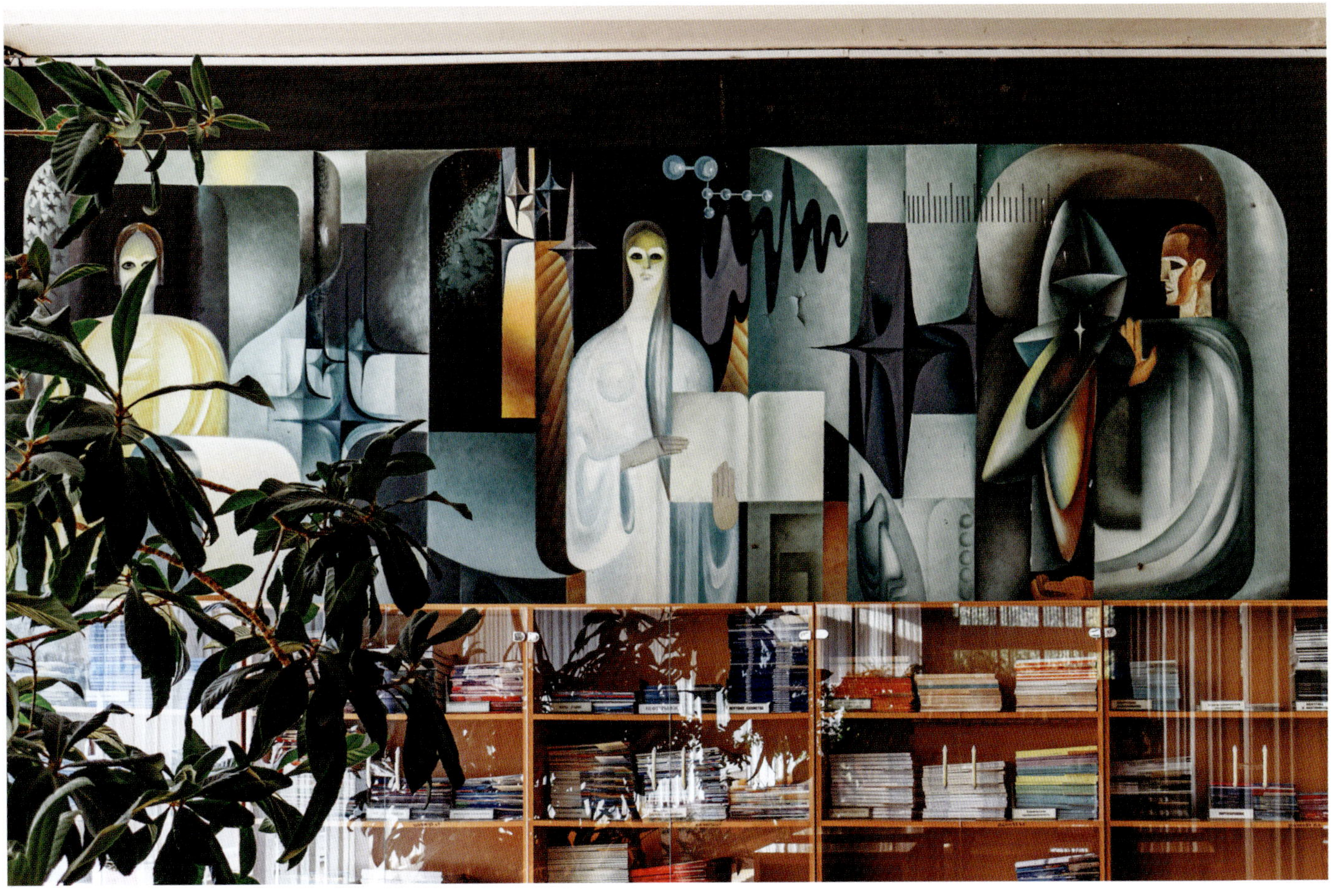

overleaf: 'Salut' Hotel
Kyiv
1979–84
Architects: A. Miletskyi, N. Slogotska, V. Shevchenko
Engineers: Ya. Shames, S. Syrota, E. Furmanov

'Salut' was originally planned in 1965 as a panelled high-rise hotel for the adjacent Palace of Pioneers (p108). After decades of design revisions its final, now-iconic cantilevered form was constructed from reinforced concrete.

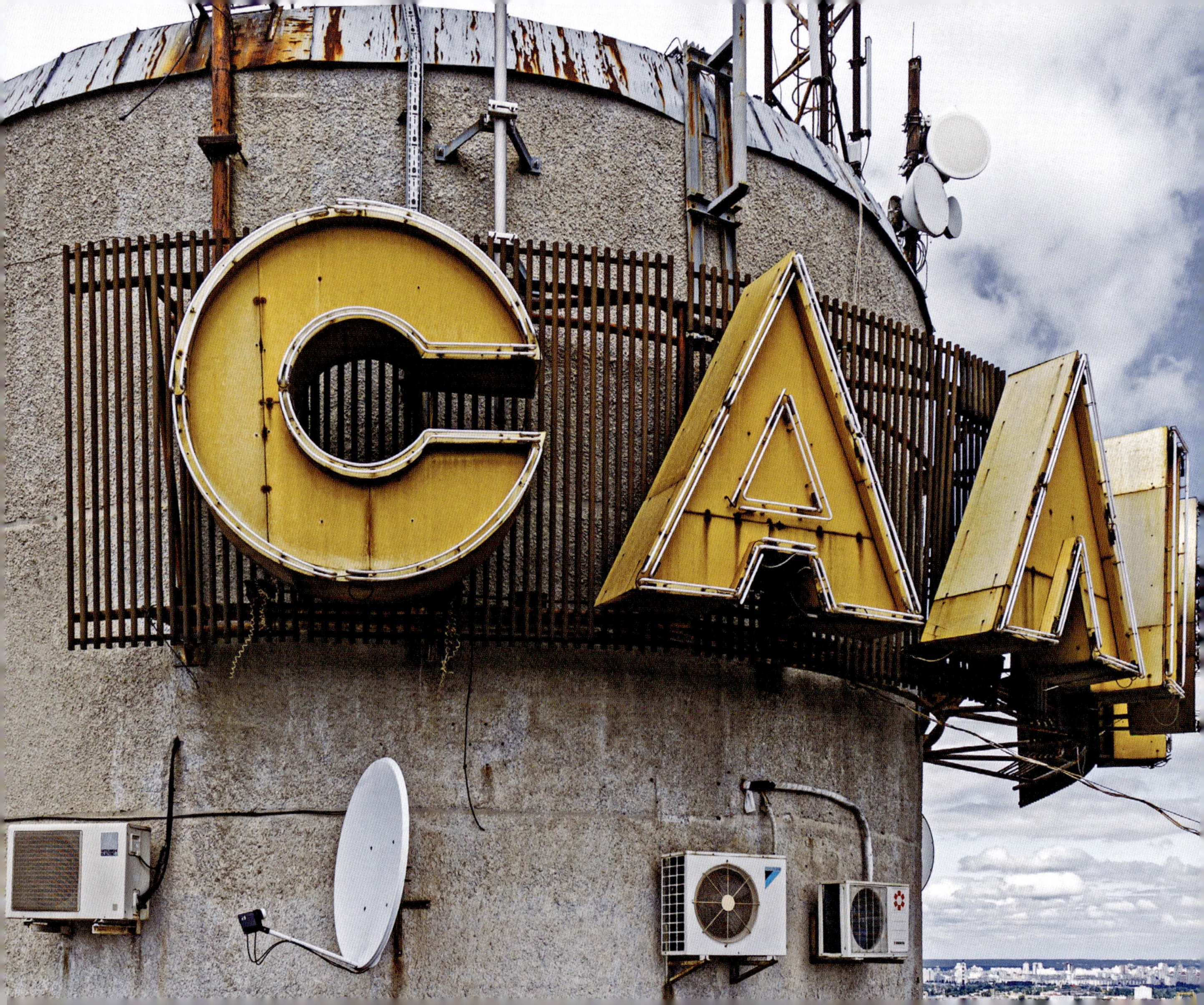

CAM

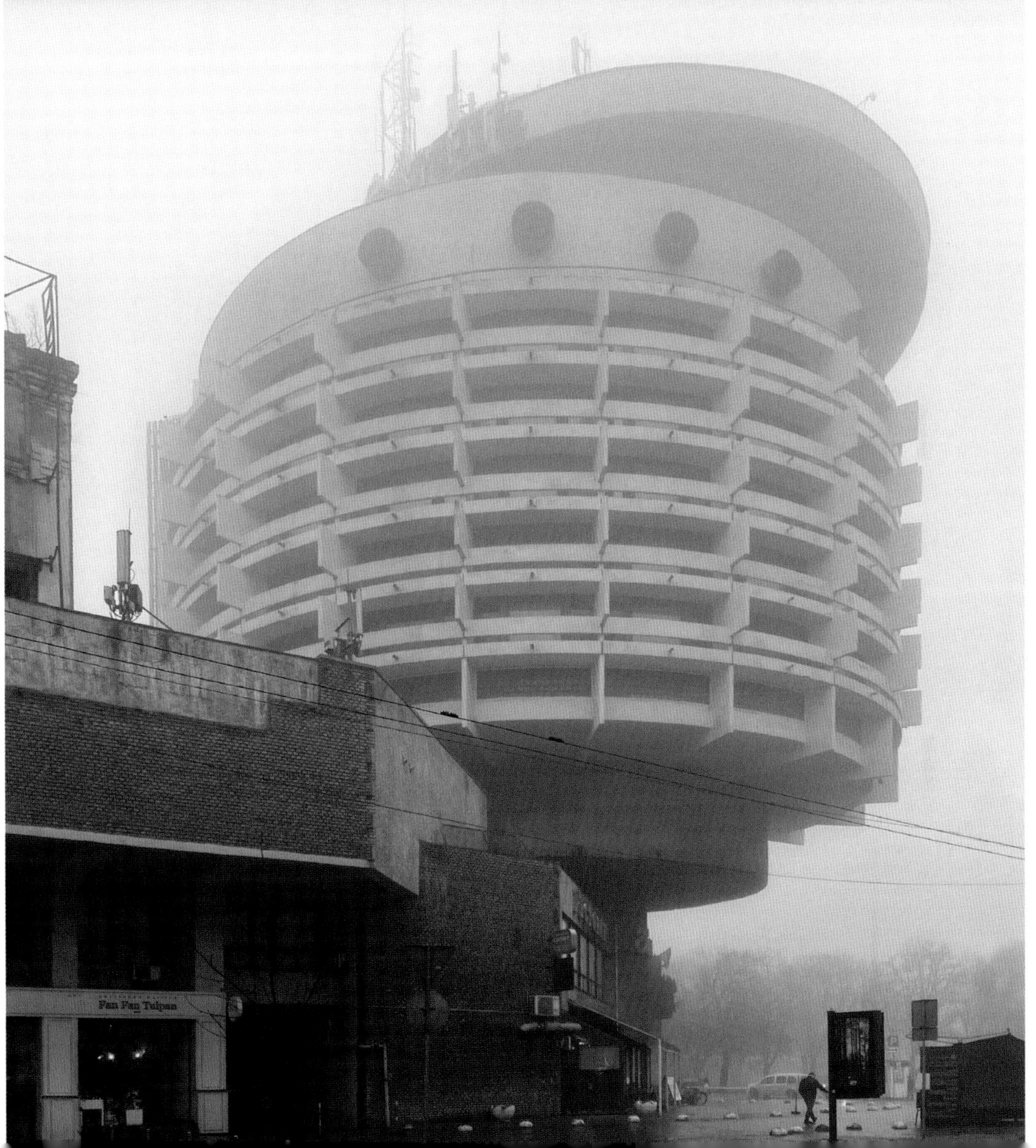
Pan Pan Tulipan

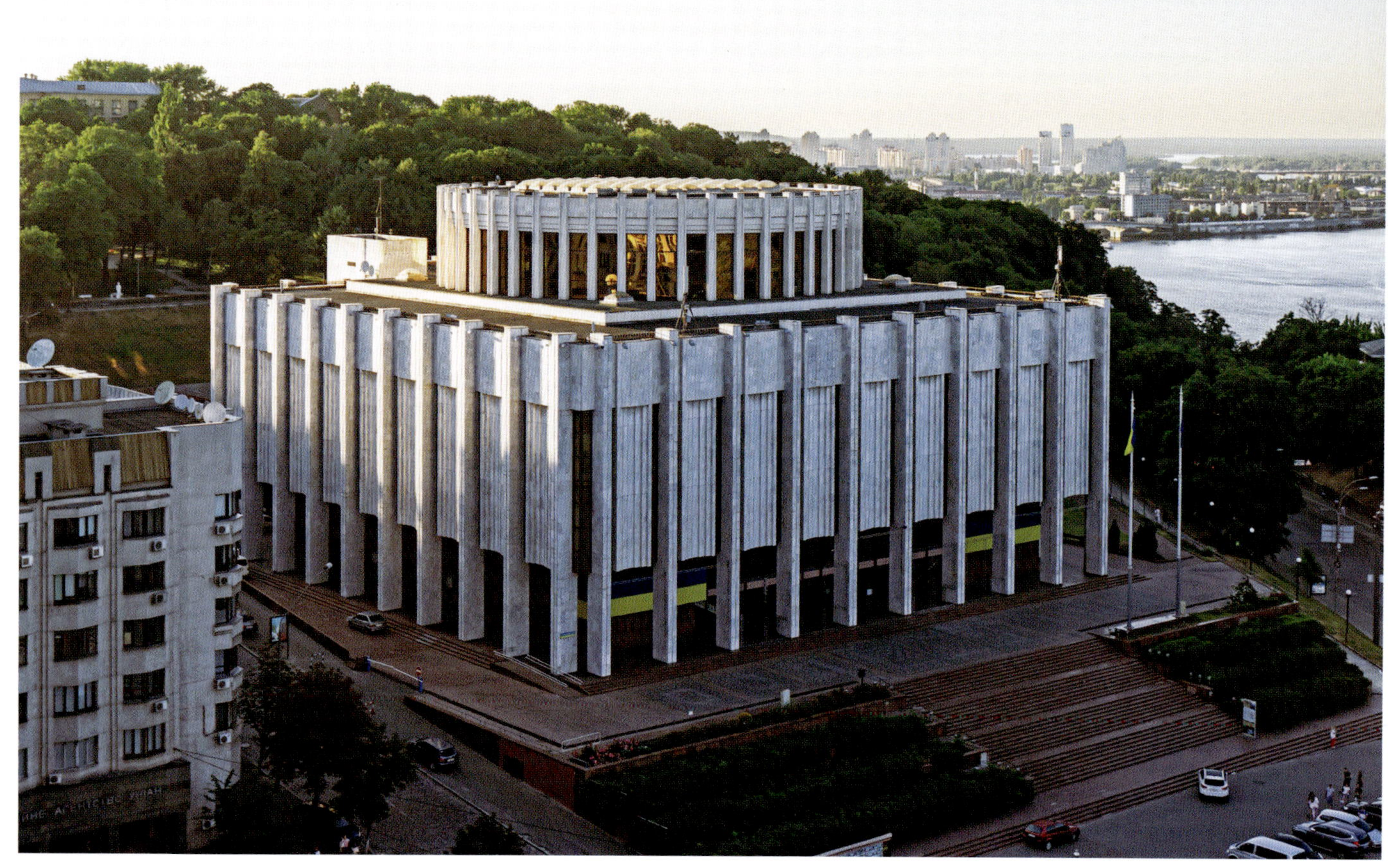

Ukrainian House (formerly the Lenin Museum)
Kyiv
1978–82
Architects: Vadym Hopkalo, Vadym Hrechyna, Leonid Filenko,
Volodymyr Kolomiiets

Engineers: Leonid Linovych, V. Koval, Valerii Barulenkov
Interior architect: Anatolii Ihnashchenko
Artists: Anatolii Haidamaka, Vitalii Miahkov, Larysa Mishchenko,
Valentyn Borysenko, Viktor Hryhorov, Volodymyr Priadka,
Olena Vladimirova

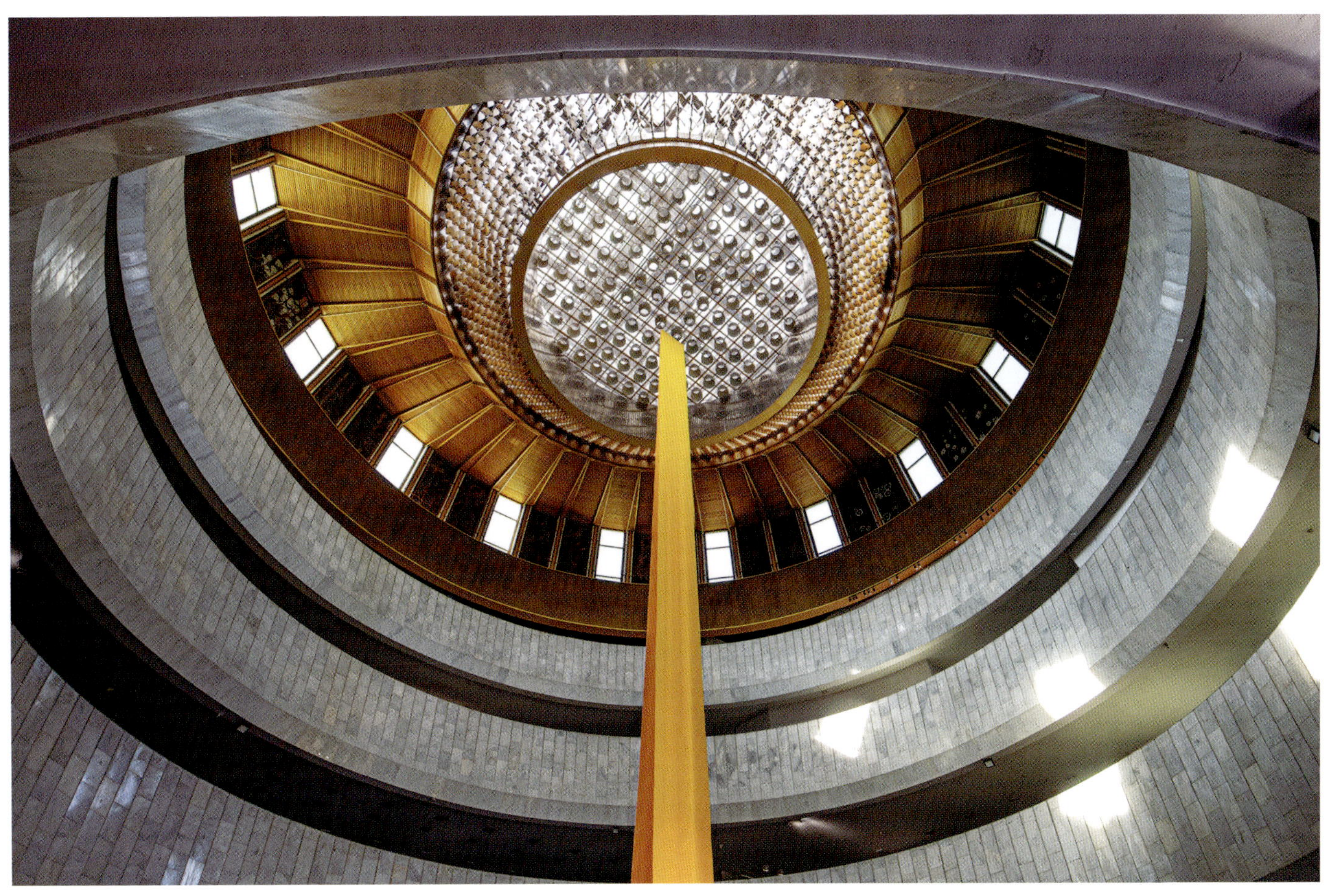

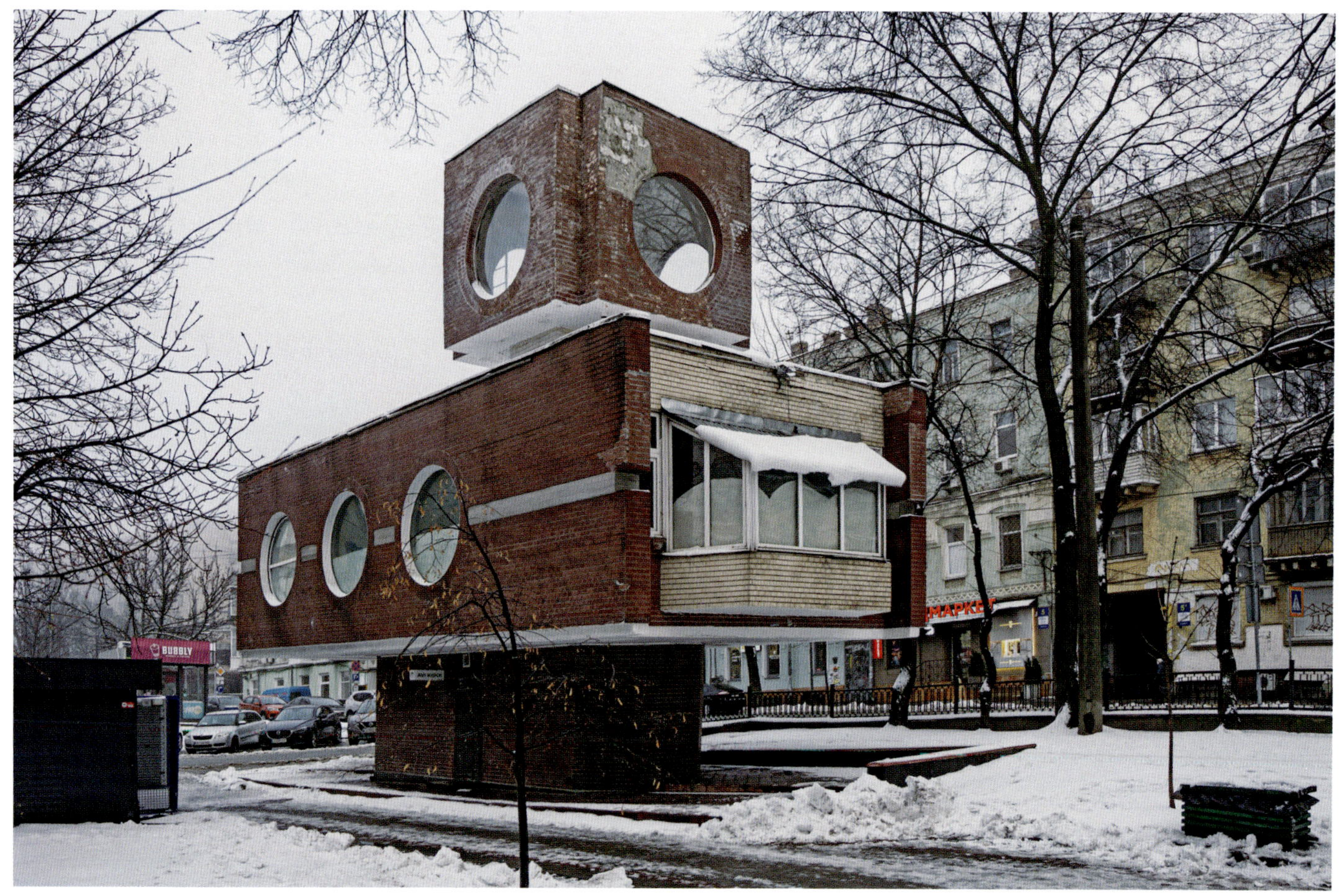

Tramway Dispatch Building
Kyiv
1982
Architects: Yanos Vigh, Oleksandr Klishchuk,
Mykola Levandovskyi, Iryna Snihur

This building originally served the tram loop at Lvivska Square. In 1996, the route between the square and Starovokzalna terminus (p158) was closed to create more space for cars. After losing its function, the building has alternated between being vacant and used as a restaurant.

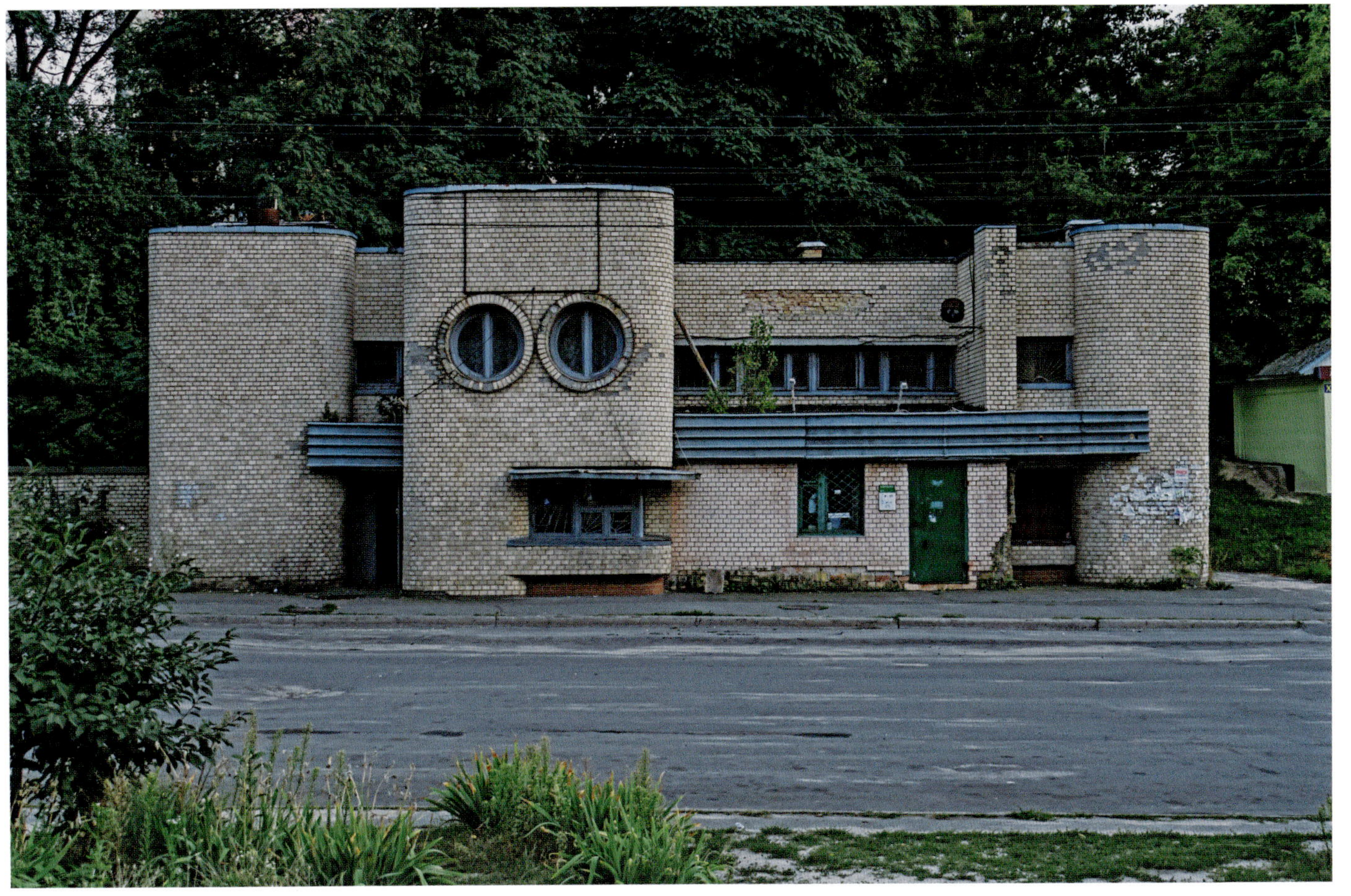

Trolleybus Dispatch Building
Kyiv
1980s

This and similar dispatch buildings were constructed following the
expansion of trolleybus routes in Kyiv during the 1980s. However, with
the later adoption of GPS navigation systems, the buildings became
redundant. This particular one is now used by drivers as a rest stop.

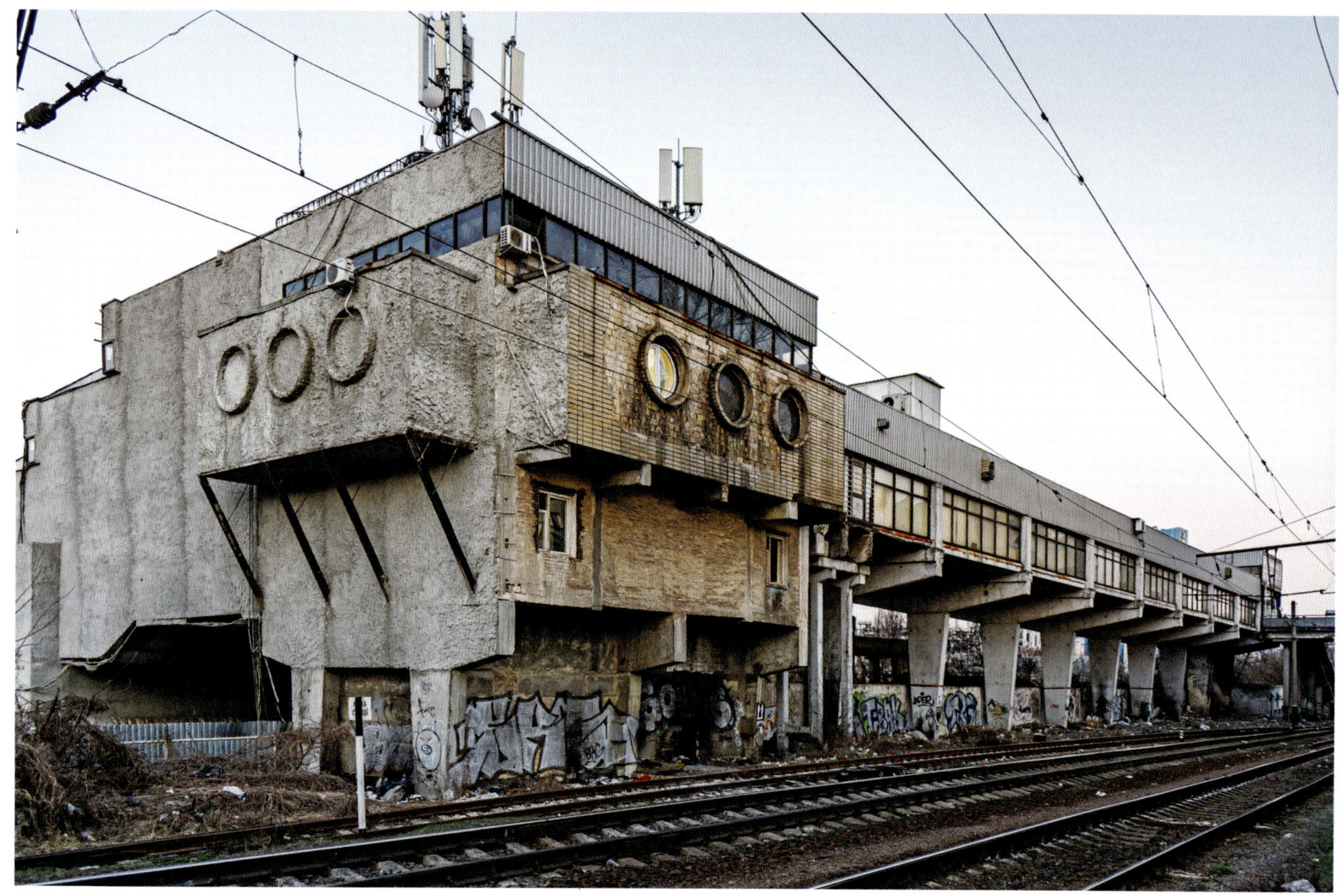

Elevated walkway, Central Railway Station
Kyiv
1988–89
Architect: Serhii Babushkin

With the emergence of capitalism this walkway connecting the Starovokzalna tram terminus with the Central Railway Station quickly transformed into an impromptu shopping corridor, necessitating its structural reinforcement to support the storage of goods.

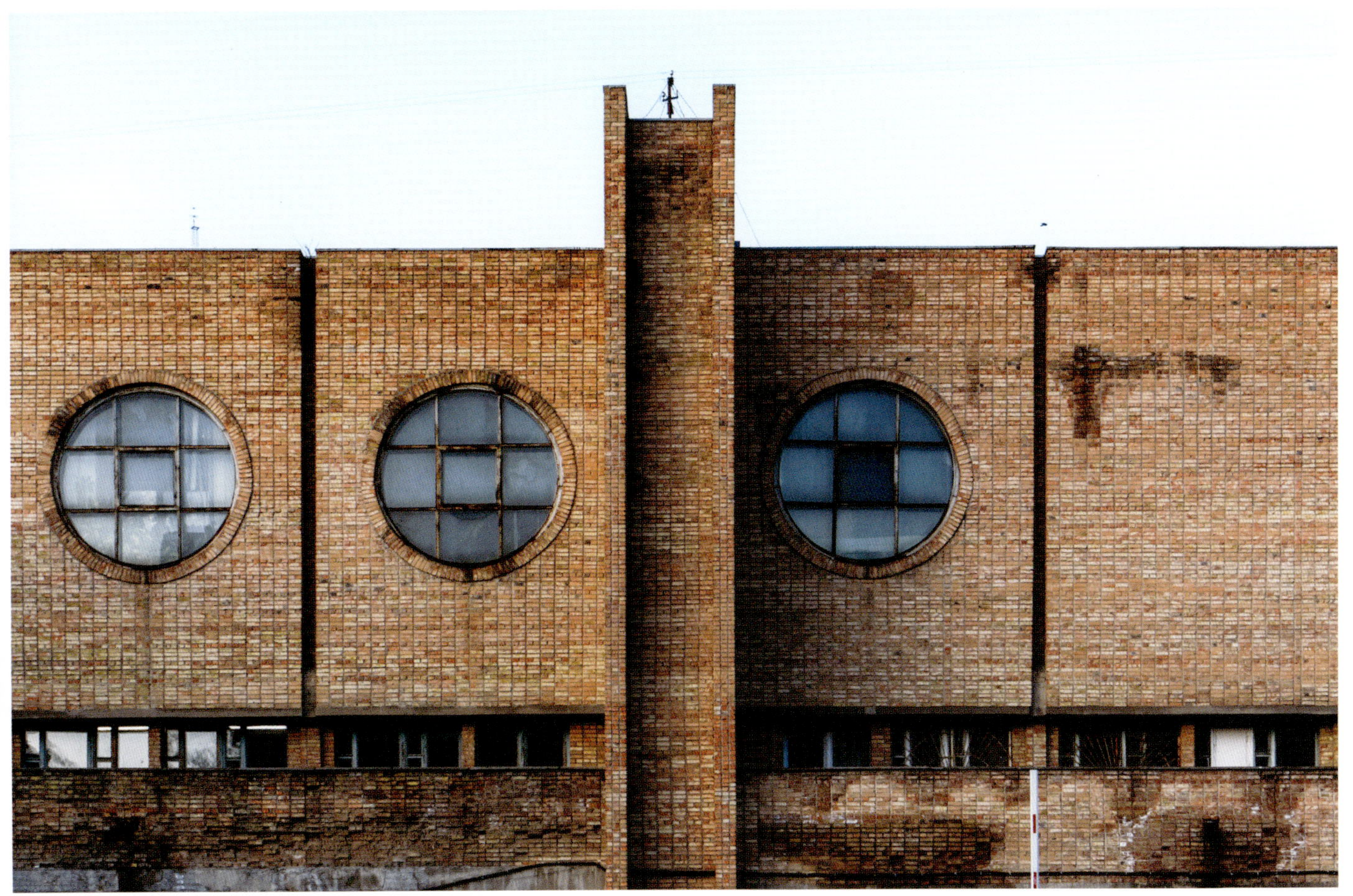

Utility Services Building, Oleksandrivska Hospital
Kyiv
1980s

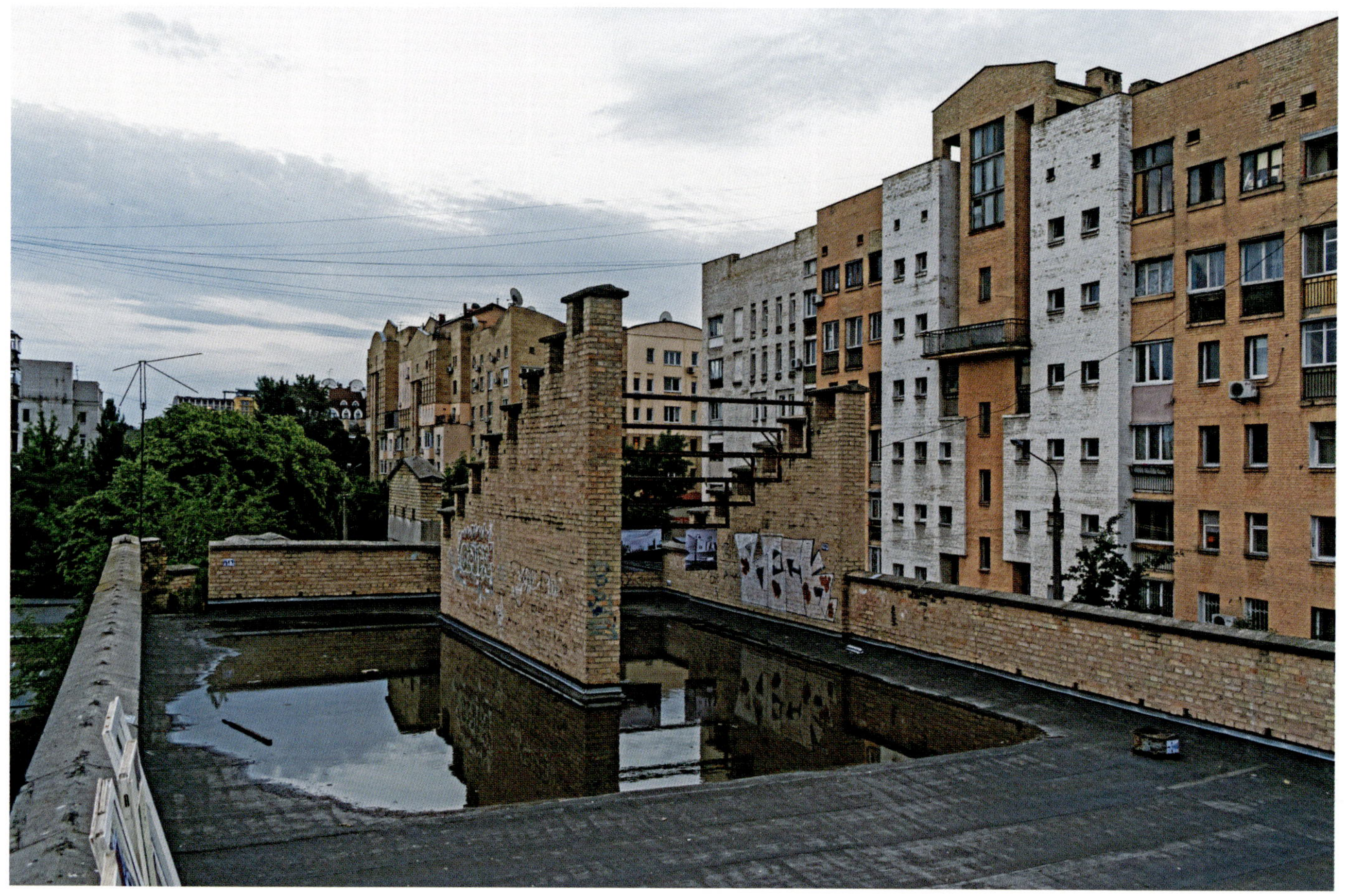

Podil Boiler Room and Residential Blocks
Kyiv
1983–93
Architects: Yurii Shalatskyi, Yurii Dukhovychnyi, Tetiana Lazarenko, Leonid Moroz, Ihor Shpara

This late-Soviet experimental project, comprising a four-block residential neighbourhood in Kyiv's historic Podil area, included a boiler room with two unique additions: an amphitheatre and a rooftop patio. Elements like these were intended to enrich and humanise

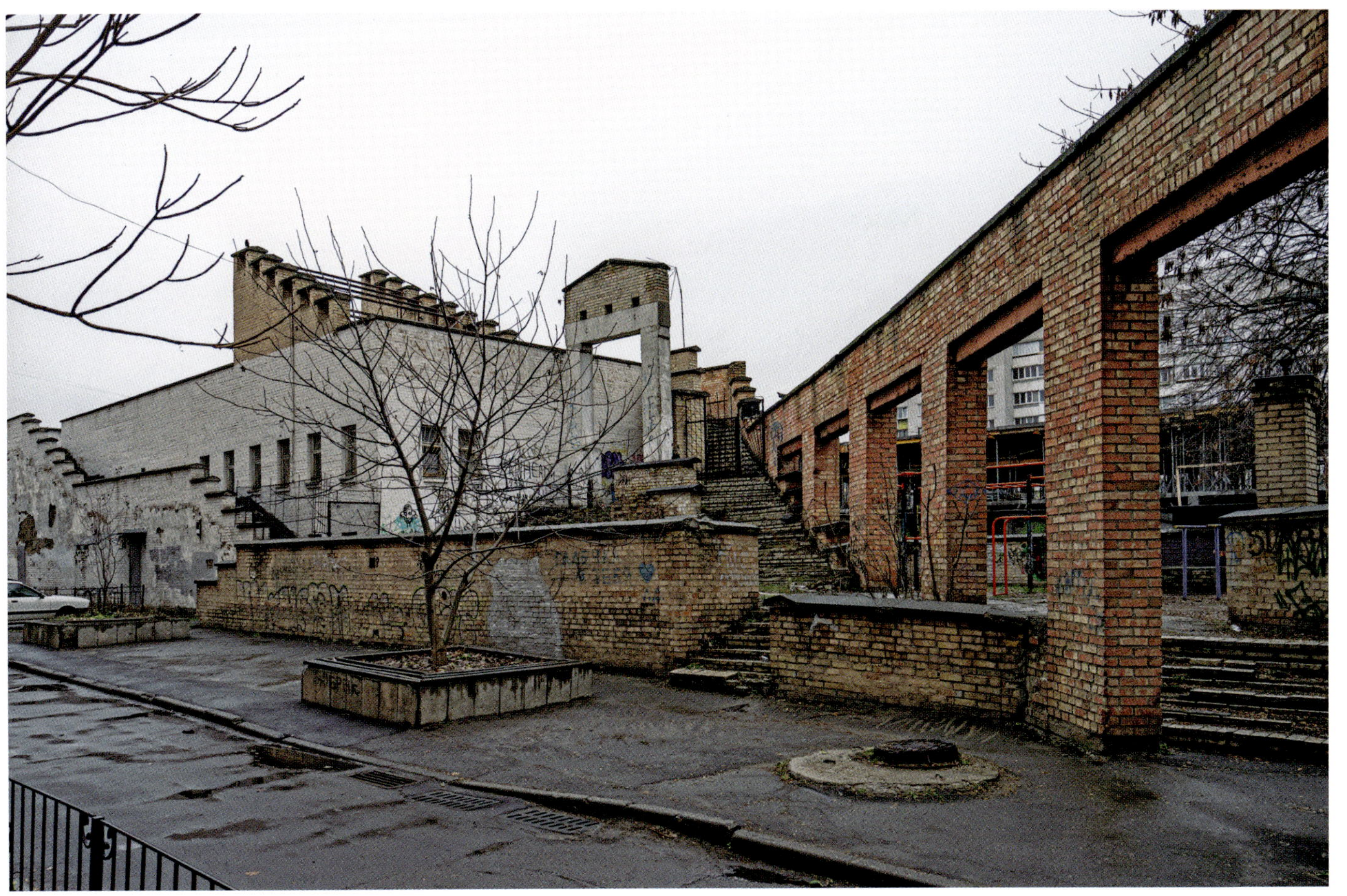

the built environment for local citizens. Following the dissolution of the Soviet Union in 1991, the patio was closed to the public and the amphitheatre, which the architects had designed to host theatrical and musical performances for the residents, quickly fell into neglect.

Activists and the local community worked together in an attempt to reclaim the patio, initially through negotiations and eventually by squatting the site; however, the municipality ensured that the site remained closed.

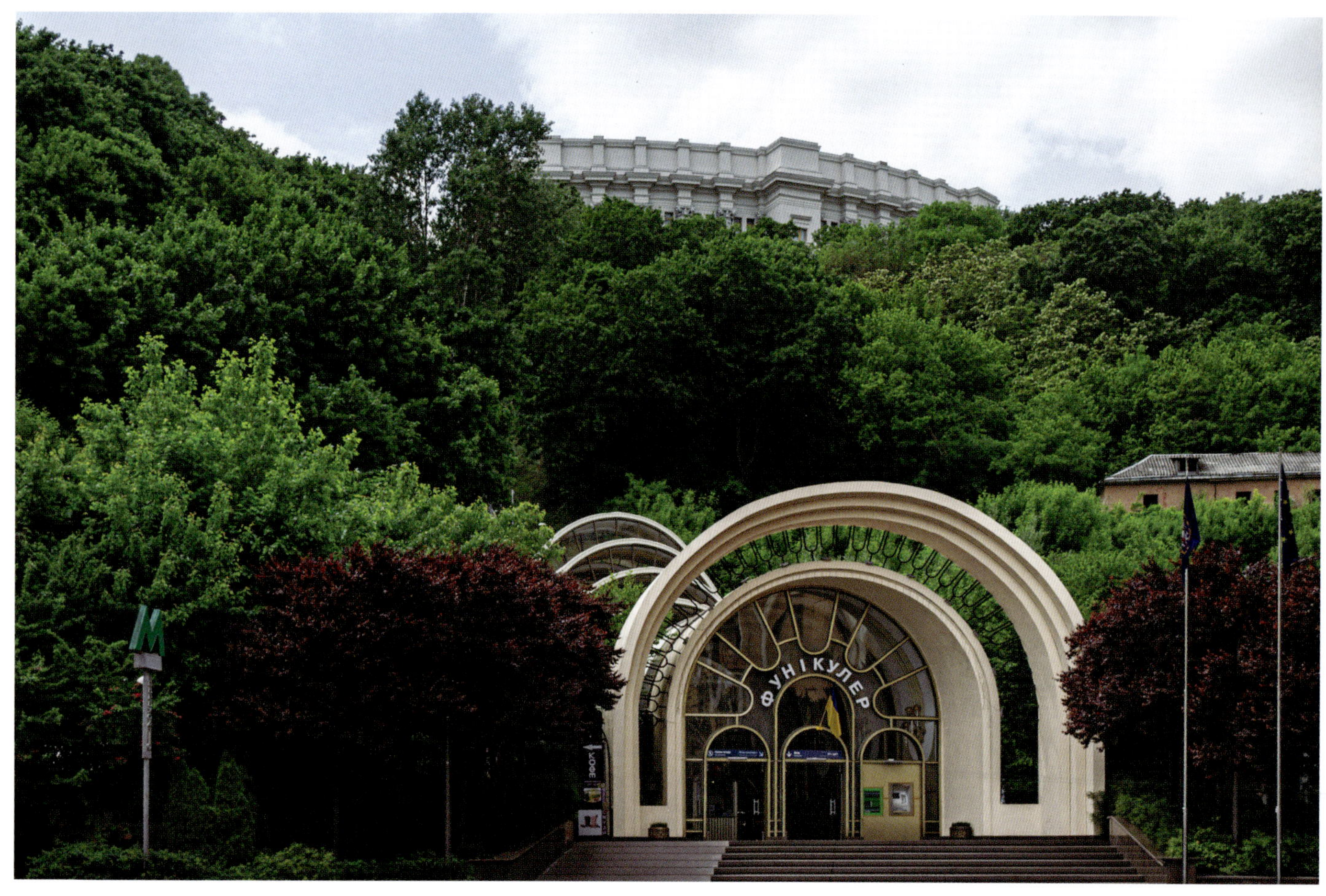

Kyiv Funicular
Kyiv
1983–84

Architects: Yanos Vigh, Valentyn Yezhov, Vadym Sharapov, A. Chupak
Engineers: V. Reznikov, N. Naiko
Artists: Mykola Shkaraputa, Ivan-Valentyn Zadorozhnyi

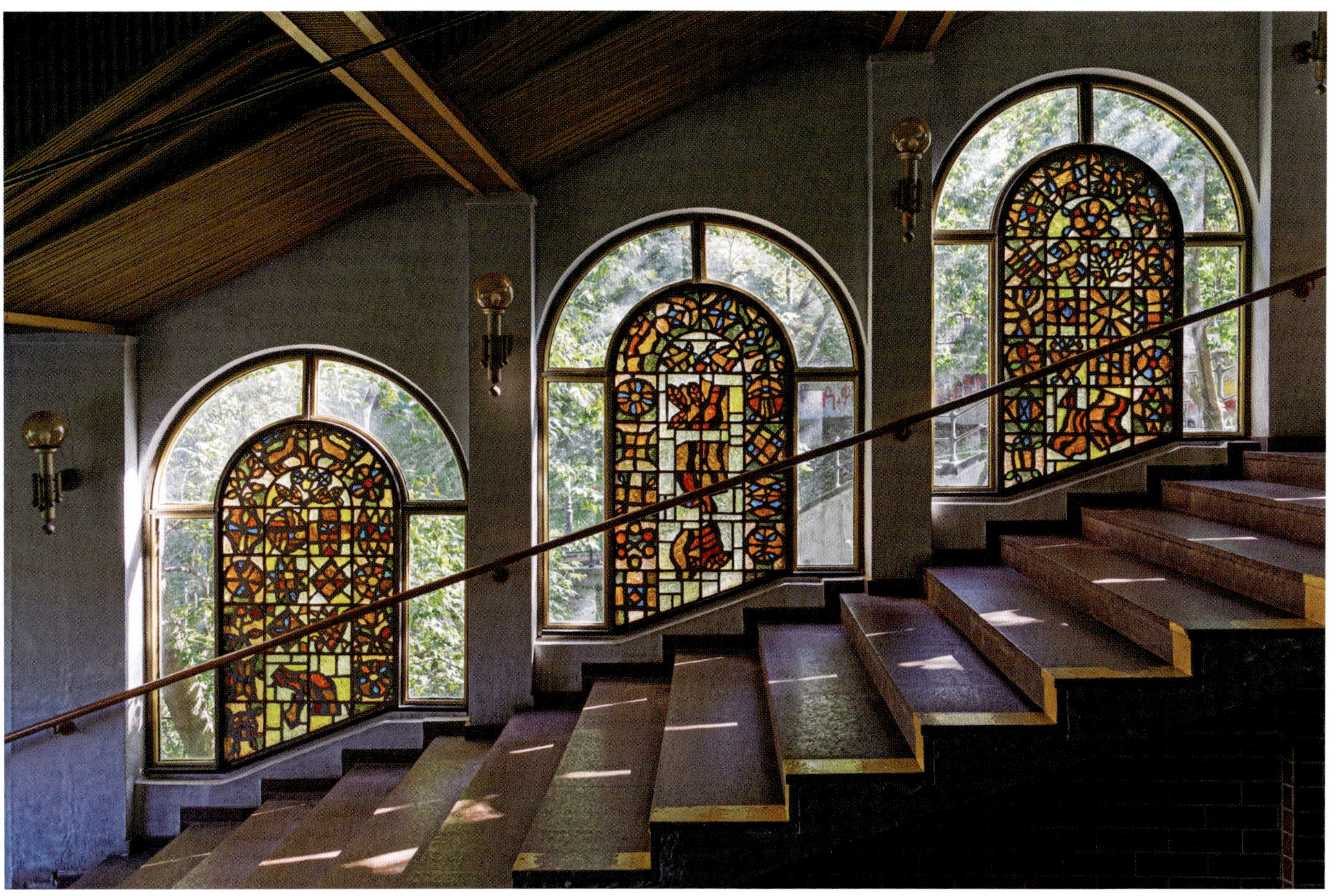

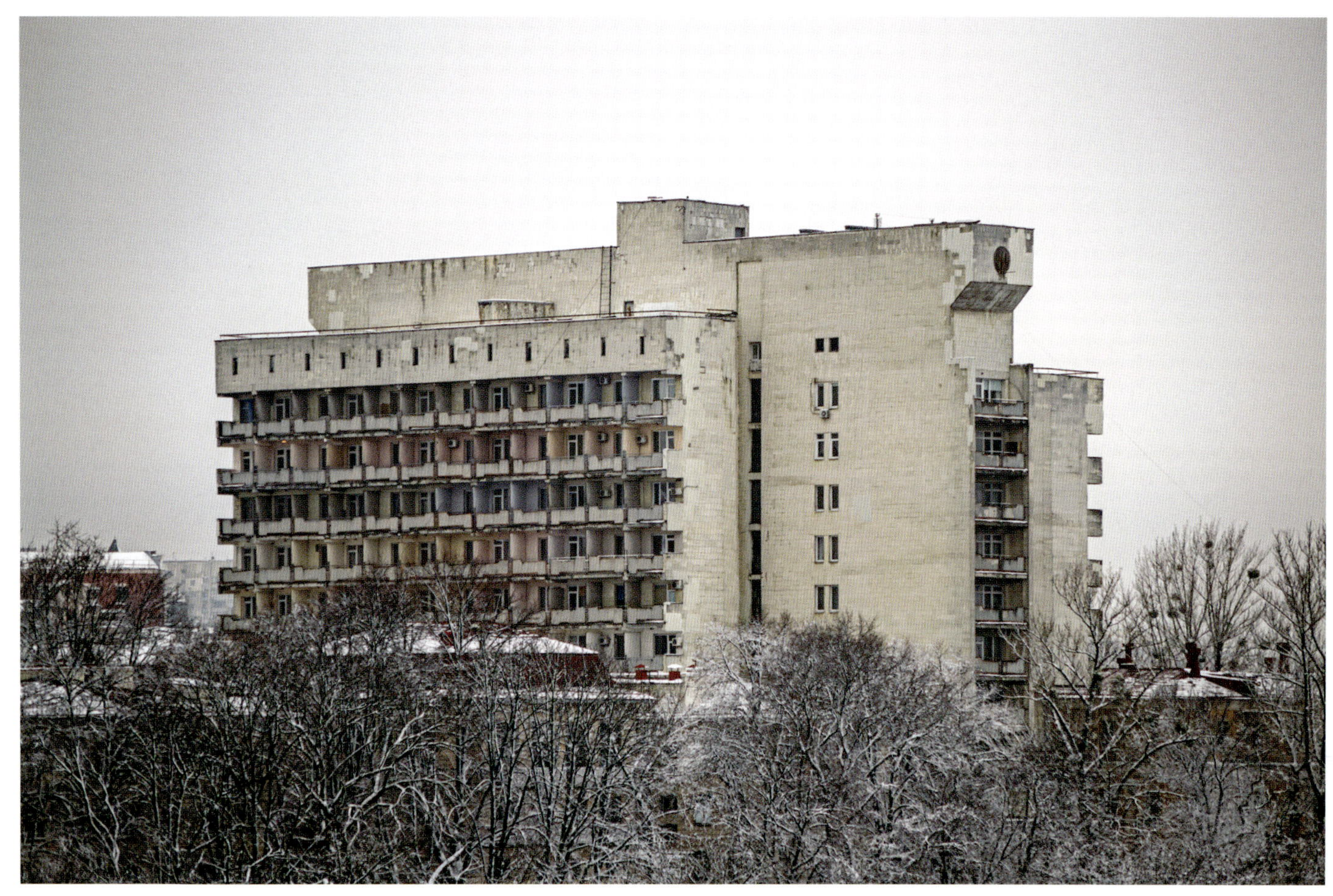

Hospital for Scientists, National Academy of Sciences of Ukraine
Kyiv
1983
Architects: Mykhailo Syrkin, V. Prach, Yu. Sedak
Engineer: V. Kyshelhof

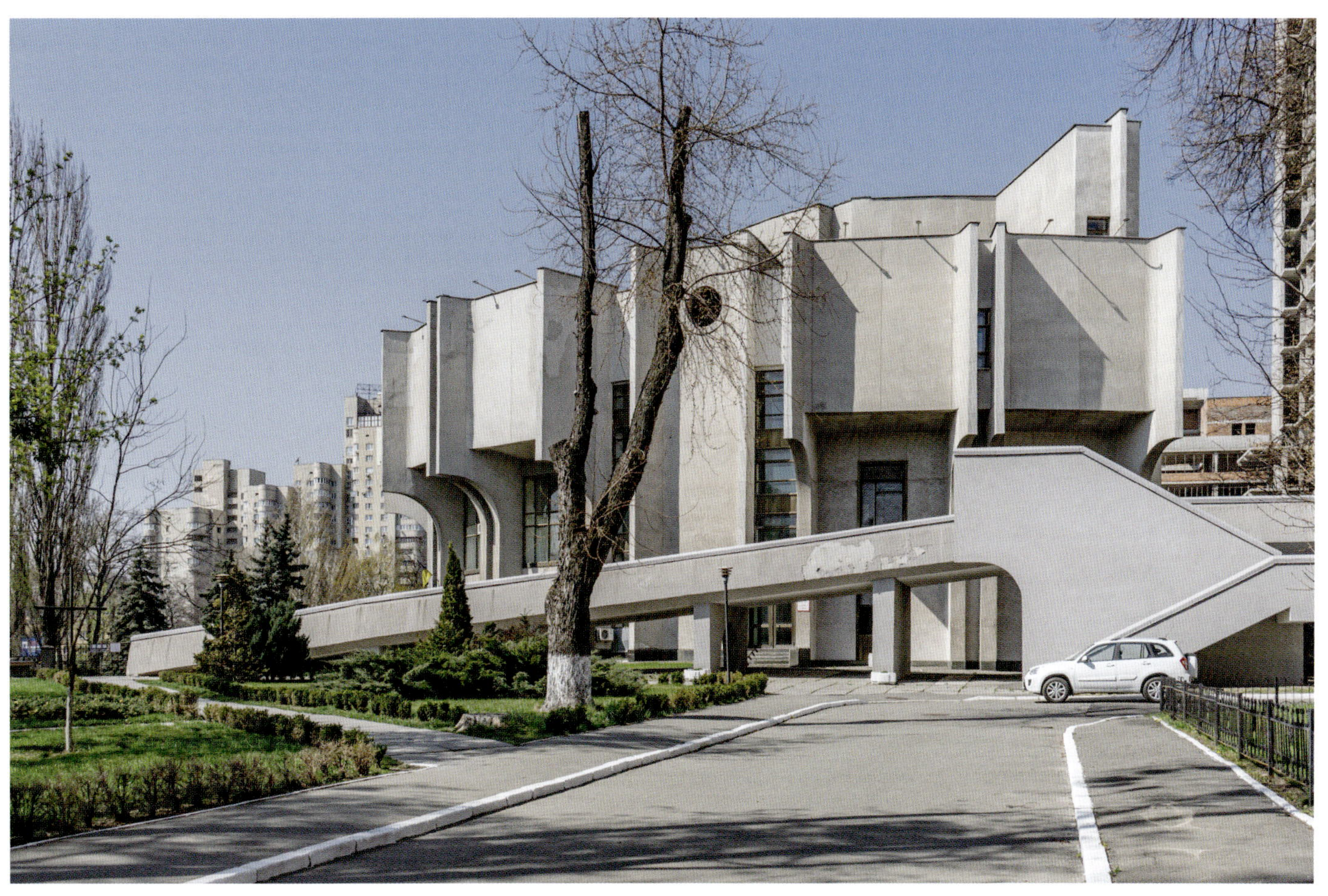

Events Hall, Bogomolets National Medical University
Kyiv
1980s

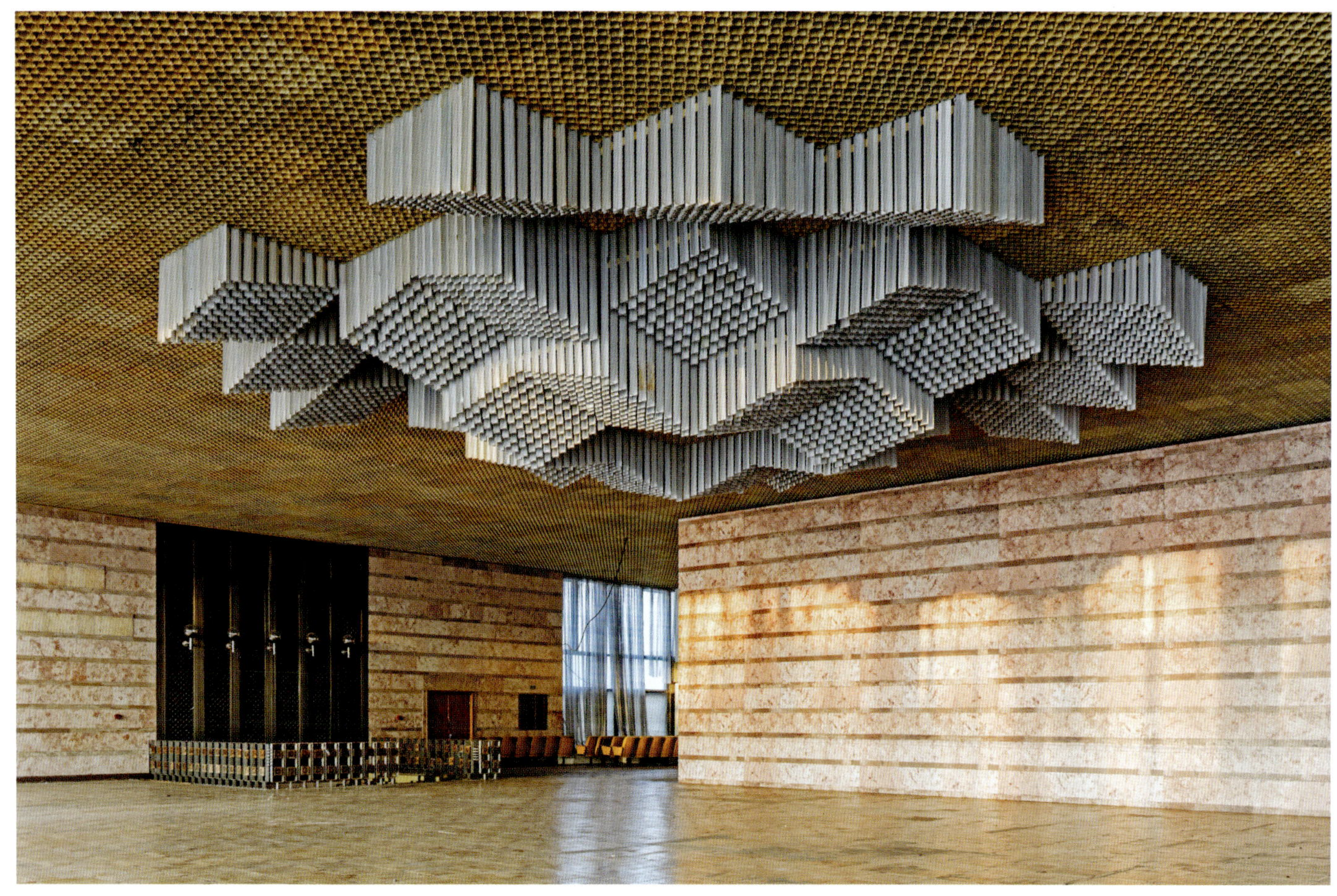

Koroliov Palace of Culture
Kyiv
1984
Architect: Valentyn Yezhov
Artists: Anatolii Karpenko, H. Terekhov, V. Dazhuk, H. Marchuk

This palace, built for the workers of the Kyiv-based Koroliov Production Association (named after Serhii Koroliov), was designed in-house by the plant's own construction bureau using plans developed by Valentyn Yezhov. The facade is clad in Armenian volcanic

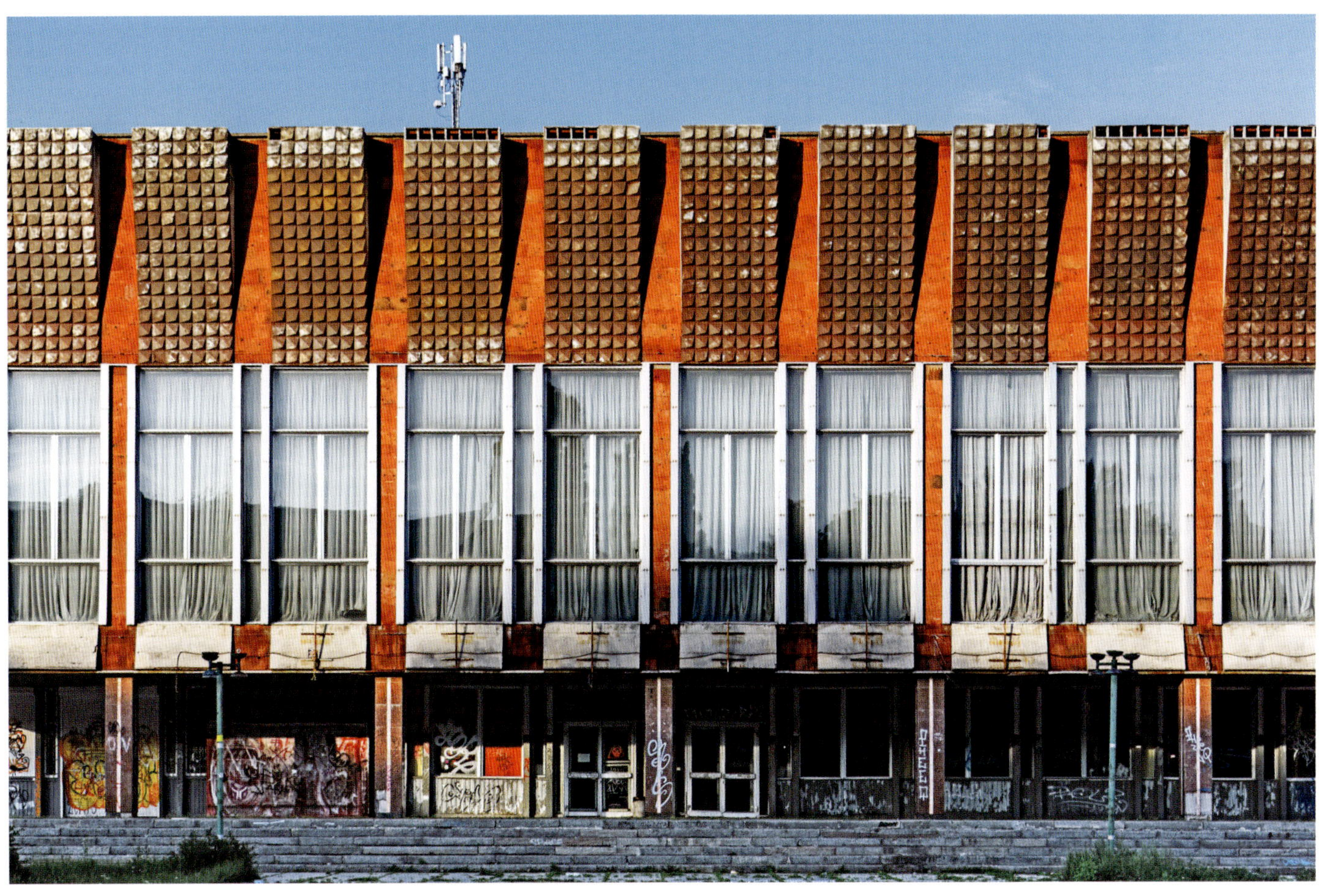

tuff, a stone rarely found in Ukrainian architecture. Inside, a futuristic metal chandelier contrasts with a painstakingly crafted wooden decorative frieze, created by a team of 15 artists and artisans. In 2020, the Roshen Corporation purchased and closed the building, announcing plans for its demolition and the construction of a new concert hall in its place. Despite public calls for its preservation, in 2023 the vacant building was left unguarded. It was soon vandalised and the interior was ultimately destroyed by arson.

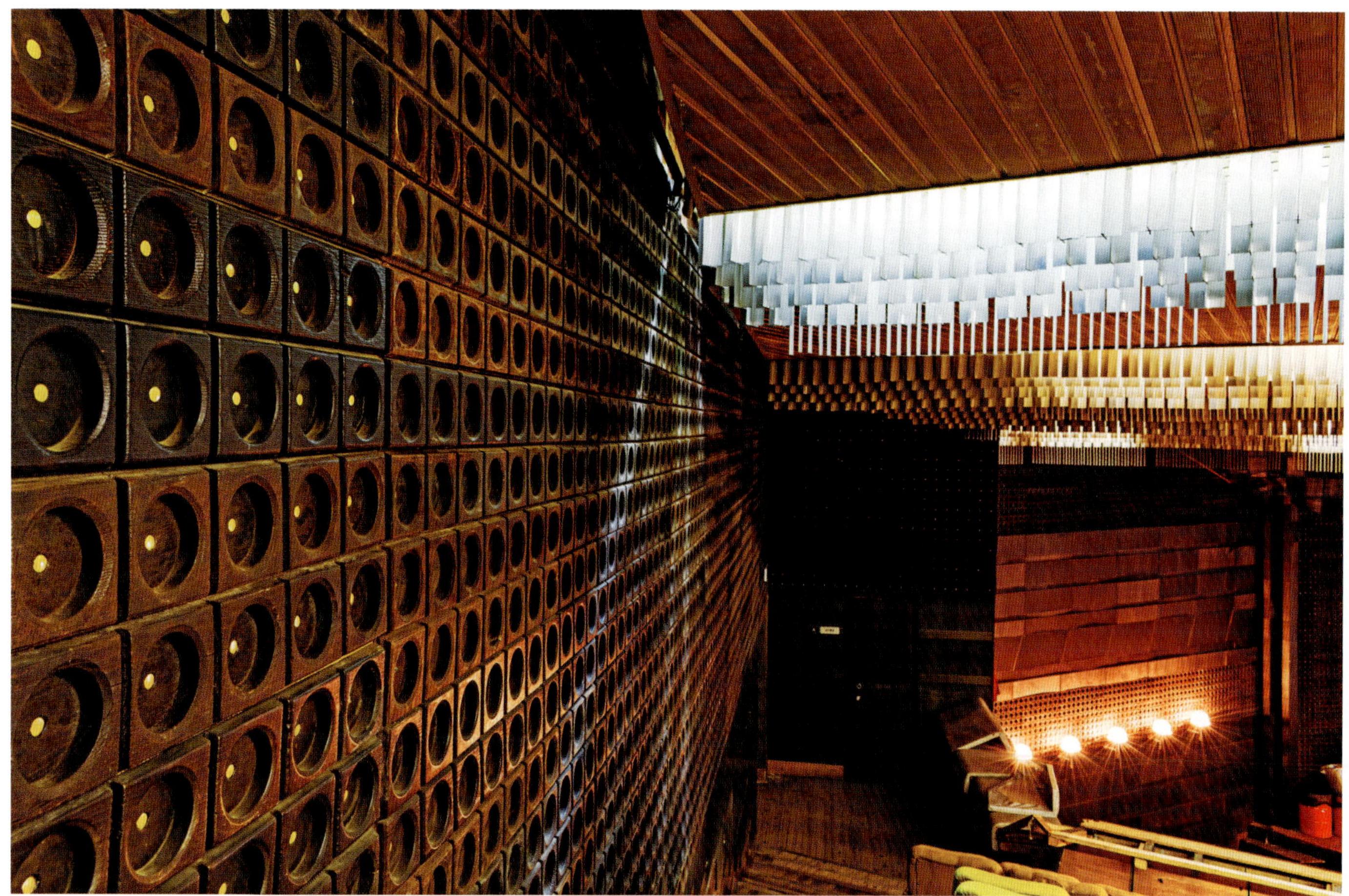

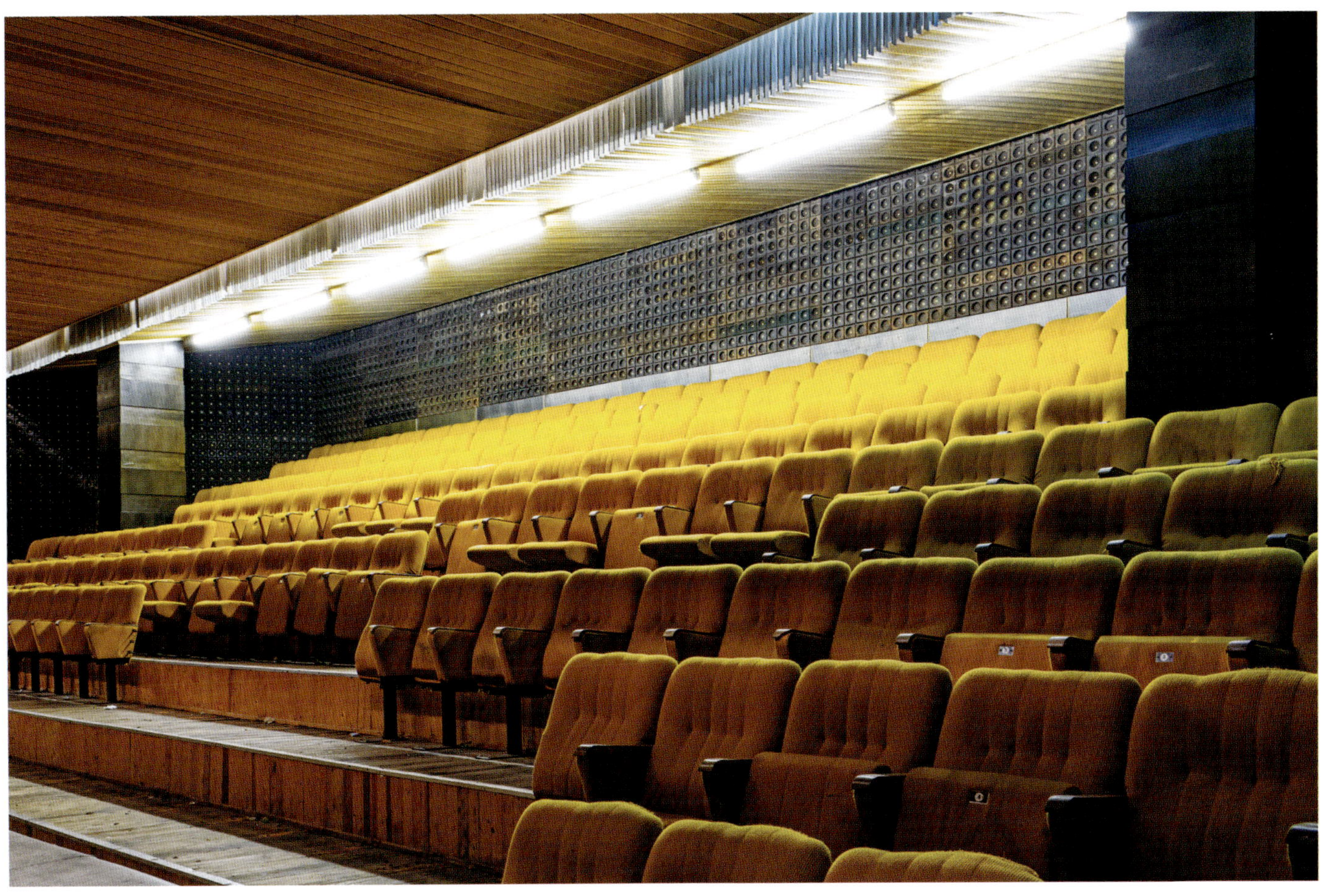

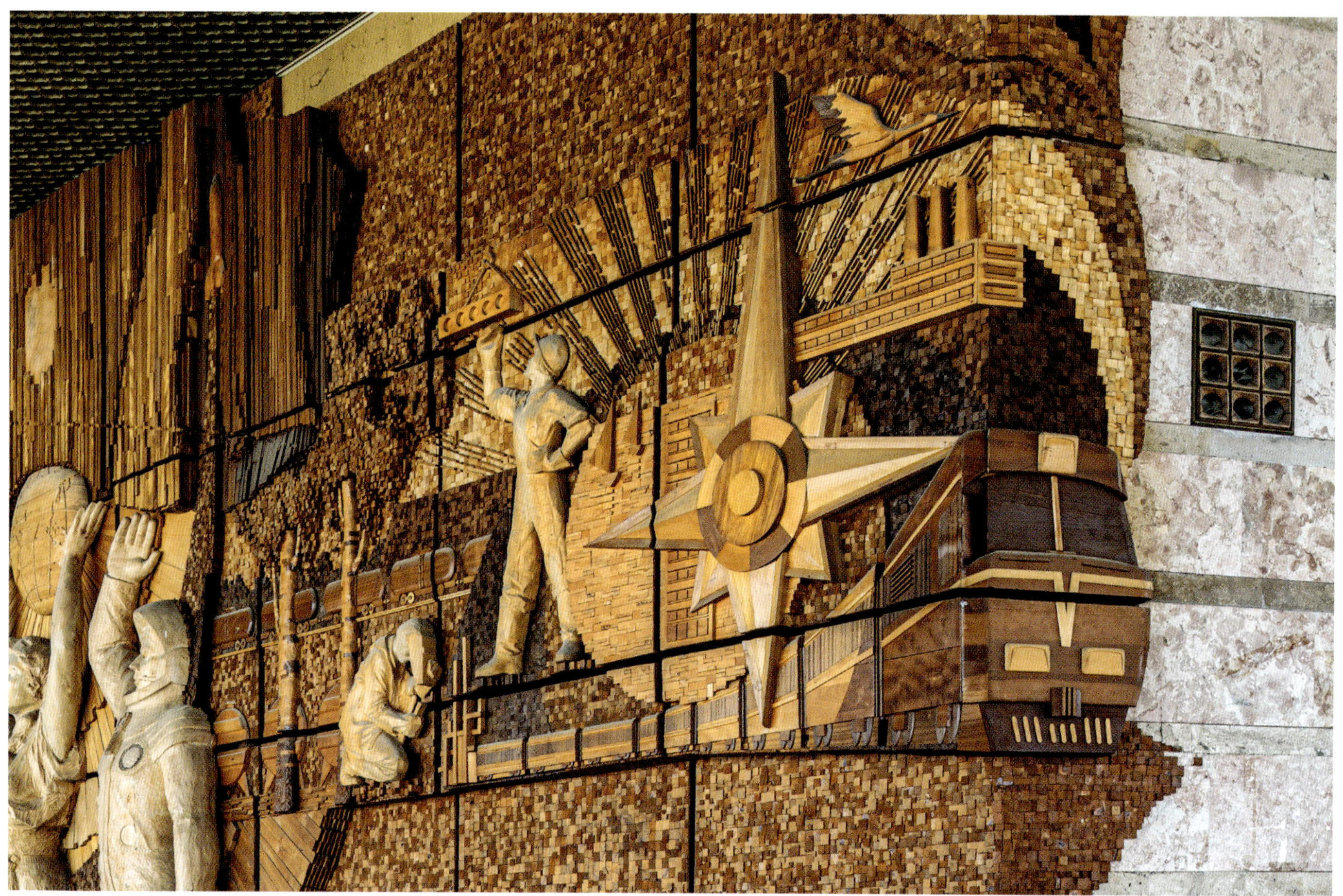

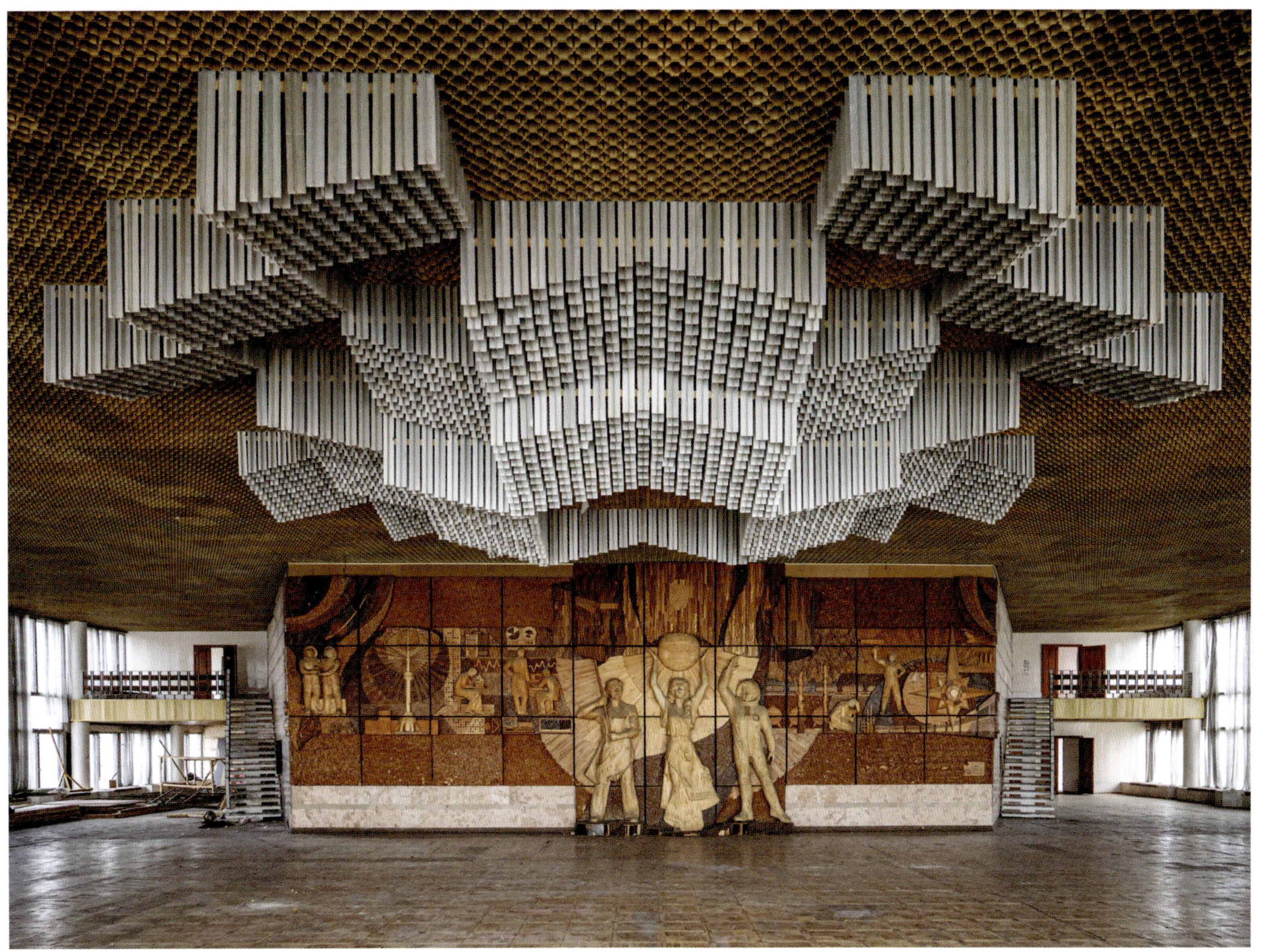

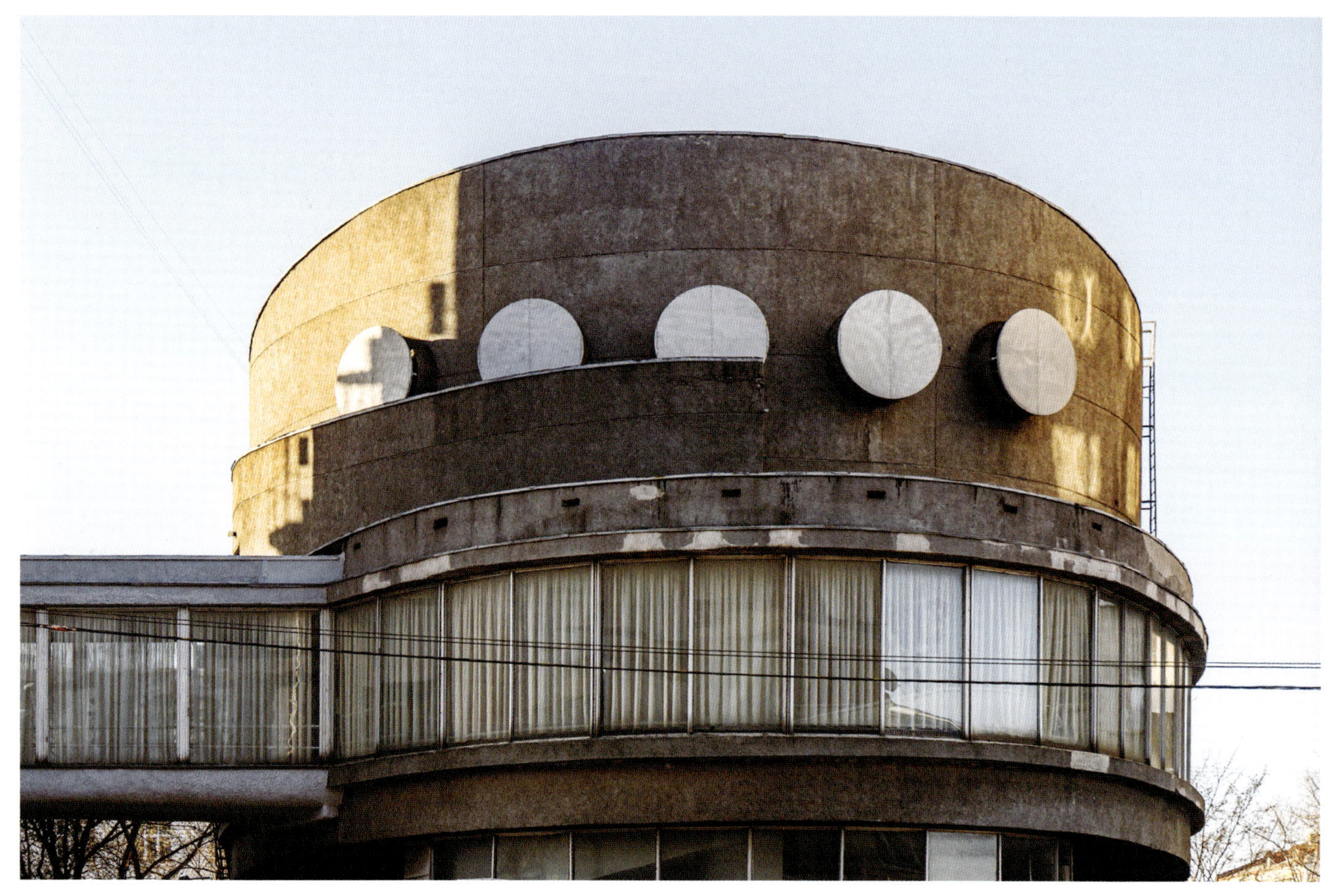

Ukravtodor building (the State Agency of Automobile Roads of Ukraine, formerly the Ministry of Roadways of Soviet Ukraine)
Kyiv
1971–76

Architects: Avraam Miletskyi, Neonila Slogotska, D. Chuzhyi
Engineers: L. Riznytska, A. Pritsker, S. Syrota

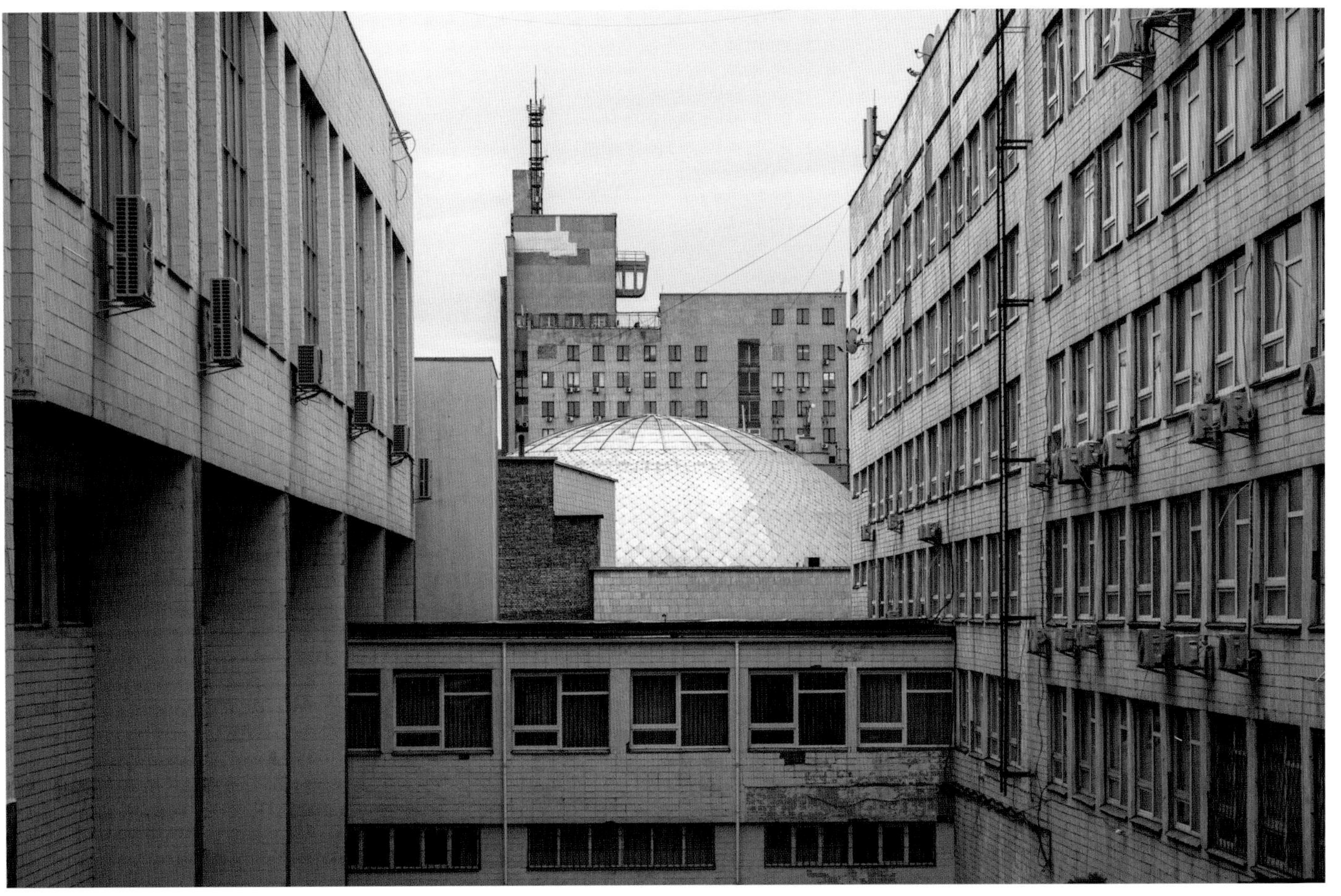

The main Ukravtodor office block stands in the background. In the centre is the silver dome of the Kyiv Planetarium (opened in 1987). In the foreground are various buildings of the National University of Physical Education and Sport.

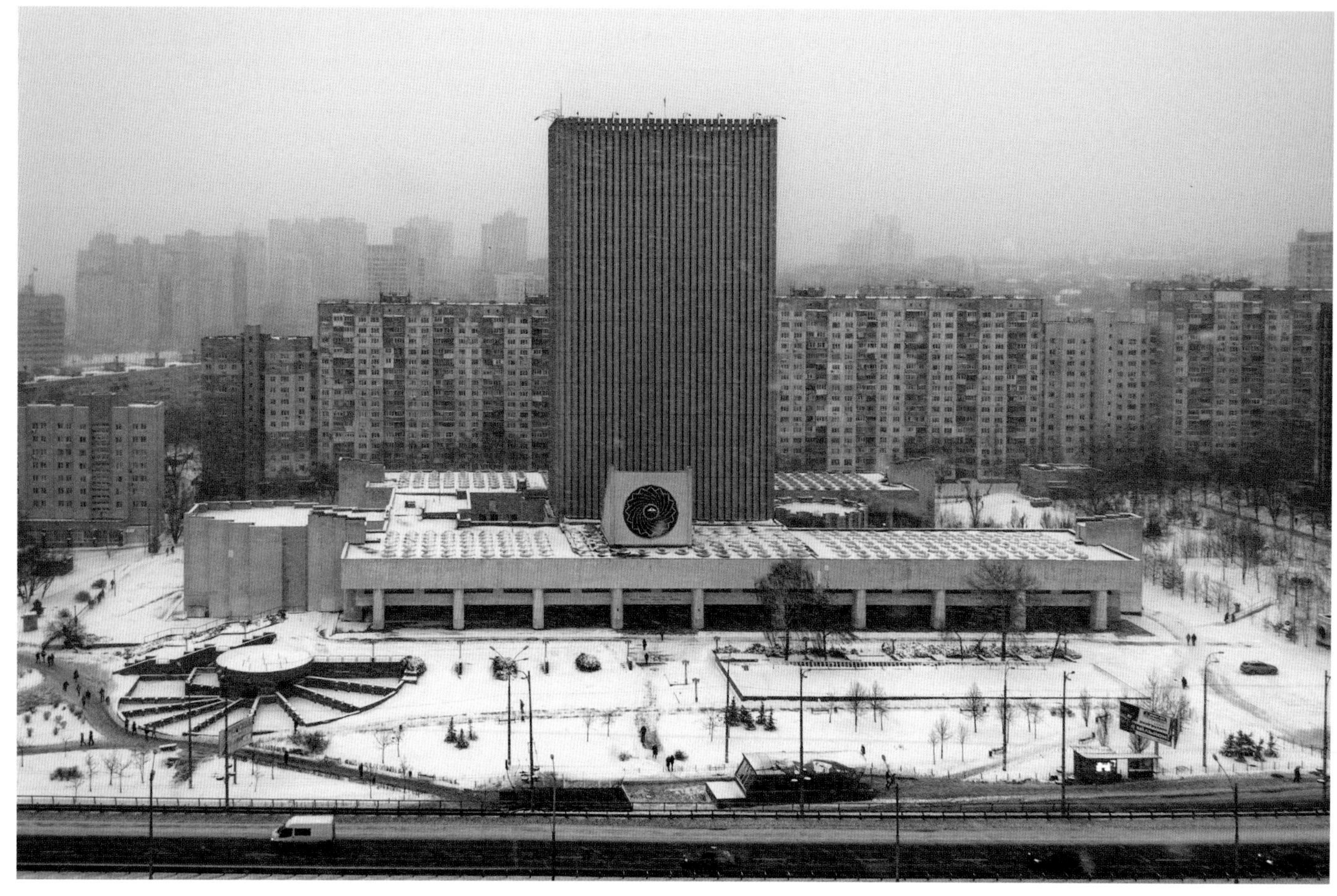

Vernadsky National Library of Ukraine
Kyiv
1976–89

Architects: Vadym Hopkalo, Vadym Hrechyna, Valerii Peskovskyi,
Volodymyr Kolomiiets, L. Prutsakova, Zh. Slavnina, L. Hlinkova,
O. Halatyn, N. Stasiuk

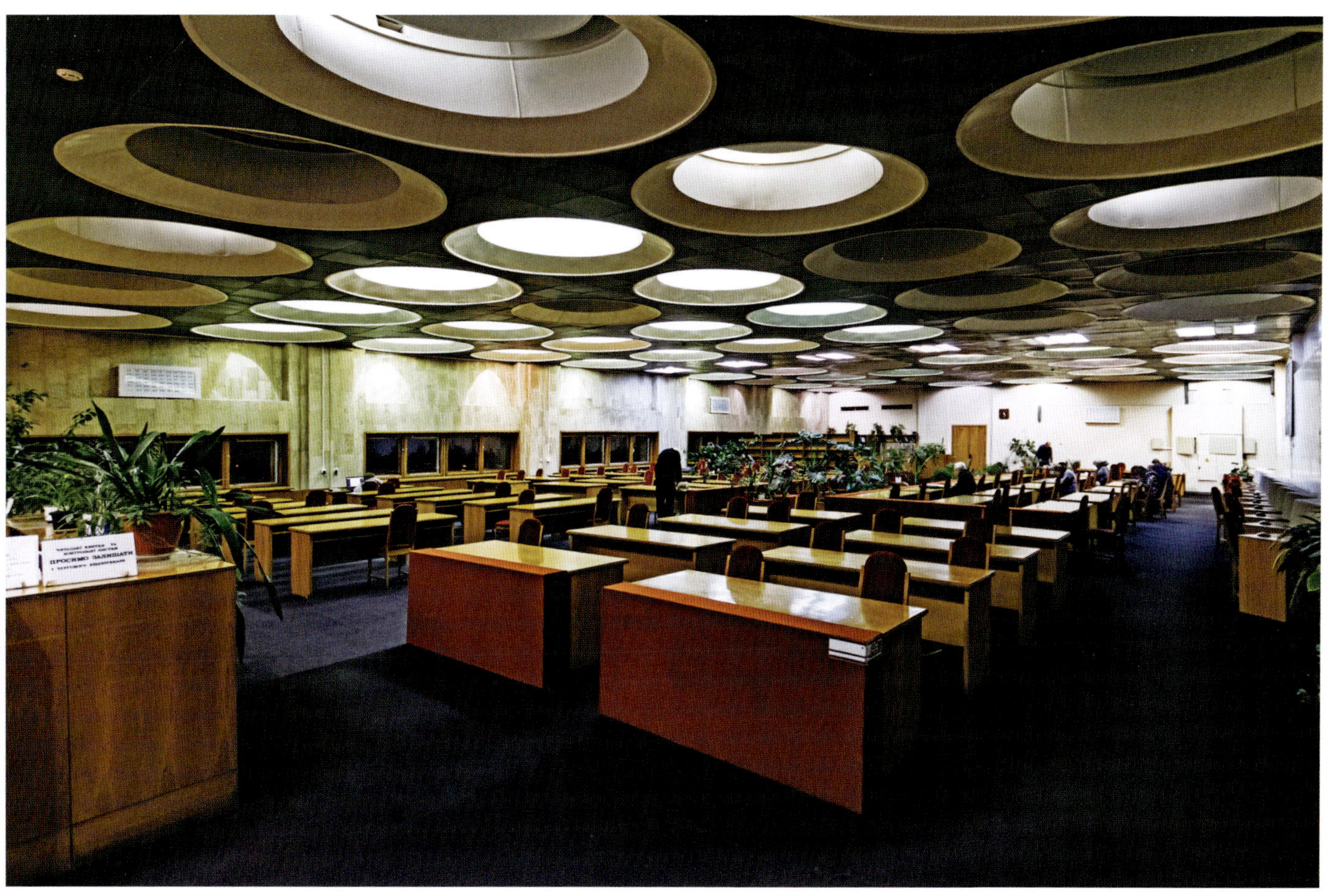

Engineers: Leonid Linovych, Kostiantyn Shvarts, A. Lepskaya
Artists: Volodymyr Pasyvenko, Volodymyr Priadka, Ivan Lytovchenko,
Mariia Lytovchenko

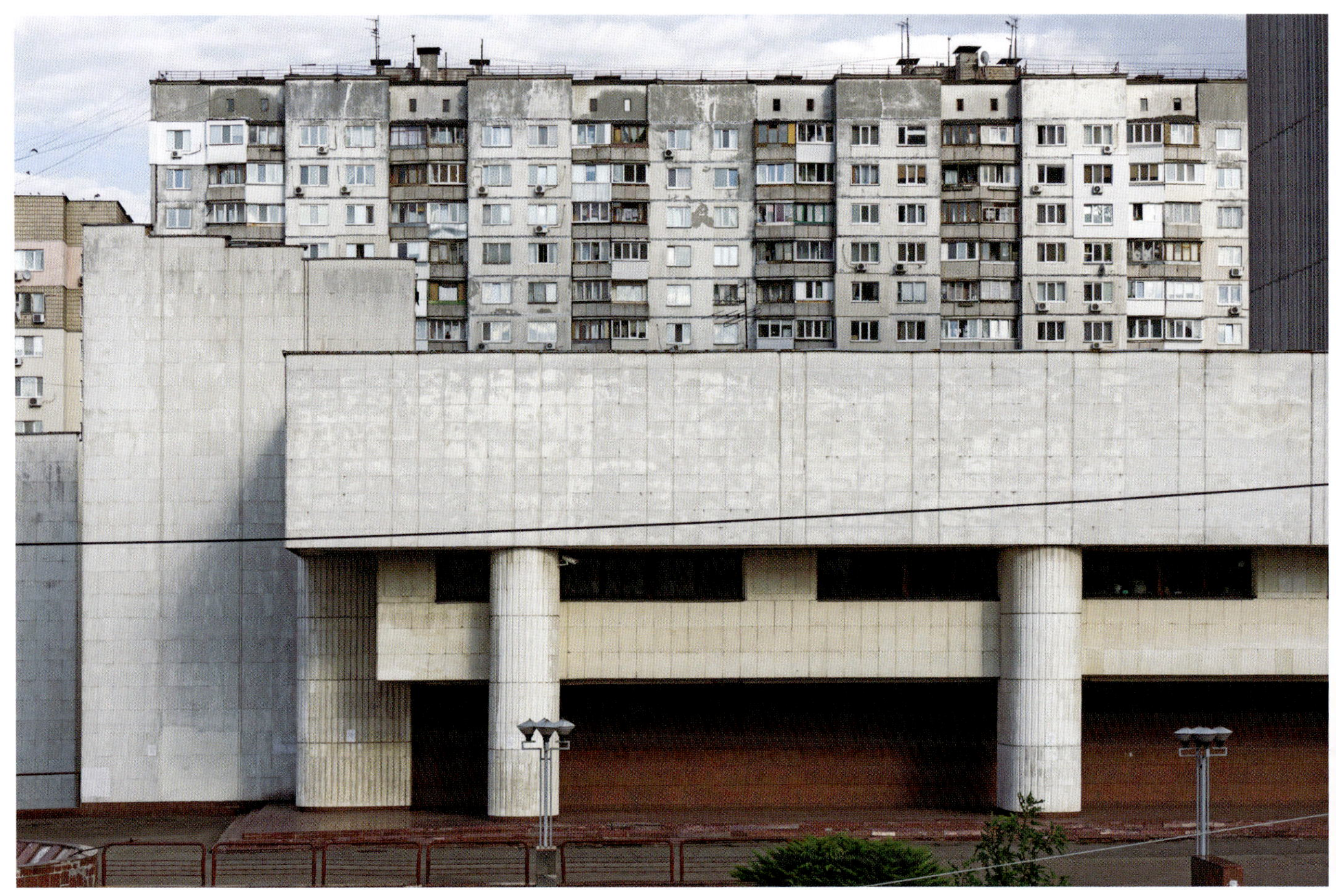

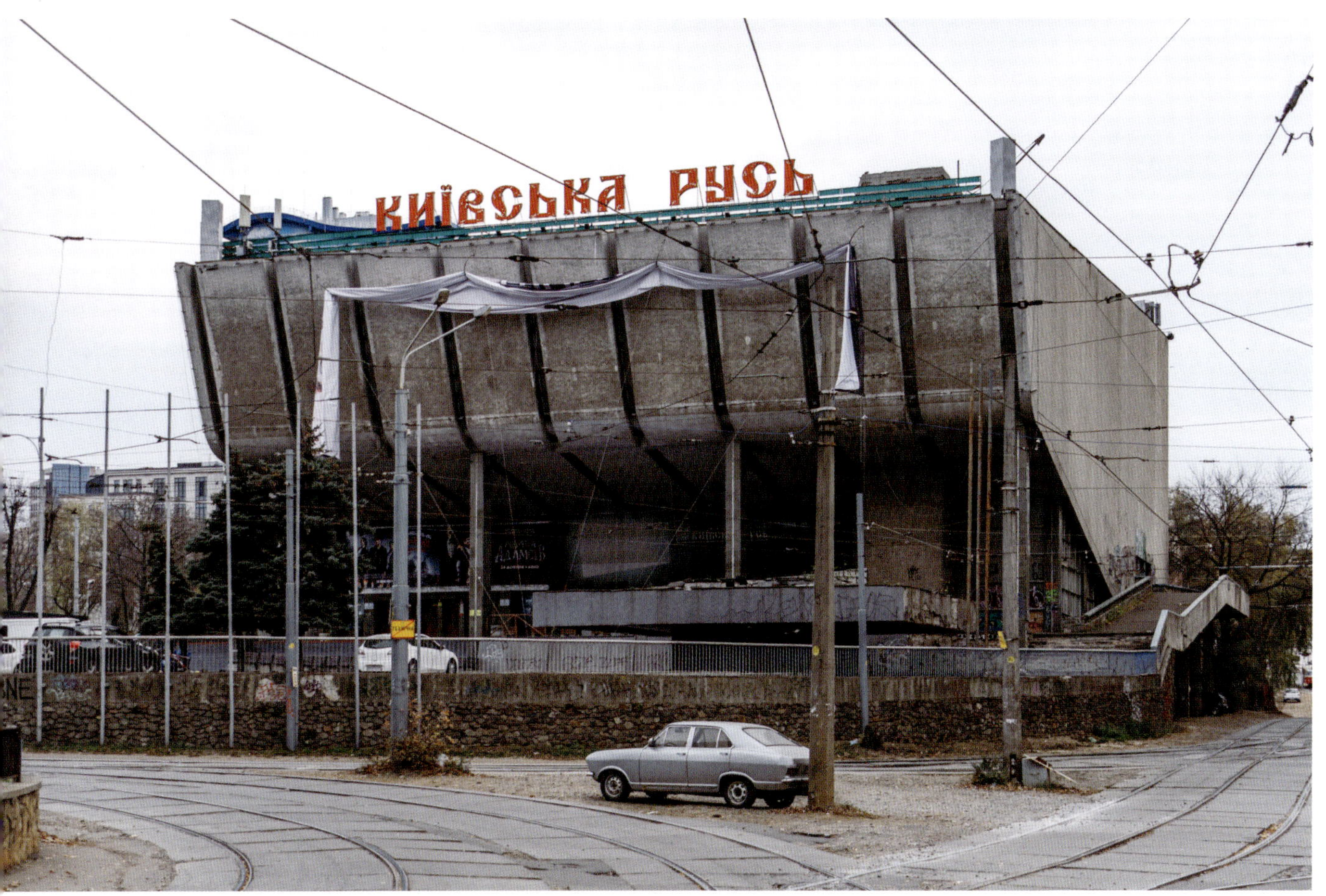

Kyivska Rus Cinema
Kyiv
1982
Architects: Volodymyr Taienchuk, Mykola Bosenko
Artists: Mykola Obeziuk, Hryhorii Korin

This brutalist building was one of many public facilities constructed in 1982 to commemorate the 1,500th anniversary of Kyiv. Renovation works were announced in February 2022, but these were indefinitely postponed following the full-scale Russian invasion later that month.

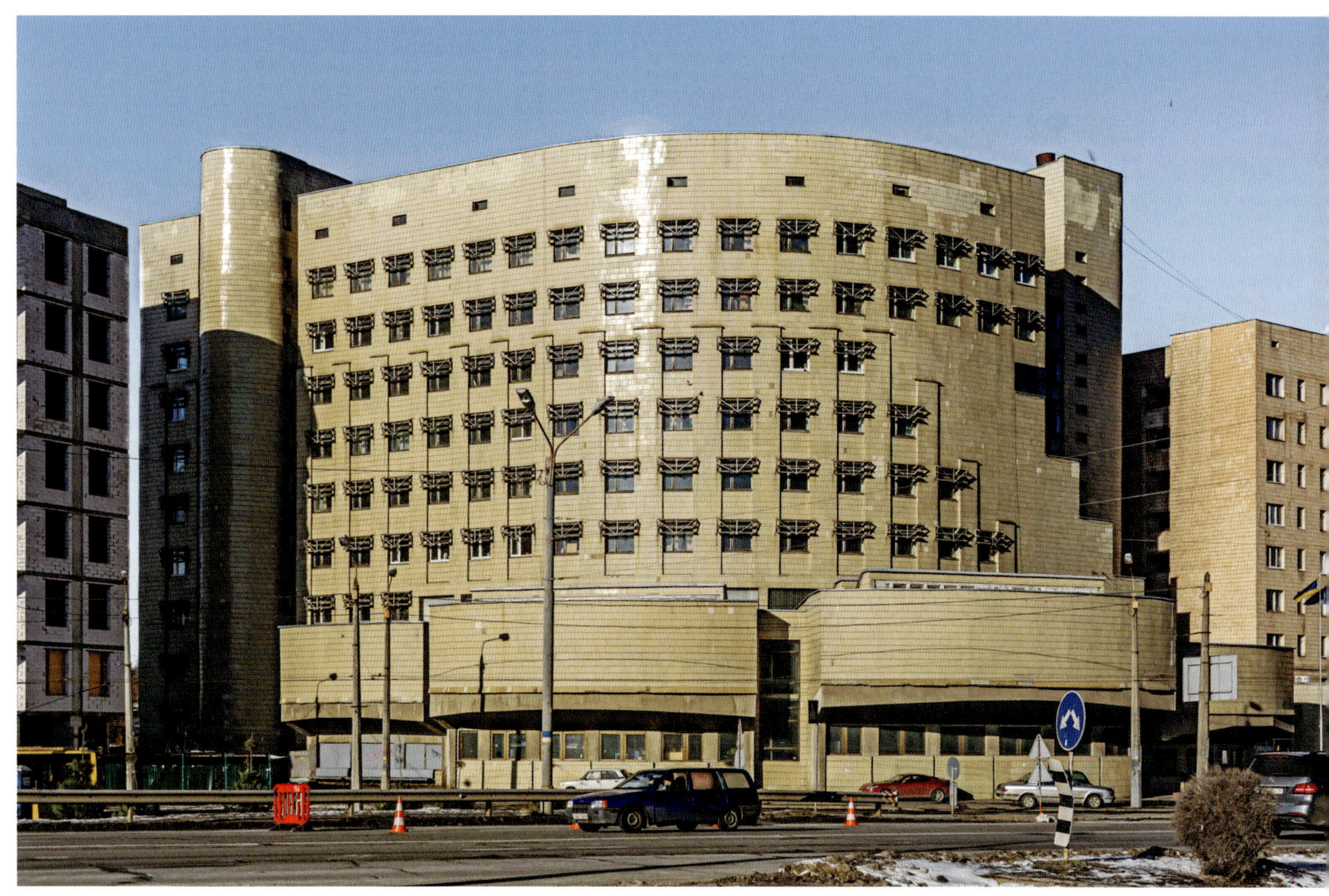

Educational and Library Building, National Transport University
Kyiv
1988

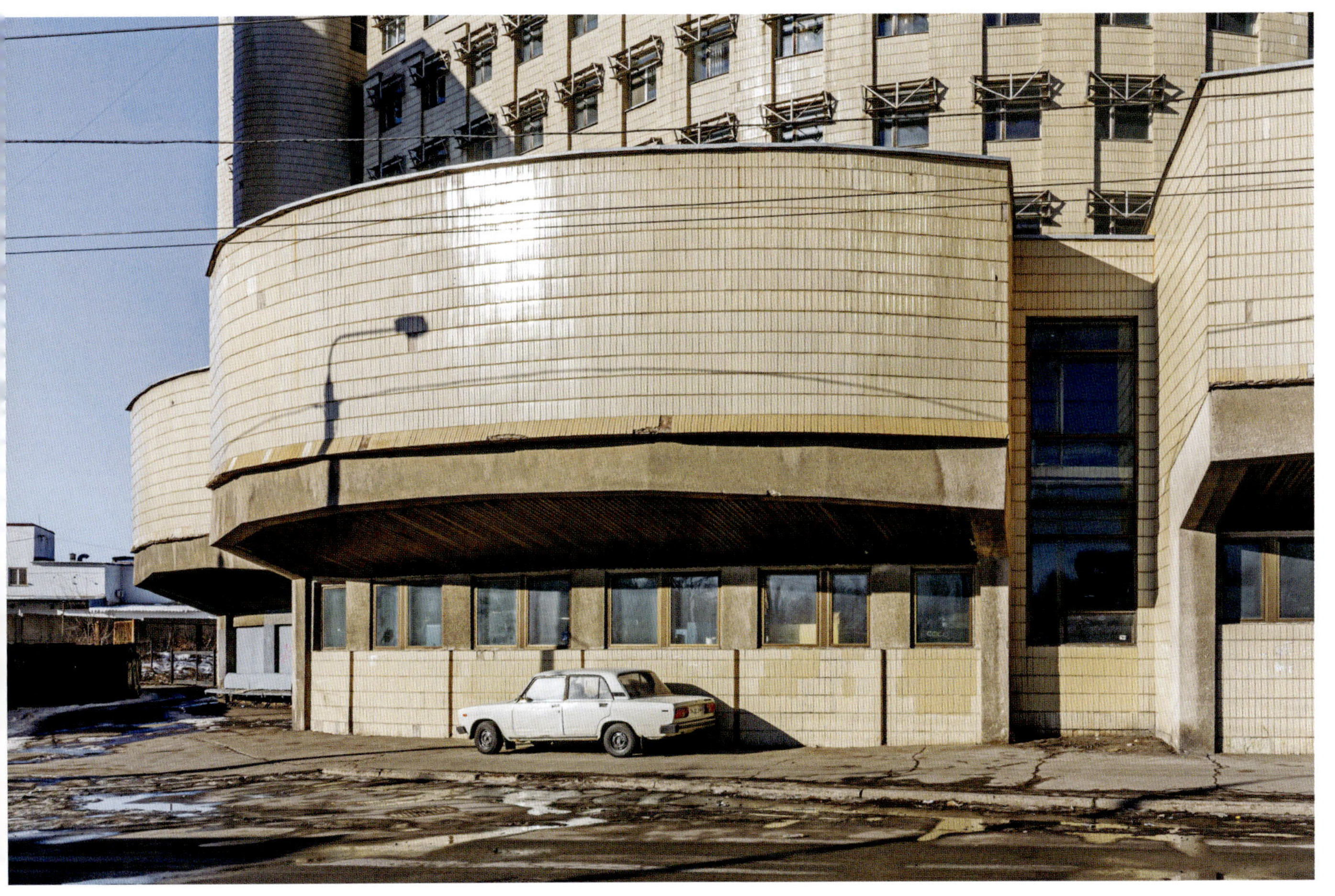

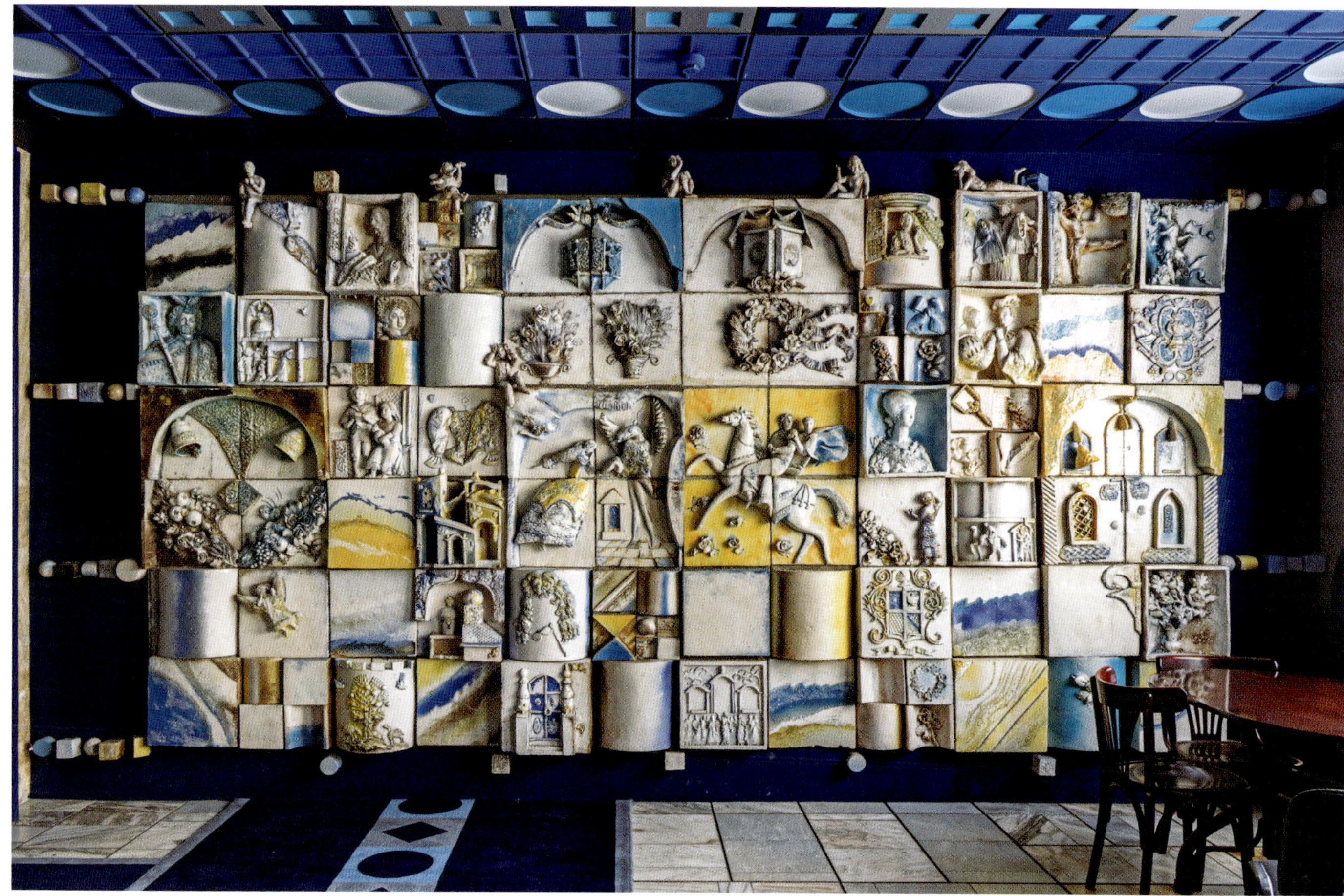

Kyiv Academic Theatre for Young Spectators
Kyiv
1987–93
Architects: Roman-Enrique Hupalo, Vira Stupnikova, Olena Yasudovych
Engineers: Volodymyr Miin, Rakhil Shukhman, Volodymyr Vysloukh

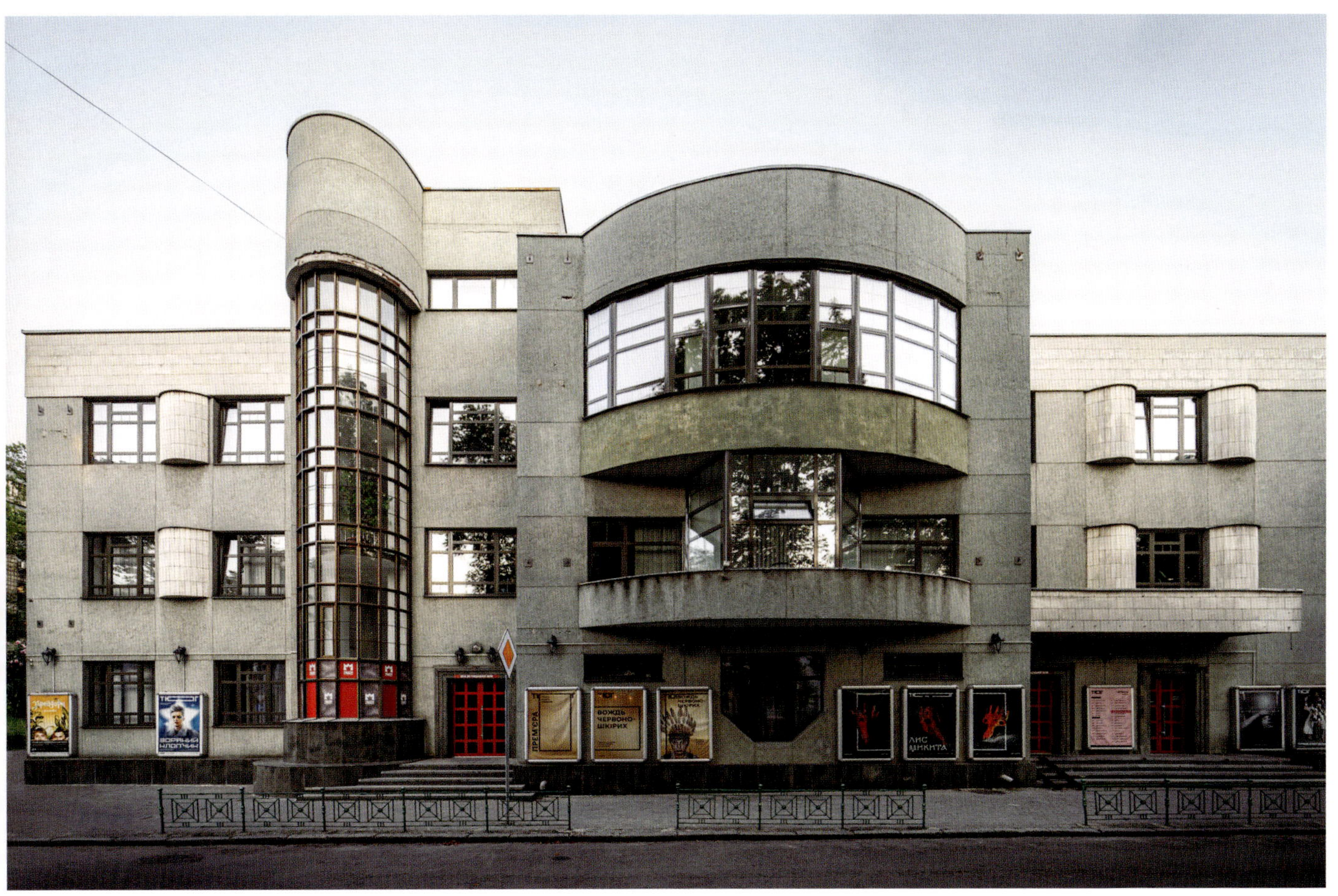

Originally designed by Vasyl Osmak in the Constructivist style as the Club of the State Political Directorate and completed in 1932, the building was repurposed in 1954 to house the Theatre for Young Spectators. In 1987 a major reconstruction project designed by Roman-Enrique Hupalo completely reshaped the structure to better serve this purpose. While the general Constructivist spirit was retained in the circular facade elements, the new postmodern design marked a complete departure from the building's original form.

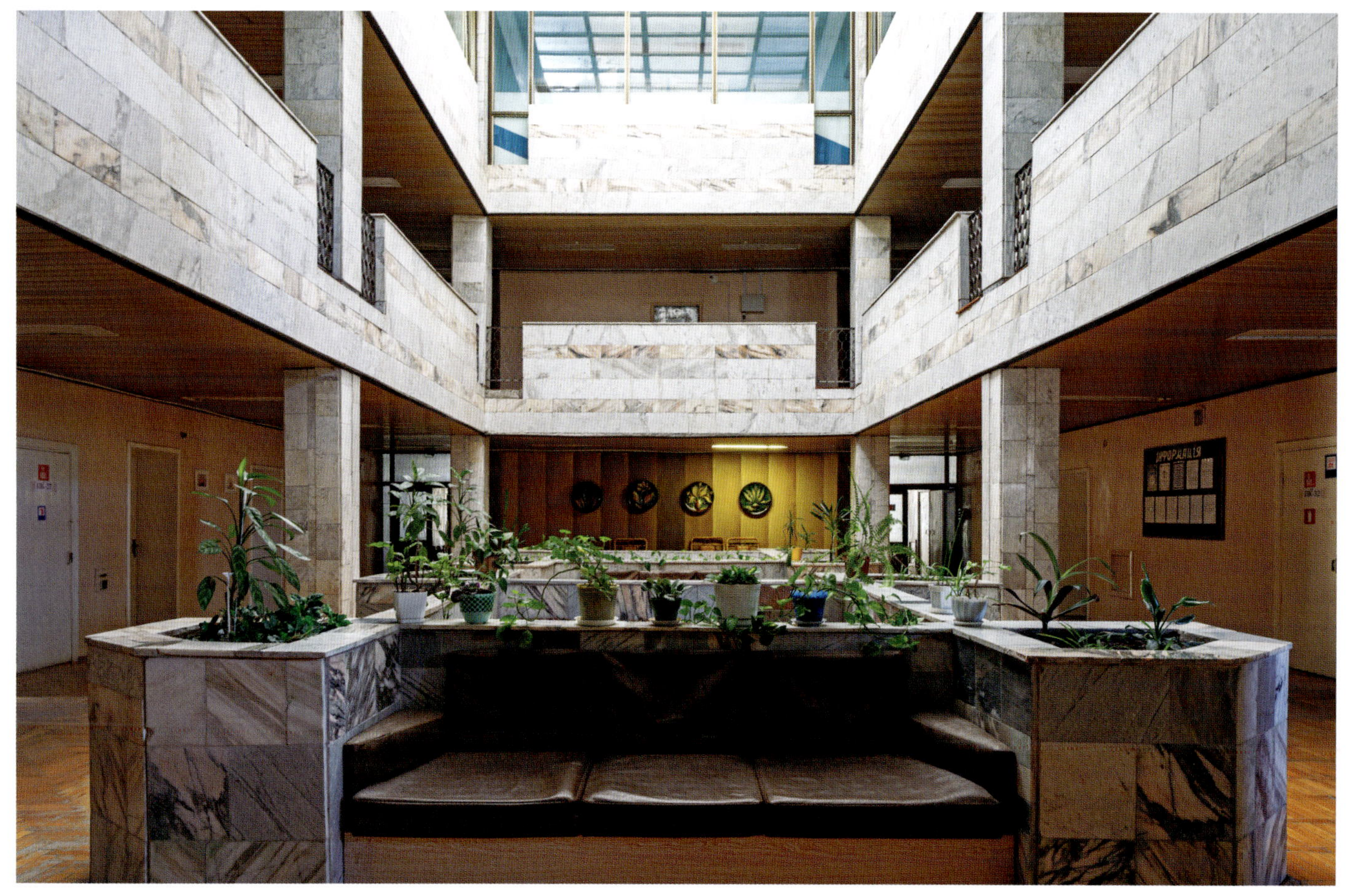

Slavutych City Hospital
Slavutych, Kyiv Oblast
1987–92
Architects: Volodymyr Buriak, Ihor Kaspert
Engineer: Adolf Kosynskyi

Slavutych, the youngest town in Ukraine, was built in the aftermath of the Chernobyl disaster to accommodate the displaced residents of Pripyat, the Atomgrad that supported the nuclear power plant. The city's master plan was developed in mere two months, and the city

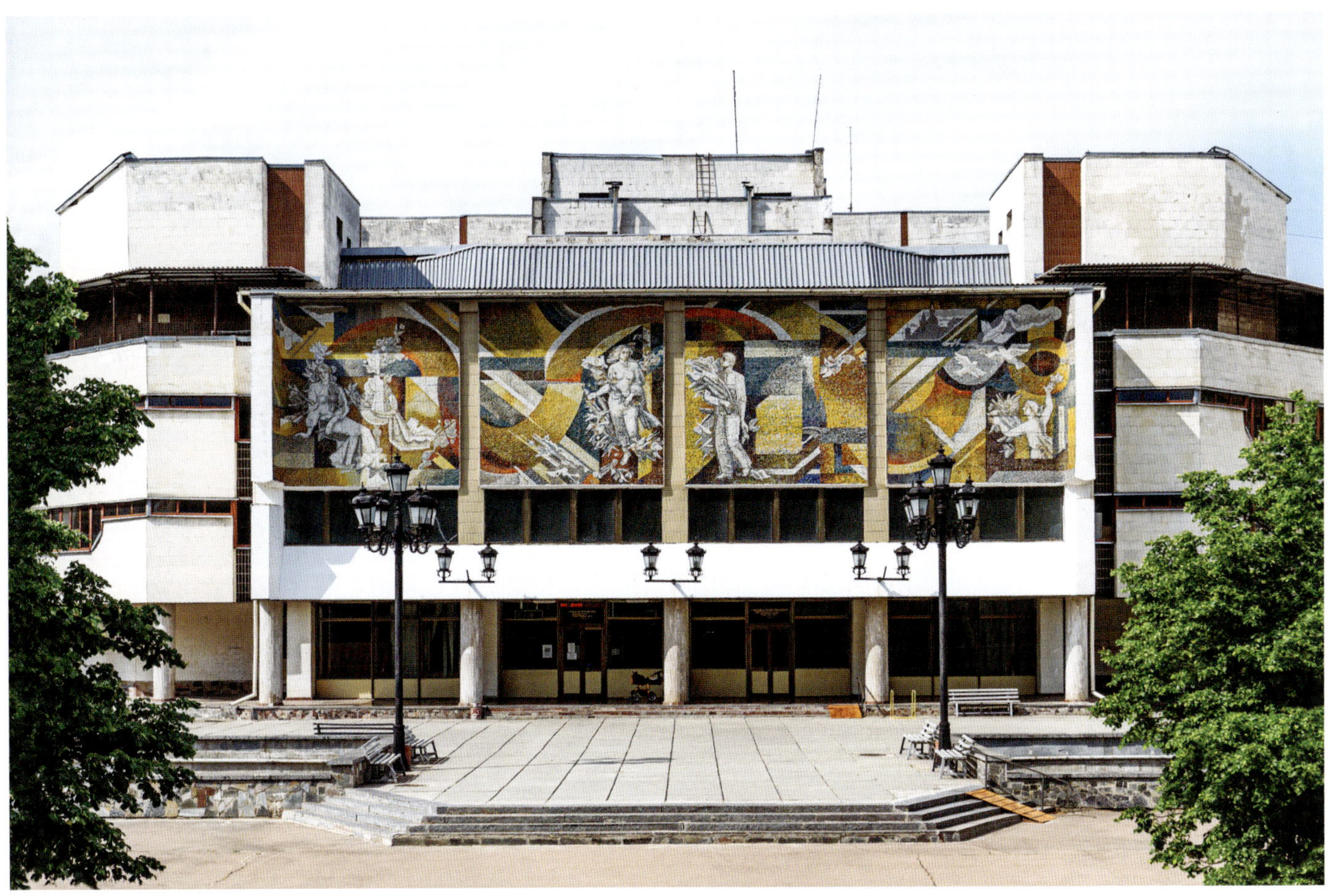

itself was constructed in just two years, through a huge collective effort involving eight Soviet republics. Each contributed distinct neighbourhoods, using the materials and architecture of their homelands to create a unique cultural mosaic – the outdoor barbecue stands of the Yerevan Quarter remain popular with locals. Today, the town is regarded as one of the most humanistic in Ukraine, with infrastructure that emphasises walkability and sustainable urban living, perhaps best reflected in its network of dedicated cycle routes.

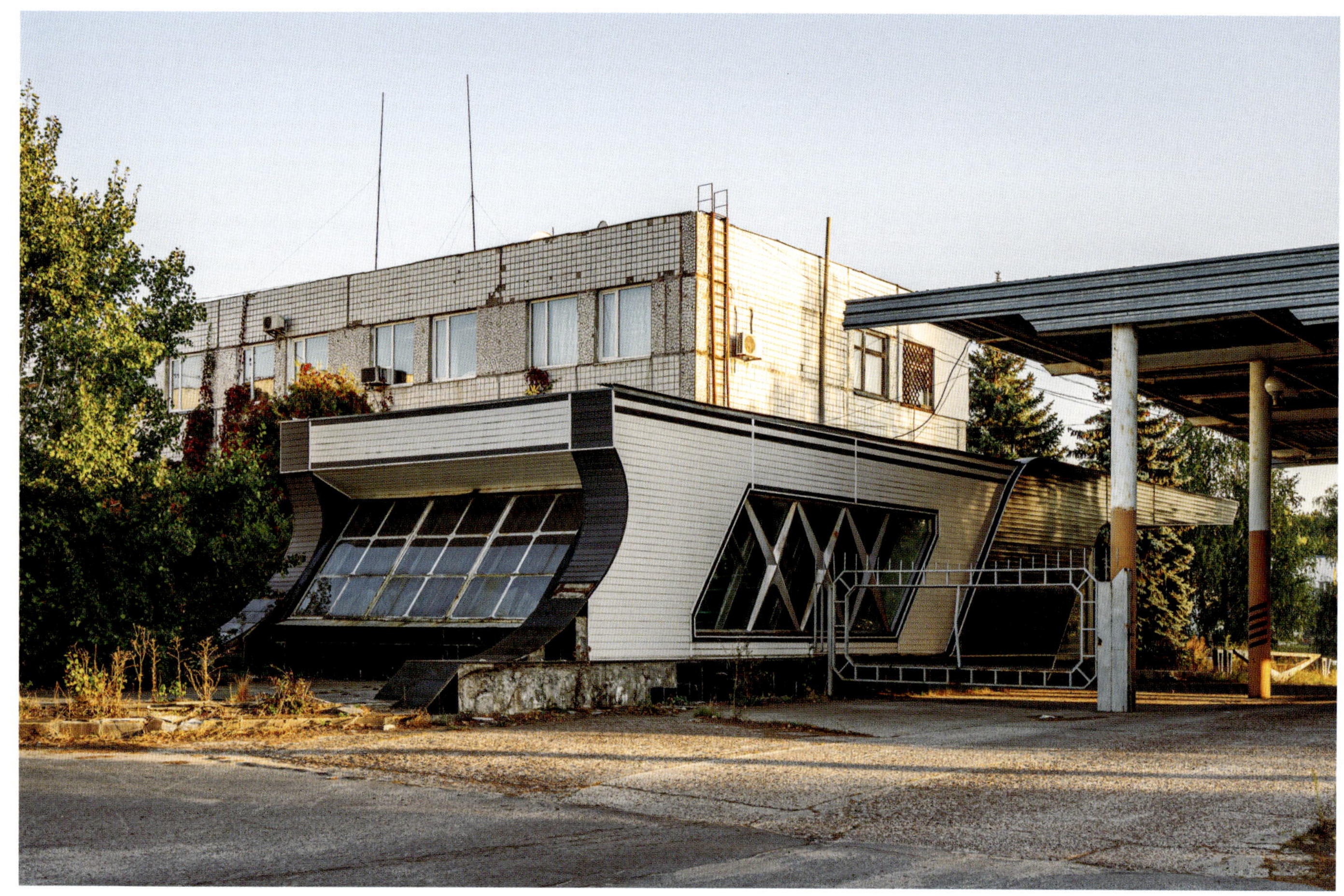

ATASS Bus Park and Repair Station
Slavutych, Kyiv Oblast
1995

The A-shaped central structure of the bus inspection areas represents the first letter of both the word for 'bus' (*avtobus* in Ukrainian) and the bus company's name ATASS (which stands for Slavutych Motor Transport Joint-Stock Company).

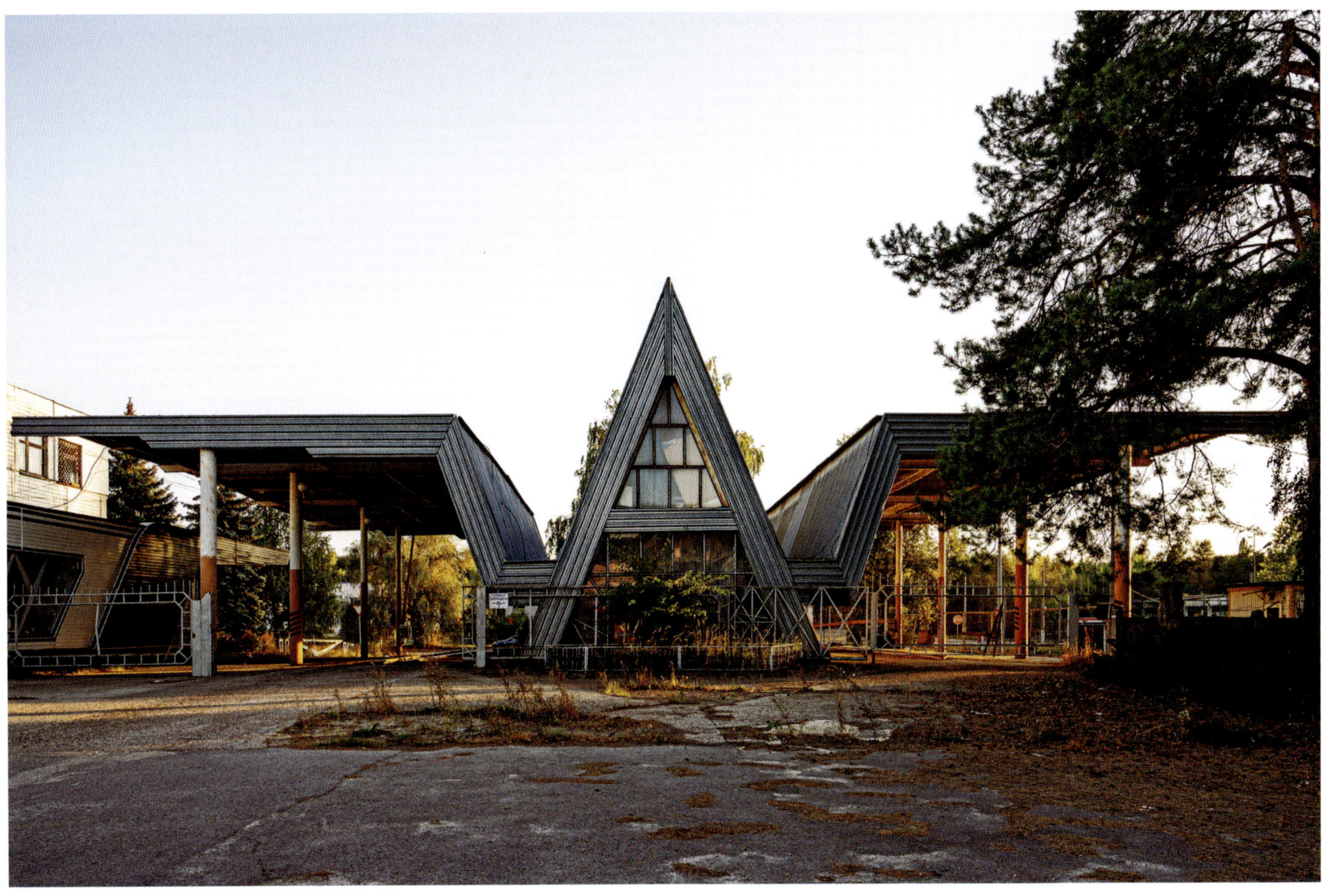

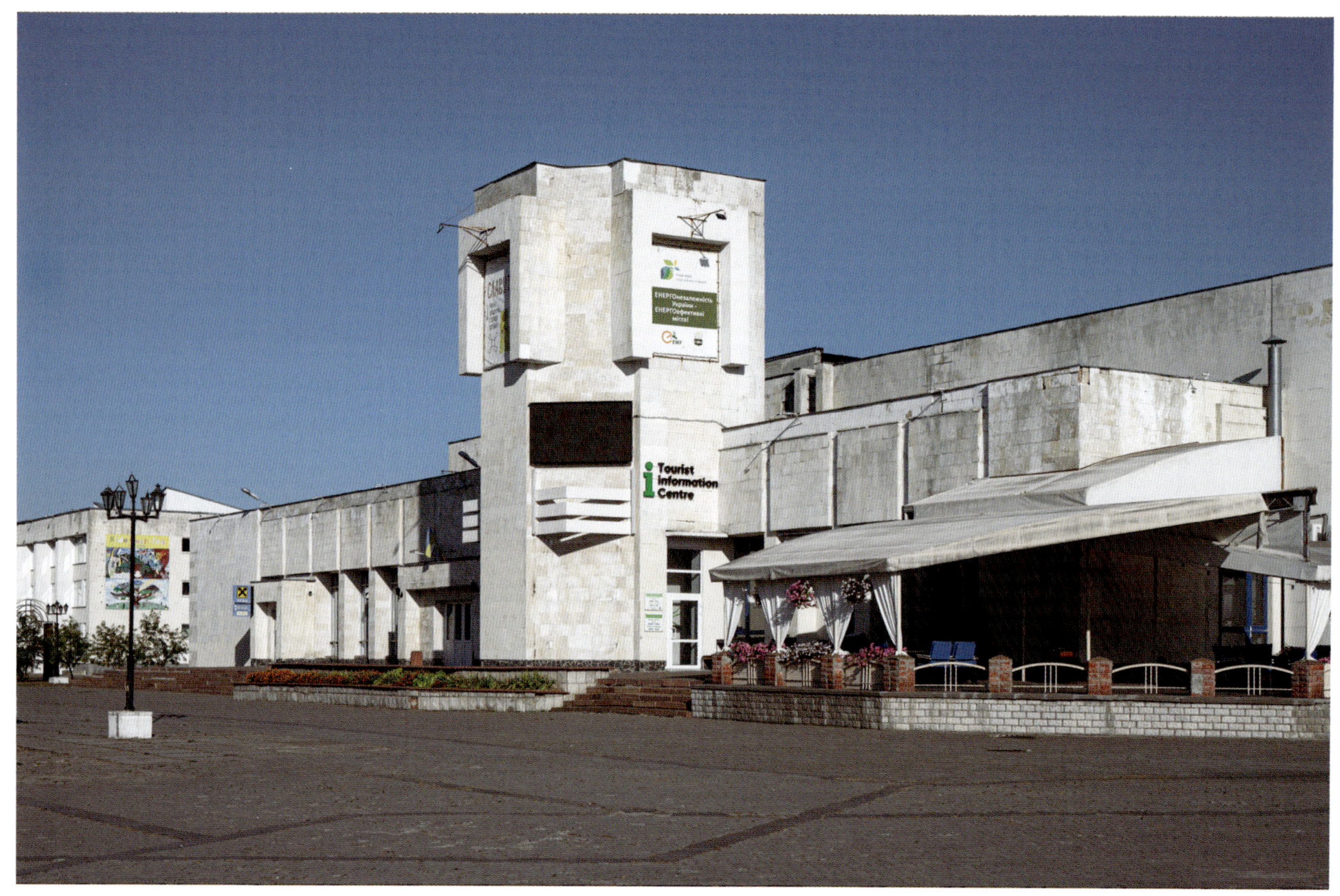

Slavutych Cinema and Concert Hall
Slavutych, Kyiv Oblast
1987–90
Architects: Ihor Dubasov, Volodymyr Petrov, Viktor Dovhaliuk,
Serhii Nivin

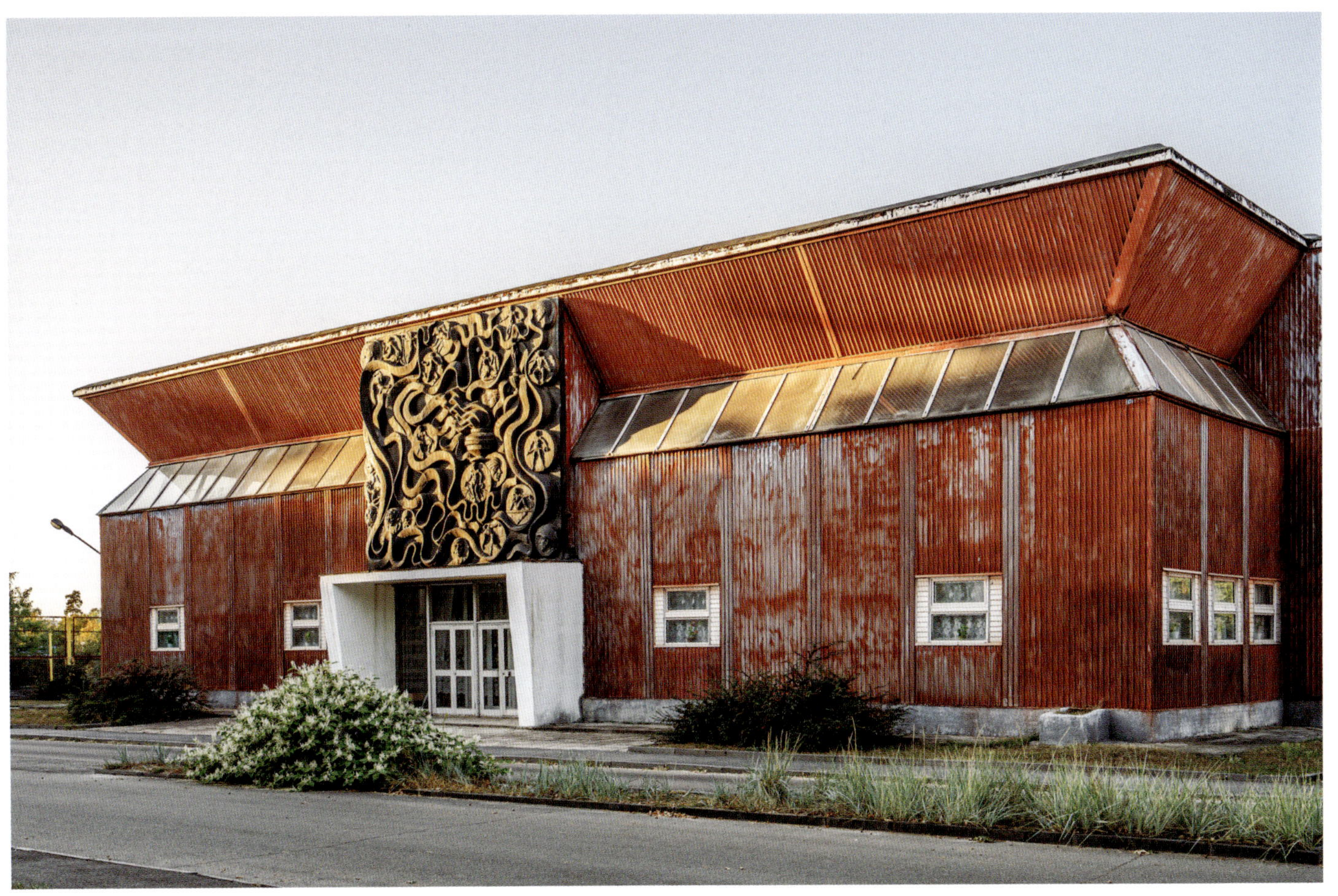

Gymnastics Sports Hall
Tbilisi Quarter, Slavutych, Kyiv Oblast
1988
Architect: V. Gaprindashvili
Artists: E. Kopadze, Z. Sakvarelidze

This prefabricated metal structure in the Tbilisi quarter was adapted by Georgian architect Gaprindashvili from the Standard Project No. 291-8-21.87, developed by TsNIIEP (see also p48). Its front and back are adorned with bas-reliefs created by Georgian artists.

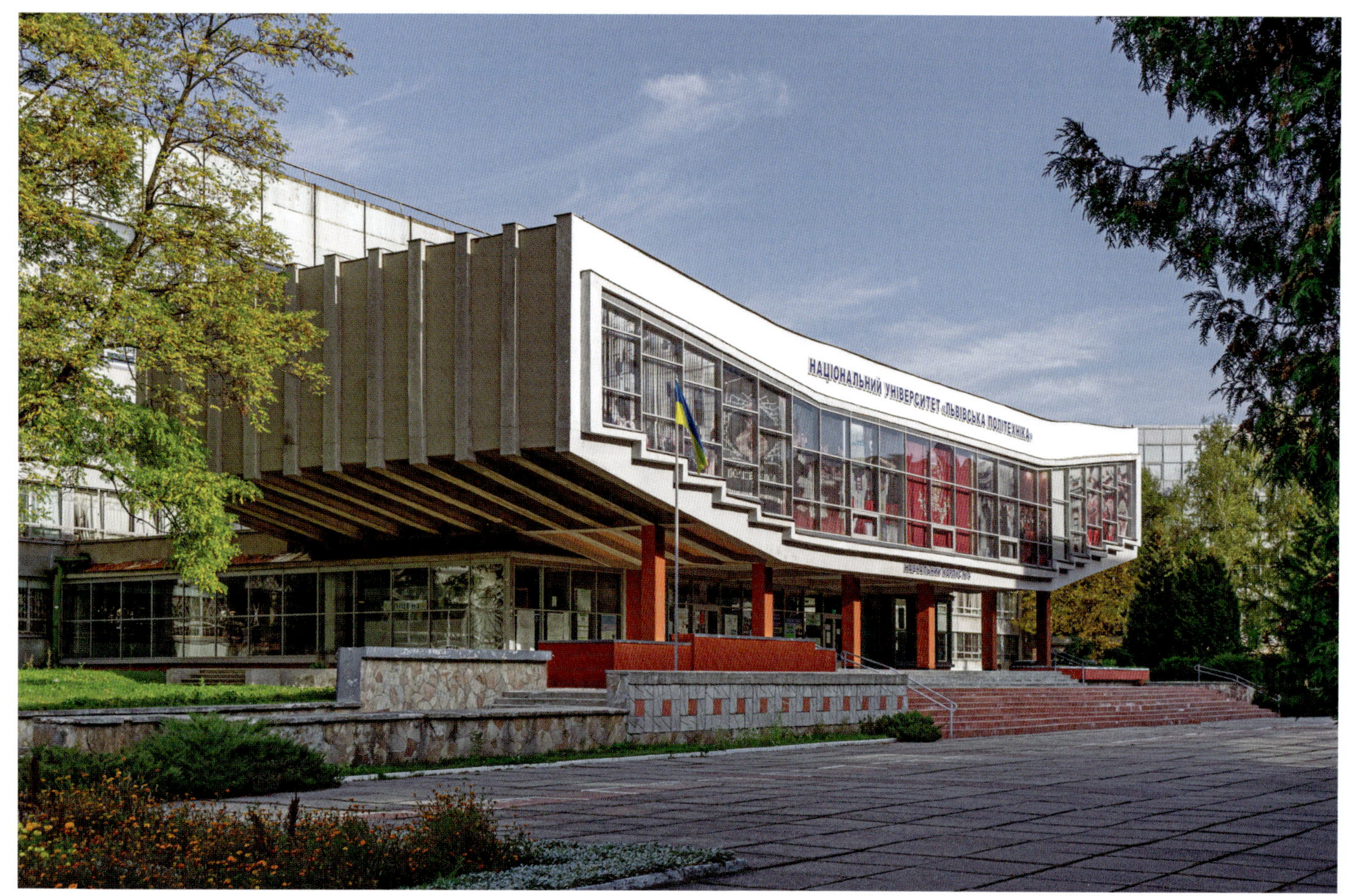

General Technical Building, Lviv Polytechnic Institute
Lviv
1971
Architects: Pavlo Mariev, H. Koziura, R. Yukhtovskii
Engineer: V. Rokach

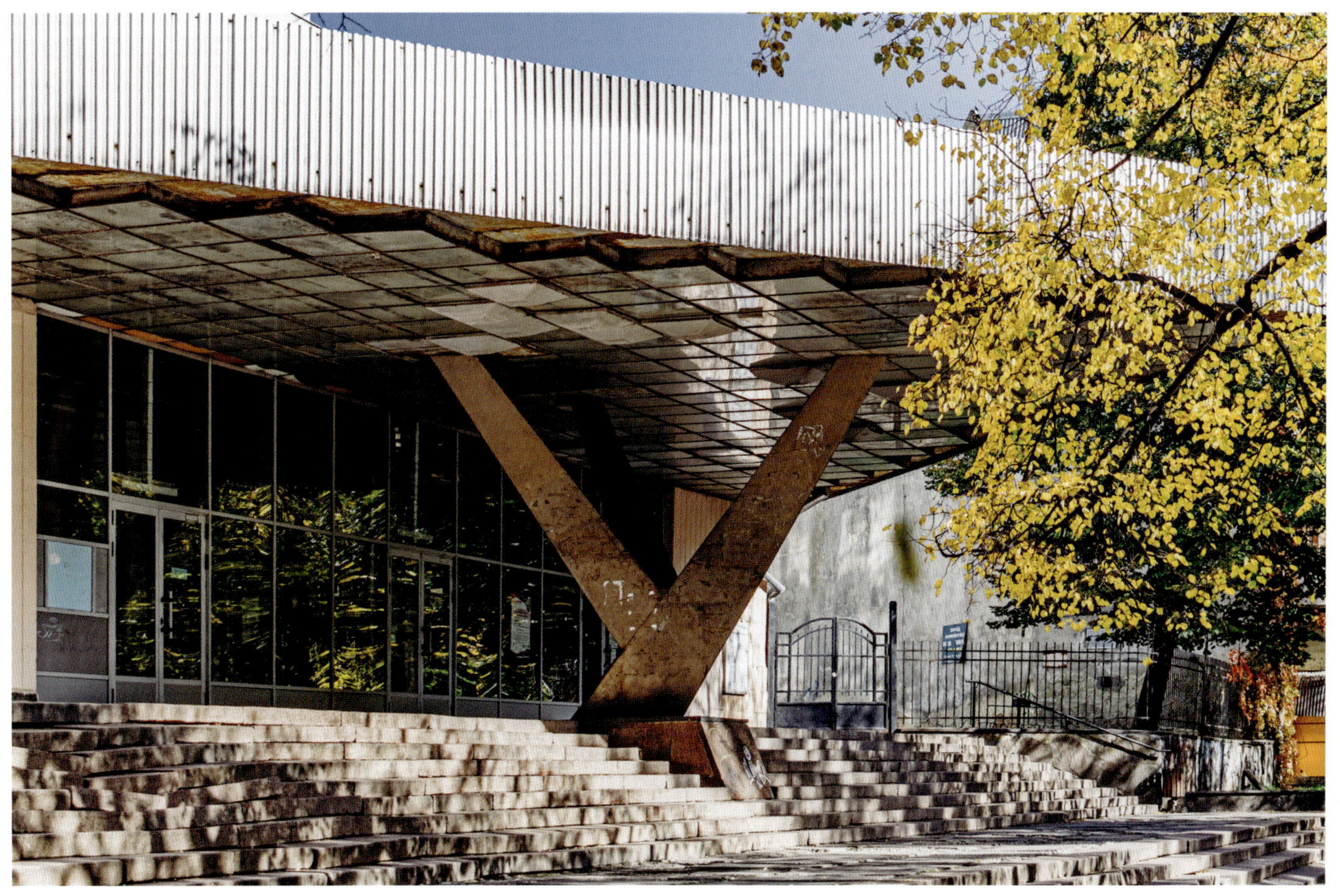

Faculty of Energy Building, Lviv Polytechnic Institute
1970–72
Architect: Muza Konsulova
Engineer: S. Sharshatkina

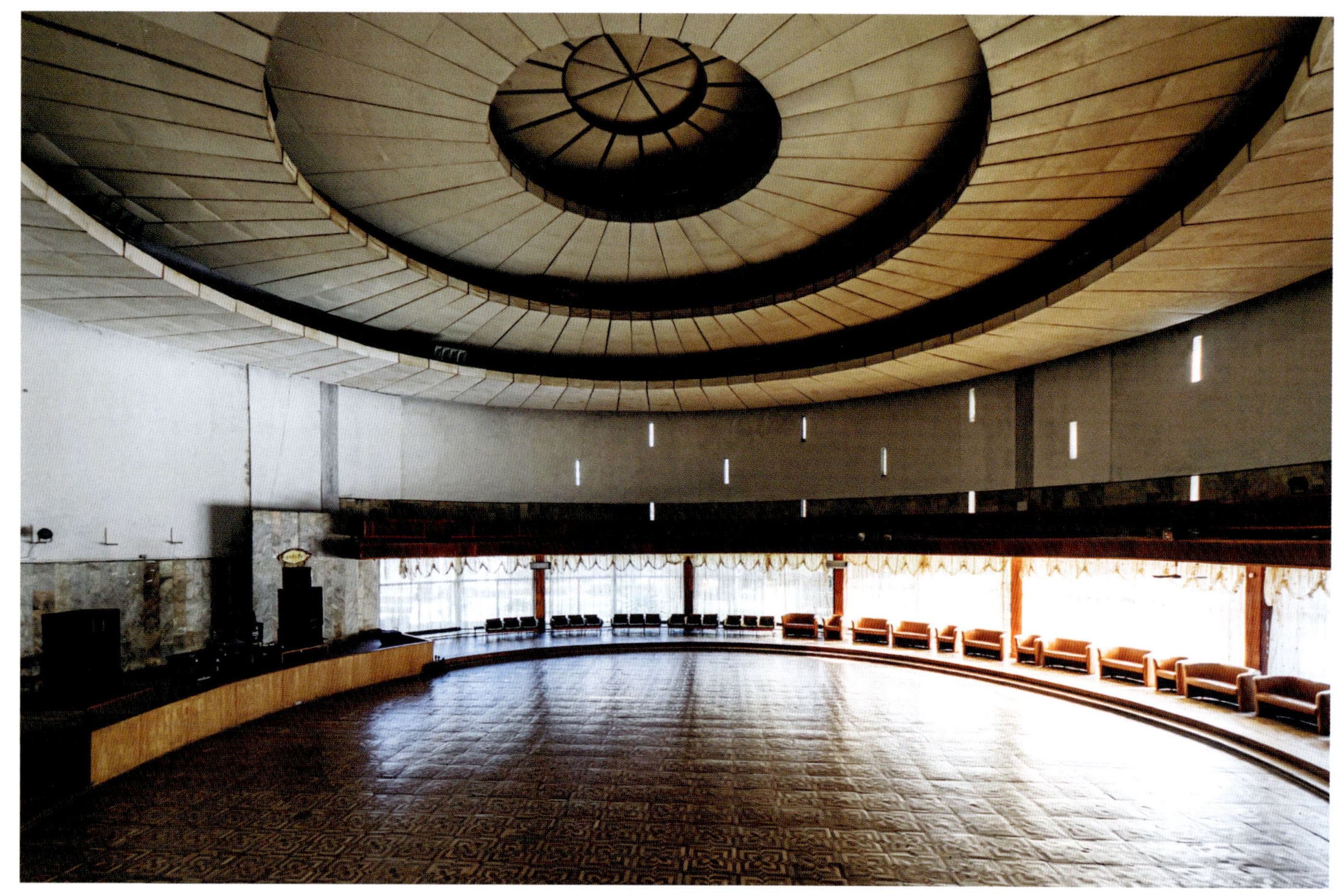

Taras Shevchenko Palace of Culture
Truskavets, Lviv Oblast
1971
Architect: Anatolii Konsulov
Engineer: L. Yefremova

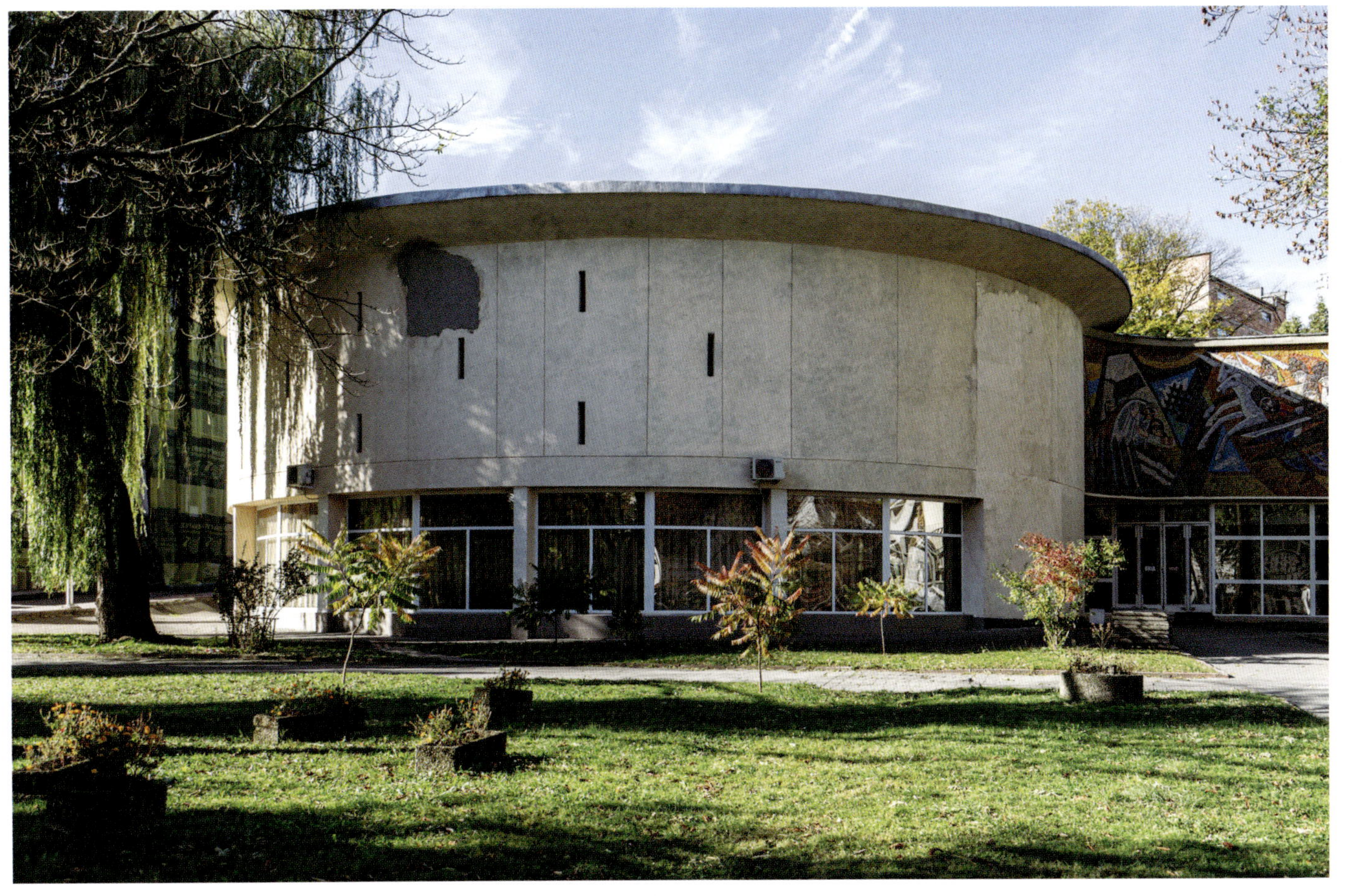

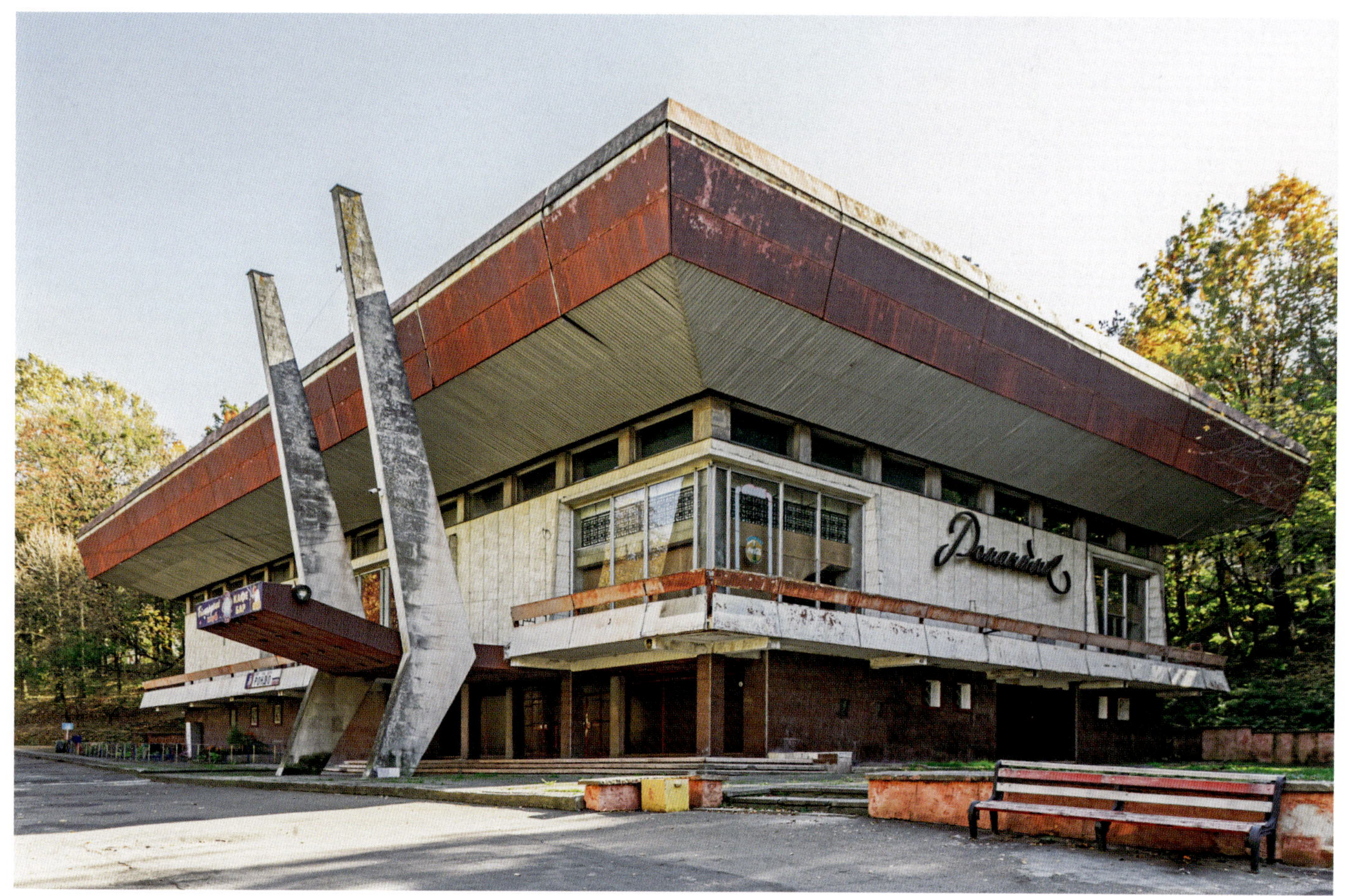

'Romantyk' Palace of Youth
Lviv
1979
Architects: Myroslav Trach, Volodymyr Bliusiuk

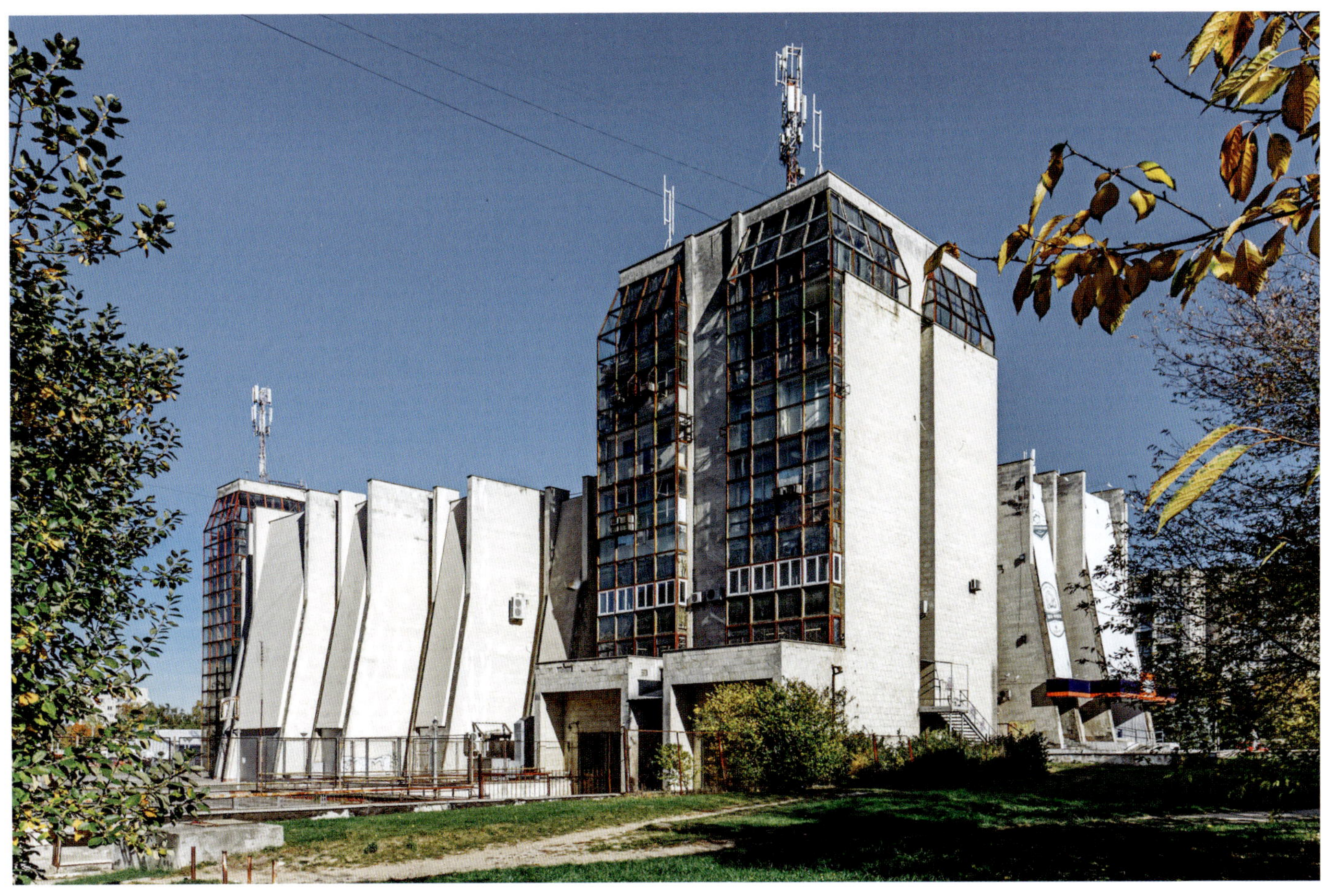

TSUM Department Store (*Tsentralnyi Universalnyi Mahazyn*
or Central Universal Department Store)
Lviv
1980s
Architects: Zinovii Pidlisnyi, Vasyl Kamenschyk, Yuliia Verblian, Vitalii Petelko

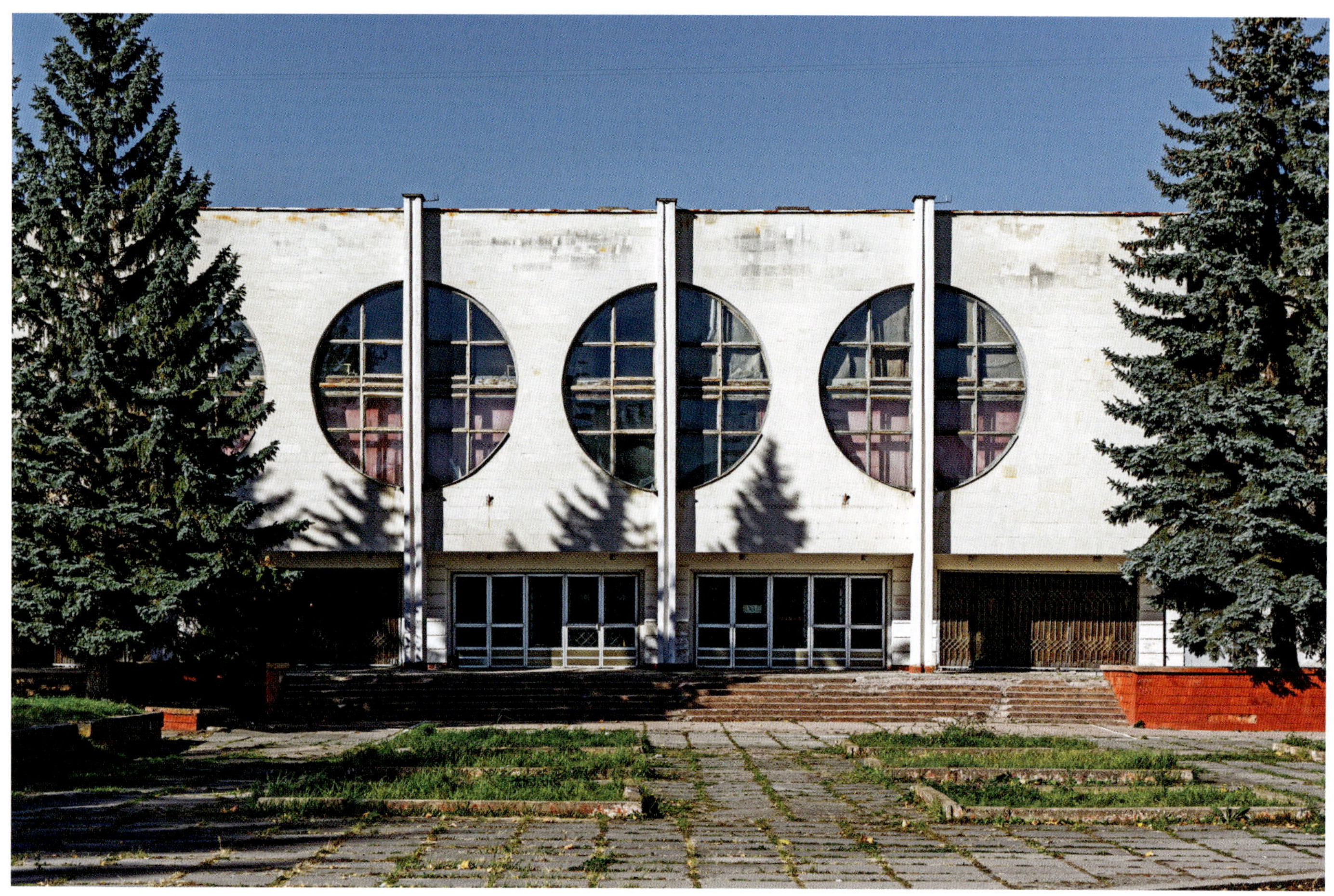

LORTA Palace of Culture
Lviv
1982

This building was designed by the in-house team at the Department of Capital Construction Design at the LORTA (Lviv Radio Equipment Association) Factory, previously named the V.I. Lenin Production Association during the Soviet era.

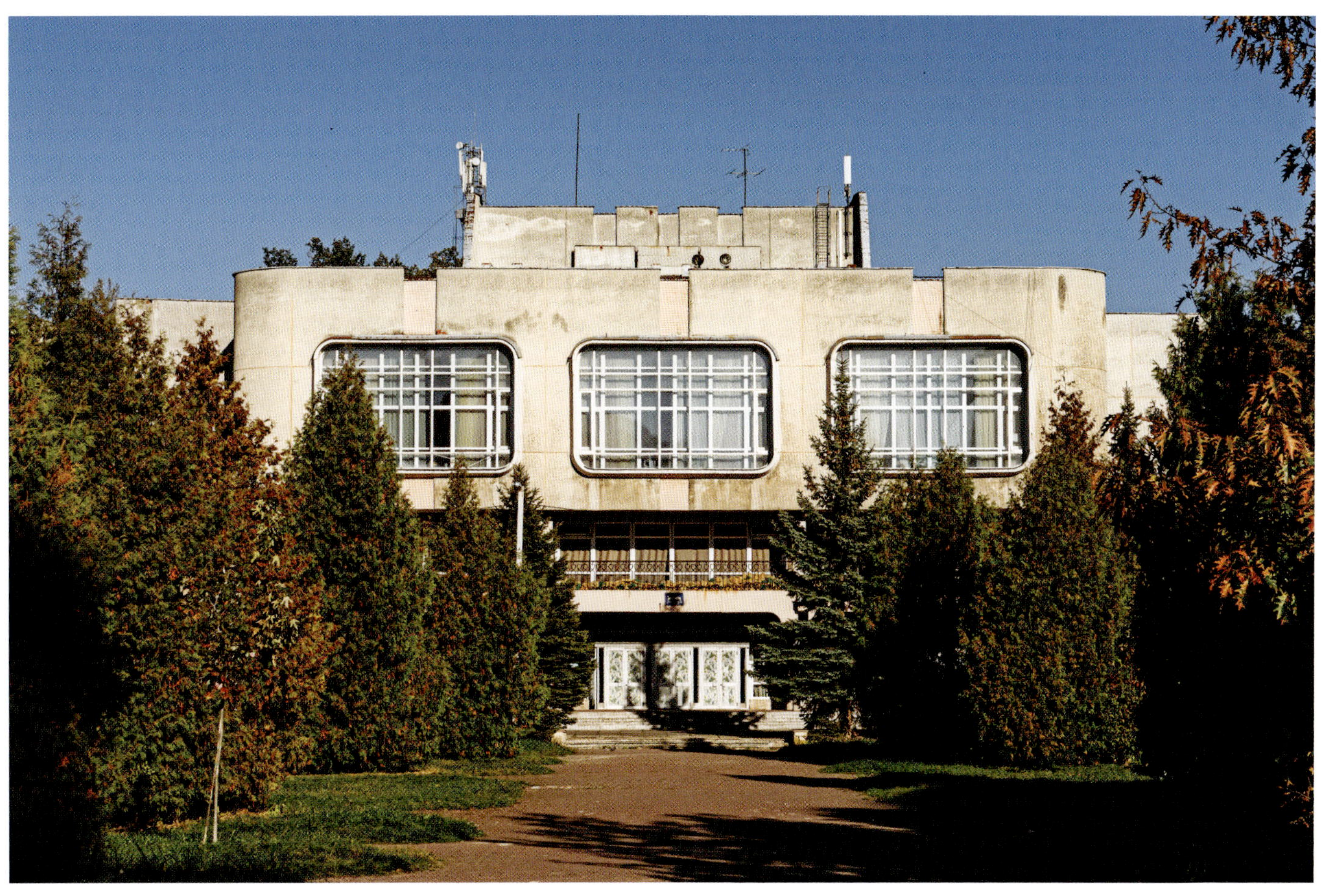

Centre for Creativity of Children and Youth of Halychyna
(formerly Palace of Pioneers and Schoolchildren)
Lviv
1984

Architects: Zinovii Pidlisnyi, Yaroslav Nazarkevych, Anatolii Vashchak,
Myroslav Smetana
Engineer: V. Sprysa

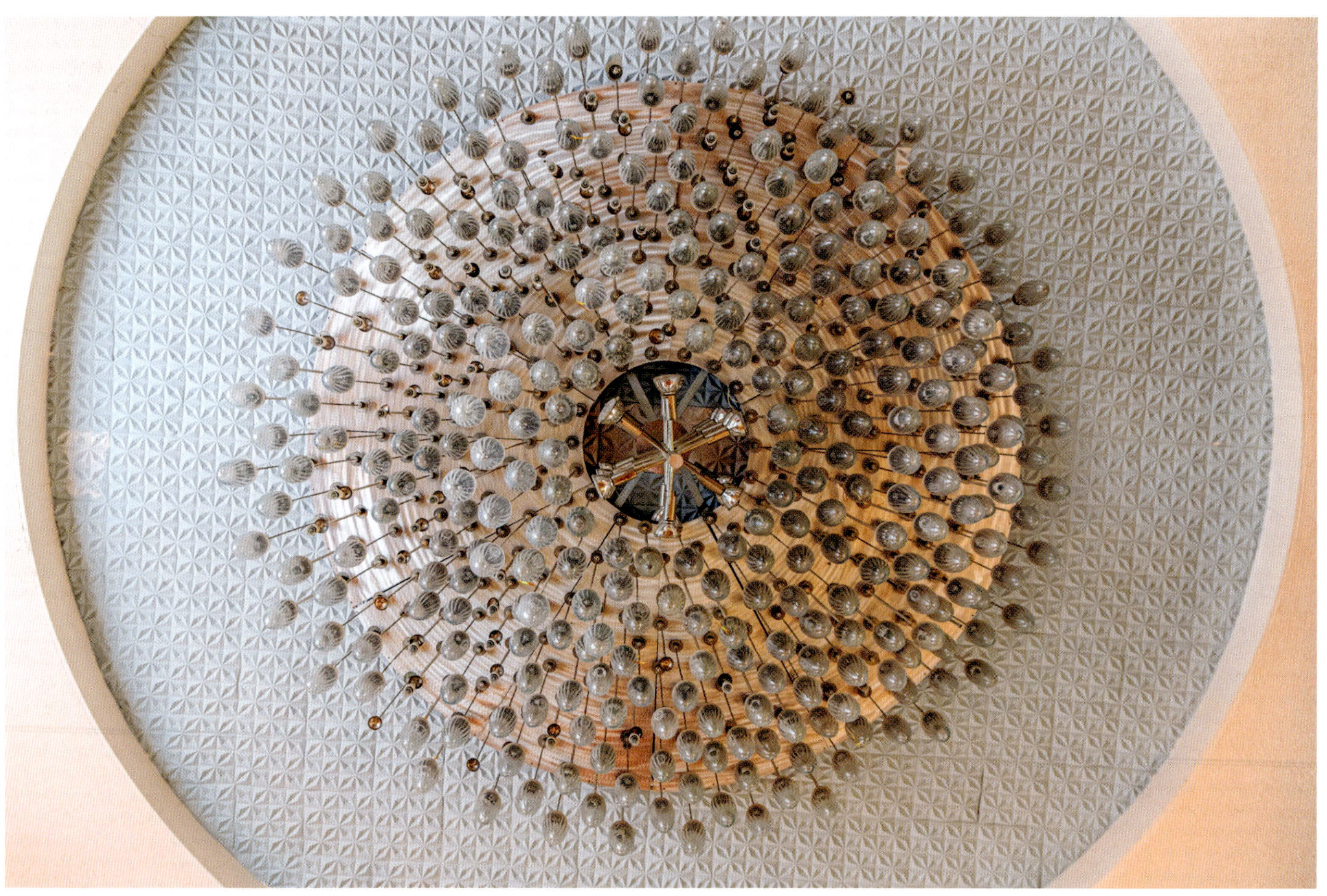

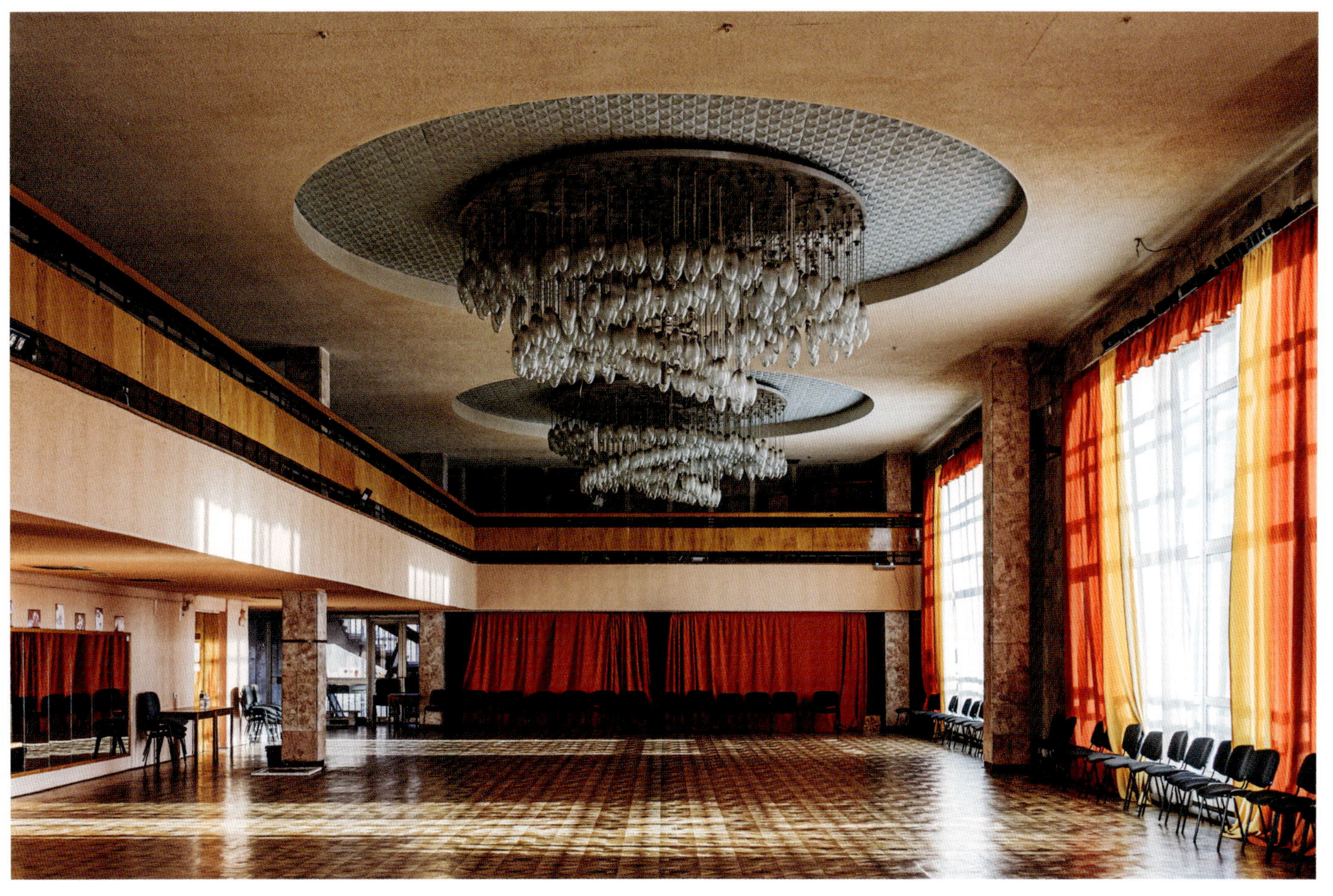

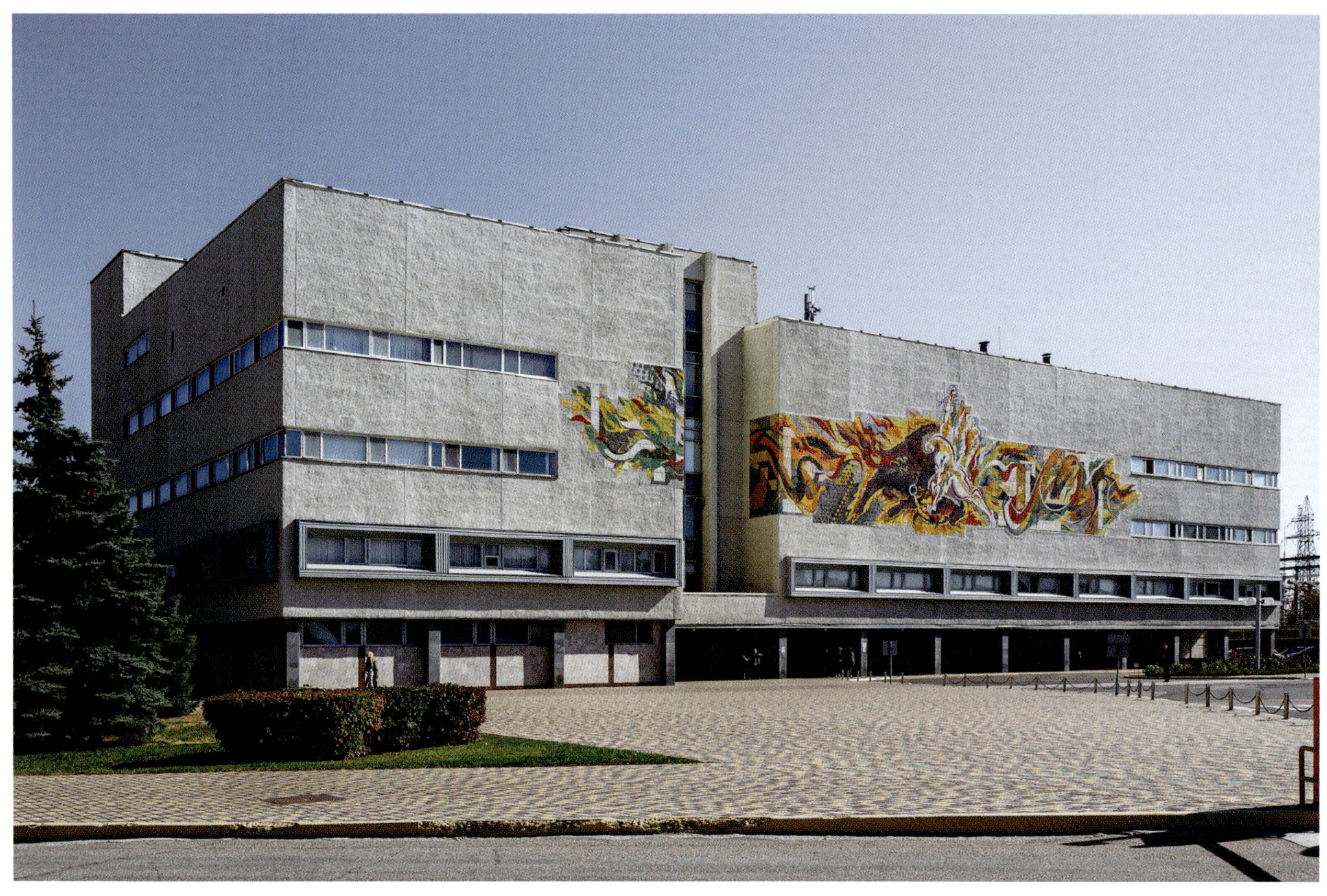

Pivdennoukrainsk Nuclear Power Plant
Mykolaiv Oblast
1975–82

Also known as the South Ukraine Nuclear Power Plant, it is the country's second largest NPP (after Zaporizhzhia), with a capacity of 2,850 megawatts. On 19 September 2022 it was damaged by a Russian missile strike.

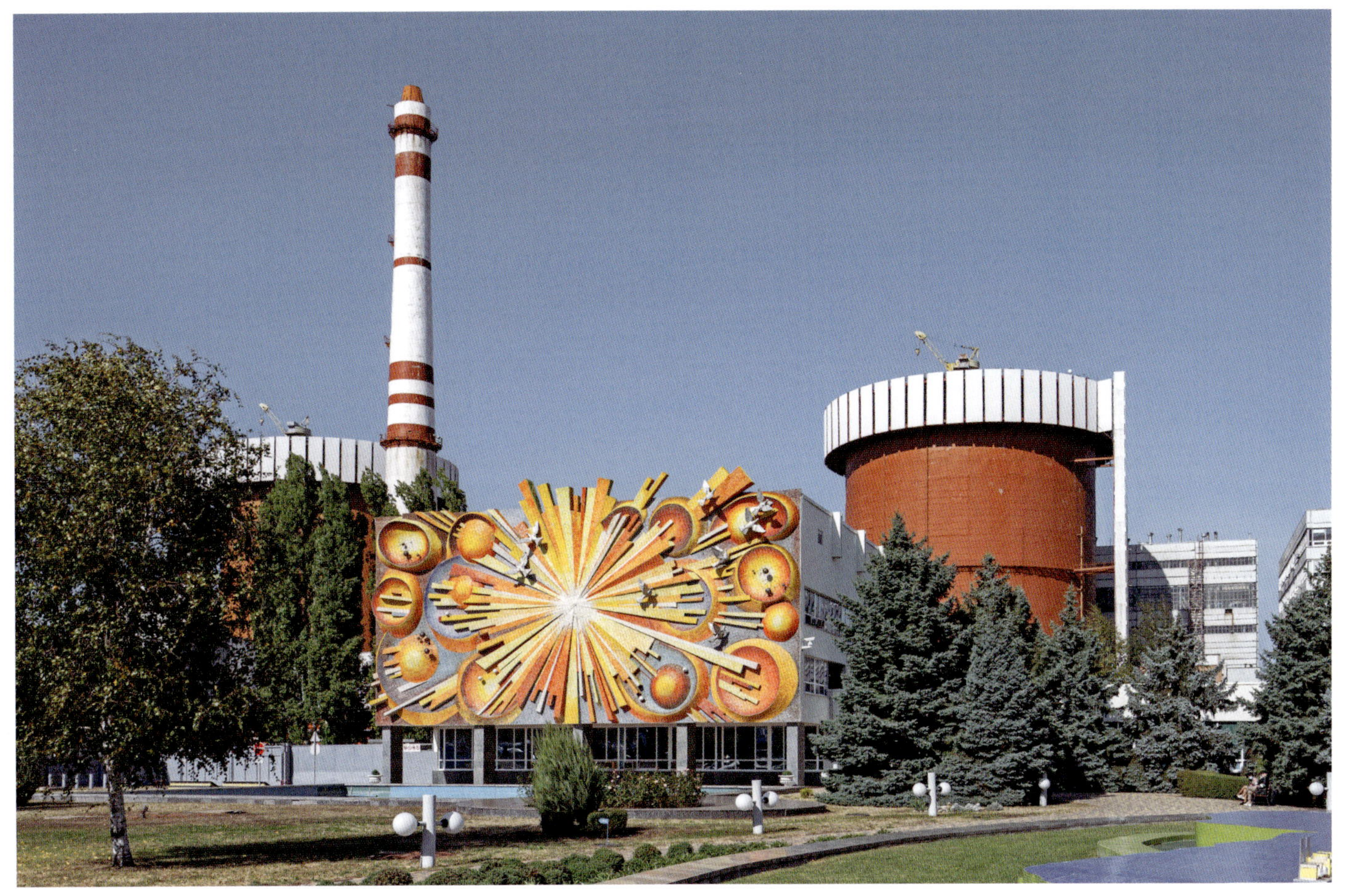

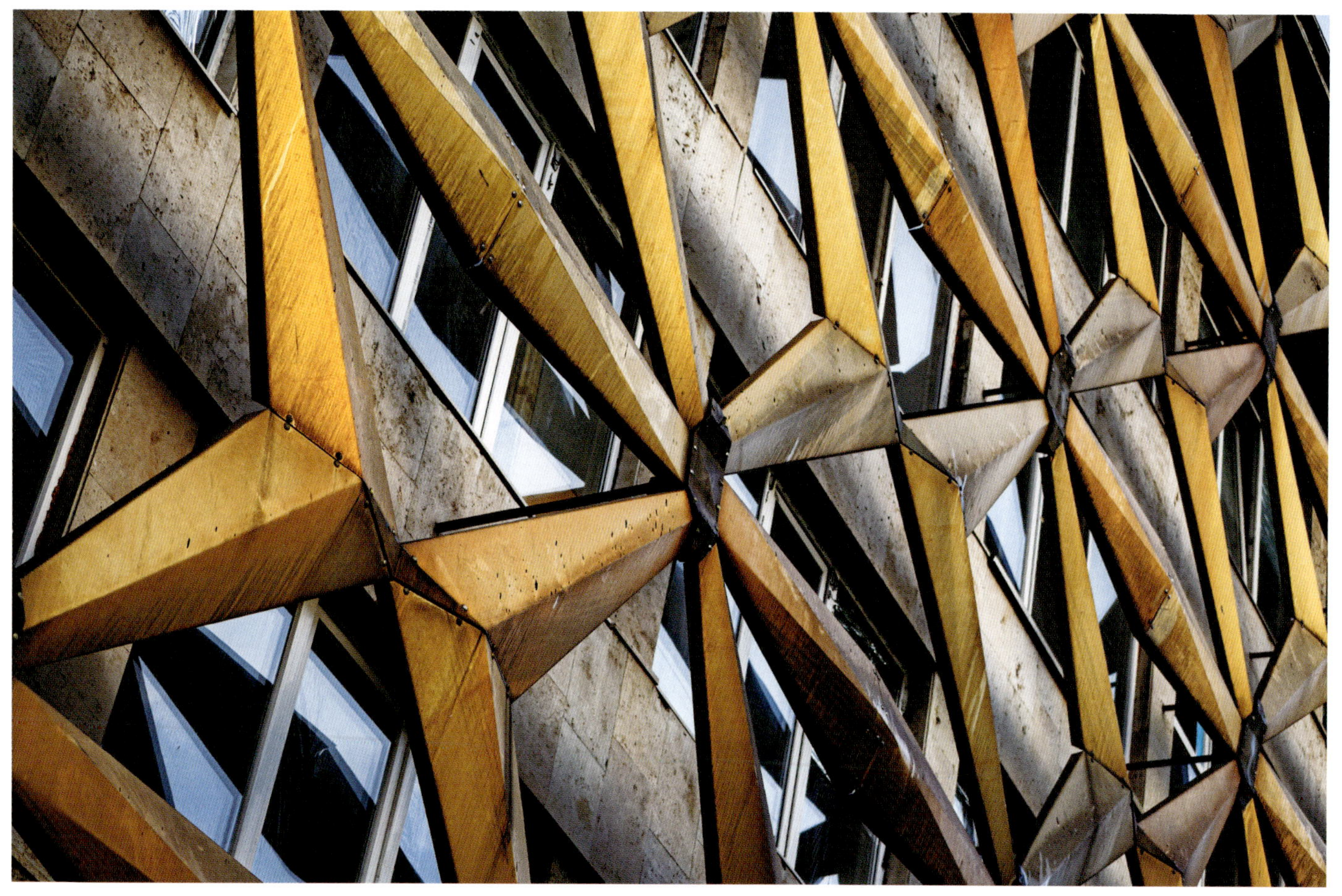

Odesa Theatre of Musical Comedy
Odesa
1981
Architect: Genrikh Topuz

Interior architect: V. Krasenko
Engineer: O. Liubovskyi
Artists: N. Abramova, I. Kulakova, V. Bubnov, A. Shaposhnikova

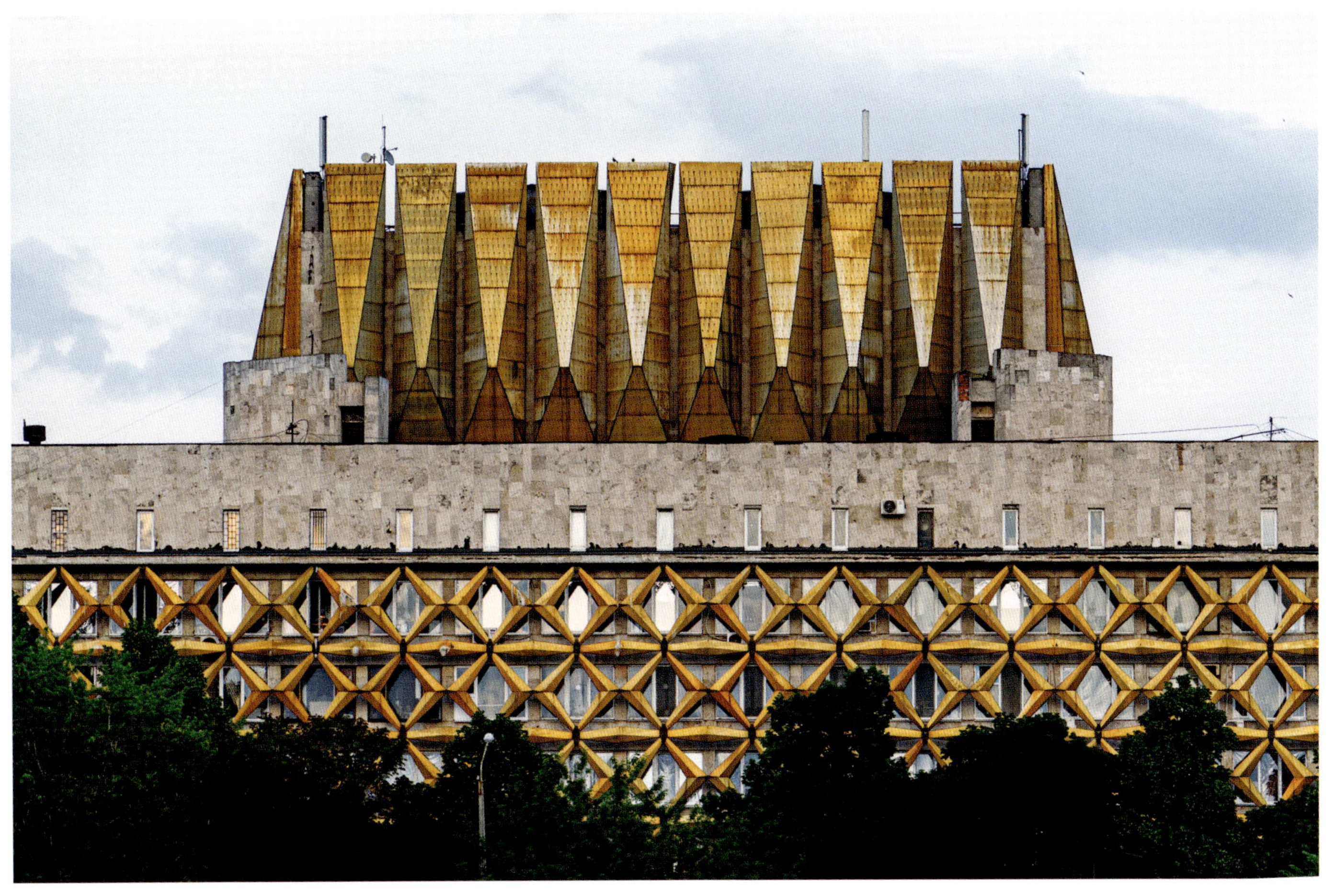

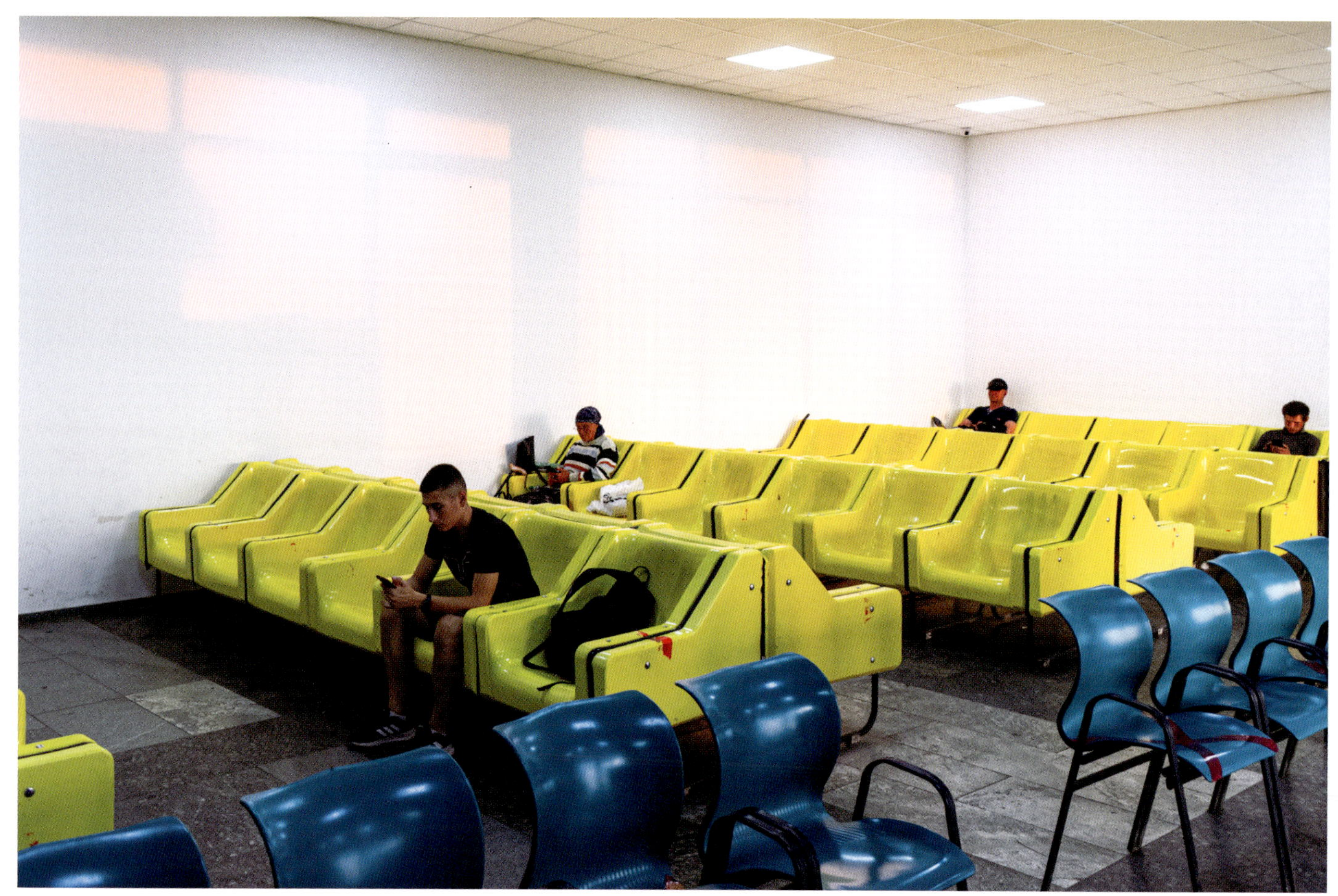

Poltava Bus Station
Poltava
1986
Architects: Valentyna Bohatenko, Mykhailo Yakovenko,
L. Gushchenska, A. Andrushkevych

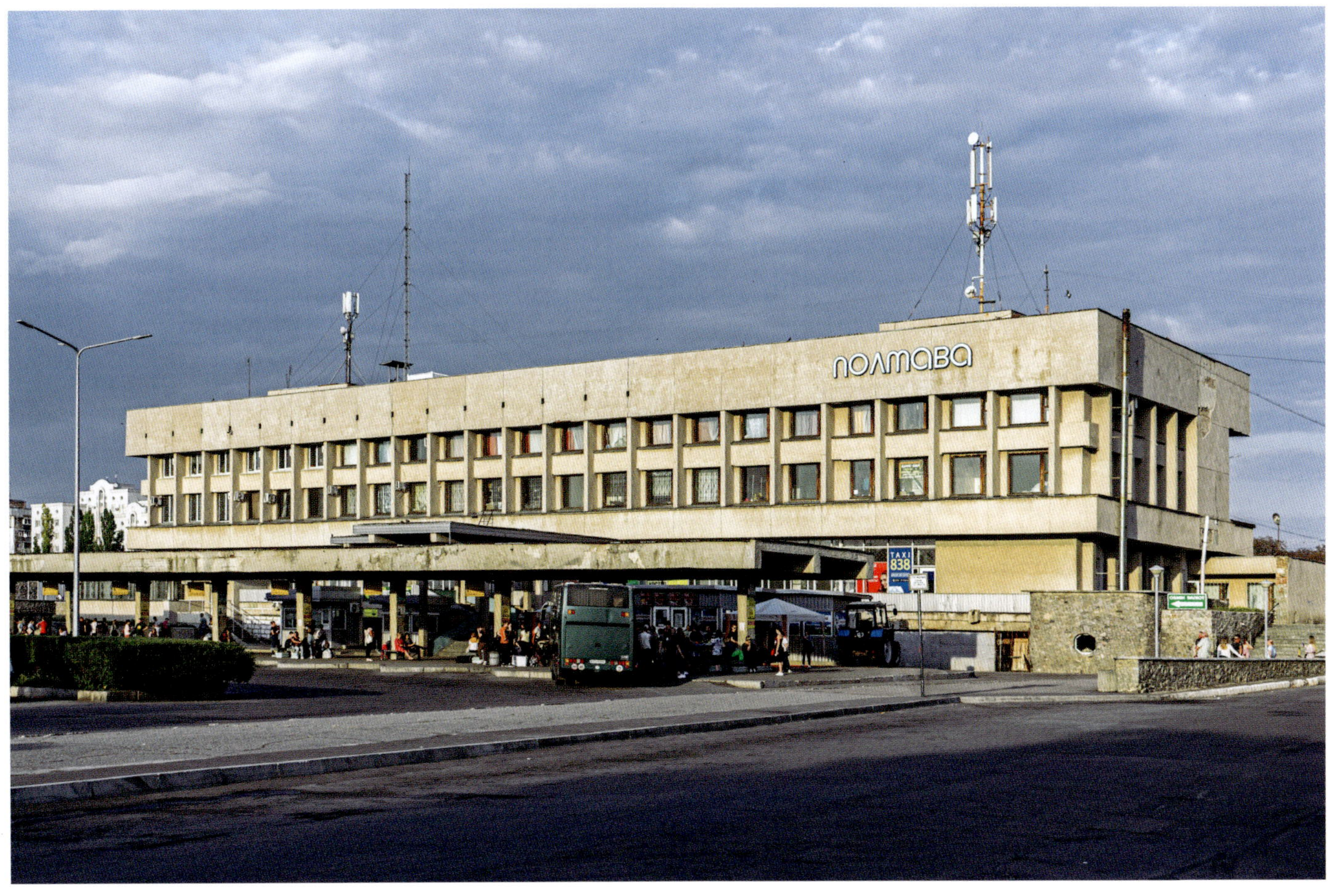

полтава
TAXI
838

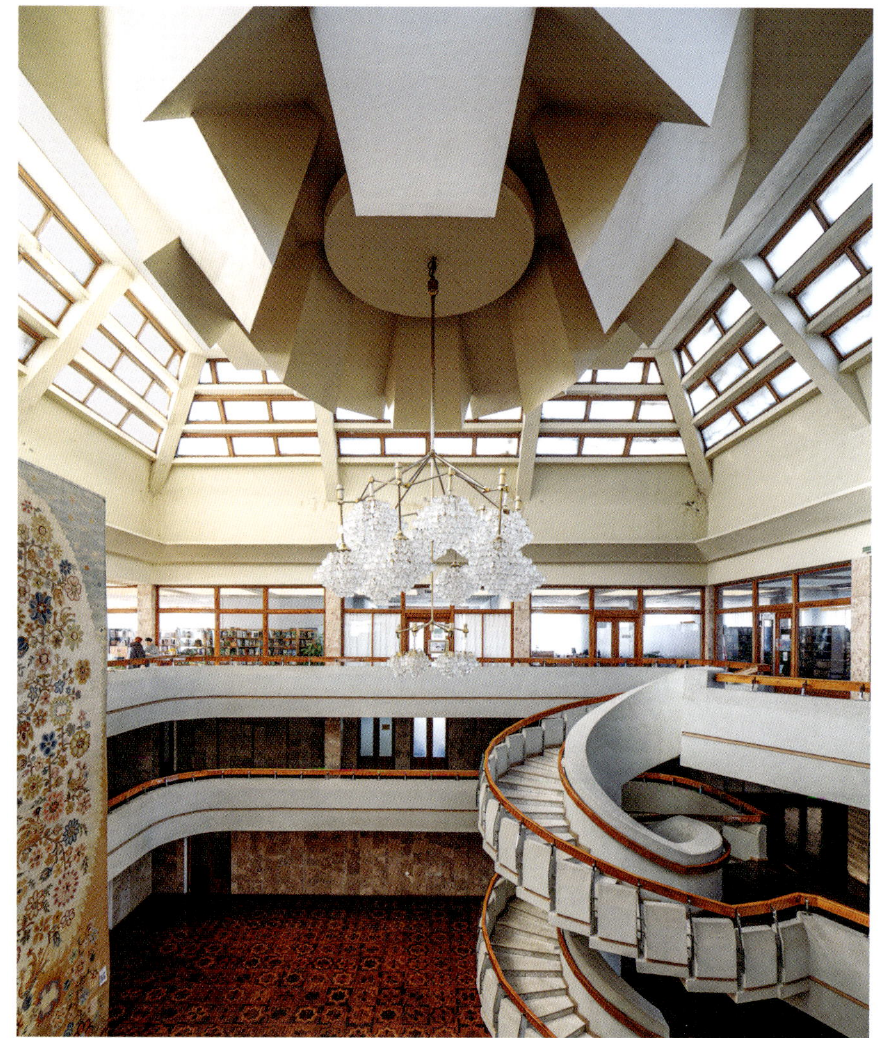

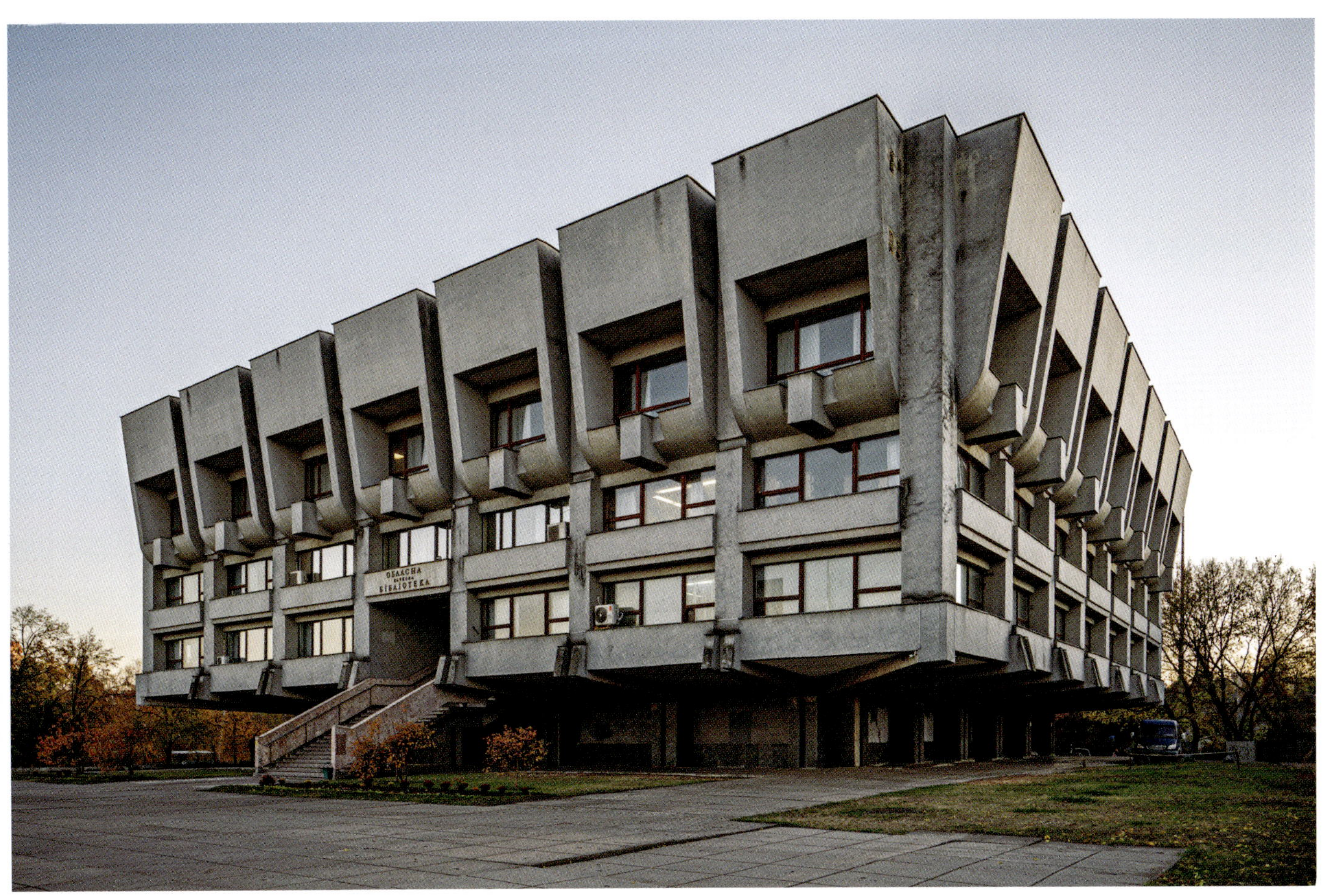

Sumy Universal Scientific Library
Sumy
1981–86
Architects: Yurii Kobyliakov, Serhii Ivchenko
Engineer: S. Morhoslip

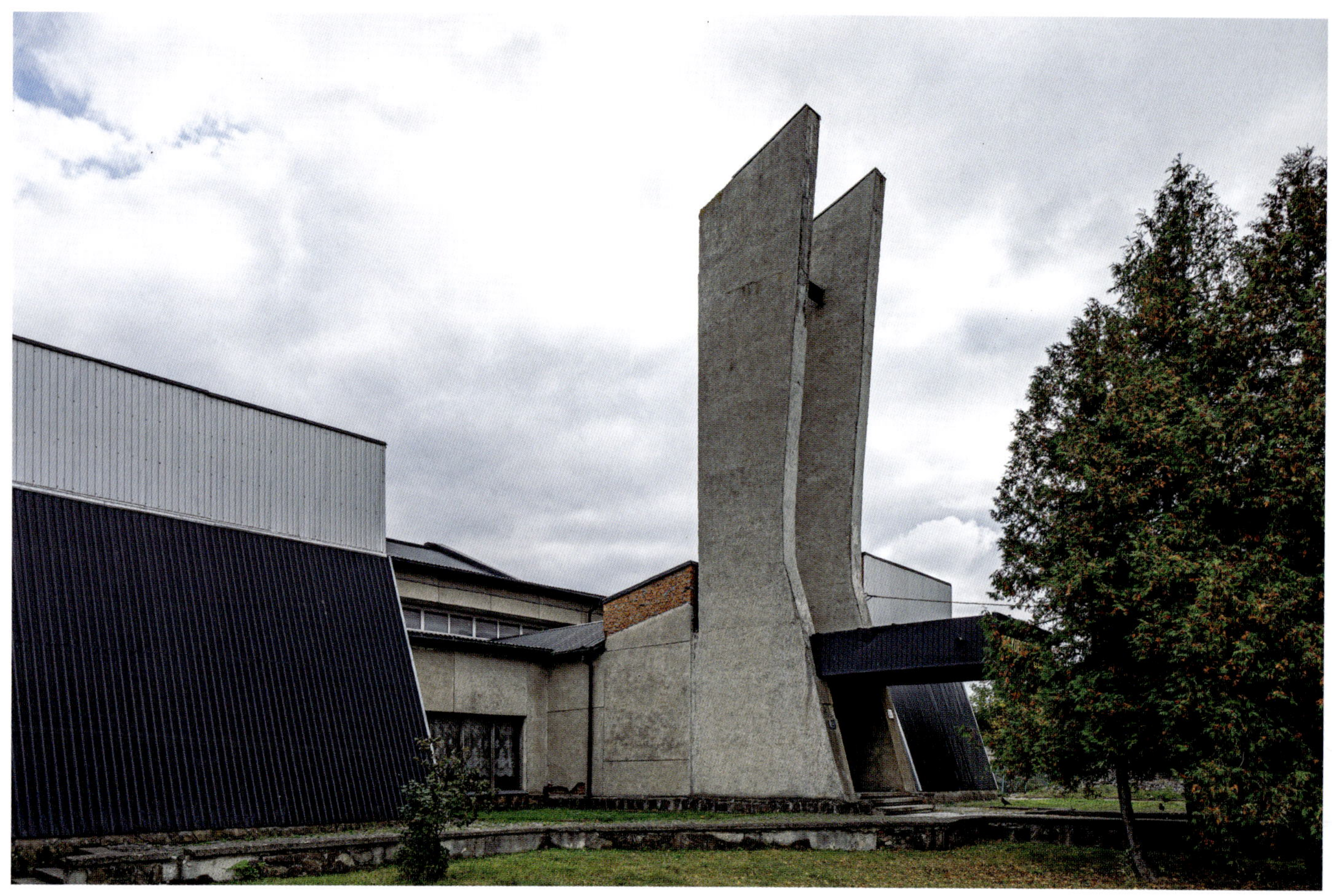

House of Mourning Rituals
Ternopil
1985
Architect: Serhii Dyriavko

Originally clad entirely in stucco, the facade has undergone a number of refurbishments since the 1990s. During this time it had been largely covered in black metal panels, which obscured the building's expressive brutalist details.

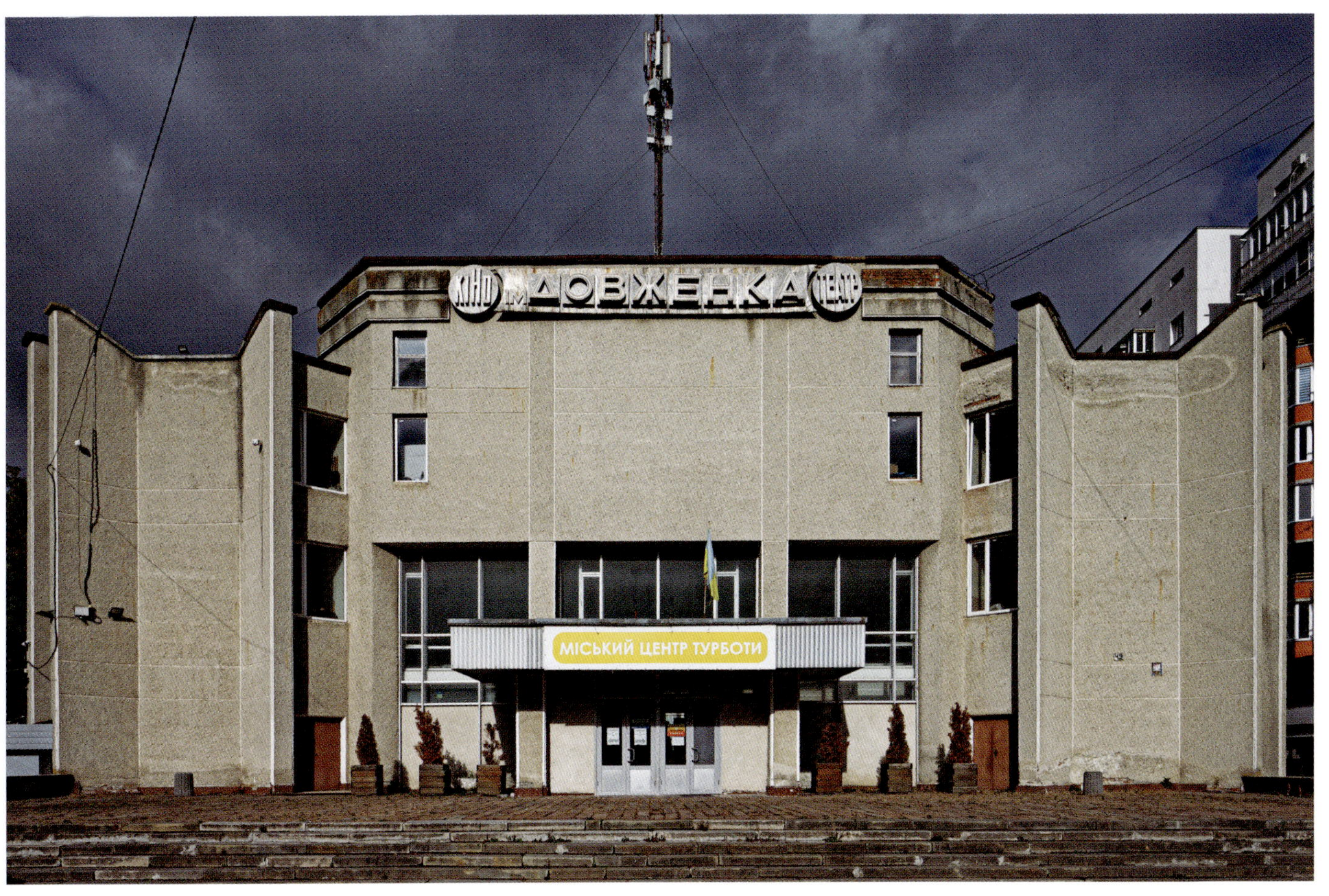

Dovzhenko Cinema
Ternopil
1980s

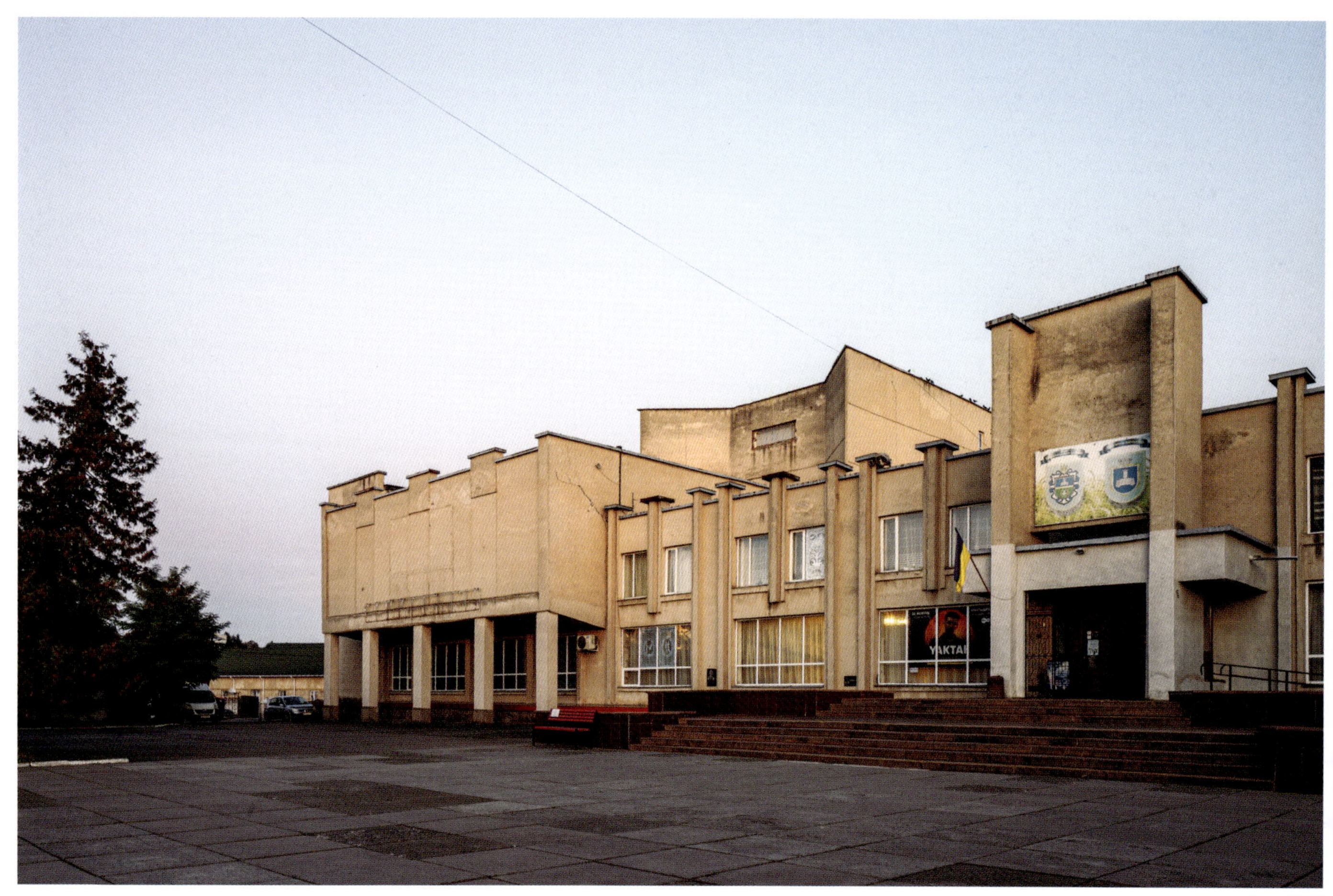

Khmilnyk Palace of Culture
Vinnytsia Oblast
1980s

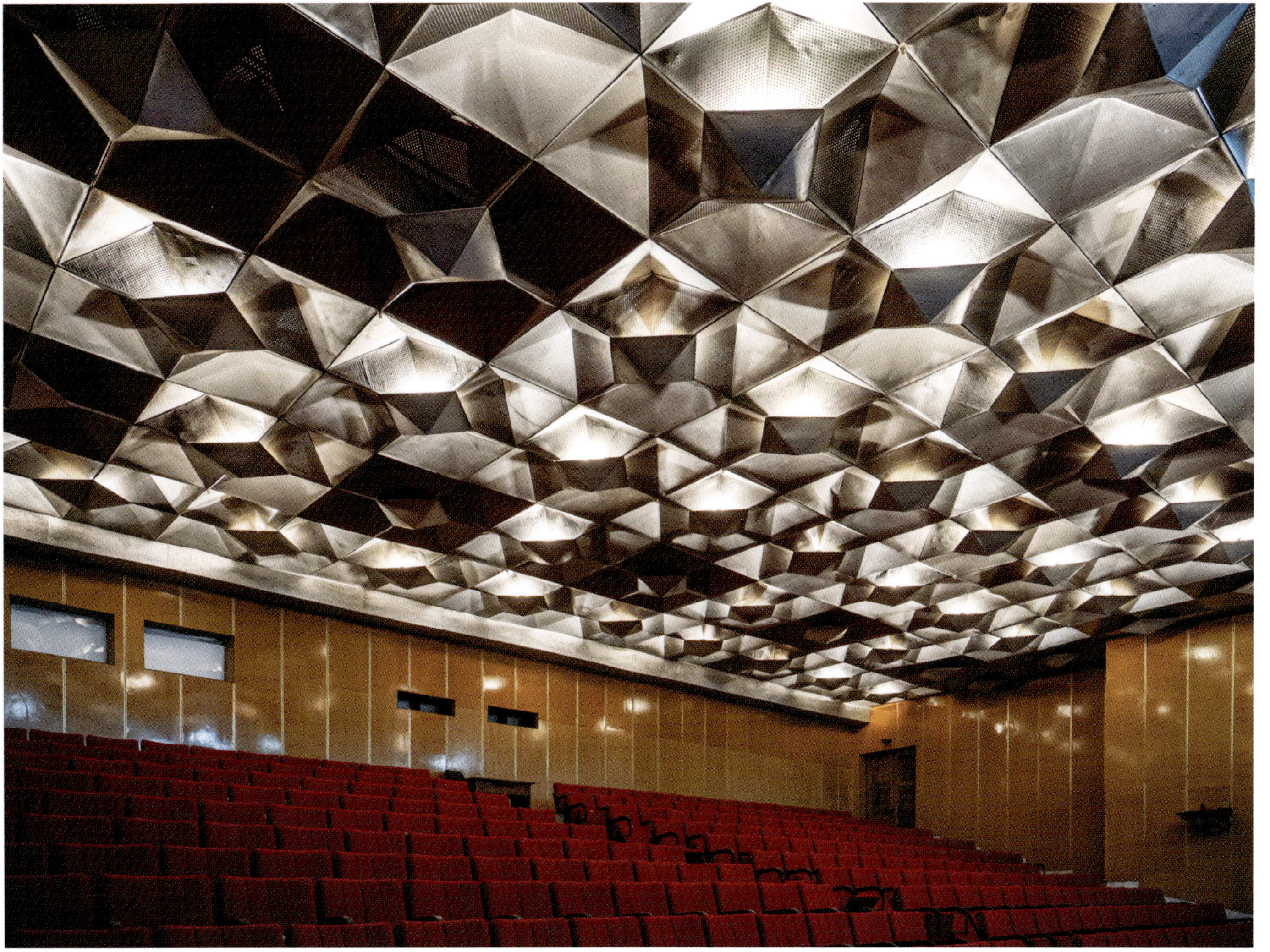

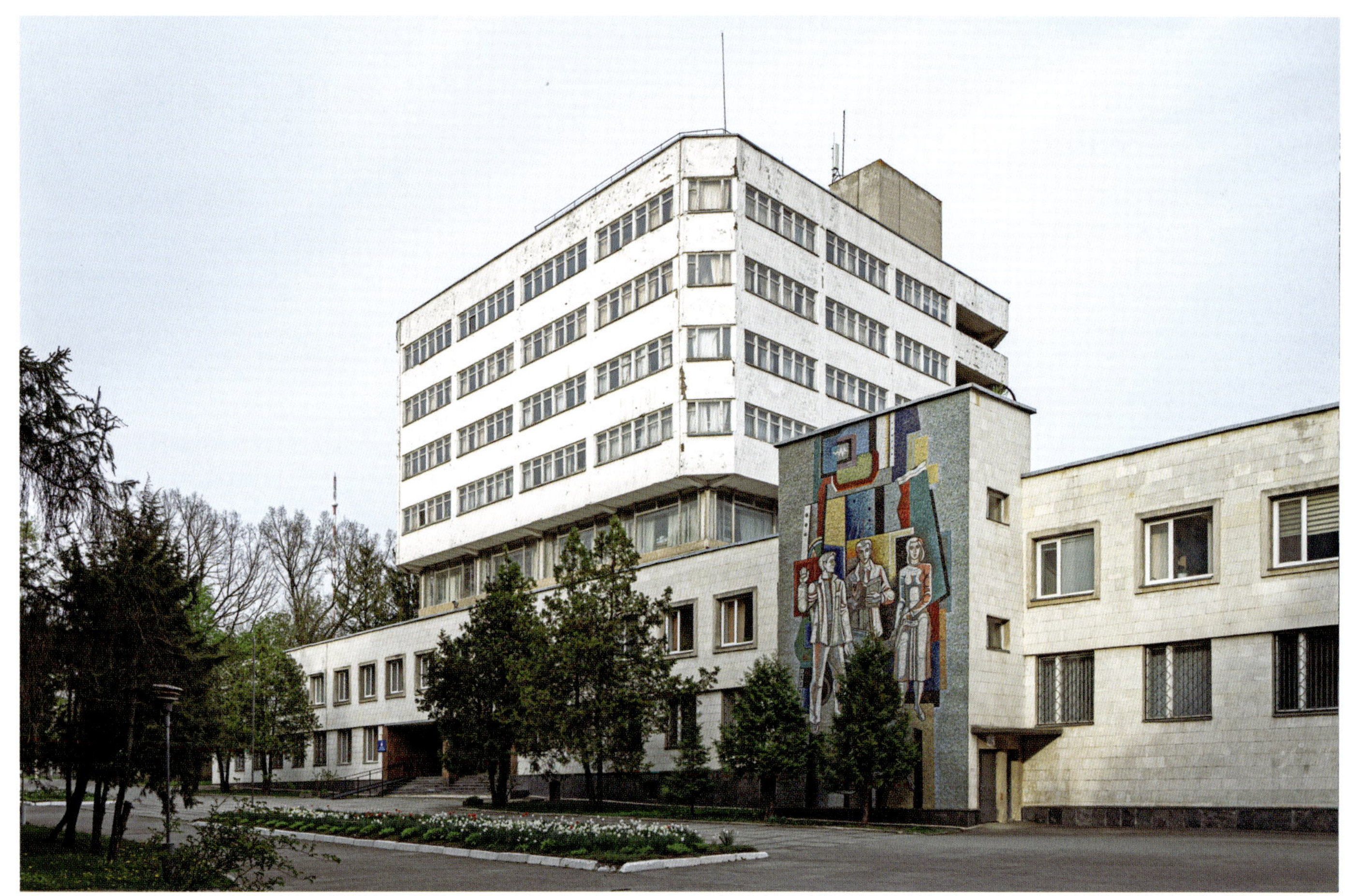

Vinnytsia National Technical University
Vinnytsia
1986
Artist: Volodymyr Yamkovenko

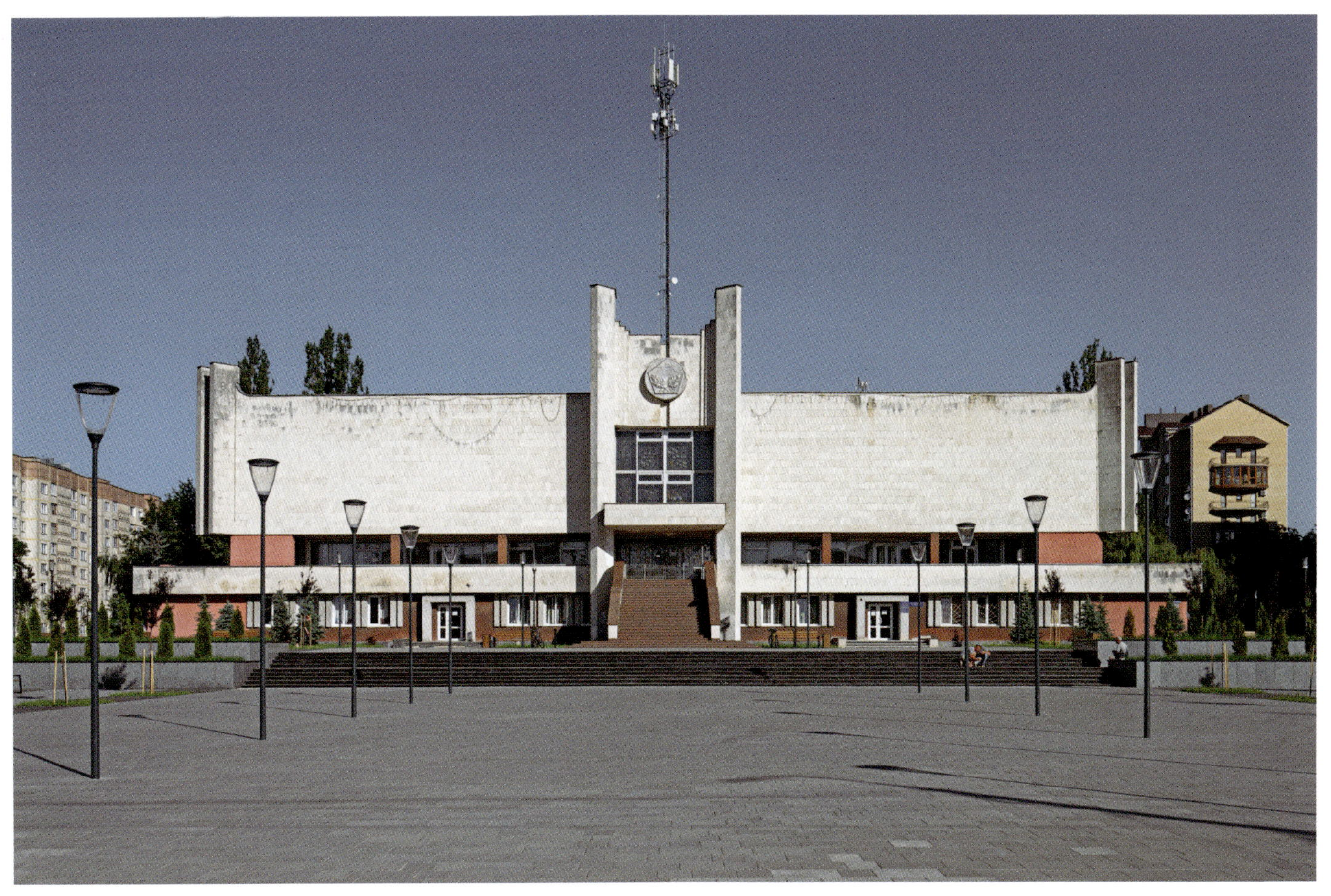

Palace of Weddings
Lutsk, Volyn Oblast
1985
Architect: Volodymyr Moroz

Engineer: A. Avdasieva
Artists: Ivan Lytovchenko, Mariia Lytovchenko

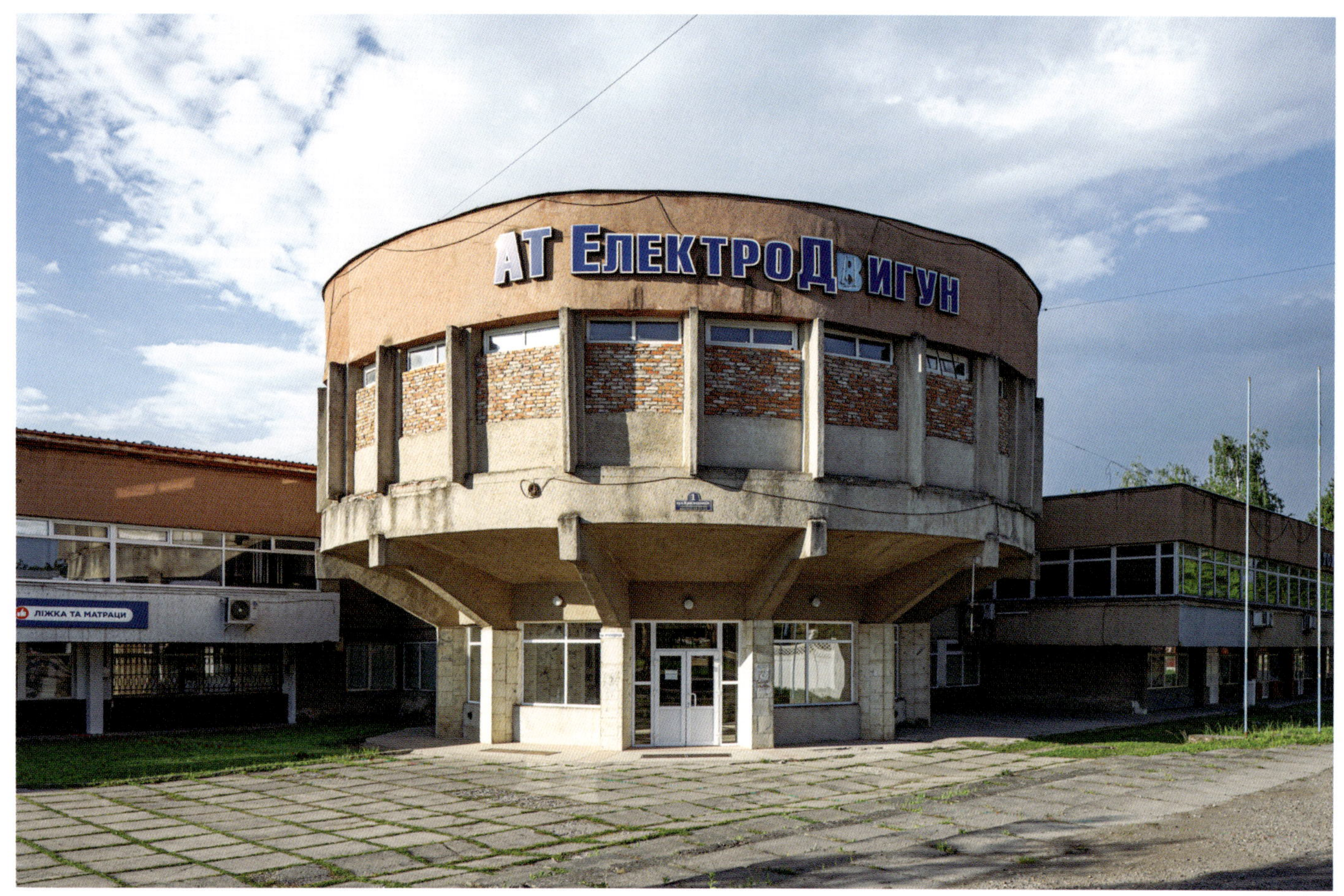

Electrodvyhun (Electric Motor) Plant Auditorium
Uzhhorod, Zakarpattia Oblast
1986

This building serves as an entrance to the factory (ground floor) and an auditorium (first floor). During the Soviet era, this was used for gatherings of workers and directors for various occasions. The windows were bricked up after the business was privatised in the 1990s.

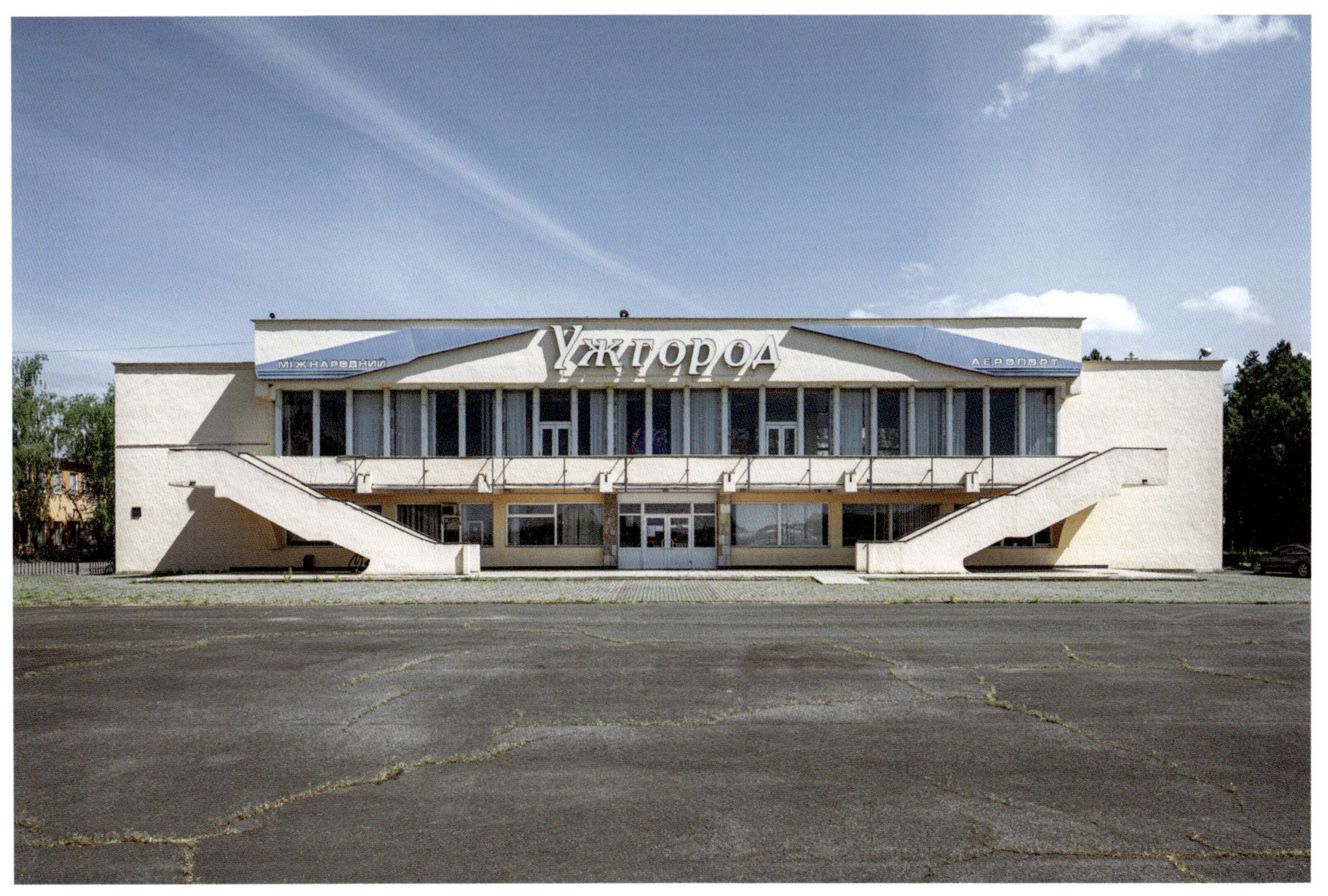

Uzhhorod Airport Terminal
Uzhhorod, Zakarpattia Oblast
1980s
Architect: Stepan Sholtes

Artists: Attila Dunchak, Mykhailo Sanych, Ivan Brovdi, Volodymyr Shchur, Petro Feldeshi

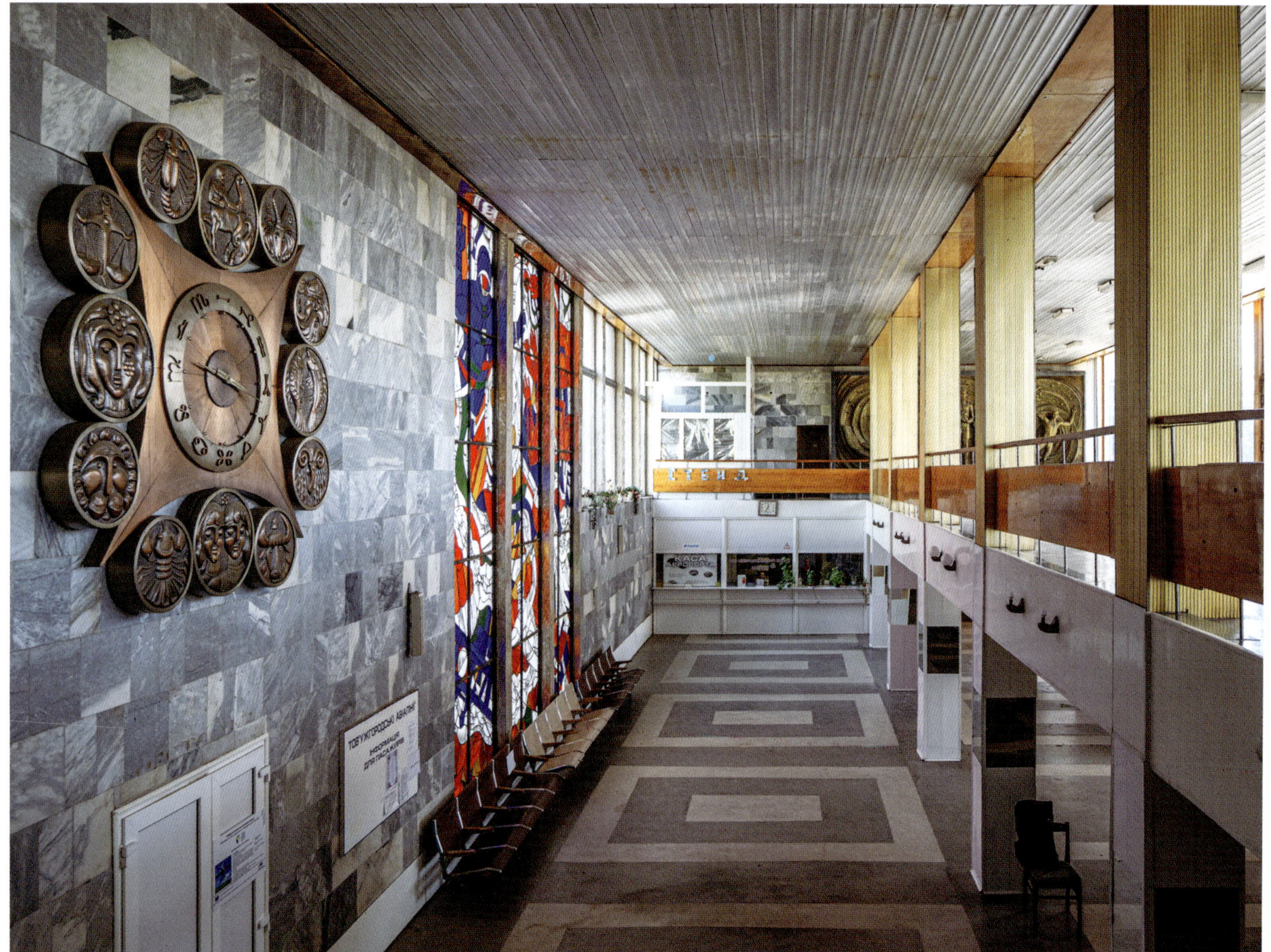

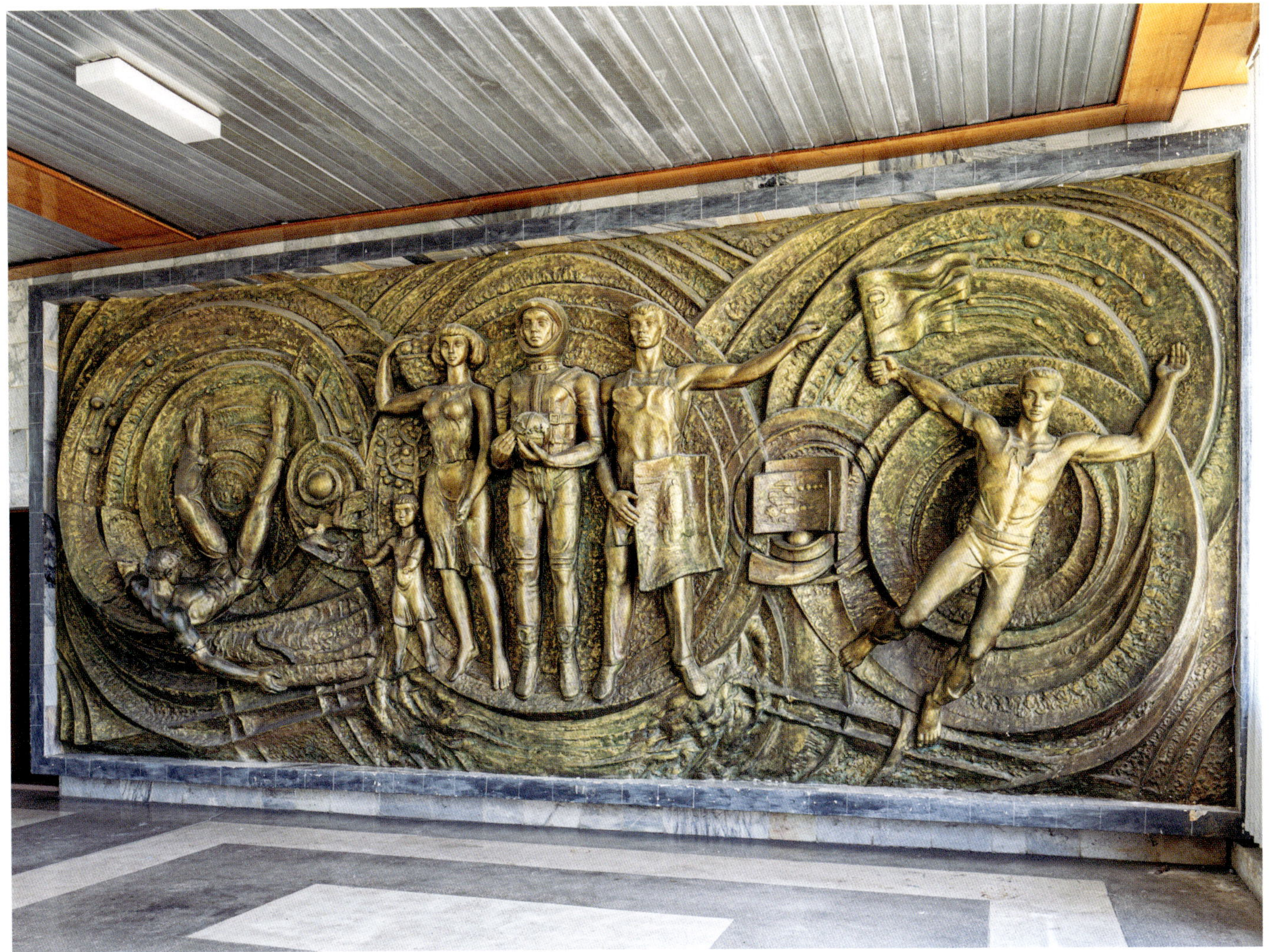

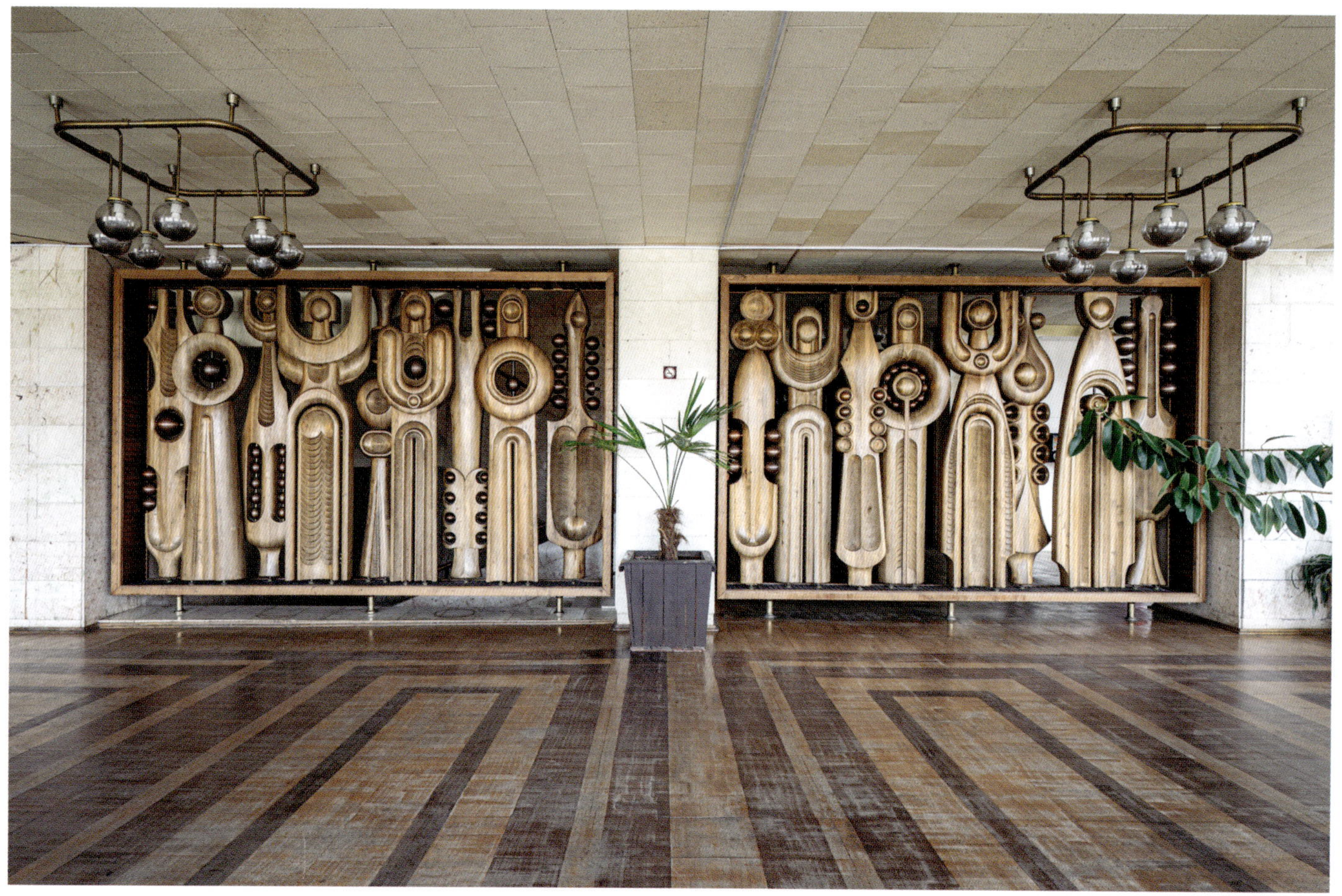

Zakarpattia Music and Drama Theatre
Uzhhorod, Zakarpattia Oblast
1987
Architects: Saniia Afzametdynova, Vitalii Yudin, Borys Zhezherin,
Mykhailo Tomchanii
Engineer: Ernest Bykov
Artists: Tereziia Chuvalova, Volodymyr Shchur, Mariia Ivancho,
Mihal Ivancho, Andrii Bokotei

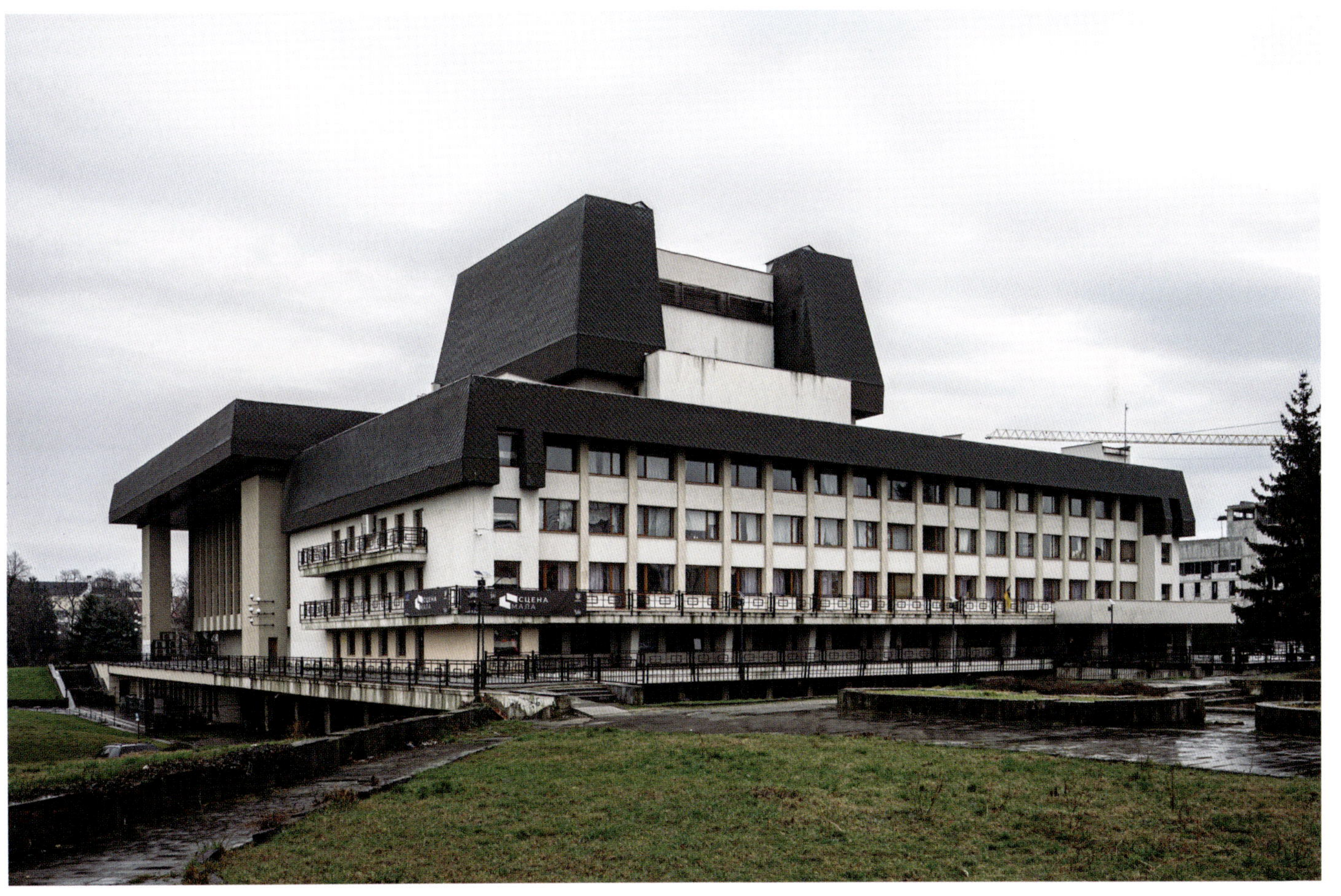

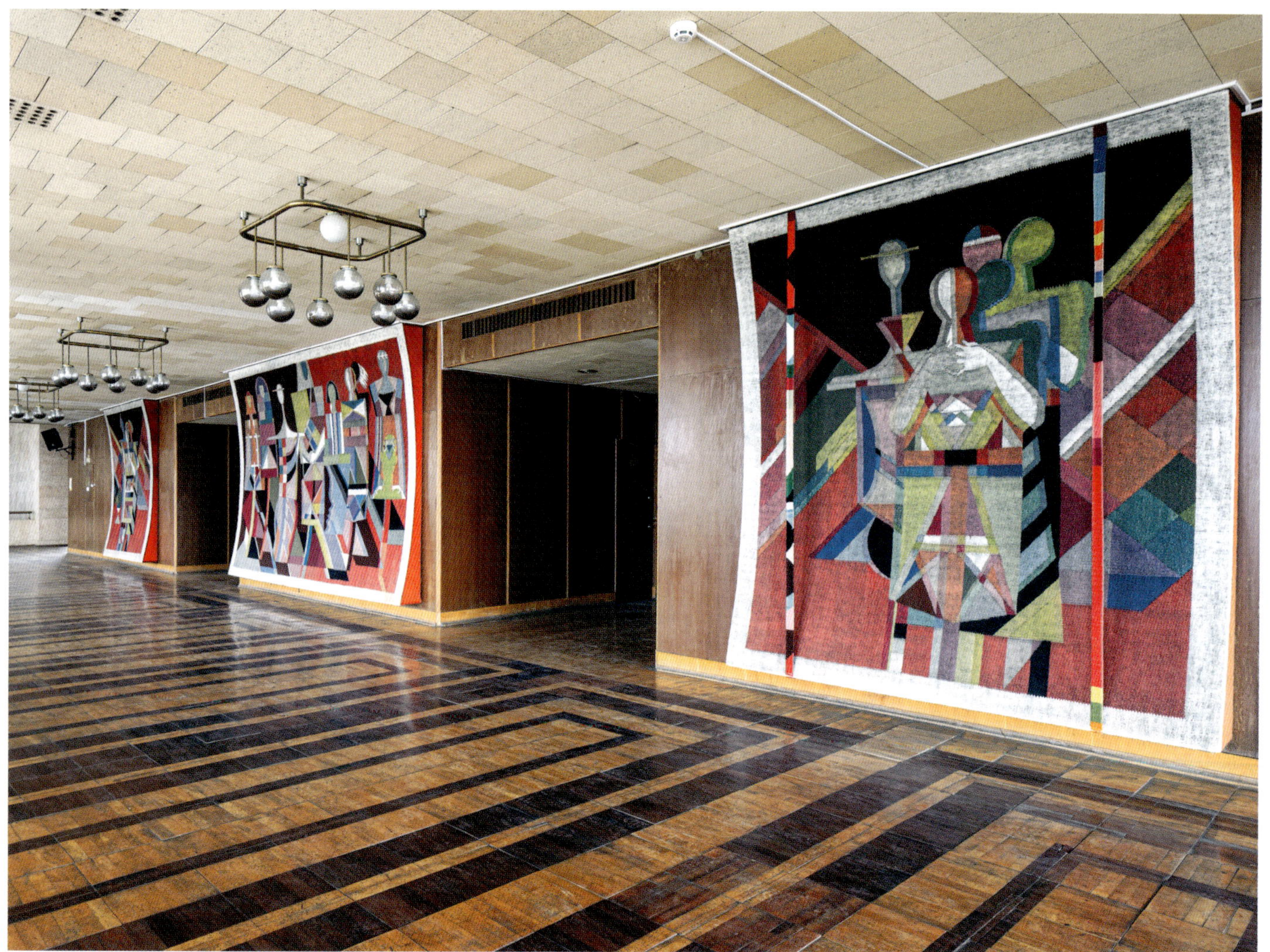

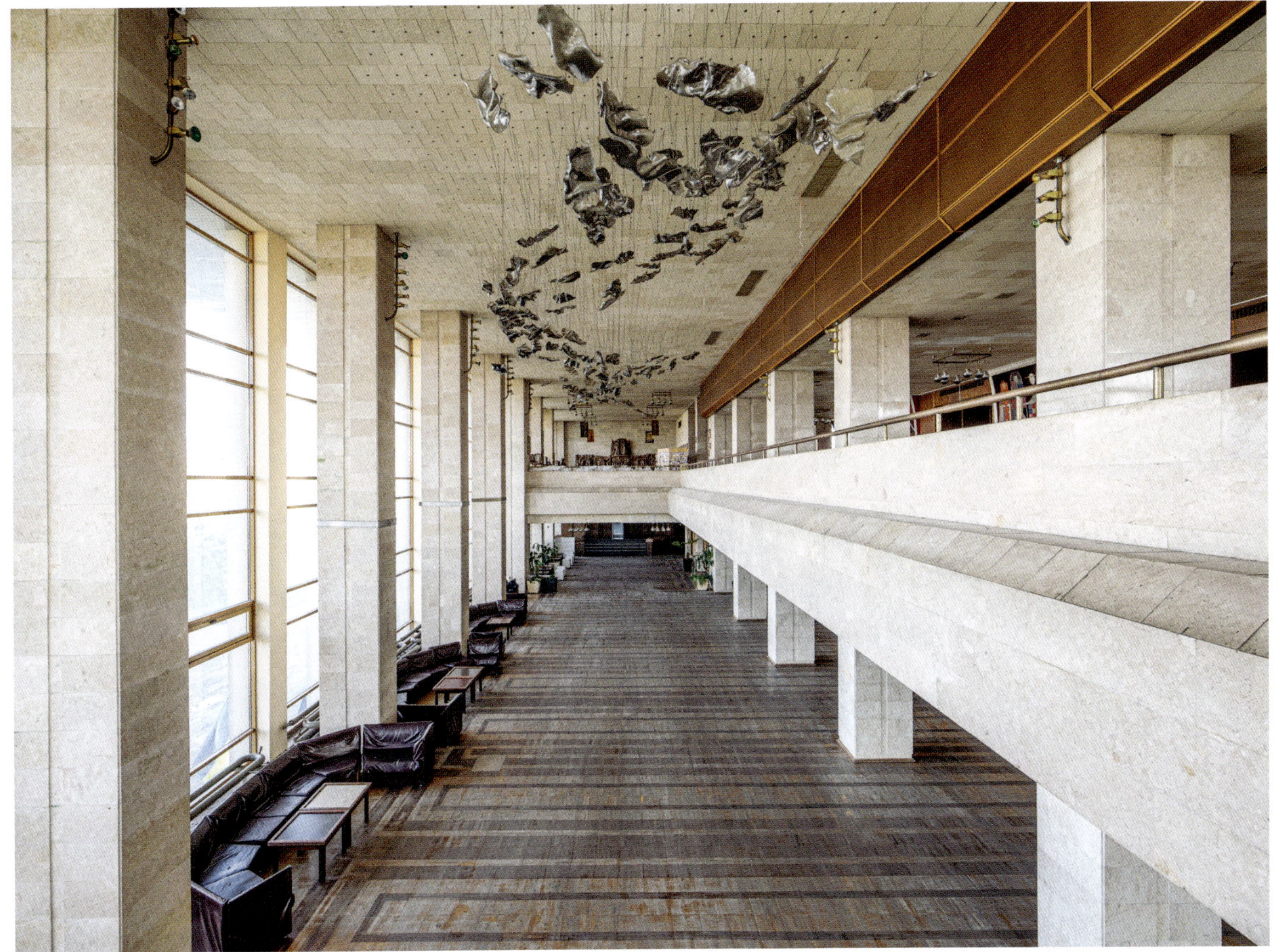

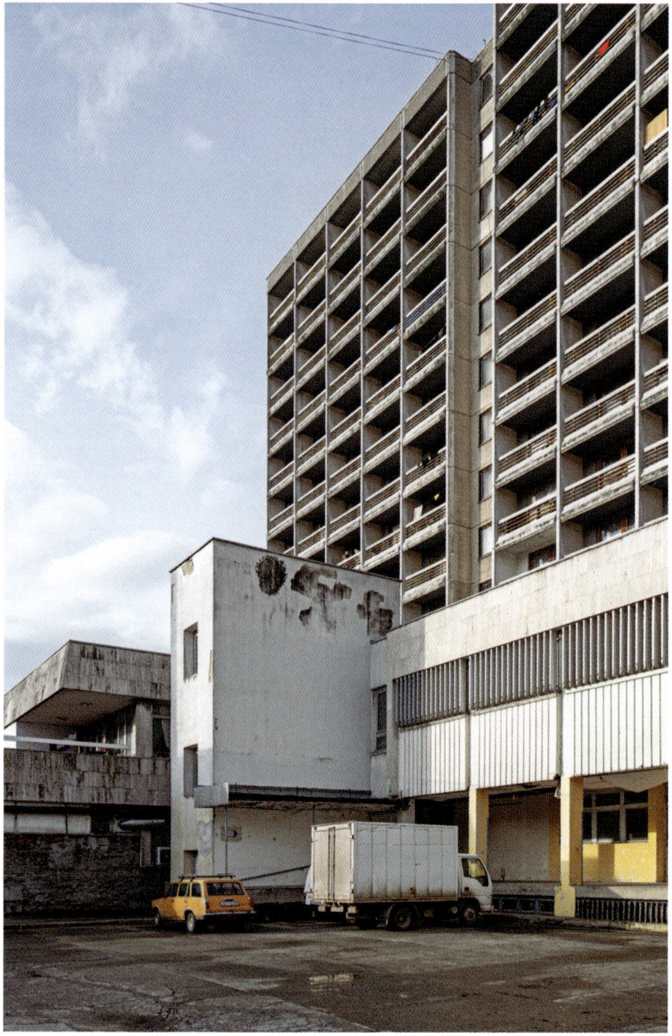

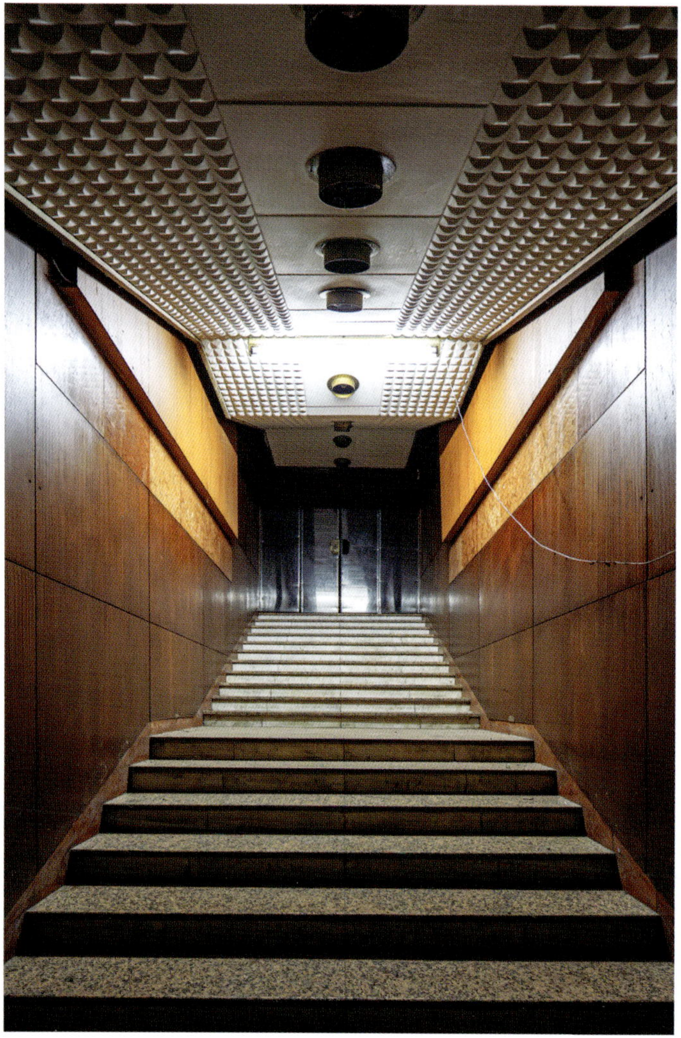

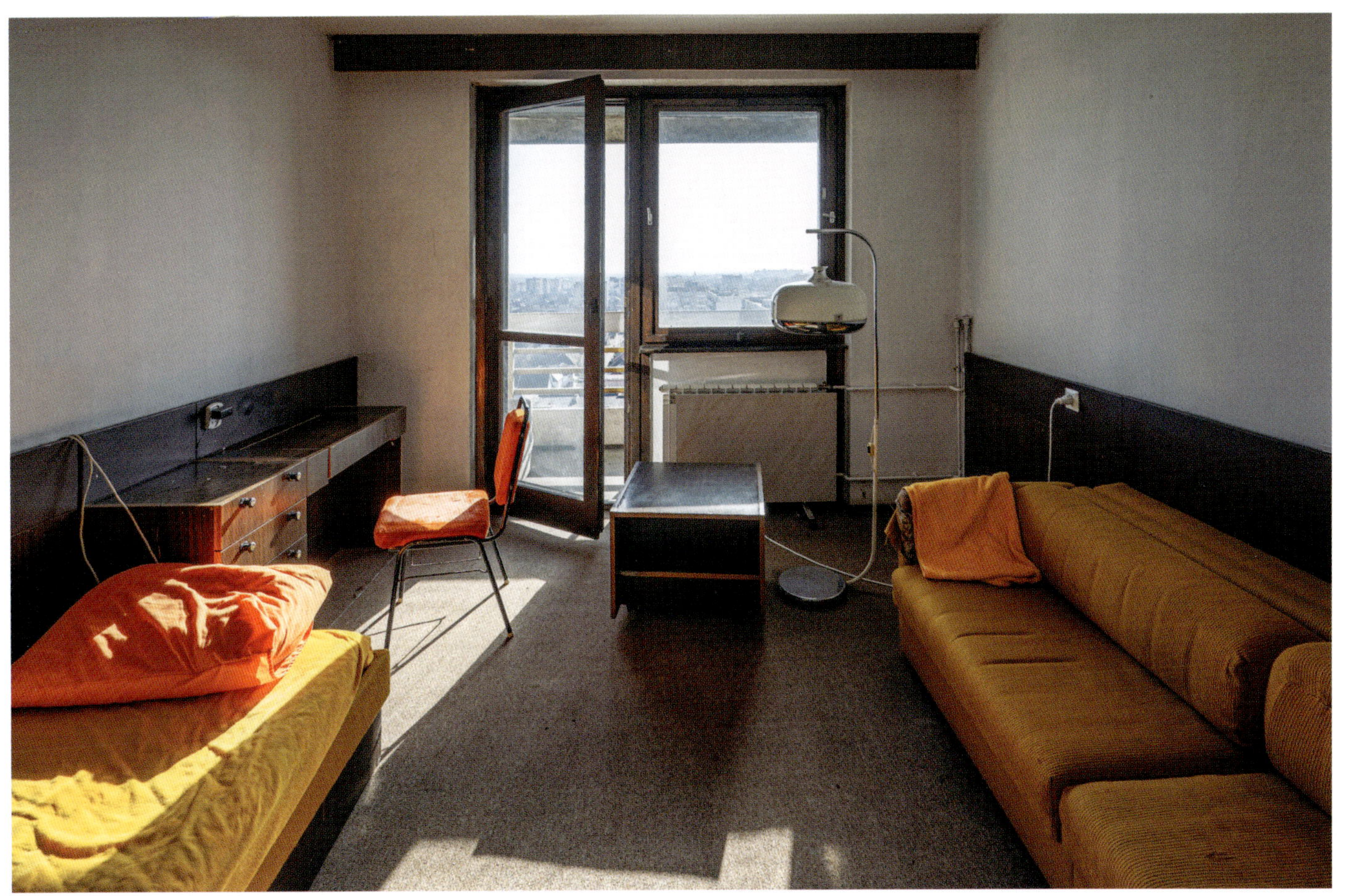

Intourist Zakarpattia Hotel
Uzhhorod, Zakarpattia Oblast
1977–79
Architects: Mihály Gere, Péter Mohácsi

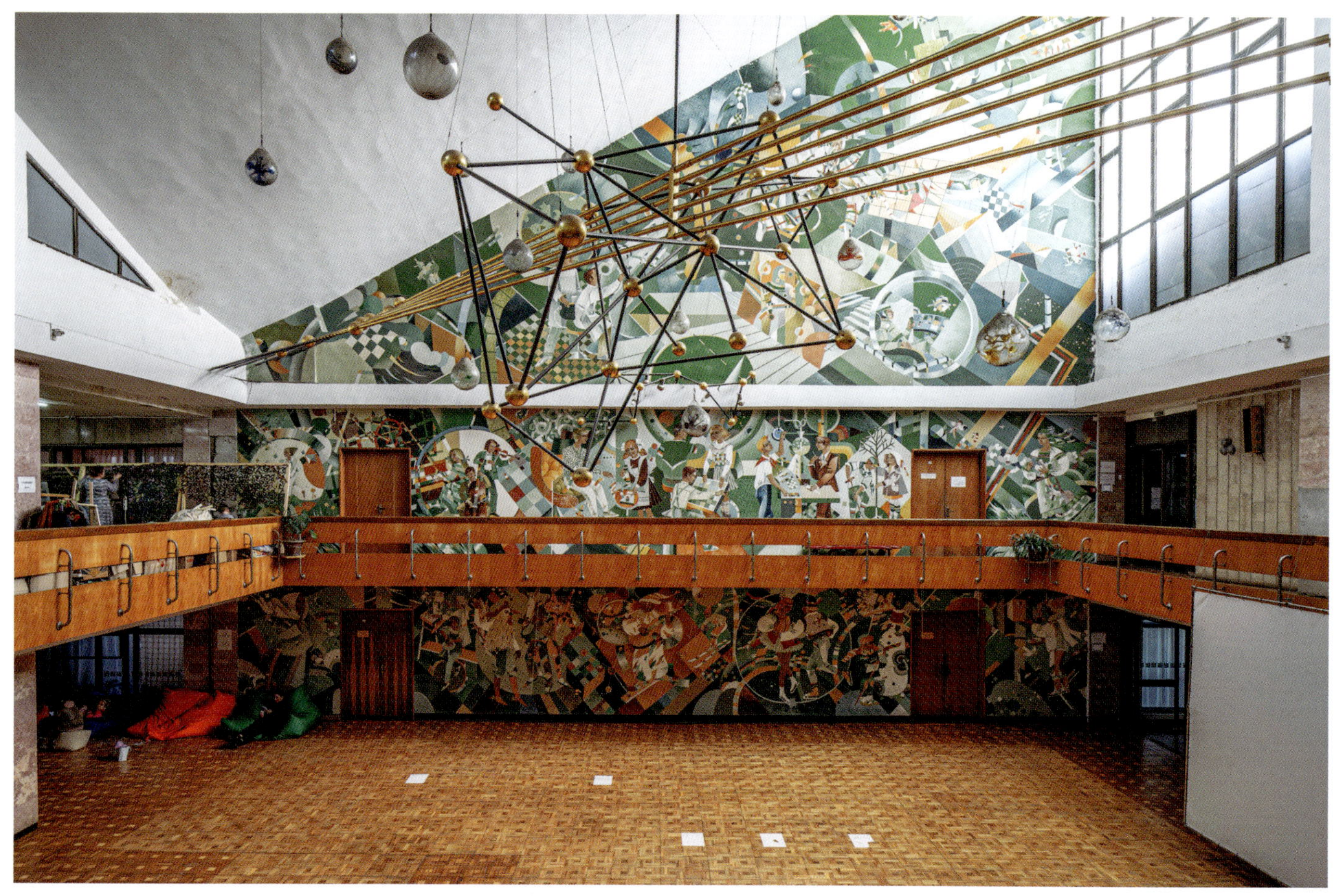

Zakarpattia Palace of Children and Youth Creativity
(formerly Palace of Pioneers and Schoolchildren)
Uzhhorod, Zakarpattia Oblast
1986

Architect: Volodymyr Bilousov
Artists: Andrii Bokotei, Nadiia Kyrylova, Petro Hulin, Vasyl Popelych

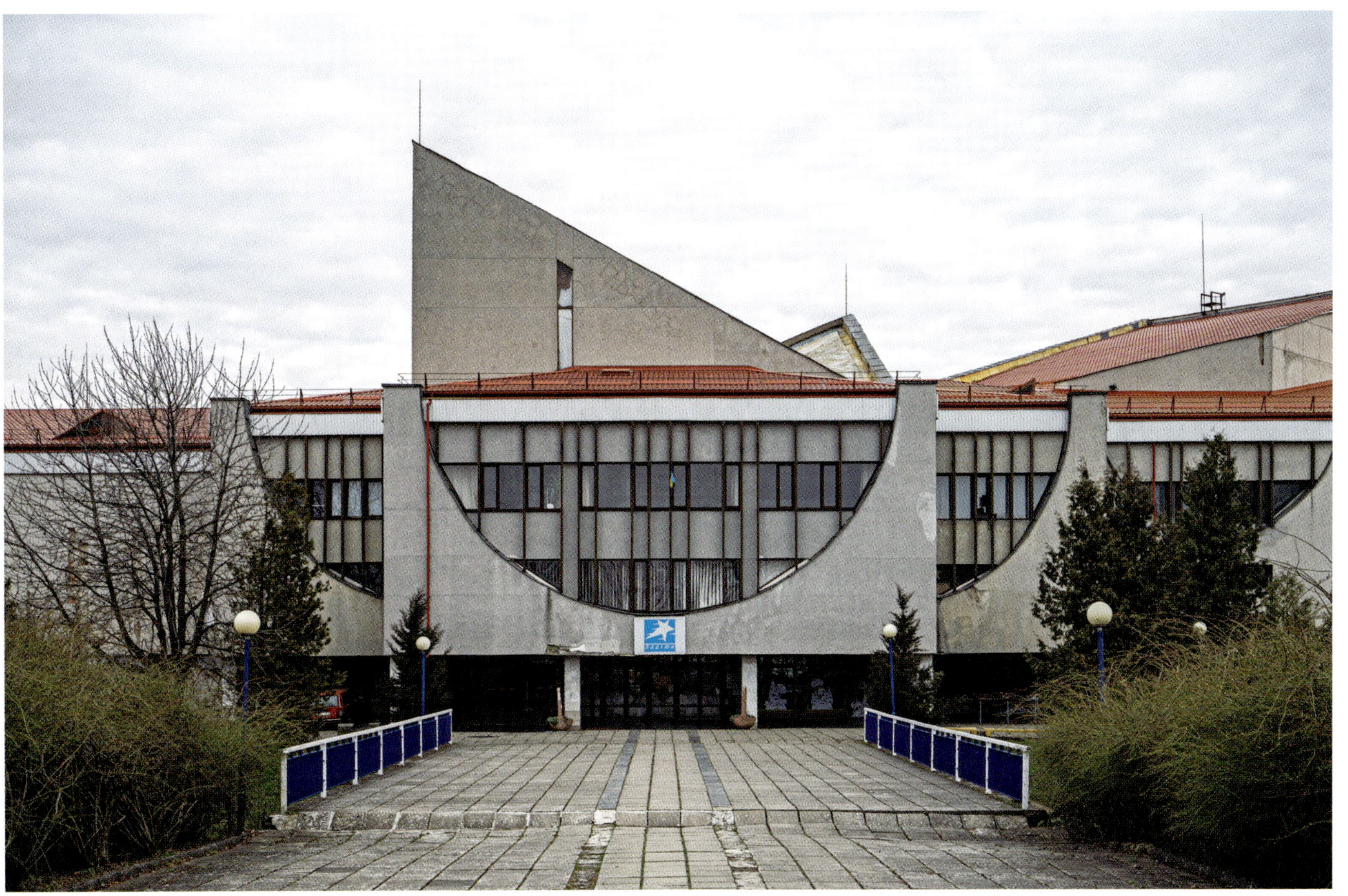

Palaces of Pioneers were multipurpose cultural and educational centres for children and youth in the USSR, designed to promote creativity, learning, and bestow an ideological upbringing. They offered spaces for activities such as science and technology clubs, arts and crafts, music, dance, theatre, sports and more. These palaces aimed to nurture a new generation of skilled, cultured and patriotic citizens. Today, they continue to serve as free extracurricular education centres, but without the requirement of uniforms or emphasis on ideology.

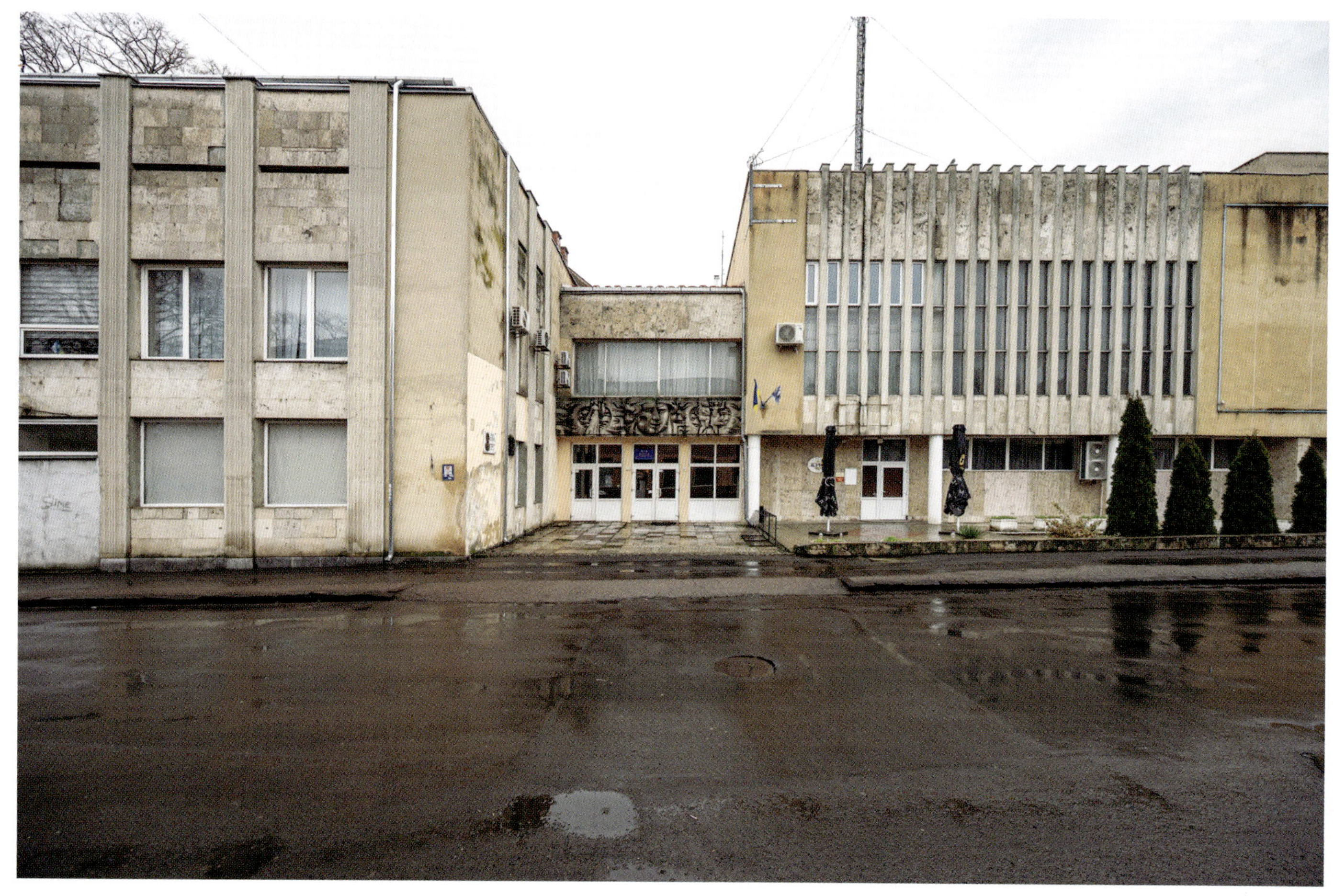

Trade Union House of Culture
Uzhhorod, Zakarpattia Oblast
1982
Artists: Attila Dunchak, Petro Bidzilia, Harri Chuvalov, Tereziia Chuvalova

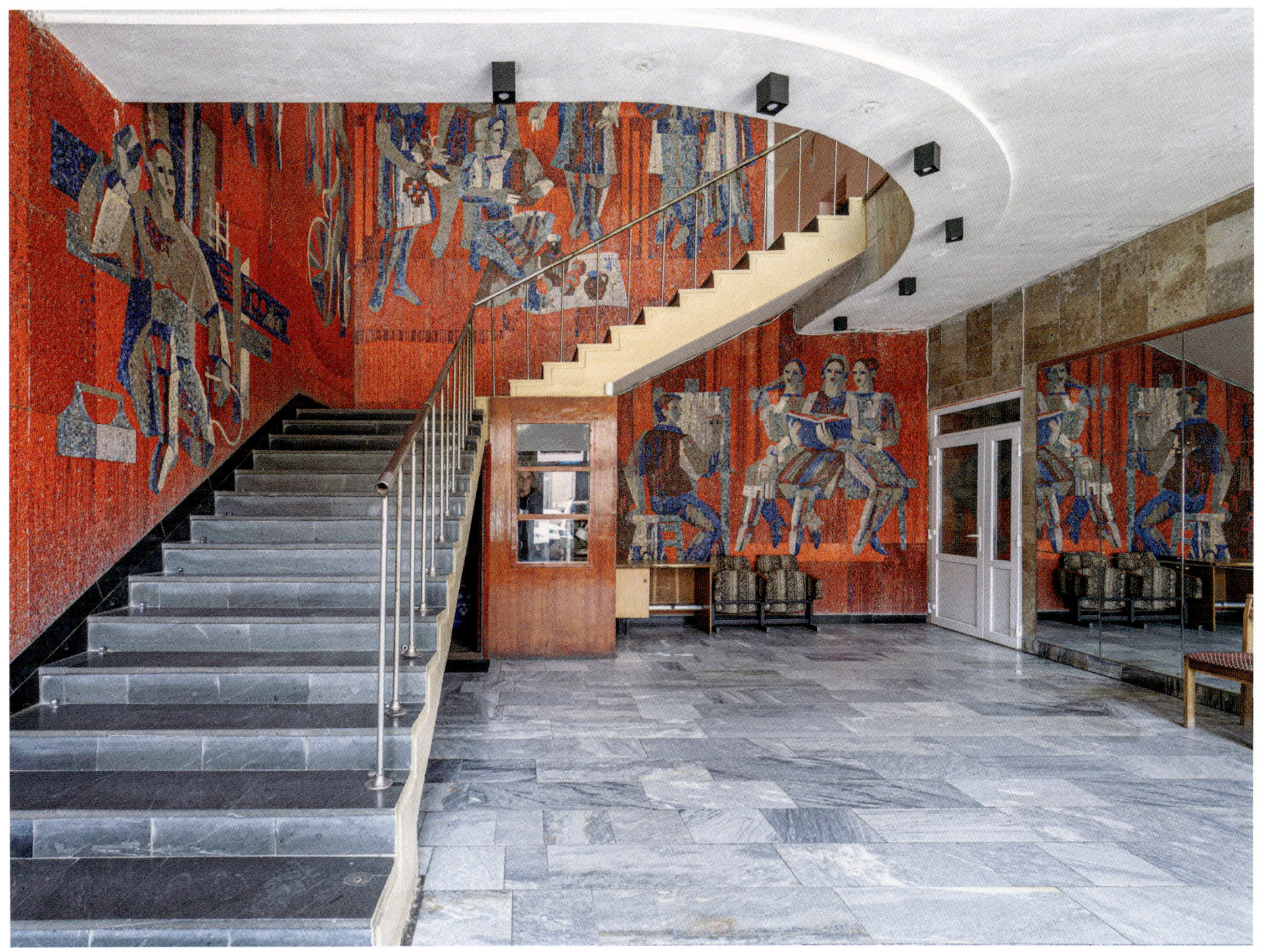

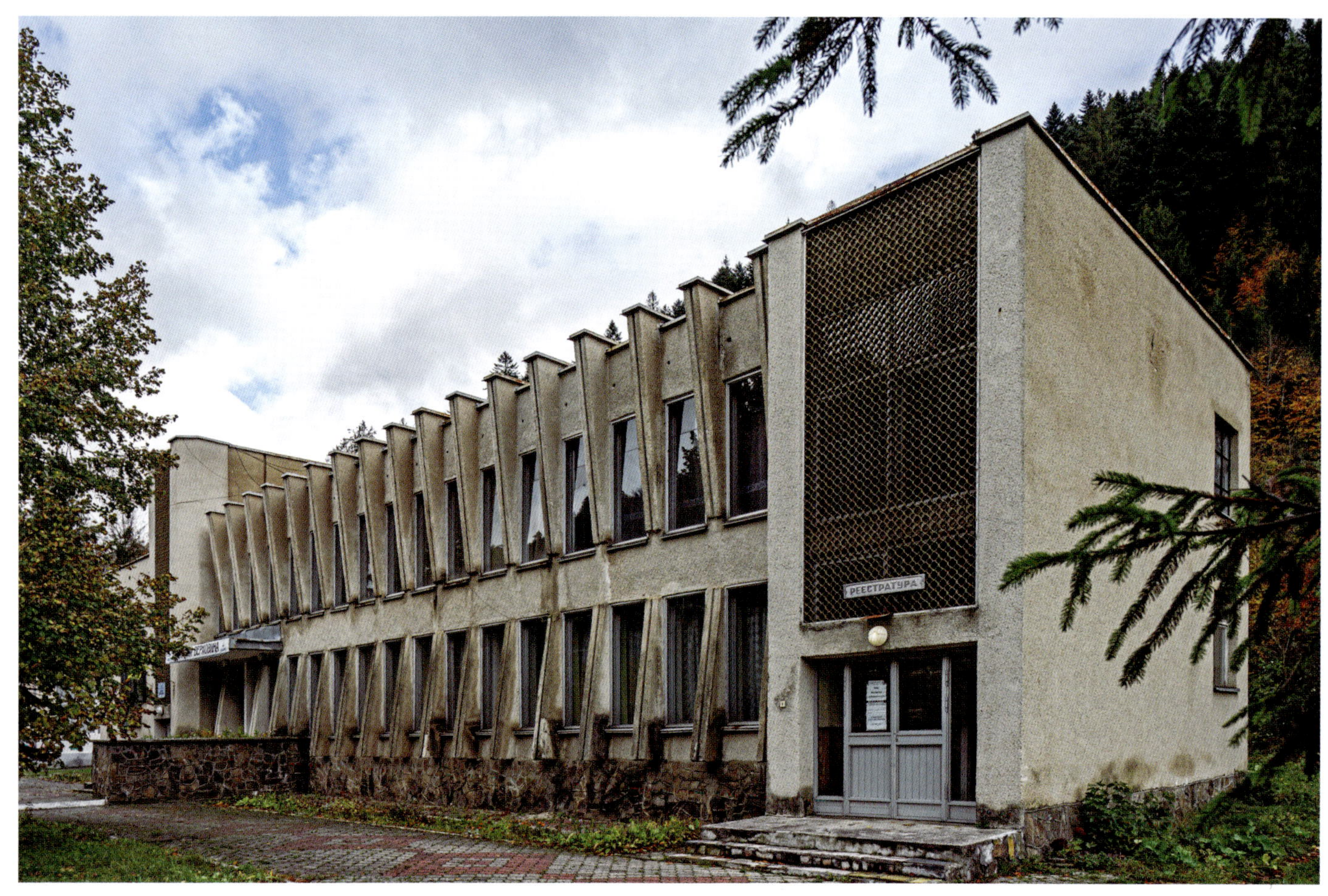

Verkhovyna Sanatorium
Mizhhiria, Zakarpattia Oblast
1980s

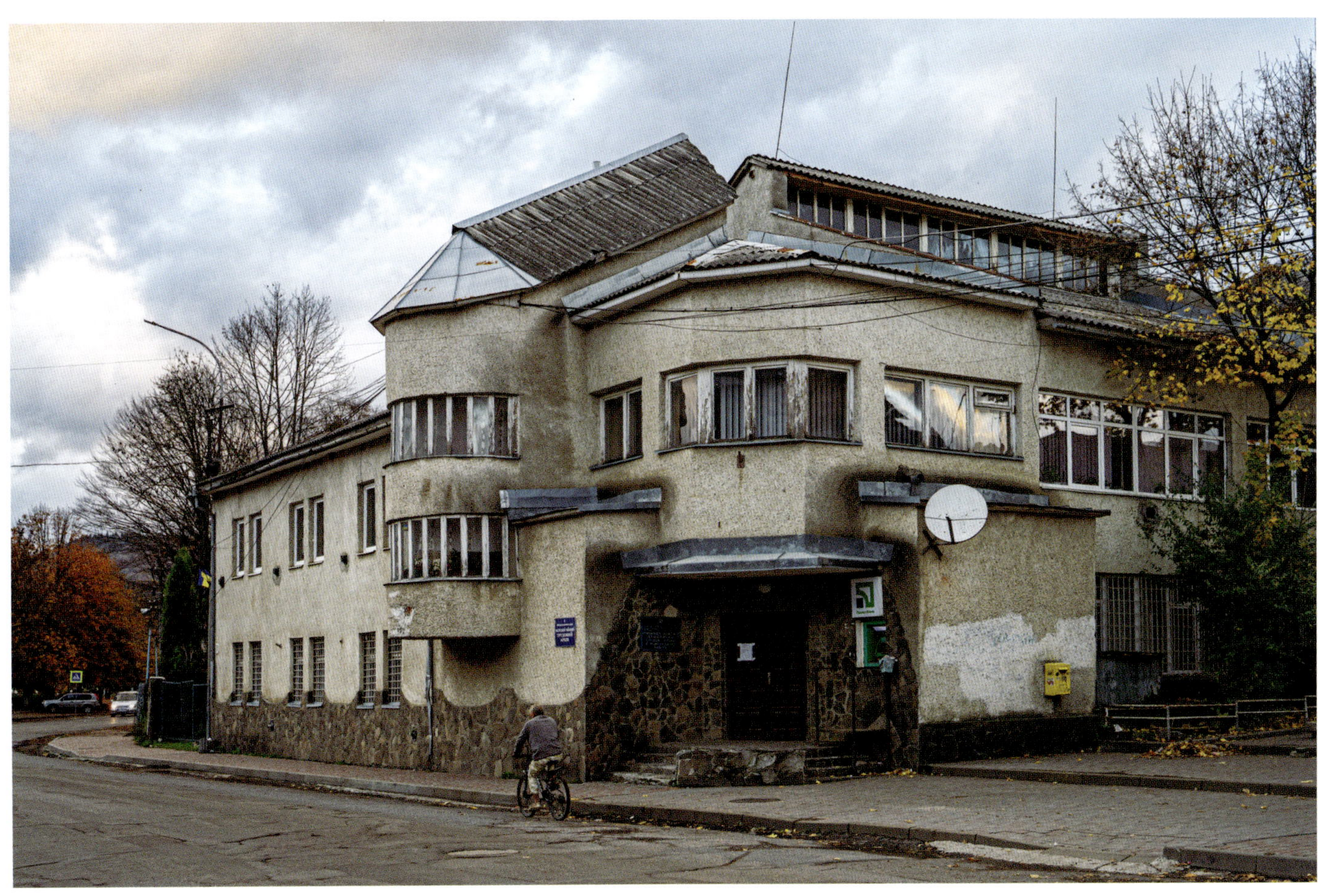

Administrative Building
Mizhhiria, Zakarpattia Oblast
1980s

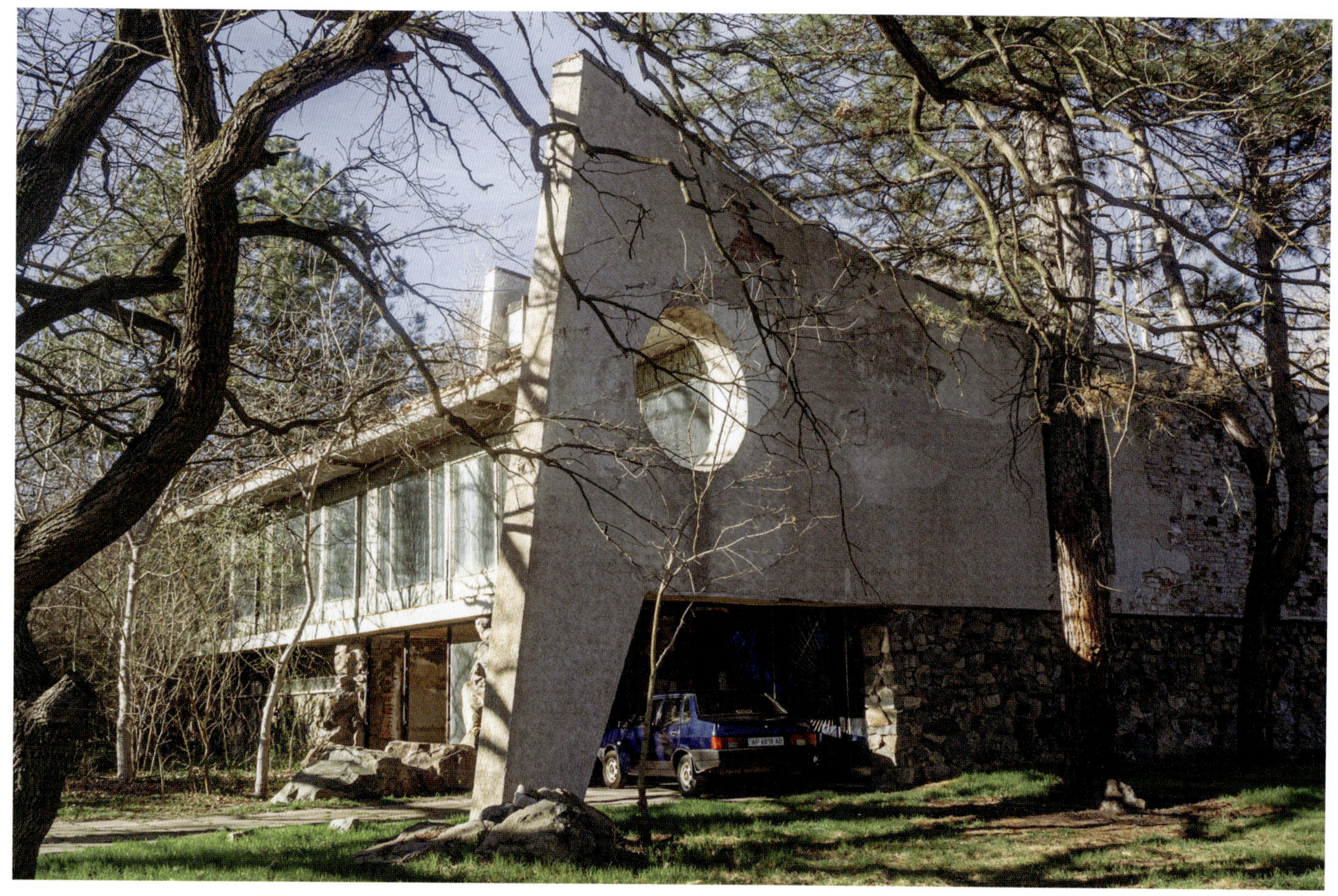

Druzhba Recreation Centre
Zaporizhzhia
1972
Architect: Mykola Zharikov

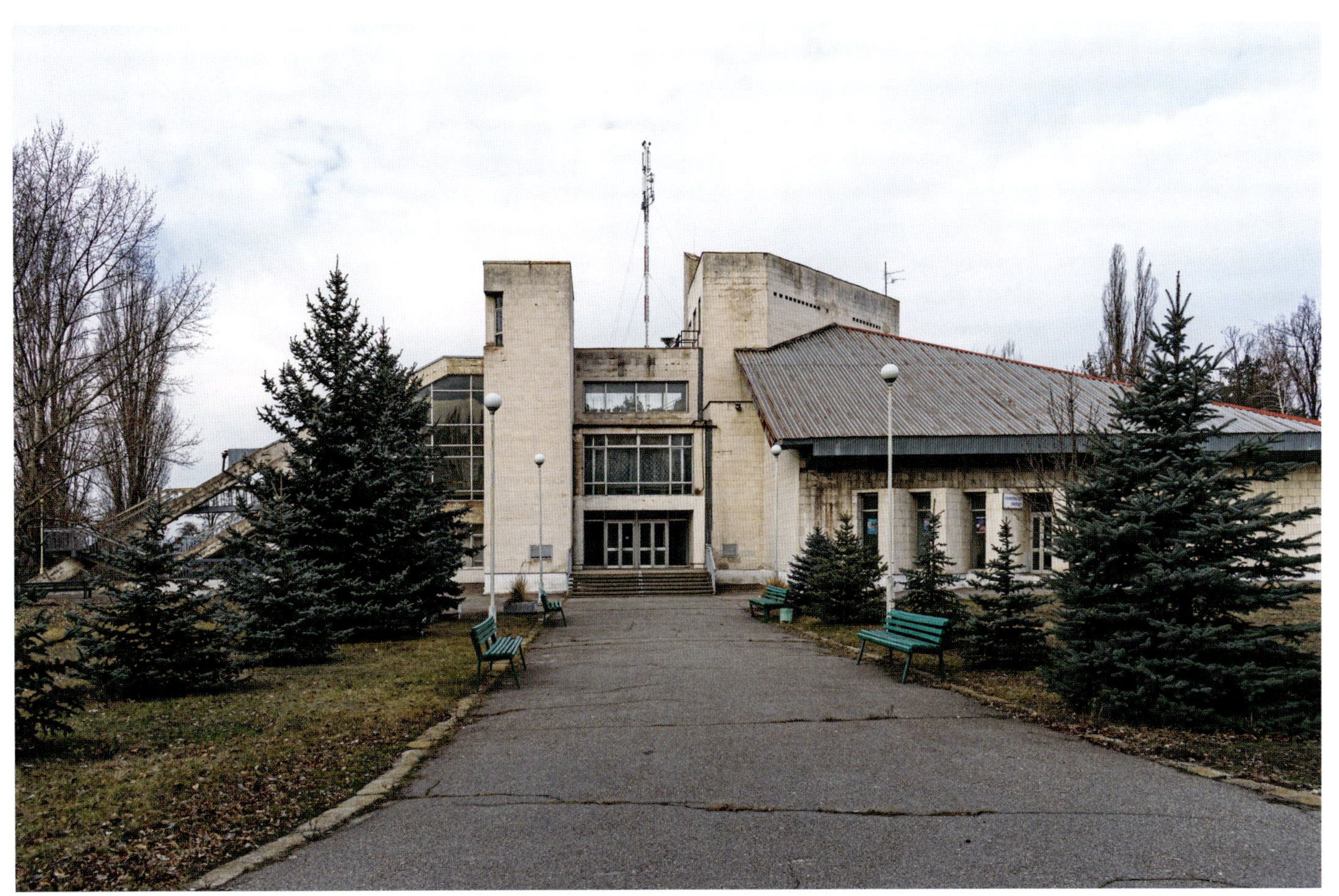

Transformer Factory Sanatorium
Zaporizhzhia
1980s
Architects: Viktor Lukashov, N. Bulakhov, L. Kurdina
Engineers: V. Nuzhnyi, V. Korotun, V. Troitskaya, L. Kartashova, A. Lyubivyi

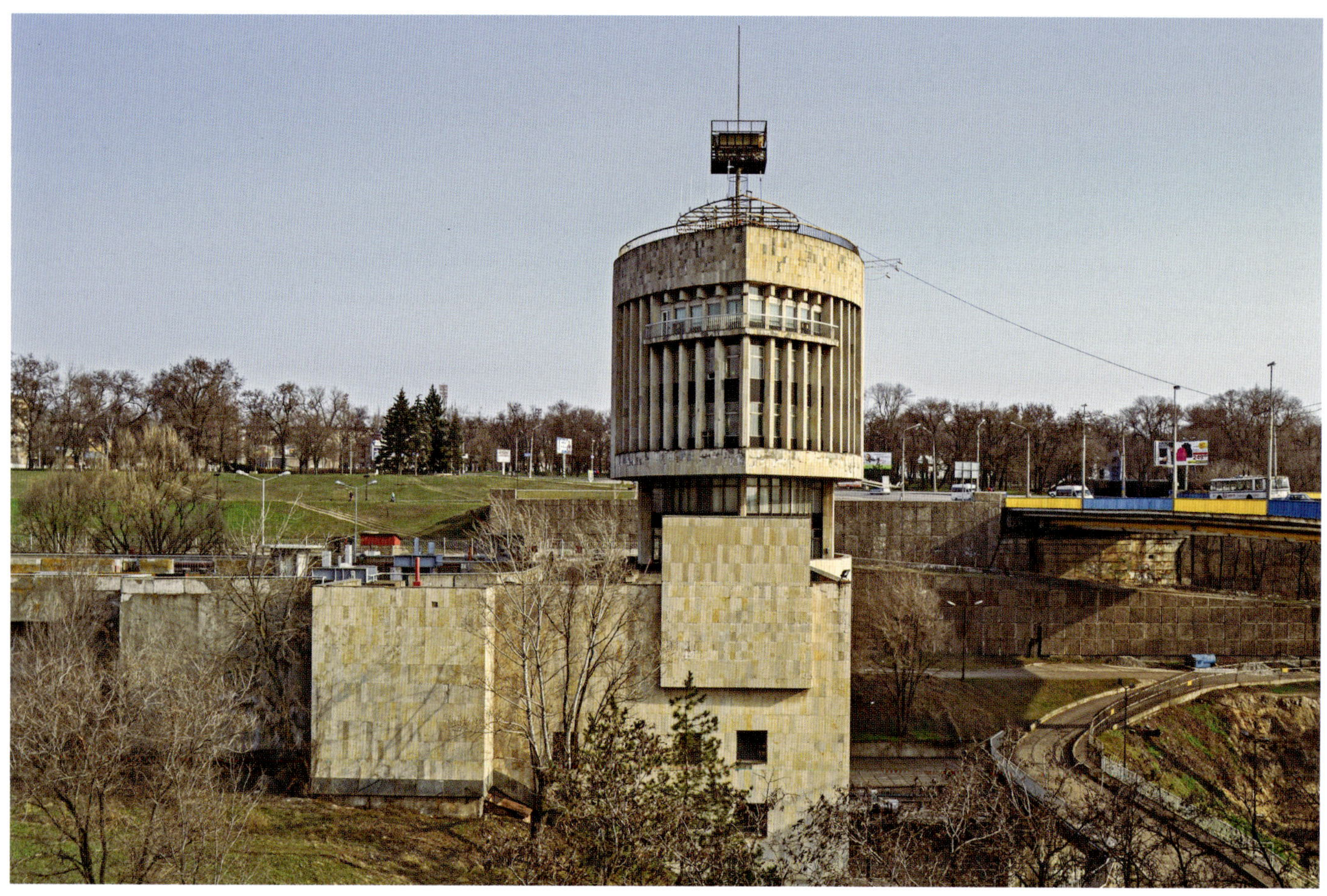

Lock control building, Dnipro Hydroelectric Station
Zaporizhzhia
1980
Architects: A. Moshenskyi, I. Okhrimenko

The largest hydroelectric station in Ukraine was built between 1927 and 1932 and rebuilt following its destruction in World War II. A new modernist power unit and lock control building were added in the 1970s. Heavy damage from Russian bombs forced its closure in 2024.

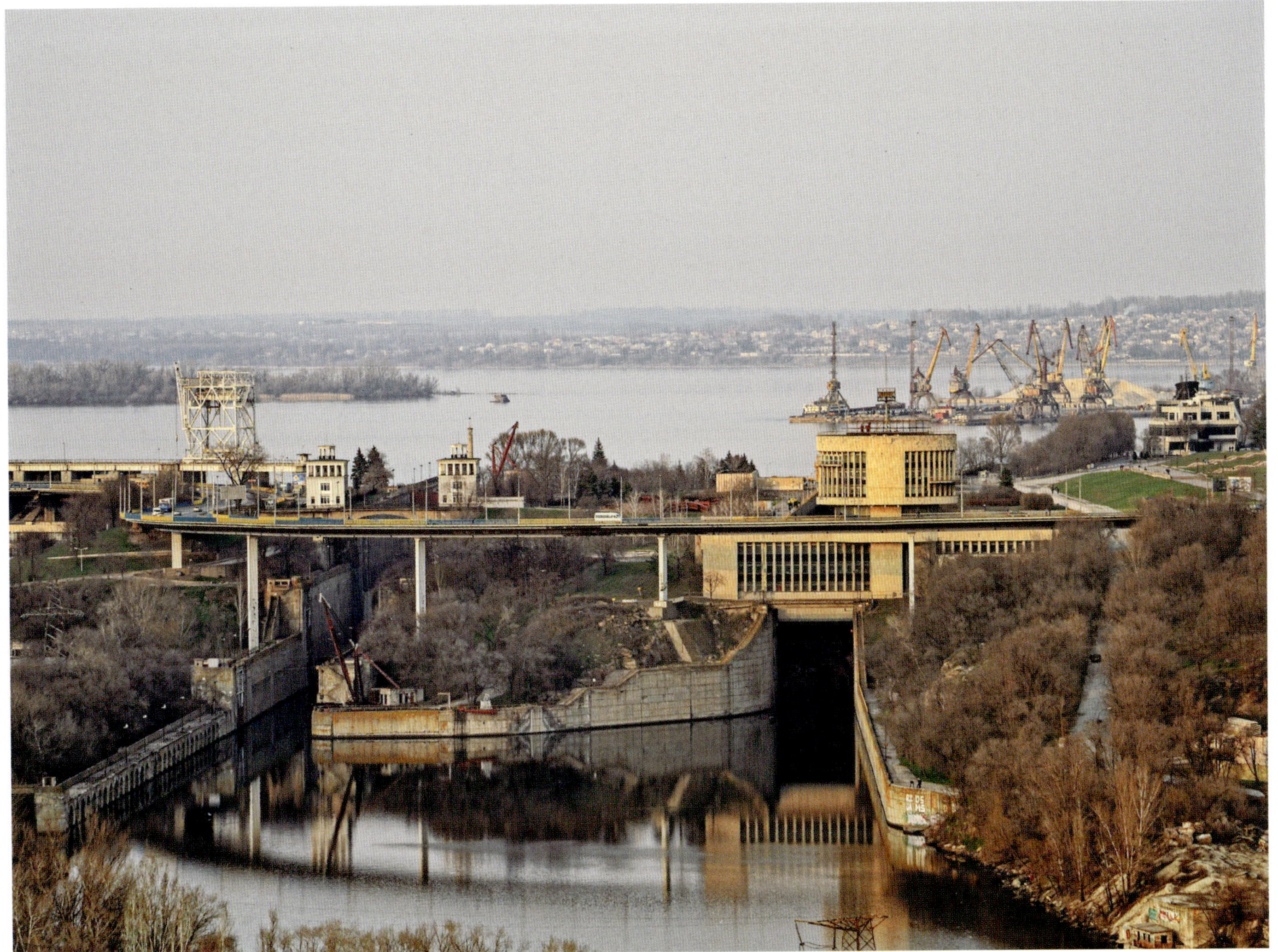

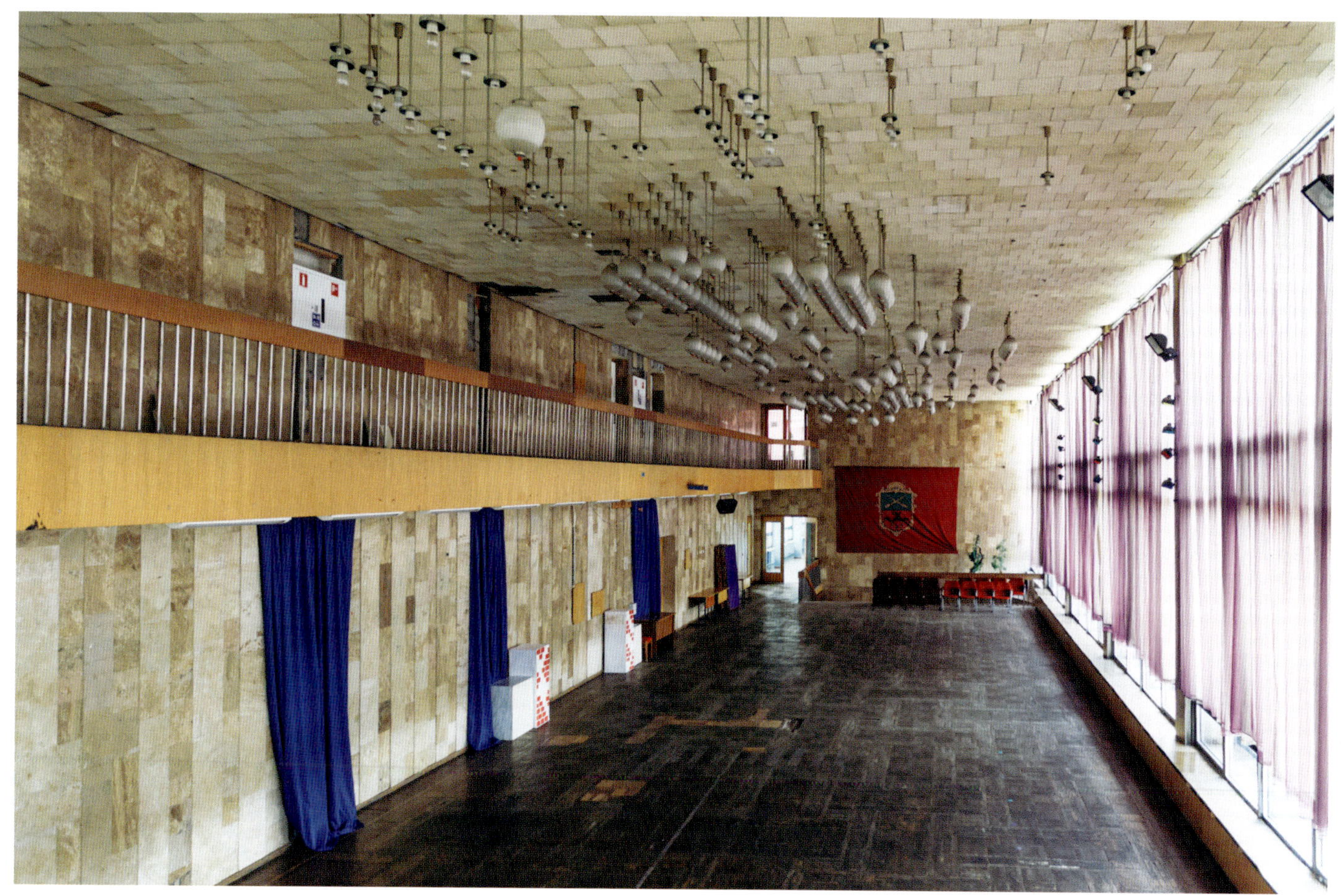

Zaporizhzhia Palace of Children and Youth Creativity
(formerly Palace of Pioneers and Schoolchildren)
Zaporizhzhia
1986

Architect: M. Drozhzhyn, I. Saskeltsev, D. Sorokin
Engineers: V. Anofriiev, L. Trushyna
Artists: Volodymyr Khomchyk, A. Bespalov, O. Zholud,
Ye. Myshevskyi, O. Shcherbyna

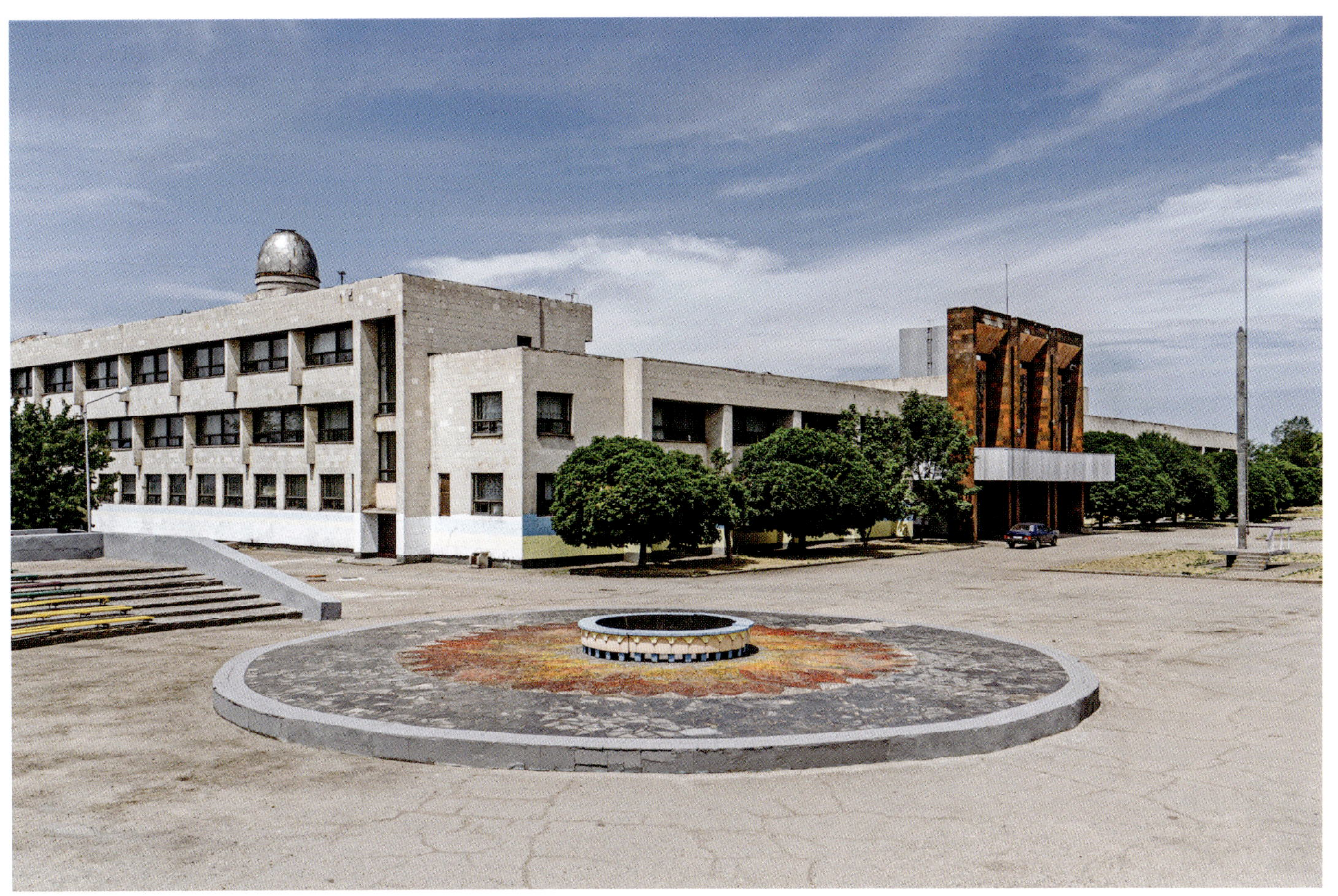

The amphitheatre, fireplace and flagpole of this Palace once hosted grand gatherings of Young Pioneers where youth, dressed in red scarves, celebrated Soviet ideals around a bonfire – a symbol of unity, enthusiasm and the 'eternal flame' of the revolution.

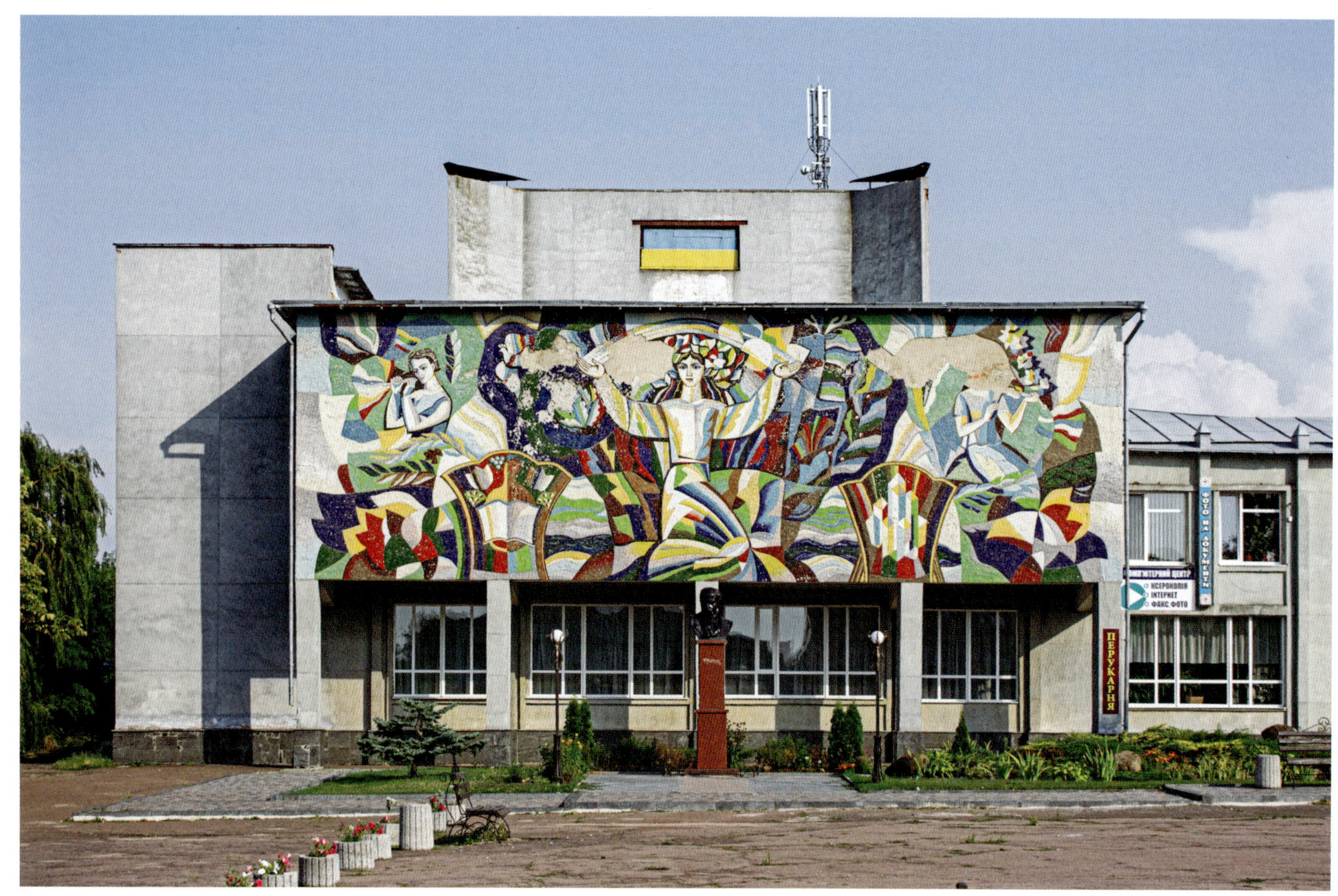

Palace of Culture
Khoroshiv, Zhytomyr Oblast
1980s

Standardised designs were widely used in the USSR during the 1960s
and 1970s. To imbue such buildings with a distinctive character, local
architects would often collaborate with artists, modify facades and
develop unique interiors, as can be seen with this example.

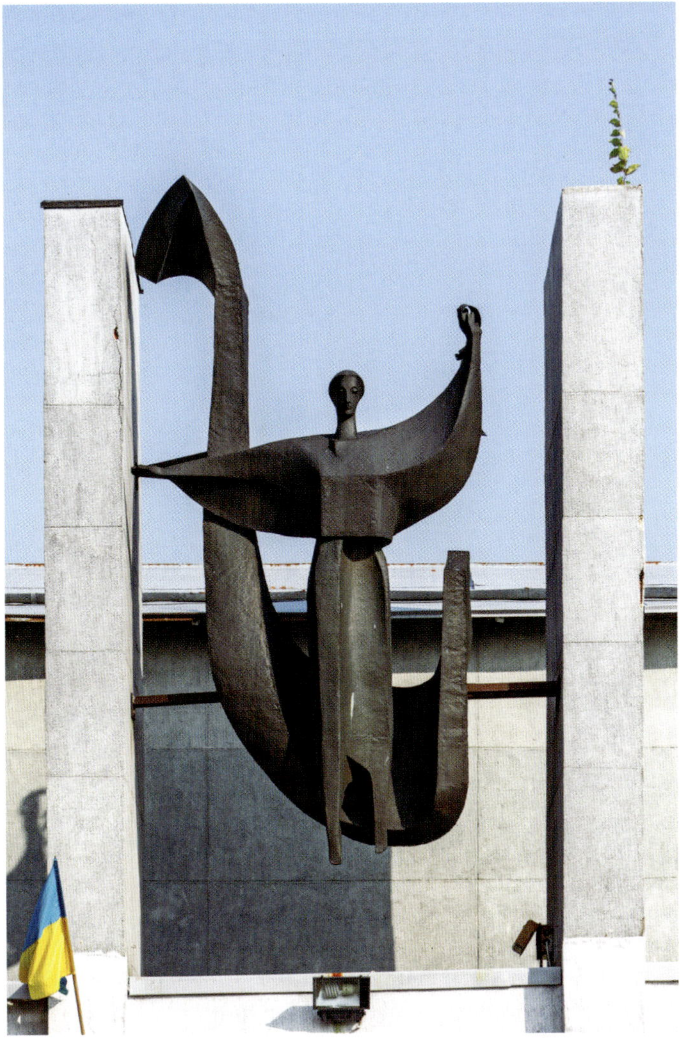

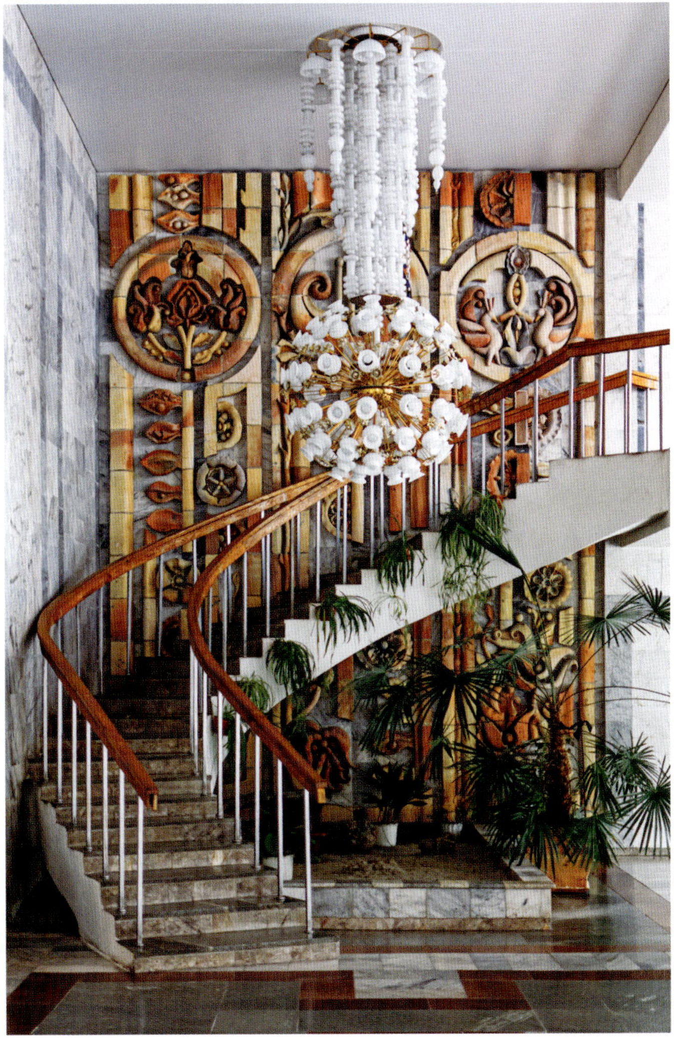

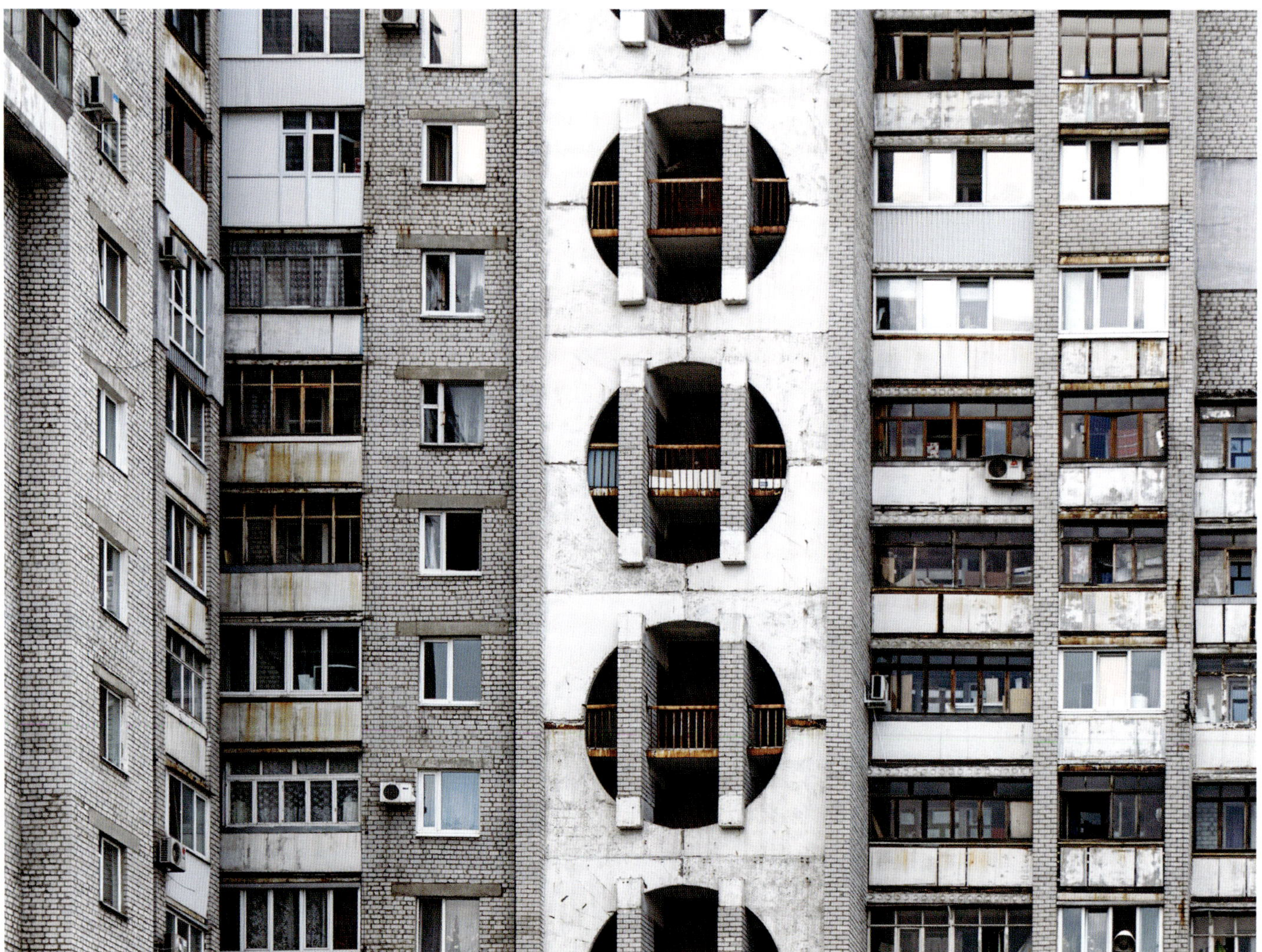

236   Residential buildings, Zaporizhzhia

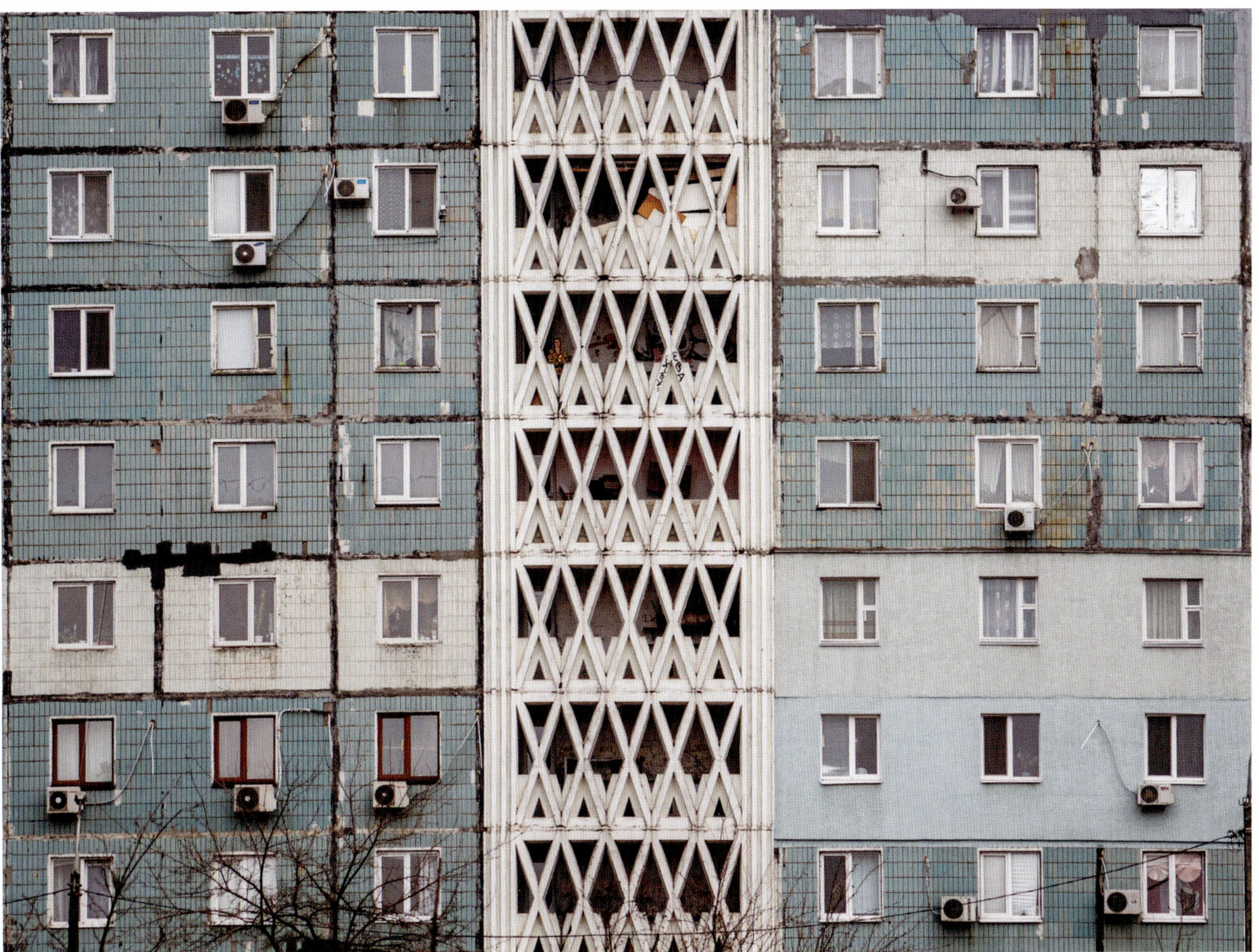

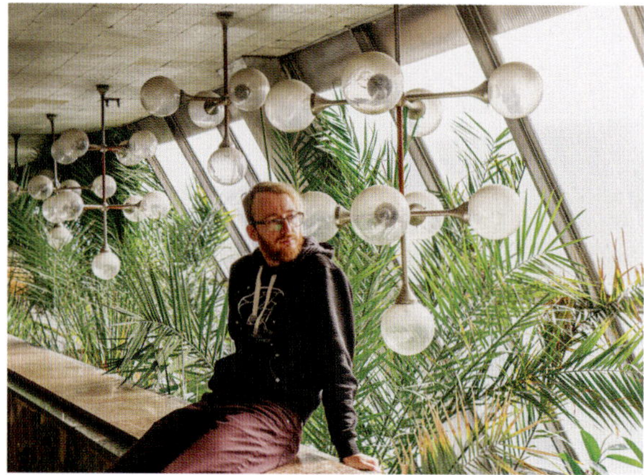

I dedicate this book to my parents, Iryna Soloviova and Valerii Soloviov.
Dmytro Soloviov, Kyiv

Published in 2025

FUEL Design & Publishing
33 Fournier Street
London E1 6QE

fuel-design.com
@fuelpublishing

Design and edit by Murray & Sorrell FUEL
Photographs and captions © Dmytro Soloviov
@ukrainianmodernism
Introduction and archive images © Owen Hatherley

Distribution by Thames & Hudson / D. A. P.
ISBN: 978-1-7398878-7-2
Printed in China

Acknowledgements:

Valerii Soloviov
Iryna Soloviova
Owen Hatherley
Damon Murray
Stephen Sorrell
Polina Korobtsova
Richard Fawkus
Oleksandr Nikitchuk
Ivan Ponomarenko
Olena Zahrebina
Aryna Starovoitova
Mykola Linnyk
Ekateryna Konsulova
Anton Marchevskii
Petro Ryaska
Oleksandr Smirnov
Semen Shyrochyn
Volodymyr Shevchenko
Volodymyr Melnichenko
Yurii Shalatskyi aka Jerzy
Yanos Vigh
Andrii Lutsik
Pavlo Kravchuk
Yevgen Nikiforov
Yuliia Levchuk
Kseniia Semenova
Viktor Poliakov
Larysa Lypkan
Olena Borysova
Tony Petersen
Adam Kovacs aka Adam Something
Nataliia Khomenko

Employees of the Zakarpattia Music and Drama Theatre, Khmelnytskyi
Music and Drama Theatre, Kharkiv Opera and Ballet Theatre, Sumy
Universal Scientific Library, Dnipro Circus, Dnipro Palace of Children
and Youth, Dnipro Medical Academy, Library of the Dnipro National
University, Burshtyn Palace of Culture, Kyiv Palace of Children and
Youth, Vernadsky National Library of Ukraine, Kyiv Theatre for Young
Spectators, Centre for Creativity of Children and Youth of Halychyna,
Uzhhorod Airport, Zakarpattia Palace of Children and Youth.

Everyone who supported me on this journey — thank you!

Endpapers:
Hradetskyi Hotel
Chernihiv
1981
Architects: Valentyn Shtolko, Alla Hrachova, Oleksandr Kabatskyi,
Volodymyr Ralchenko
Engineers: Volodymyr Sloboda
Artist: Halyna Sevruk

Back cover:
'Meteor' Palace of Sports
Dnipro
1983
Architects: Yurii Khudiakov, Viktor Sudorhin
Engineer: Leonid Sandler

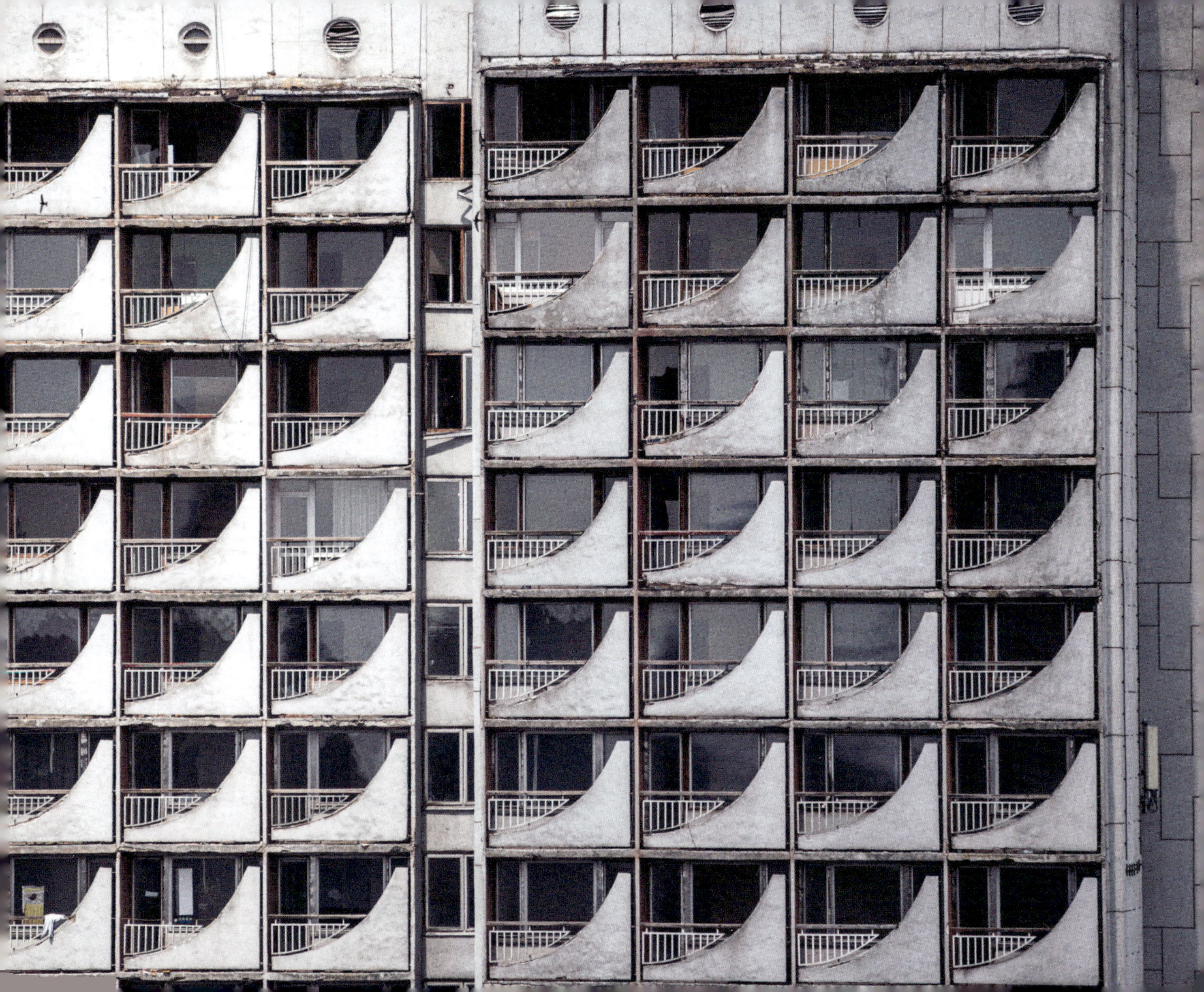

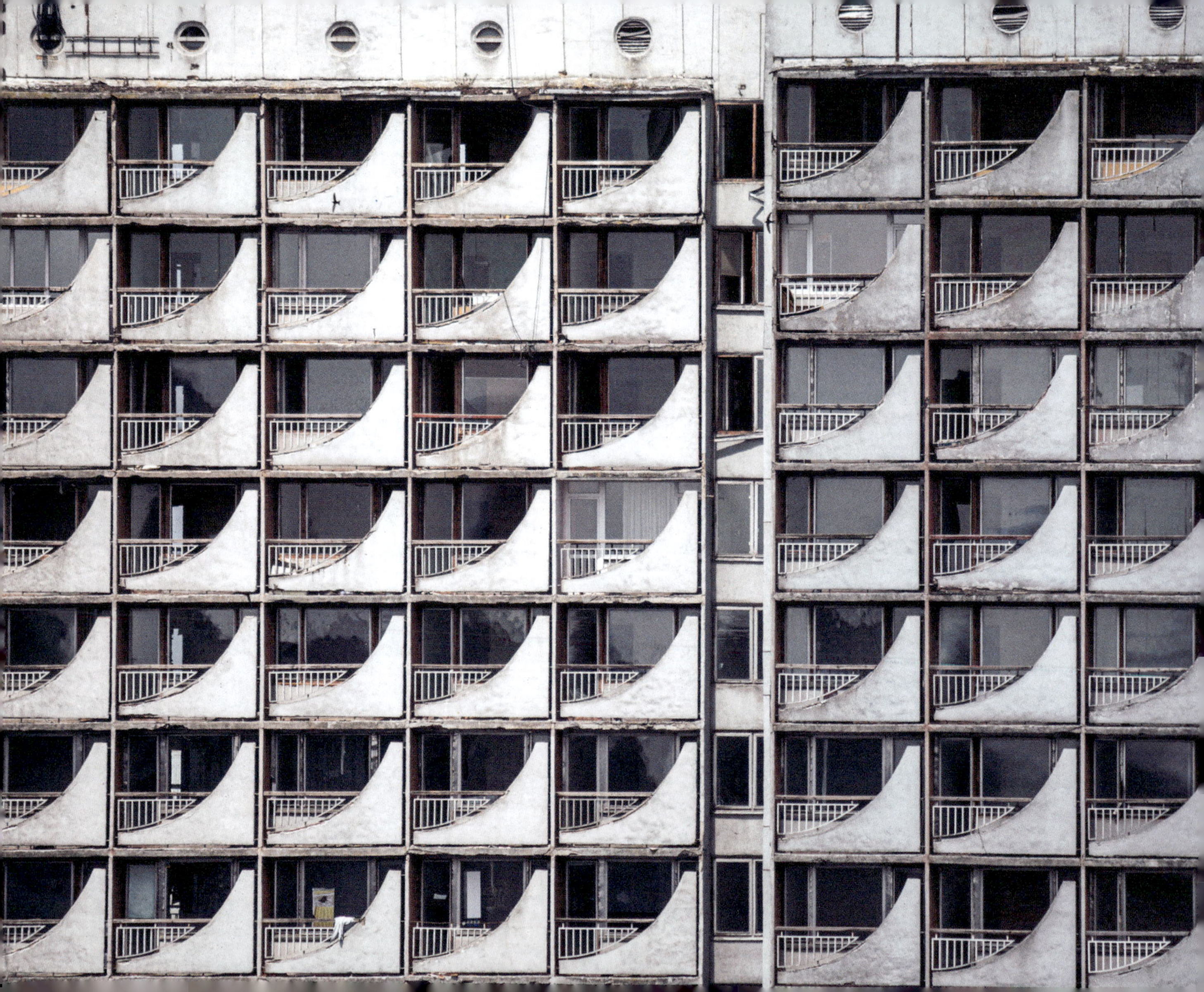